DISCOURSES OF MODERNITY

DISCOURSES OF MODERNITY
The Case of Estonian Literature

Piret Peiker

Helena History Press

Copyright 2024 © Piret Peiker

All rights reserved
Published in the United States by:
Helena History Press LLC

H P

A division of KKL Publications LLC, Reno, NV USA
Publishing scholarship about and from Central and East Europe

www.helenahistorypress.com

Distributed by IngramSpark and available through all major e-retail sites

info@helenahistorypress.com

ISBN 978 1 943596 44 7

Editor: Gábor Tamás Molnár
Graphic design: Sebastian Stachowski

Contents

Acknowledgements	vii
Introduction	1
Modernity	3
The Notion of Modernity	3
Modern ideas of time, history, and change	8
Modernization: plural paths or convergence?	11
Modern legitimation of power and popular sovereignty	15
"Belated" and postcolonial modernization	18
Estonian	21
Literature	23
Modus Operandi and Chapter Overview	29
Chapter One. Another Road to Modernity	33
Creation ex nihilo? Re-reading the Warwick Debates	34
The formation of Estonian modernity	37
The power of communication	47
Ethnocultural and civic nationhood	52
The Estonian Republic	57
The Soviet model of modernity and its failure	68
Soviet (Post)colonialism?	73
Post-independence Estonia through the postcolonial lens	83
Coda	94
Chapter Two. Decolonizing Translations: Lydia Koidula's *The Last Inca of Peru* (*Peruama wiimne Inka*, 1866); *Martinique and Corsica* (*Martiiniko ja Korsika*, 1869); *Juudit, or the Last Maroons of Jamaica* (*Juudit, ehk Jamaika saare wiimsed Maroonlased*, 1870)	99
The value systems of German/Estonian New World stories: discourses of legitimation of power, history and change	106
The postcolonial aspects of translation	106
Slaves and savages	109
Conceptions of colonial space and historical change	111
Estonian New World literature	116
Story and narration in *Huaskar/Inca*	119
Narrative situation and strategies of communication	119
Histoire and discours	122

The thought-worlds of *Huaskar* and *Inca*	124
Nobility, serfs and savages	125
Space, time and change	129
The curses and blessings of the elders	133
The power of knowledge	137
The power of marriage	138
Adapting a Fellow Spirit: Koidula's *Juudit* and Mügge's *Eduard Montague*	143
Slaves and savages in Juudit *and* Eduard Montague	146
From slaves and savages to an agent of history: the creation of a people	148
From a Historical Romance to a Political Tale of Warning: Koidula's	
Martinique and Corsica and Mühlbach's *The Empress Josephine*	152
Geography and History: Koidula's Adaptation Strategies	153
A People Grown Savage	155

Chapter Three. *Bildung* in the Image of Modernity:
Estonian Narratives of Formation, 1896–1993   161

The Western European *Bildungsroman*	164
The Postcolonial *Bildungsroman*	168
Estonian *Bildung*-narratives and the postcolonial model	173
Juhan Liiv's The Shadow	173
Soviet period Bildungsromane	179
Silvia Rannamaa's *Kadri* and *Stepmother*	180
Jaan Kross's *The Czar's Madman*	190
Emil Tode's Border State	198
Anton Hansen Tammsaare's *Truth and Justice*:	
A post-postcolonial *Bildungsroman*?	210

Chapter Four. Self-Colonizing Translations? The Modernist Language
Renewal Project of the Young Estonia Movement (1905-1915), and Andrus
Kivirähk's *The Man Who Spoke Snakish* (*Mees, kes teadis ussisõnu*, 2007)   227

Young Estonia as a modernist project: debates	233
Young Estonia, modernity and modernism(s):	
a reading in contribution to the debates	238
Language, Abject and Imagination in *The Man Who Spoke Snakish*	255

Afterword	269
Works Cited	273
Index	299

Acknowledgements

This book draws on a long period of thinking about modernity, postcolonialism and sociopolitical change that took place in several forms. It involved writing a doctoral dissertation at the University of Turku and a number of articles on the related topics, as well as research, teaching and seminar discussions at the Estonian Institute of Humanities, the School of East European and Slavonic Studies – University College London, the University of Tallinn, the Institute of Advanced Studies Kőszeg. The thought-provoking international summer schools in Tallinn and Kőszeg played a special role.

I wrote the book in the framework of the European Research Council project "Between the Times: Embattled Temporalities and Political Imagination in Inter-war Europe" (TAU17149), based at the Institute of Humanities, University of Tallinn. I am grateful to the leader of the group, professor Liisi Keedus, and to all the other members of the group: Johannes Bent, Tommaso Giordani, Henry Mead, Daniele Monticelli, Ksenia Shmydkaya. I was generously welcomed to the team of erudite intellectual historians and benefited immensely from our thorough discussions of each other's work. I am also very grateful for the postdoctoral research grant awarded to me by the Institute of Advanced Studies Kőszeg at the final stage of my study. Special thanks to my supervisor Professor Attila Pók for his guidance and for the conversations on inter-war period Estonia in comparative context.

The book owes a lot to my years as a doctoral student at the department of Comparative Literature, University of Turku. I feel special gratitude to my supervisors, Professor Liisa Steinby and the late Dr. Marja-Leena Hakkarainen for their insightful comments and friendly support throughout my studies. I am likewise grateful to other professors and fellow students who participated at the doctoral seminars. In particular, I would like to thank Pirjo Ahokas, Kaisa Ilmonen and Aino Mäkikalli for their stimulating intellectual presence, as well as for their kind practical help to me as a foreign student. Many thanks also to my thesis reviewers, professor Gregory Jusdanis, professor Ann Rigney, and professor Jaan Undusk whose critical remarks helped me to carry on the work in a renewed spirit.

I am also deeply obliged to many other colleagues and friends who took interest in my work during its different phases, contributing useful critique, information, and ideas. I would specifically like to thank the people who found time to read parts of my manuscript and comment on them: Epp Annus, Mirjam Hinrikus, Tarmo Jüristo, Linda Kaljundi, Tiina Kirss, Eneken Laanes, Mikko Lagerspetz, Krista Mits, Ilona Pikkanen, Peeter Selg, Marek Tamm. I am most grateful here to my copy editor at Helena History Press, Gábor Tamás Molnár, who proved to be an insightful and inspiring fellow scholar, as well as a thorough and demanding editor.

Finally, I wish to express my utmost gratitude to my late husband George Schöpflin. He was my first and foremost reader, proofreader, critic, and discussion partner.

Introduction

This book is a study of the emergence and evolution of what is today known as modern Estonian culture as it has been reflected in and constructed by Estonian-language literature from the mid-19th century to the early 21st.

One major ambition in this research was to identify new or forgotten lines of the sociopolitical imaginary that would contribute to the cultural capital of the 21st century, potentially useful not only to my compatriots, but also to other co-humans facing the challenges of the present-day global world and looking for fresh resources to manage them. Being a young student in late 1980s and early 1990s I was part of the extensive and—seemingly—very sudden changes in Estonia. As I was trying to make sense of this experience and, later, as a scholar, trying to contribute to my society to seek best (least bad) outcomes, I needed to research the phenomena of profound social change more generally and put Estonia in a comparative context. The present book is one of the results.

As will be explored in more detail in the beginning of Chapter One, Estonia has been discussed by scholars of nationalism and modernization studies as a sort of an anomaly/test case, as it seemingly jumped into modernity *ex nihilo*, not having had a pre-modern state or elite culture. This book takes another look at the meaning of the notion of (pre-modern) history, and the connections between the fashioning of a modernity and the characteristics of its particular pre-modernity. The goal is to offer a new understanding of the modernization processes not only in the Estonian area, but also in a more generalizable way.

In that context I employ the term and the insights of Postcolonial Studies throughout the book. Doing that, I side with those scholars who argue that this field ought to analyze imperial structures and ideologies in a greater variation than it has done traditionally, mainly focusing on Western Europe and its overseas colonies. While the knowledge of Postcolonial Studies is very helpful to gain better understanding of a case like Estonia, it also works the other way round. Neither the geographical location of the society studied nor the political colors of the ovelord that witholds the society's pursuit of self-determination should prejudice the researcher against considering them in the comparative frame work of global postcolonialism. I hold that close-up investigation of particular stories of modernization, including the self-interpretations of the modernizers involved, *together* with the awareness of the particular cases' embeddedness in the global, is a fruitful strategy in the studies of modernity and postcolonialism.[1]

The term "discourse" is used in a great variation of meanings, so it is in order to shortly clarify my own. I use it in the overlapping sense of a particular group of statements that can be analysed as united by their common themes, and vocabulary, as well as the beliefs, values, impetus in the world etc. implied by them. In my analysis, discourses are not disembodied but are always enacted in a particular social and institutional world. They are shaped by it and simultaneously interactively shape its processes and peoples' perceptions of them.[2] In my definition the operation of discourses involves dynamic processes, they transform in time and space and can sometimes function reflexively. They do not occur in discursive isolation, but in dialogue, imitation, contrast, and opposition to other discourses.

When discussing Estonian discourses relatable to modernity, my main focus is on those that directly address the concerns and aspirations of modernization itself: on the ways how the Estonian *lettres* have narrativized, conceptualized, troped, questioned, and also *created* modernizing change in interaction with their shifting national/imperial and international political, economic and socio-cultural contexts. While the circumstances of the Estonian case are to a certain extent idiosyncratic, they also raise important questions about latecomer and post-

---

1   I use "postcolonial" as prevalent in Postcolonial Studies: to refer to "the consequences of colonialism from the time of its first impact—culturally, politically, economically" (Nagai 239), i. e. in the Estonian case covering the relevant aspects of both the colonial periods and the periods of independence. I subscribe to Anne McClintock's broad definition of colonialism as "direct territorial appropriation of another geo-political entity, combined with forthright exploitation of its resources and labor, and systematic interference in the capacity of the appropriated culture (itself not necessarily a homogenous entity) to organize its dispensations of power" (295). I will return to this problematic in Chapter One when discussing Soviet colonialism.
2   This understanding is broadly in accordance with Michel Foucault's in *The Archaeology of Knowledge* (see especially 72).

colonial modernities much more generally[3]: the dynamics of catching up with earlier modernizers; the ongoing endeavor to create such models of modernity and visions of historical change that would fit local needs; the relationship between political and military power, and cultural hegemony; the boundary between colonial mimicry and creative reception in processing outward influence.

In what follows in the introduction I will open up the rest of the central nodes in the title: "modernity", "Estonian" and "literature". After that I will explain the rationale of the choice of the texts selected for analysis, the disciplinary context of the work, and give an overview of the structure of the book.

Modernity

The Notion of Modernity

The stem "modern" goes back to Latin *modo* and *modus*, meaning "just now, currently" and "a certain way of doing or being" (a fashion, so to say). It has often been used to contrast past and present—in the late fifth century, for example, the Latin *modernus* refered to the Christian present in opposition to the Roman past. Charles Baudelaire's essay "The Painter of Modern Life" ("Le peintre de la vie moderne", 1863), an evocative piece for modernity studies in a number of fields, agrees with this historical stem in that he describes 'modernity' (*modernité*) as "the transient, the fleeting, the contingent". Yet his character, the painter of modern life (based on Baudelaire's contemporary artist Constantin Guys), is in no way a free-floating idler, quite the opposite—"walking or quickening his pace, he goes his way, for ever in search", in order to draw upon the fast-paced contemporary world for his work. His genius is in his acute sense of historicity, he does not base his creativity on earlier models in more than most general terms, because "every age has its own carriage, its expression, its gestures". Baudelaire's piece dramatizes a number of features that have come to be associated with the modern, or at least modern Western, sense of self: the pursuit of knowledge in an intelligible and potentially masterable (global) world; inwardness, self-fashioning and affirmation of ordinary everyday life; a vocational ethic as a driving force for action and basis of existential identity; a new

---

3   My notion of "latecomer" or "belated" modernities (I use the terms interchangeably) is derived from Jusdanis, *Belated,* Jusdanis, *The Necessary,* and Schöpflin, "Nationhood". The idea and its connection to the perception of time as linear and progressive dominant in modernity will be further discussed later in this introduction.

perception of historical temporality that views time as discontinuous and constant change as a norm, with a specific modern attitude that humans can and ought to deliberately transform the present.

As this book approaches modernity in a comparative perspective, not solely focusing on the Western experience, it is important to note Charles Taylor's 1996 article "Two Theories of Modernity". The Canadian philosopher and theorist of modernity argues there that all the approaches that have developed since the 19th century to assess the phenomenon of "modernity" can be divided into two broad categories. These are the "cultural" and the "acultural" ones, of which he considers the latter strongly dominant at the time of his writing. According to the "acultural" perception, there are particular "culture-neutral" transformative operations, whether intellectual or social, such as e.g. rationalization, secularization, industrialization, technologization, democratization, increased social mobility and division of labour, acceleration of time, etc. Any traditional culture could go through them, even if many "acultural" theories do consider the historical reasons why the modernizing changes started earlier in some cultures ("the West"), or why certain cultures modernize more easily than others.

Cultural theories, on the other hand, describe modernizing changes in terms of specific cultural thought-worlds. Modernization is analysed as a movement from one particular constellation of cultural understandings to another, considering how notions such as e.g. the self, the society, the good are transformed and repositioned there. Nietzche's reading of modern scientific culture "that paints it as actuated by a constellation of values" and Weber's reading of the Protestant ethic are given by Taylor as examples of the "cultural" approach ("Two Theories" 4). Here one might also consider many of the culture-specific accounts that developed since 1980s by scholars, often anthropologists who talk about multiple modernities, rather than modernity in singular.

Taylor advocates greater prominence for the cultural approach, as it would enable both to grasp what is culturally specific about the thought-world of the modern West without universalising it, and to preclude the imposition of "a falsely uniform pattern" ("Two Theories" 8) on the multiple non-Western experiences of science, industrialisation, struggles for democratic reform etc. Taylor does not deny the impact of Western post-17th-century natural science and "accompanying technological efficacy" on the rest of the world ("Two Theories" 7-8), yet he argues that the "acultural theory" alone offers an incomplete and therefore distorted picture of the global processes of modernization.

Taylor's examples of "acultural" theories are the classical theories of modernity, e.g. Max Weber's theory of rationalization, Durkheim's account of societies developing from "mechanical" to differentiated, "organic", forms of cohesion ("Two Theories" 3). Even if these theories sometimes make global references, they are in real terms dealing with their own place and time: the *fin-de-siècle* West undergoing rapid modernizing change.[4] Other, even more paradigmatic examples of "acultural" approach are offered by the convergence and modernization theories (discussed in more detail below) that emerged post-WWII in 1950s and 1960s in the West and built on the ideas of the 19th-century classics. The liberal modernization theorists[5] saw the West as the source of modernization and the non-West as a recipient of a particular clutch of "modern" phenomena from the West that would eventually help them "catch up" with it.

Taylor's distinction between "acultural" and "cultural" approaches to modernity repeats and inflects itself in a variety of discussions about the appositeness of "modernity" as an analytical category in scholarly work. The political theorist Bernard Yack criticizes the conflation of "substantive" and "historical" definitions of modernity in much academic literature (*The Fetishism*). A "substantive" definition defines modernity as a bundle of certain distinctive traits, while in "historical" terms modernity comprises an era starting about 1789 and *everything* related to it. In actuality, so Yack, traits that can be considered specifically modern always exist side by side with other features, pre-modern or non-modern, building different cultural constellations in different localities (*The Fetishism*). Frederick Cooper agrees with Yack's diagnosis (123-124) and holds that the value of "modernity" as a scholarly concept is seriously in doubt (113). While "modernities" have proliferated in the academic literature since the 1980s, "the formulation of alternative modernity is empty unless one can demonstrate both the alternative and the modernity" (130). For "alternative modernity" as a concept to be convincing, the historian should be able to specify what the distinctive differences from other forms and discourses of modernity are, and what the reasons are to still call it a modernity, rather than simply a society undergone some kind of extensive innovation (114, 130).

Peter Wagner's *Modernity: Understanding the Present* (2012) that combines political theory and historical sociology forcefully addresses the difficulties of defining modernity as singular and acultural/Western or plural and endlessly particularized, and opens up frameworks for research crucially helpful for the present thesis. Wagner takes up Foucault's differentiation between modernity as

---

[4] It should be noted though that these classical social scientists themselves never claimed to be scholars of "modernity" and used this term seldom. Rather, their work was a response to the particular period of rapid modernization in the *fin de siècle* Western Europe and North America.
[5] E.g. Eisenstadt, *Modernization*; Levy; Parsons, *Societies*; Smelser.

a set of historical intitutions and modernity as "an attitude and experience" that "demands the exploration of one's self, the task of separating out 'from the contingency that has made us what we are, the possibility of no longer being, doing, or thinking what we are, do or think'" (Wagner, *Modernity: Understanding* 21). Every society, says Wagner, attempts to deal with a set of interrelated basic epistemic, political and economic "*problématiques*": What is accepted as "certain knowledge" that the society's self-understanding can be based upon? Are the same sources accepted by the whole society? How to set the rules for common life (questions of power, legitimization and governance)? How to meet the material needs of the society? (See especially *Modernity: Understanding* 74-76.) A modern society is one that sees these questions, at least theoretically, as "truly open" (*Modernity: Understanding* 74), and one where people "do not accept any external guarantors—that is, guarantors they do not themselves posit—of their knowledge, of their political orders or of their ways of satisfying their material needs" (*Modernity: Understanding* 22).

The above is the core of Wagner's conceptual definition of modernity. Earlier theories of modernity have also emphasized the modern assumption of autonomy and mastery, but they have tied the implementation of these to particular classical Western institutions, mistaking this institutional link for universal principles of modern development (*Modernity: Understanding* 43). In actuality, there are multiple possible and equally valid answers or solutions to these *problématiques*, even if some can be considered—for a time being—more effective or beneficial than others. Customarily any solution to a situation of dissatisfaction leads to side effects and unintended consequences, thus provoking new critiques and social transformations to come (*Modernity: Understanding* 28-63). Thus Wagner's approach sets up a framework by which multiple, including temporally successive, models of modernity can be compared from the viewpoint of their arguments over and responses to the *problématiques* and the expression of these in various institutional forms.

From that perspective, Wagner sides with the scholars (e.g. Giddens, Habermas, Heller) who do not see "postmodernity" as a new era that marks the end of modernity in the West (as argued by e. g. Lyotard, Baudrillard). Even if the rise of digital communication, post-industrial economy and a multi-polar world in which the West does not have a hegemony[6] marks a profound historical trans-

---

6   The loss of clear hegemony in practical terms only happens from the beginning of the 21st century, not at the high point of the postmodernity debates in the 1980s and 1990s (cf. Schöpflin, "The Small States").

formation that calls for radically new intellectual and institutional responses, this is still a successive phase of modernity, one marked by a sense of crisis, unpredictability, self-reflexivity and various forms of critique. "The debate over the end of modernity and the rise of postmodernity during the 1980s and 1990s may not have had a clear conclusion," Wagner writes, "but by now one can see how the center of discussion has shifted towards the exploration of forms of modernity rather than the end of it" (*Modernity: Understanding* 31).

Wagner's central account places a strong emphasis both on human agency and *potential* openness to *any* historical change in all models of modernity. However, very importantly for my argument in this book, he also recognizes the role of history, earlier choices taken ("path-dependancy"), as well as external influence and the impact of global power disparities on different societies' options to respond to the basic *problematiques*. Although from my perspective Wagner does not pay enough attention to the instances where (an unacceptable model of) modernity is imposed on a local population by force, he does make this short comment (in a footnote):

> [A] major difference between expectations of the future may be related to the issue whether a society can see itself plausibly as a creator of its own modernity or whether it sees itself as forced to respond to a modernity that unfolds outside of itself but exercises a strong impact (*Modernity: Understanding* 29).

Wagner references Ibrahim Kaya's work (*Modernity: Understanding* 25) on the strongly outwardly oriented Turkish society after the Kemalist revolution, as well as his own case studies of Brazil and South Africa in the global framework. In doing so, he differentiates himself from the culturally isolationist assumptions that inform the work of some scholars of the "multiple modernities" school, and also implicitly seem to underlie Taylor's short article I discussed above. Although the central gist of Wagner's argument is elsewhere, in this aspect his theory of modernity anchors and theoretically illuminates, rather than contradicts, "cultural" definitions of modernity. Such situationally grounded definitions often emerge from the perspective of latecomer modernizers, such as the one by the anthropologist scholar Bruce Knauft:[7]

---

7   Wagner stays within the disciplines of sociology and political theory, thus his engagement with the work that approaches modernity in terms of plural models is restricted to the sociologist Shmuel Eisenstadt and his followers. Wagner does not discuss scholars in other disciplines, much of whose work preceeds Eisenstadt's (see footnote 15 for examples).

for the purposes of the present book, *modernity can be defined as the images and institutions associated with Western-style progress and development in the contemporary world*. The images of "progress" and institutions of "development" in this formulation do not have to *be* Western in a direct sense, but they do resonate with Western-style notions of economic and material progress and link these with images of social and cultural development—in whatever way these are locally or nationally defined ("Critically Modern: An Introduction" 18, Knauft's emphases).

Modern ideas of time, history, and change

The British comparativist global historian Christopher Bayly argues that an essential part of one's "being modern is thinking you are modern", having an "aspiration to be "up with the times"" (10), assuming that constant rapid change is the way of the world that one ignores only at one's own risk. This sensibility has often been described using the metaphor of modern technological icons: one worries about catching the train of modernity "frantically trying to get on board" (Sztompka 140; cf. Heller 7-11) or, more "postmodernly", the aeroplane is used as the figure for endless pursuit (e. g. David Lodge's novel *Small World*). Modernity is not only an epoch or a collection of traits; on the level of experience it is importantly also a claims-making strategy, a reference point for individuals and communities to argue that past experience need not and, moreover, cannot fully define future expectations.

To emphasize a particular perception of history and change as specifically modern does not mean to argue that non-modern people do not go through processes of radical change, or that they are unaware of them, or that these are without exception rated in negative terms. However, in non-modernities change is not perceived as an open ended, progressive or regressive movement. Rather, change is either seen as a return to an earlier situation, or is conceptualized in "the millenarian mode", with the sense of divine forces leaking into human history (Bayly 11). In the first case, we can talk about a cyclical perception of history, while in the second, a simultaneous, timeless embodiment of the divine (Koselleck 10-11). One of the most important intellectual historians of modernizing change, Reinhart Koselleck reminds us in his *Futures Past: On the Semantics of Historical Time* that "until well into the sixteenth century" Christians lived in the expectation of the Apocalypse (11). This, of course, in itself carries a degree of future-oriented perception of history, but not one identical to the modern sensibility of open-ended progress: it is a matter of a single, transcendental transformation, rather than ongoing change, and it does not involve human agency.

Koselleck also provides an evocative comparative citation of Luther and of Robespierre, important in the context of this book, illustrating the sea-change between modern and pre-modern perceptions of change in relation to human agency. The epoch of the Reformation was widely believed to be introducing the Apocalypse at any moment, and Luther believes that "for the sake of the chosen, God would shorten the final days, 'towards which the world was speeding, since almost all of the new century had been pressed into the space of one decade'" (quoted in Koselleck 12). Robespierre, in contrast, says in his speech on the Revolutionary Constitution: "The time has come to call upon each to realize his own destiny. The progress of human Reason laid the basis for this great Revolution, and you shall now assume the particular duty of hastening its pace." (quoted in Koselleck 12) Despite the strong providential overtone in Robespierre, it is clear that in his case it is the humans, not God, whom he believes to be the agent of speeding up time and accelerating historical change.

Building on Koselleck and also on his readings of the thinkers Weber, Durkheim, Marx and Simmel, the sociologist Hartmut Rosa emphasizes the importance of the emergence of the novel temporality so far, as to make "the acceleration of time" the defining feature of modernity. "[T]he Enlightenment developed a characteristic form of impatience as a result of the separation of the historical space of experience from the horizon of expectation" (*Social* 44), Rosa argues in Koselleck's terminology. "This impatience, and associated ideas of Progress, a belated Reason, and an acceleratable History, are constitutive presuppositions for the triumphs of the natural sciences and the industrial revolution that follow" (*Social* 44).

Rosa outlines three separate but connected forms of social acceleration which each feeds the others in a circuit, creating a self-propelling spiral of progressively accelerating change. Technical acceleration boosts the acceleration of social change which in turn accelerates the pace of people's lives which in its own turn creates a demand for ever-increasing technical acceleration in order to save time. Technical acceleration is about technical and technological advancement and driven by the economic imperatives to maximize the production of sellable output per unit of time and to be the first to innovate. The acceleration of social change relates to what Rosa, following Hermann Lübbe, calls the "contraction of the present" (*Social* 76): the accelerated transformation of social circumstances, institutions and human relationship patterns shrinks the period of time in which experiences and expectations based on the past are still valid and relevant for the future. Psychologically, the dynamics of acceleration feeds upon the human perception of the "discrepancy between a limited [individual] lifetime and the perspectivally unlimited time of the world" (Trejo-Mathys 11) which is no longer bridged by religion or other long-termist value systems that would make individual life histories meaningful parts of larger history.

Rosa notes that although in the modernized societies acceleration has been continuously increasing, this has not happened "*in linear fashion but in phases interrupted by pauses and small trend reversals*" (*Social* 122; emphasis in the original). An estimate shared by most scholars, Rosa argues the phases of the sharpest acceleration have been the *fin de siècle* period (1880s-1920s) that as a response spawned artistic modernism as well as classical social theory, and the 1980-1990s that reacted with postmodernism and theories of modernity and globalization (*Social* 42-44; Rosa and Scheuerman 5). It is customarily the case that major waves of acceleration are accompanied by debates in which "cries for deceleration in the name of human needs and values are voiced but eventually die down" (Rosa, "Social Acceleration: Ethical" 89) after which a new surge of technical innovation starts.

Although Rosa considers social acceleration a constitutive part of modernity, he holds it possible that it "crosses a critical threshold in "late modernity" [turn of 20th-21st century]" beyond which the necessarily time-consuming processes of deliberative democracy cannot control the speeding fields of economy and technical innovation anymore. The profound processes of modern acceleration, so Rosa, were "firmly grounded and enabled by the stability of *some* modern institutions like law, democracy, the industrial work regime" ("Social Acceleration: Ethical" 94; emphasis in the original). Paradoxically, as there is no *directed* change with long-term perspective anymore, history may once again appear static in a "hyperaccelerated standstill" ("Social Acceleration: Ethical" 95; my emphasis): whereas there are a lot of events and alterations, they are all superficial and leave the deeper problems untouched (*Social* 270). Hyperacceleration fragments and erodes stable institutions and identities, which postmodernists may consider liberating, but which in real terms are undermining the "capacity to exercise ethical and political autonomy", whether individual or collective, in any meaningful sense (Rosa and Scheuerman 16).[8]

---

[8] This section concentrated on the hegemonic epistemology of time in modernity. However, perceptions of time as cyclical are in some contexts smoothly combined with those of linearity, and appear at the everyday level (repetition of daily activities, yearly festivities, biological cycles and rites of passage, etc.), as well as in a range of philosophical and even sociological conceptualisations of historical change (e.g. by Johann Gottfried von Herder, Vilfredo Pareto, Oswald Spengler, Arnold J. Toynbee). The modern Western sacralization of canonical works of art and

Modernization: plural paths or convergence?

Rosa's theory is self-admittedly Western-centric, primarily interested in understanding "the essence and the developmental dynamic of modernity following Western patterns" (Rosa, *Social* 29). However, he also holds that elsewhere as well, the "processes of modernisation" will bring about a uniform pattern of acceleration converging with the Western one. Modern societies may look multiple on the surface, developing different "material structures, social associations and cultural convictions", yet "when it comes to the depth-structural logic of global transformation, they all invariantly follow the dictates and logic of the social acceleration", Rosa argues ("The Universal" 59). Thus, despite its critical and bleak disposition, the universalist and deterministic overtones of Rosa's account notably resemble those of the optimistic modernization and convergence theories of the 1950s and 1960s mentioned above—a period onto which Rosa looks back with a certain nostalgia for the stability of classical modern institutions and related convictions—as well as, of course, those of the classical 19th-century social thought that shares Rosa's alertness to the dark side of modernity.[9]

Theories of modernization and convergence emerged immediately after the Second World War, primarily in the United States. These theories had very strong academic and political credibility until the 1970s, both in the West and elsewhere.[10] The theories responded to the situation where there had developed three separate but interdependent "Worlds": the First World of the industrially developed democratic societies in the West, and soon also in the far East; the Second World "socialist" bloc rapidly industrializing in its own vein; and the Third World of the decolonizing societies, many of which had not been industrialized, where different political and economic ideas and influences competed.

Modernization and convergence theories are teleological in the sense that they set their contemporary Western countries (the United States particularly foregrounded) as "model countries" (Bendix) which the traditional, backward, underdeveloped ones ought to imitate in order to reach the same standard of modernity, to catch up, liberating themselves—and this is important—from impedimental local traditions. They take modernizing change to be unilinear

---

literature as timeless/simultaneous can be pointed out as a ubiquitous example of a conceptualization of time as simultaneous in Western modernity.

9 Rosa writes that social acceleration may well be identified with Weber's famous notion of the "iron cage" of modernization, the staightjacket of rationalisation driven by the motor of the increasing efficacy of technology, production and bureaucracy ("The Universal" 59).

10 For examples of highly acclaimed works in modernization theory see footnote 7. E. g. Huntington, Kerr, and Rostow can be mentioned as important contributions to the convergence theory.

and irreversible, assuming that "less developed societies have to follow the same path that more developed societies have already trodden" (Sztompka 131). Although there is also a sense that the transformation in the image of the West is somehow a natural evolutionary process, modernization is prevalently viewed as something that can be engineered by small "enlightened elites, determined to pull their countries up from backwardness" (Sztompka 131), rather than something that must be resonant with the aspirations of, or draw upon the agency of, large parts of society.

If modernization theory is applied primarily to the "Third World", the convergence theory concerns mainly the Soviet bloc, arguing that the Soviet social, political and economic systems will ultimately converge with the Western ones, because the logic of industrialisation and technological development *per se* leads to close conformity of societies (Streeck 3). This would not mean the collapse of the Soviet system, but rather a "slow evolution of 'real socialism' embracing western patterns" (Sztompka 141) of democracy and elements of market economy, whereas the West will further develop the institution of the welfare state. Soviet official standpoint was strongly hostile towards the ideas of convergence, emphasizing the ideological distinctiveness of the communist party-lead "dictatorship of the proletariat", and its status as a higher stage of historical development in comparison to capitalist societies (Kelley).[11]

Both Soviet and Western theories of modern progress described above build on the seminal thought of the Enlightenment period and in the 19th century. Thus the liberal and the Marxist thinkers of the post-WWII period have much in common. They posit a broadly analogous timeline of development from the 16th century to their own time and tend to privilege technological development and economy as the principal forces driving modernizing change and impacting on socio-cultural progress. However, American scholars, such as Talcott Parsons saw their own society, rather than Soviet Union as the "lead society" of his time, having "come to play a role approximately comparable to that of England in the seventeenth century" (Sztompka 122; cf. Parsons, *The System* 87).

It is noteworthy that in the early 1990s, the eminent Polish sociologist Piotr Sztompka saw a hopeful potential in neo-modernization or "post-modernisation" theories responding to the stimulus of the post-1989 situation of Central-Eastern Europe (136-141). The fundamentals of mid-century modernization theory

---

11 Some of Soviet dissident underground press was appreciative towards theories of convergence (Brockmann 59). The Soviet Union also tried to compete for the hearts and minds of the Third World, yet on the whole lost out to the United States, and even to China which became the third superpower (Boden).

would be entirely revised, he believes, resulting in approaches "purged of all evolutionist or developmentalist overtones" (140), as well as from economic determinism, prejudice against local traditions, political elitism, etc. Rather, modernization would now be viewed as "a historically contingent process of constructing, spreading and legitimating" institutions of modernity like democracy or free market (140).

The change in perspective at the turn of the century resulted not only from the academic discreditation of earlier convergence theories, but also the "postmodern" ideological climate where the West lacked its earlier triumphalism and almost seemed "as if ready to jump off the train of modernity"—the same one that the post-Soviets would so like to board (140). However, the following years showed that the new approach to modernization relating to de-Sovietization discussed by Sztompka gained little currency in the social sciences or practical politics. It was largely supplanted by studies in "transition", the term's implication on a progressive movement of change towards catching up with the model West of universal values—much like the Parsonian modernization theories of the mid-century.

However, roughly from the 1980s, but more noticeably during 1990s and 2000s, scholarly discussion shifts from 'modernization' to 'modernity', or, significantly, rather to the plural, *modernities*, with concepts "multiple modernities", "alternative modernities", "counter-modernities", "coeval modernities", "entangled modernities", or also "postcolonial modernities", "Islamic modernities", "African modernities", "Asian modernities", etc. being suggested and by varying degree gaining currency. "Belated modernity" and "latecomer modernity" are frequently also employed in specific reference, and in the singular, yet they as such always imply difference in respect to an "on-time" mainstream modernity and thus they connote pluralization.

It can be observed that modernization theories, as well transition theories, are dominated by economists, sociologists and political theorists, but it is rather anthropologists, historians, literary and critical theorists, often involved in the cross-disciplinary field of postcolonial studies, who produce most of the scholarship of pluralized modernity.

If modernization theories were characterized by a belief in unilinearity, teleological development towards Western exemplars, the shift towards the term modernity comes with an emphasis on plurality and the implication of parity and contemporaneity. At the same time, as mentioned above, that sort of usage has justly been criticized for frequent conceptual vagueness and lack of historical specificity when characterizing either different "modern" social structures and thought-worlds or different people's interpretations of what modernity is and what it encompasses (Cooper, especially 126-135). Thus, to my mind, the most useful recent approaches to modernity (e. g. Bayly's, Knauft's and Wagner's) are those that next to the belief of modernity's plurality foreground the empirical historical dimensions of the development of modern societies, such as the long-term interconnectedness of human cultures, and the idea of "successive modernities" within one society (thorough-going changes in the models of modernity beyond the initial modernization).

It can be argued (as does Wagner, *Modernity: Understanding* 3-4) that "a key event in the formation of what we consider to be modern Europe was the so-called discovery of the Americas with their hitherto unknown populations, and this event triggered European reflections about the nature of humankind [...] provided a background to philosophical speculations about the 'state of nature'" and the proceeding development of science and social thought.[12] The axiological and political turbulence associated with Enlightenment and the following political revolutions, however, did not follow a clear "first in the West, then elsewhere" (Chakrabarty 6; cf. Anderson) pattern, but reverberated much across the world (America, Europe, the Caribbean, India, South America, etc.). Ideas, events and slogans at different places were variously locally triggered and lead to a variety of outcomes, yet at the same time also feeding off and bouncing back from one another (for a good amply sourced account see Bayly, especially 86-169).

The 19th century, writes Wagner,

> is, in the global perspective, not the beginning of the diffusion of European modernity but rather the onset of parallel processes of world-making, inspired by the modern imaginary but pursued under conditions of considerable power differentials (*Modernity: Understanding* 163).[13]

Frequently, and precisely to attend to their oppressed position, many (former) colonials are inspired by "the principles of individual and collective self-determination" (Wagner, *Modernity: Understanding* 162), in addition to (and usually linked to) the attraction of the material progress and lifestyle associated with modernity. However, as noted above, the shared broad horizon of modern ideals can lead different postcolonial modernizers to a variety of successive solu-

---

12 The figure of the native American in the Western European, overseas and Estonian social imagination will be explored in Chapter Two.
13 It could be added that the processes unfolding in complex global networks can be parallel, but also overlapping and certainly interlinked (cf. Bayly 476).

tions to the locally inflected *problematiques* that they attempt to address. This is also the reason why Wagner would consider too limited the depiction of late modernity as a self-propelled and globalizing process towards ever further accelerated time and fragmented institutions. Even, if in some aspects illuminating and astute, it is too inattentive to the range of particular social experience and too deterministic (Wagner, *Modernity: Understanding* 152-153).[14] The essential dynamic of modernizing change draws upon "collective creativity", of the ability of a society to mobilize any existing cultural resource in order to (re)think the relevant *problematiques* and come up with superior solutions.[15]

What is more, the classical modern institutions developed from the 19th century and especially in the aftermath of World War II, the disintegration of which Rosa deplores, are idiosyncratic to certain Western societies. Most of the world never experienced such a widely legitimized and institutionally stable form of modernization, though many societies did and still do see it as a positive example to aspire to. It ought not to be assumed (as Rosa seems to do) that it is up to the West to develop the answers to present-day global threats. It may turn out that societies with more, or more recent, historical experience of steering drastic institutional change in a situation of unfortunate socio-political heritage and strong outward pressures are more tuned to the current global environment (cf. Wagner, *Modernity: Understanding* 165-167).

Modern legitimation of power and popular sovereignty

From the beginning of its debates, the image of modernity has had a split and double reputation. One wants to get "on" the train of modernity, which stands for the Enlightenment belief in the perfectibility and redeemability of human beings, for political emancipation, individual and collective self-fulfilment, material prosperity, a future which is happier than the present; as early Barack Obama put it, for the "audacity of hope". On the other hand, there is the coercive, instrumentalist and alienating modernity where the national or impe-

---

14 Wagner talks in terms of global "time-space compression" rather than acceleration, and critiques David Harvey rather than Rosa (*Modernity: Understanding* 152-153).
15 Wagner's analysis's emphasis on the collective creativity of innovating societies interestingly dovetails with the description of decolonizing nationalisms as movements of individual and collective *"Bildung"* drawing upon the local "culture" by the postcolonial theorist Pheng Cheah (discussed in Chapter Three). He understands "culture" as a dynamic force, a source of artistic, political and other kinds of imagination. A successful cultural *Bildung* is rooted in the everyday life and traditions of "the people", yet forward-looking and aligned with critical reason, appropriating European influences and turning them into something new (Cheah, *Spectral* 217, 286, 290).

rial elites use the new modern forms of knowledge and administration for disciplining and punishing their populations with a self-righteous sense of being progressive and rational.

The elites certainly have an important role in putting forward and framing important questions for their collectivities. Yet I do not want to reduce my approach to the pre-supposition that there are "people" who are modernized and "elites" that are either celebrated for liberating and civilizing the masses or unmasked as manipulating and oppressing them. Instead, at least in the present context, it is more fruitful to pose questions in the framework of "struggles over popular sovereignty" (Winks and Neuberger 1) and related processes of legitimation or delegitimation of power.

Thus, one needs to enquire into the particular instances where people—different kinds of people, individuals and collectives in a variety of social status and roles—claim their rights and voice their aspirations or fears by discourses relating to modernity (e.g. evoking estate society *vis-à-vis* emancipation and nationhood; progressive change *vis-à-vis* sacred tradition; experience of technological change and urbanization, etc.) in their specific political and socio-cultural contexts. In each instance it has to be asked what grounds the participants axiologically, what they want to achieve, how their discourses and practices fare in interaction with others, what kind of individual and collective identities are constructed, challenged or rejected in the process.[16]

Approaching the issue of perceptions of legitimate power in modernity, it is useful to start with the broad acknowledgement of the scholars of modern history that the turbulence of the revolutions and radical political change at the end of 18th century as such can be described as a cluster of legitimation crises. These crises built up and escalated in reaction to the preceding significant increase during the 16th-17th centuries in the capacities and ambitions of states to condense power, i.e. to keep control over their populations, to tax them, to draft them for compulsory army-service, etc. "The shift took place for a number of interlocking reasons, mostly to do with the new technologies of information storage, military potential and methods of organization" (Schöpflin, "Nationhood").

Schöpflin emphasizes the significance of the information revolution following the invention of printing, launching a rapid increase in the rate of lit-

---

16 There is a substantial pedigree in this sort of enquiry. Some of the very different studies that I was inspired by and draw upon in this book are Chakrabarty, George, Hroch, *Social*, Jansen, *Eestlane*, Jusdanis, *Belated*, Raud, *Japan*, Schorske, and Steinberg. These studies build their innovative socio-cultural and political generalizations on attentive readings of a variety of literary or other cultural texts.

eracy and formal education among the populations of many parts of the world, which made it possible to institute large-scale state bureaucracies and, on the other hand, enabled large groups of people also to organise, if necessary, *against* established authorities ("Nationhood"). Bayly puts special stress on the globally present financial pressures caused by warfare, as the costs of competitive military technology had risen fast, forcing the governments to lean heavily on their subjects. This was frequently provoking resentment and throwing "doubt on the capacity and, ultimately, legitimacy" of the "old regime" (Bayly 86).

Thus, nationalism (in the sense of national mobilization) historically developed in response to the tensions of modernization and the ambitions of modern states to condense power and to place tighter rule over their populations. The echoes of the principles of "no taxation without representation" and "rights of man" as the proper basis for legitimate power (in themselves extraordinary ideas against the background of previous history) continued globally "down through the nineteenth century" (Bayly 87) and ever since. As argued above, this is true not only in the West. The universalist ideas of political emancipation were introduced in the works of French and Scottish thinkers, but they did not remain contained there. These ideas inflected locally in many places of the world, intertwining with local discourses and initiatives, often used to engage with indigenous issues with long histories or to challenge the premises of European colonialism and its civilizing mission.

However, it is equally true that for a while the early modernizing states (Britain, France, the Netherlands) had the lead not only in condensing coercive military and bureaucratic power. They were also the most efficient in the legitimation of those two by *condensing cultural power*, developing civil societies engaged in critical intellectual exchange, but also increasingly more cohesive national identities, built on shared cultural norms, memory, a shared thought-world, and linked to particular state territories. This enables modernizing states to redistribute power, yet avoid major disruption (Schöpflin, "Nationhood"). A degree of cultural homogeneity is needed in order to allow a modern state to function— a state which is politically heterogeneous, without being unstable and constantly ready to fall apart, Schöpflin argues.

Manuel Castells makes much the same point in a similar context, when he writes: "Legitimation [of power] largely relies on consent elicited by the construction of shared meaning; for example belief in representative democracy. Meaning is constructed in society through the process of communicative action." (12) Despite the similarity, Schöpflin would add that universalist civic concepts like "representative democracy" are not enough to make the rule of a modern state perceived legitimate: "Citizenship is a cold concept. Legal regulation, administrative procedures, rights and entitlements do not build solidarity and trust. Citizenship needs a cultural foundation." ("Nationhood") Modern states are based both on the political and the cultural, and thus it follows that their universalist premises like "democracy" or "citizenship" are always culturally tinged. This includes the early modernizers—even if they see and represent themselves and the world in civic terms, these very universalist assumptions are never "culturally innocent". (Schöpflin, "Nationhood")[17] Metaphorically speaking, the civic contracts that underlie modern state governance are always coded in particular national languages. Thus, they embody a tension beween universalism and particularism.

"Belated" and postcolonial modernization

The success of the early Western modernizing states in being able to condense large amounts of political, economic, military and cultural power made them disproportionally and threateningly dominant in relation to other states and cultural communities. The mass incorporation of colonial territories, the Napoleonic Wars, as well as the "opening" of Japan in 1851 are all manifestations of that dominance in the 18th and 19th centuries. The weaker communities had "no option but respond or vanish" (Schöpflin, "Nationhood"), the result being a frenzy to modernize as quickly as possible, whatever the previous cultural, economic and sociopolitical situation. Germans, though politically fractured in small states, are the first large cultural group in Europe to contest the hegemony of the early modernizers; the formerly loosely ordered multi-ethnic Austro-Hungarian, Ottoman and Russian empires make rapid attempts to centralize and nationalize top-down. Many smaller ethnic groups of these empires, perceiving themselves oppressed in unprecedented ways, as well as sensing new opportunities, and increasingly aware of the discourses of popular sovereignty and national identity, in their turn aspire to condense power and to claim rights.

When trying to understand the "national awakening" movements of the latecomer groups (including Estonians) it is essential to note here how social, political and economic aspirations, and cultural ones in the narrower sense (development and promotion of language, literature, folklore, history-writing, music,

---

17 Thus I do not agree with Schöpflin that "citizenship" or "democracy" are necessarily cold concepts. They can and do become part of a particular culture's "myth-symbol complex" (Fredrik Barth's term Schöpflin uses), inspiring trust and solidarity in their local inflections. Furthermore, even the bureaucratic procedures of a particular state, once predictable and customary, can become part of everyday culture and a source of popular identification.

etc. of the group), are intertwined and interdependent. The historical sociologist Miroslav Hroch studied 19th-20th-century national activism comparatively among a number of small European ethnic groups. These groups all share the characteristics of being part of a larger political unit with a ruling class of a different ethnicity and lacking continuous indigenous traditions of political independence and high culture. Miroslav Hroch's work's main reception has been confined to Nationalism Studies. However, to my mind, his account would be a very helpful comparative source for Postcolonial Studies. Essentially, Hroch is an insightful theorist of decolonizing national movements whose findings could be highly relevant also for studying postcolonial societies overseas.

Hroch is interested in the activists' respective success or failure in mobilizing broad-based popular movements. He establishes that very similar forms and scales of typical patriotic agitation are present in every group, drawing upon cultural attributes of ethnic culture (literature, history). However, he also finds that the agitation can lead to very different results among different groups, and that it does not, *by itself,* ever take a movement into a mass phase. On the one hand, cultural empowerment is essential—on no occasion does a mass movement mobilize itself, if the respective ethnic group does not have (or achieve during the "awakening") high levels of literacy in a shared language and a strong system of communication (Hroch, *Social*, especially 184; cf. Anderson, Deutsch). On the other hand, a movement never mobilized either if the "content that was mediated through this communication system" did not resonate with significant proportions of the group (Hroch, *Social* 185). It did resonate only, Hroch's concludes, when a) the ethnic-linguistic lines coincided with the major socio-political and economic antagonisms at the time of transformation to modernity, and b) when the fledgling national movement was perceived as successfully addressing the relevant indignations and aspirations (*Social* 185-186).

In other words, at least in relation to the circumstances Hroch is studying, the possible impact of 'elite manipulation' by romantic intellectuals ought not to be over-rated. Yet, Hroch's study also implies that the aspect of cultural agitation, though never the sole trigger of a mass patriotic movement, is still one of the essential factors of its success. In my terms, a mass national movement is a modern political body legitimized by the ideal of popular sovereignty. Thus it needs to construct shared meaning and condense cultural power, so that it is not disrupted by the internal heterogeneity and difference of opinion that are its integral characteristics by definition.[18]

---

18 I will discuss Hroch's work particularly on Estonia in more detail in Chapter One.

Having thus far considered the internal mechanisms of latecomer modernization, it is now important to call to mind that latecomers, even those with independent states, can never afford fully to concentrate on their internal resonances and condensation of power. In their endeavor to modernize, they always face the uneasy issue as to what extent they ought to adopt early Western models as the universal blueprint of "modernity", or otherwise aspire to create their own modes of modernity, which would build upon such local structures, traditions and patterns of change that are compatible with and advantageous for modernization. The issue presents itself as a powerful tension, rather than as a definitive dilemma (though it can create conflict and deep divisions in the modernizing collectivity), and respective latecomers solve it in a variety of ways and not necessarily once and for all (Jusdanis, *Belated*; Raud, *A Comparative Analysis*). Yet, at least in the beginning of their endeavors, latecomers cannot but turn to the same pool of ideas, narratives, methods and practices that successful early modernizers had already used. This is so not only because these building blocks are already "around" and that it would be hardly possible to think outside the established frames of reference. It is so also because it is necessary to be seen to be following the "correct" blueprint to get recognition, to get accepted as a moral agent, as a civilized, not backward, culture, by already successful modernizers.[19]

Without doubt, modernization is often socio-culturally disruptive for the early modernizing groups too; it does not happen smoothly, as a self-sufficient and organic unfolding. All modernizing processes, as, indeed, presumably all human cultures, are to some degree triggered and shaped by external forces. However, the outward, yet also internalized, pressure on the latecomers rapidly to conform to a superimposed model, is specific in its character and its forceful impact. On the one hand, the sudden rupture in relation to previous tradition threatens to lose resonance with and alienate much of the population (elites included) and imperil modernization in that way. On the other hand, latecomers tend to feel that their modernities are forever unsuccessful for the opposite reason—because they are different from those of their reference cultures, they continuously consider them as flawed copies of a proper original (Jusdanis, *Belated*, especially xiii-xiv; Pilv; cf. Naipaul, *The Mimic Men*).

Thus there is an in-built tension here between the exigencies to resonate outside on the one hand, and inside on the other. The long-term success and viability of a latecomer mode of modernity depends on its resonance and acceptability both in the domestic framework, and in the regional and international

---

[19] As noted above, the example need not be a Western society.

framework. The mode need not be coherent in the sense that it ought to be able to do away with all inconsistency and struggle e. g. between indigenous and Western, or religious and scientific thought-styles and practices. One can only agree with Chakrabarty that this is neither possible, nor necessary, nor desirable. It is not the issue here with how much consistency or inconsistency a society can live with (this depends on its particular cultural thought-world), but, importantly, with how much *conflict* it wants to, or can afford to, live with, both nationally and internationally. One knows from experience that one *can* combine democracy with "traditional" gender roles, disadvantaged ethnic minorities, imperialism, or even slavery, as long as this is internationally viable, or as long as no affected group arises and demands that equality, fraternity, freedom ought to apply to them too.

Estonian

Inhabited by loosely associated (both cooperating and feuding) tribes, the present day Estonian territory was conquered and formally Christianized during the 13th century Baltic Crusades by the Teutonic Order and the Swedish and Danish crowns. A small German-speaking elite (never more than 10%) of landed nobility and clergy gradually increased its privileges and came to dominate the area. In 1721 Peter I won the territory from the Swedish Empire and incorporated it in the Russian Empire. It remained under Czarist rule until the First World War, continuously locally governed by the Baltic Germans who maintained all their privileges as the ruling class almost to the end of the 19th century. During the 16th-19th centuries the Estonian-speakers mostly belonged to the peasantry of the Baltic German landowners. Particularly since the introduction of serfdom—partially in the 17th and comprehensively in the 18th century—they constituted a by-and-large socially homogeneous land-bound group until the abolishment of serfdom 1816–1819. The freedom of movement and the opportunity to purchase land (from the mid-19th century) opened avenues of accelerated change. In 1918 Estonians declared independence and governed an independent republic during the interwar period. Estonia was coercively annexed by the Soviet Union during the Second World War while *de jure* remaining independent under international law. It reclaimed *de facto* independence 1991 and joined the European Union 2003 and NATO 2004.[20]

---

20 An overview of Estonian history in English can be found in Raun, *Estonia* or Kasekamp, *History*.

Ea Jansen, one of the most eminent Estonian historians places the people's history before the First World War in the postcolonial framework. "When dealing with the history of Estonians from whatever aspect", she argues,

> it ought to be definitely taken into account that, on the one hand, geopolitically and economically the territory has since pre-historicity been part of the Europe, on the other hand, for a long time it has also been a colony of Europe, and this fact has impacted on the whole development in the locality. As claimed by Wilfried Schlau, the editor [...] of an overview of the social history of Baltic Germans, the history of the German colonisation and decolonisation of the Baltic area followed the same model as the general development of European "overseas" colonialism (*Eestlane muutuvas ajas* 12-13).[21]

A slightly unusual peculiarity in the Estonians' case, Jansen continues, is the double, shifting, power arrangement in the provinces of Estonia and Livonia whereby the power was varyingly shared between the local German nobility and (since the Northern War) the Russian Empire. Despite that, "the colonial power over the indigenous people" and a model of European estate society lasted in the Baltics for centuries and "started to crack later than elsewhere in Europe" (13).

The "cracking" evolved into the Estonians' rapid modernization at the intersection of the two hegemonic cultures, German and Russian. Within roughly fifty years from the mid-19th century, the small semi-literate peasant estate speaking various "Estonian" dialects, lacking a "high" culture or a substantial social network, without any historical memory of access to political power and thus without significant symbolic and mythic underpinning for action, transformed itself into a complex, modern society with a national consciousness, ready to establish a nation-state when the opportunity presented itself. As Chapter One will show, this was influenced by important features of pre-modern and early modern heritage feeding into the Estonian modernization processes. This heritage, and experience and aspirations developing from there, entangle with the impact of earlier or stronger modernizers, as well as with that of the changing world at large.

---

[21] All translations into English are mine, unless otherwise referenced. At the recommendation of the publisher I opted for translating closely and only supplying the original language version or other translation versions if it was relevant for the discussion (as it is in Chapter Two and in a few other cases). If the translation is not by me, the reference that is provided is to the translated version of the source and the information about the translator is given in "Works Cited" together with the rest of the information about the source.

While circumstances of the Estonian case are to a certain extent idiosyncratic, they also raise interesting theoretical questions about latecomer and postcolonial modernities much more generally: the dynamics of the "catching-up" with early modernizers; the outcomes and viability of an ongoing endeavor to create and sustain such models of modernity and visions of historical change that would fit local needs; the relationship between political and military power, and cultural hegemony; and the boundary between colonial mimicry and creative reception in processing outward influence. Frequently a group is "late" to develop an indigenous version of modernity because of its history of colonization. However, after the earliest fast spurt in modernization by England, France and the Netherlands in the 18th century, at different periods of modern history most societies have felt "backward" and disadvantaged in relation to their competitive neighbours or (potential) colonizers.

Finally, I want to emphasize that the aim of analyzing the Estonian case in terms of postcolonialism is not to add to the competing victimhood claims abundant in the world. Rather, I want to propose it as a useful frame of reference which would enable us to consider the Estonian discourses of modernity within the global context of different kinds of unequal power relations, colonial formations, and projects of national mobilization. This offers new insights by throwing into relief both historical connections and situational analogies, rather than leaving one with viewing Estonia as a unique case, a regional case, or as a somewhat deficient version of Western normality. As chapters Two, Three and Four will show, the poetics of Estonian literary works analyzed has important correspondences with that of the postcolonial paradigm outlined by scholars in Postcolonial Studies (e. g. Ashcroft et al., *The Empire Writes Back*; Bhabha, "Representation") both in the structural and in the thematic aspects. This recognition enables novel readings of some significant Estonian texts which otherwise remain opaque in important dimensions, as well as add insight into the broader postcolonial paradigm.

Literature

People have been writing texts that today are called literature for at least 25 centuries, and if we count equivalent genres in oral traditions (e.g. songs, tales, myths), presumably throughout the whole of human history. However, these were not gathered under any separate category or differentiated from another kind of, non-artistic, type of texts until the late 18th and early 19th century.

Until about the beginning of the 19th century the European derivatives of the Latin word *litteratura* were used in the sense of "letters", "book learning", rather than in the sense of creative writing, *belles lettres* (Widdowson 31). At the end of the 18th century Romanticists start to use "poetry" (or, in German, *Dichtung*) much in the same sense as "literature" is used today, but privileging verse forms. When the importance of prose, especially the modern novel increased, literature becomes the umbrella word, to cover the "creative" genres in both verse and prose (Williams, *Keywords* 187).

With a variety of emphases, scholars of literary history and scholars of modern nationhood broadly confirm that it is far from a coincidence that "literature" in the modern sense emerges hand in hand with the emergence of nations. Modern nationhood is based on the ideas of mass mobilization and popular sovereignty. Literature, made from the material of a specific vernacular, more than other genres of art, is seen as a strong force for condensing national culture, a new adhesive to help replace older ties created by the discourses and practices of religions. Indeed, observes Widdowson, the concept of literature first takes its form with the primary sense of "national literature"; it is altogether "difficult to discuss 'Literature' abstracted from its determining national conditions of being" (37).

In my analysis, literature participates in creating, as well as enacts in its form, *both* twin characteristics of modern nations discussed in previous sub-chapters —the increasing political heterogeneity, multiplying voices and fora of debate, emergence and broadening of the public sphere on the one hand, and the strive towards the construction of shared meaning, condensing cultural power, on the other. Or to use Mikhail Bakhtin's terminology, there are always both centrifugal and centripetal forces active in the field of literary creation and reception (as well as in the literary works themselves).

To illuminate the relationship between literature and nationhood further, it is useful to consider Benedict Anderson's argument in the now classical *Imagined Communities: Reflections on the Origins and Spread of Nationalism*. According to Anderson, the "old-fashioned" realist novels are in an important sense *like* nations in their form. The kind of novel that Anderson has in mind presents numerous different characters engaged in their various activities, who may be even "largely unaware of one another", yet they are all "embedded in the minds of the omniscient readers" as part of the novel's plot as a whole. One never meets more than a small percentage of one's fellow nationals, yet one has the confidence in their steady simultaneous existence and of the presence of communal ties within a nation. Thus Anderson sees the novel (as well as the newspaper, which has a quintessentially analogous form) as unprecedented forms of imagining, which correlates with large groups of people starting to think of themselves and their society in a new, national, way.

In addition to the overall novel form, Anderson also discusses at length the poetics of introducing local communal agenda in three particular 19th-20th-century novels. The novels make references to actual shared social spaces and social concerns. Anderson is right to emphasize that the works by a José Rizal, a Charles Dickens, a Harriet Beecher-Stowe, or a Lydia Koidula fuse the worlds inside the texts with those on the outside. This is so not only because the texts discuss issues relevant for extra-textual communities, but also because the text-worlds are in their turn widely discussed, and often acted upon, in the "outside" world by large numbers of people—in press, journals, societies, coffee-houses, pubs, homes, activist groups, schools, government institutions, and many other places. The latter result cannot be considered completely extra-literary in its nature, as it is promoted by particular devices *in* the novels, which aim, for example, to entice a multiplicity of different readers into a debate on what are presented as issues of common concern, or to make the readers empathize with characters who belong to social groups they might never meet in the "outside" world.

Having for a while concentrated on the national embeddedness of the novel it is, however, again, important also to emphasize, that like modern cultures themselves, national literatures are not nationally autonomous, self-sufficient, or preoccupied only with internal communal matters or with a fixed group of fellow-nationals. Firstly, as Jonathan Culler points out, a shared vernacular does not necessarily coincide with a shared national community. A book in Spanish can be read, and often directly addresses, a variety of speakers of the language, both in the (former) colonies and in Europe (27-30). Furthermore, what was said above about modern cultures in general is also true of national literatures —a national literature is judged in its domestic framework, yet also in the international one. The latecomer modernities in particular depend on the validation of early successful (literary) modernizers. National language being "at once an affair of the state and the material out of which literature is made" (Casanova 34), *belles lettres* is the most important among art forms on which a latecomer's international acceptance as a respectable, civilized culture, relies. Thus, once again, there is an in-built tension, first and foremost for latecomer literatures, between the exigencies to resonate outside on the one hand, and inside on the other.

Pascale Casanova's *The World Republic of Letters* argues that although literatures are national, they are also part of a world system, which is, among other things, very importantly one of unequal power relations. It "is based on the opposition between a capital, on the one hand, and peripheral dependencies whose relationship to this center is defined by their aesthetic distance from it" (12). That means that to be successful, latecomers must, to an extent, conform to earlier existing models. Essentially, in the literary field too they need to "catch up"—in order to break "into the ranks of established moderns", they must become "up-to-date", familiarize themselves "with the most recent innovations of technique and form" approved by the center (91).

The (unequal) power in the literary world system that Casanova is talking about is partly specifically aesthetic and literary, yet she allows that the latter forms of power are never fully independent from more general cultural value systems, nor from political or economic power. A literature's place in the world (which affects the reception of new works of this literature) depends on the fame and age of the literature's tradition and existence therein of international classics; the prestige of the literature's language; and the nation having a wealthy cultivated literary "milieu", involving education, publishers, critics, prizes, etc. (Casanova 14-18). Clearly none of these factors is a purely aesthetic one. Paradoxically, one of the cultural norms prescriptively associated with "great", high cultural literature (especially strongly since literary modernism) is its autonomy from national, political and economic concerns. The central, most prestigious literatures are most autonomous at least in the sense that they can afford to be "most exclusively devoted to literature as an activity having no need of justification beyond itself" (Casanova 85). This does not mean that the universal, free and timeless "literary capital" cannot be or is not put to national political uses in these cultures (34). Actors in peripheral literatures can win autonomy if they are sufficiently compatible with the central values in order to become internationally recognized, "consecrated" by the center (126-163).

The power relations of the literary world system are not unchanging. The work of Johann Gottfried Herder (1744-1803), or rather, the rippling "Herder effect" he triggered (Casanova 77) undermined the cultural capital of French Enlightenment norms and ideals, earlier viewed as universally valid. Herder located the ultimate source of artistic fertility not in the "high" culture, but in folklore—the soul of any national literature was the "authentic" tradition of its people in its vernacular. Thus oral traditions became (to a degree) an acceptable alternative source of cultural capital, able to lend a young literature the much-needed nobility of age. The national and popular notion of literary "legitimacy" introduced by Herder "was inseparably political and literary" (Casanova 77)—it "encouraged all peoples who sought recognition on equal terms with established nations of the world to stake their claim to literary and political existence" (75).

The Herderian strategy undoubtedly makes powerful claims, and the assumed deep link between an author and his/her native tongue has become an unexamined commonplace of national cultural thinking. However, to my mind, Herderianism has altogether only weakly shifted the power relationship between center and periphery, including the dominance of "central" natural languages. This is among other things testified by the fact that bilingual authors from former European colonies tend to opt for writing in the colonizer's language with its cultural capital, not in a local vernacular, and those who do not, are necessarily less prominent in the world system. "All literary authors in small languages", Casanova observes, "[...] are caught in dramatic structural contradiction" that "forces them to choose" between orienting themselves towards the world, and the presently most powerful values of literariness, which can cut them off from their compatriots, giving them however "literary existence" (257). On the other hand, they can "retreat into a small language that condemns them to invisibility or else to a purely national literary existence" (257).

For all her cool-headed insightfulness, between the lines Casanova without reflection prefers, even valorizes, international-aesthetic literary ambition over a nationally or politically conditioned one. She elaborates on the international constraints on the actors of "small literatures", but not on the internal communal and civic role or functions that literature may fulfil for the national audience in latecomer modernities.[22] On the other hand, numerous critics and authors of "peripheral" latecomer modernities have highlighted exactly those concerns, criticizing and re-defining the "central" notion of the aesthetic. To parallel his own case for Greece, Jusdanis refers to the Kenyan novelist Ngũgĩ wa Thiong'o's statement that art for art's sake has no meaning in Africa (*Belated* 7). The Nigerian author Chinua Achebe emphasized the interconnection between his sociopolitical and aesthetic goals: "Perhaps what I write is *applied art* as distinct from pure. But who cares? Art is important, but so is education of the kind I have in mind. And I don't see that the two need to be mutually exclusive" ("The Novelist" 162; my italics). For Achebe, an African creative writer who avoids his/her contemporary social and political issues "will end up completely irrelevant [...] like that absurd man in the proverb who leaves his burning house to pursue a rat fleeing from the flames" ("The African Writer" 8).

---

22 This perspective, I believe, is also reflected in Casanova's (non-spelled-out) aesthetic judgements—modernism is swiftly preferred to realism, and only "high" cultural works come under her consideration at all.

In early modernities too the "world of letters" was an important realm socializing people into the participatory forms of modern politics. However, there literature quite soon (from about the 19th century) becomes simultaneously commodified and aestheticized, a consumer good on the market and—allegedly—a differentiated sphere of beauty and disinterest. The tension in this discrepancy is resolved by separating "high" literature (valued by people with fine tastes, subject to specialist discourses, not subject to the mechanisms of the market) and low "popular" literature, something indiscriminately consumed by masses, incapable of analyzing their own tastes (cf. Bourdieu, *The Field*).

However, the Western doubled concept of literature (in English "Literature" and "fiction") is not, nor has it ever been, absolute. Firstly, the bourgeois public sphere experience of literary discussion and the proceeding drive to "'literarify' society" at large (Grimminger, qtd. in Jusdanis, *Belated* 97) was early on channelled in the general formal education system, where it is one of the fundamental elements to the very day. Secondly, Jusdanis is right to observe (concerning the West), that "art could not forget the ambition of the Enlightenment—it still aspired to some sort of social effect" (102). "High" literature was supposed to be autonomous from society, above it, an end to itself—yet authors and critics have continuously been seeking social relevance, wanting art to matter in the world. Furthermore, with the influxes of new kinds of voices in the sphere of Western cultural discussion, postcolonial ones among them, towards the end of the 20th century Western attitudes towards the "high"/"popular" art divide have become gradually undermined and relativized.[23]

In postcolonial and/or authoritarian states the cultural sphere in the narrow sense (literature, film, theatre, etc.) often for long periods remains the central realm where *broad-based* civil discussions are carried out and claims for political power can be made. It should be recalled in the context of this book that in the Soviet bloc art, especially literature, performed many if not most of the functions carried out by the media in democracies, as it was less heavily censored, and more usable for speaking between the lines. I also claim that literature's role in the public sphere does not have a uniform history in all societies. It does not automatically disappear in a certain phase of modern development

---

23 Raymond Williams's *Culture and Society* (1958) and *The Long Revolution* (1961), and Pierre Bourdieu's *Distinction* (1979) are early examples. Among the significant ones that have emerged since the 1980s there can be mentioned the projects of New Historicism (e.g. Greenblatt, Butler), Mieke Bal's interdisciplinary cultural analysis based on "travelling concepts" in the humanities, Franco Moretti's "distant reading", and the interdisciplinary studies of cultural memory, including the role various "creative" texts play in its production (e.g. Erll and Nünning).

(expansion of the public sphere) or with decolonization, but rather it also depends on the civic traditions and political socialization in a particular society. Jusdanis attests to a long continuing mass appeal and public visibility of poetry and criticism in Greek society, and resistance to strict fencing-off of the aesthetic sphere by specialists (*Belated*, especially 139-140). In the present book especially Chapter Four will show that the literary sphere has not lost its role as a domain for sociopolitical debate in Estonia in the 21st century. Even if people may read fewer books, the literary-cultural field is by and large accepted as a realm relevant for public matters, and even its internal debates are frequently disseminated through mass media to a broader public.

Modus Operandi and Chapter Overview

Though not practising the particular methods outlined in Mieke Bal's *Travelling Concepts*, this book has been stimulated by its approach to study aesthetic texts "*in view of* their existence in the culture". This means they are not seen as isolated jewels, but as things always-already engaged, as interlocutors, within the larger culture from which they have emerged" (*Travelling Concepts* 9; Bal's italics). Simultaneously, Bal's approach involves the essentiality to pay close attention to a cultural object studied, detailed concentration to its particular characteristics and means as a cultural interlocutor, including literary ones. Indeed, she proposes "a qualified return to the practice of 'close reading'" (10): only thus can be understood how particular cultural texts participate in cultural debates and in the wider patterns of cultural communication, reproduction and change.

Further, the "Estonian literature" considered by this book is not limited to literature in the confined sense but encompasses Estonian writing more generally. Taking the approach habitual in discourse analysis, the primary sources include both fictional and non-fictional texts, involving the fields of historiography, literary criticism, journalism, political speeches, and more. However, whereas I trace the main discourses of modernity across a number of different genres, I put a relatively strong focus on the role exactly literature has played in trying to work through the rapid processes of modernization in their national and transnational context. Creative writing, especially prose, has been dominant over visual arts and music in the Estonian canon, and central for cultural memory and nation-building.²⁴ Since the Estonian-speaking population became almost fully literate during the second half of the 19th century, fiction with its captivating plot lines, empathy-inspiring characters and figurative power became an important field where modern narratives of collective and individual selfhood and historical change were imagined, debated and circulated (cf. Hennoste, "Heroism" 1146).

Discussing the circulation of the discourses of modernity in literature I consider "high cultural" literary texts next to popular adventure stories, romances and "girl books". While some of the works studied here have enjoyed international critical acclaim for their literary qualities, others have not been translated into Western languages, yet have exerted important influence on the Estonian popular consciousness intraculturally. The choice of the texts for extended analysis, while partly subjective, proceeds from the principle that the selected texts are (or were) widely read by Estonians and important in terms of their long-term impact on the processing and construction of the experience of modernization. By these criteria, many more works could have been added to the selection under consideration, but I was satisfied that the set was varied and historically representative enough to let me discuss what I consider the most important facets of the topic.

My aim is "to transcend a purely aesthetic approach and go beyond the methodological textualism (the idea that individual texts are the natural unit of analysis) that has held literary criticism for too long in its grip" (322), as the scholar of Cultural Memory Studies, Ann Rigney, suggests. The main object of attention is discursive formations and the socio-cultural work they perform, rather than "isolated literary highpoints" (cf. Rigney 322). At the same time I consider attentively the individual literary qualities and genre poetical specifics of the texts studied, as well as the (usually institutionalized) contexts in which the different genres occur. For the purposes of the argument in this book it is important to note how different texts are received, interpreted and maintained in the culture: their particular poetic and thematic features influence how they resonate or (sometimes temporarily) lose their resonance with their cultural interlocutors.

Chapter One discusses the history of Estonian modernization, providing a relatively broad account of the discursive and institutional aspects of its de-

---

24 I agree with Epp Annus's judgement that in Estonian literary sphere prose has been the main means for the construction of collective narratives, whereas lyrical poetry has played a supportive role, adding some evocative figures and images ("Kirjanduskaanon ja rahvuslik identiteet" 10).

velopment with specific attention to the role of the literary sphere. It addresses the international and national critical debates relevant for the topic: the alleged rootlessness of the Estonian pattern of modernization that involved in the 19th century; the specific features, tropes and mechanisms of circulation of the discourses of modernity in Estonia across time; the significance of the civic and ethnic models of nation-building; the characteristics and collapse of Estonian liberal democracy in the interwar period; the question of the appropriate theoretical paradigms for understanding Sovietization and its aftermath in the global context; the discursive and institutional entanglement of neoliberalism, nationalism and democracy in the 21st century.

Against that background chapters Two, Three and Four each focus on a particular literary-cultural nexus providing in-depth analyses of fictional and non-fictional texts illuminating the construction and circulation of Estonian discourses of modernity during different periods of modernization. At that, I want to emphasize that the organization of the book is thematic, rather than strictly chronological. The texts, sometimes coeval, sometimes not, are discussed comparatively to allow insight into key aspects of modernization across time.

Chapter Two studies the mechanisms of change in the thought-world of Estonian culture during the second half of the nineteenth century, as the Estonian-speaking community was emerging from the domination of the Baltic German upper class. This is explored through the case study of two historical novellas about anti-colonial uprisings in Peru and in Jamaica respectively, translated loosely from German into Estonian by one of the key figures of the Estonian National Awakening, the author and journalist Lydia Koidula. Outlining the intriguing pattern of changes made by Koidula in comparison to the German versions, the analysis draws upon ideology-critical methods of Translation Studies closely associated with the Postcolonial Studies, as well as the close reading strategies of the Descriptive Translation Studies. The reading makes "translation" function as an extended figure for the modernizing and decolonizing discursive change in Estonia more generally.

Chapter Three discusses Estonian *Bildungsromane*, a genre troping and "domesticating" the challenges of modernity and modern selfhood (Moretti *The Way*). The historical space in this chapter stretches from the end of 19th to the end of the 20th century, highlighting both the big differences and the subtle continuities in the protagonists' life worlds and endeavors of self-realization. The works discussed come from the Czarist period, the interwar republic, the Soviet period and its immediate aftermath in the beginning of 1990s. The Estonian texts will be analyzed both in comparison to Western and postcolonial *Bildungsroman* models. Among these readings most space is dedicated to *Truth and Justice* (*Tõde ja õigus*, 1926–1933) by A.H. Tammsaare, a five-volume novel considered one of the most significant texts for the Estonian culture. It is discussed as an idiosyncratic example of the *Bildungsroman*, a poetic *tour de force* that forges a model of modern Estonia acceptable both intra- and internationally , as it inflects Western, Russian and postcolonial models. The analysis provides further insight into the discursive strategies that can be employed when culturally working through belated rapid modernization, as well as to explain the canonical position and continuing relevance of Tammsaare's novel in Estonian society.

Chapter Four considers the discourses of national language and national literature among the Estonian discourses of modernization. One of the two foci of the chapter is the Young Estonia movement's early-20th-century project to radically "renew" the Estonian language and Estonian culture inspired by an array of foreign influences. The polemical reception of this project and its impact on Estonian society has lasted until the present day. The case of Young Estonia is placed in the comparative framework of international literary and cultural modernism that developed in the 1880s–1920s, in response to the challenges of the period that social scholars (such as Hartmut Rosa) see as one of the two most rapid phases of modernization until now. There emerges the question how Young Estonian postcolonial reformism and openness to foreign "languages" (both literally and metaphorically) relates to the modernist desire to create new languages and generally "make it new" in the cultures with long literary traditions.

Secondly, I outline the intense intellectual debates still going on in the 21st century on Young Estonia, starting with the movement's 100th anniversary in 2005. I treat the debate not as a reservoire of secondary authority on how to judge the movement, but rather as a primary source that highlights a pervasive controversy in the society over the topical pressures of globalization and related competing visions of modern Estonian statehood. In this connection, the debate is placed in dialogue with Andrus Kivirähk's novel *The Man Who Spoke Snakish* (2007), a historical fantasy of the black-humor type, featuring the last human speaker of a dying language as its main character. The novel's publication and reception coincided with the Young Estonia debate, and also with a serious crisis in the relationship between ethnic Estonians and the ethnic Russian minority in Estonia amid the global economic crisis.

The Afterword will shortly revisit the main concerns of this book and connect them to the present-day context.

Chapter One. Another Road to Modernity

The chapter sketches the development of Estonian modernization, aiming to create a preliminary broad picture of the discursive and non-discursive aspects of this history with special attention to the literary sphere. The central concerns of the chapter are signalled by its title, which alludes to Liah Greenfeld's *Nationalism: Five Roads to Modernity* (1992), a history of the modernization of England, France, Germany, Russia and the United States, a study that will be mentioned again in this chapter, and to Johann Gottfried von Herder's polemic against universalist historiography, *Another Philosophy of History for the Education of Mankind* (*Auch eine Philosophie der Geschichte der Menschheit*, 1774).

The chapter has two interrelated foci. On the one hand, it introduces the basics of the Estonian discourses of modernity: the cluster of cultural thought and communication patterns that emerge as central for narrating collective and individual selfhood, historical change and rupture in the Estonian writing. While the subsequent chapters dedicate more space to closely reading the varied enactment of the discourses in the poetics of particular texts, here I pay more attention to the social embedding of the discourses and the dynamics of their circulation among the different groups of Estonian speakers. Secondly, the chapter addresses the internationally impactful theoretical debates that I see as most crucial for the topic: the formation patterns of "latecomer" and postcolonial modernities; the civic and ethnic models of nation-building; the theoretical paradigms for understanding Sovietization and its aftermath in the global context; the impact of neoliberalism on the models of nationhood and democracy. Such a double focus helps to put the Estonian case in the global framework and illuminate it from aspects that remain invisible, if treated simply as national or regional history. At the same time it contributes to the international debates through the case study, scrutinizing *their* underlying assumptions and blind spots.

Creation ex nihilo? Re-reading the Warwick Debates

The rapid emergence of an Estonian-speaking modern nation at the end of the 19th century where there had been no history of high culture or statehood before presents a useful concentrated case for studying modernizing social change. Thus in Nationalism Theory the Estonian "anomaly" has been a frequent example and a point of debate, although rarely in the form of studies focusing on Estonians in particular, but rather as a figurative illustration to different theoretical arguments. "Estonia has been dragged into nationalism theory as a kind of offstage actor," observes George Schöpflin, an "emblematic case" (Schöpflin, "Nationalism Theory"). One of the intriguing, as well as prominent, occurrences of Estonia in that role are the so-called Warwick Debates (1995–1996) between two influential scholars of nationalism and modernity, Ernest Gellner and Anthony Smith.

The Warwick Debates concerned the formation patterns of modern nations, their relationship (or lack thereof) with the pre-modern communities (*ethnies*) that preceded them. Gellner and Smith belong to the "modernist" camp in Nationalism Studies that argues that nations in the modern sense (i.e. political nations based on the ideal of popular sovereignty and citizenship) are not to be perceived as ancient "slumbering" communities "awakened" by the national patriots but, rather, as forms of modern organization that develop in response to "specifically modern conditions—those of early industrialism or its anticipations, social mobility, the need for mass literacy, public education and the like" ("The Warwick Debates", A. Smith summarizing Gellner's views).[25]

Yet, whereas for the "ethno-symbolist" Smith, modern political nationalisms and nations are still rooted in and influenced by their particular pre-modern pasts—certain ethnic communities and identities, which typically have a sense of shared history, myths of common descent, etc.—, for the "pure modernist" Gellner "the genealogy of the nation" is entirely "located in the requirements of modernity, not the heritage of pre-modern pasts" ("The Warwick Debates", A. Smith summarizing Gellner's views). Nations, so Gellner, do not have "navels", they are like the biblical Adam who was not born from certain parents but was

---

[25] "Modernist" theorists do not agree on an exact list of the necessary conditions for modern nationhood.

created by God as a grown man. Or if some nations seem to have navels linking them to a pre-modern past, this is rather irrelevant for the argument, because it can be shown that some modern nations live very well *without* navels, thus the navels where they do exist are purely ornamental. ("The Warwick Debates") At this point Gellner introduces the example of the Estonians as an entirely navel-free and parentless modern nation:

> There are very, very clear cases of modernism[26] in a sense being true. I mean, take the Estonians. At the beginning of the nineteenth century they didn't even have a name for themselves. They were just referred to as people who lived on the land as opposed to German or Swedish burghers and aristocrats and Russian administrators. They had no ethnonym. They [had no] ethnic self-consciousness.
>
> Since then they've been brilliantly successful in creating a vibrant culture. [...] It's a very vital and vibrant culture, but, it was created by the kind of modernist process which I then generalize for nationalism and nations in general.[27] And if that kind of account is accepted for some, then the exceptions which are credited to other nations are redundant.

According to Gellner, modern nations are based on literary "high" cultures and formal education, not folk cultures, whatever nationalists may claim. Thus, to counter Gellner's arguments, Smith first enumerates modern nations (English, Russians, Israelis, etc.) who have strong links to *pre-modern* "high" cultures, elite cultures. Then he moves on to Estonians and Finns:

> Now, we may admit that in the case of the nations I have cited, it makes sense to explore their genealogies. But, what of modern nations that have lost their parents or never had them, or are not quite sure who their parents were? This poses considerable problems for nationalists attempting to create nations. It is certainly one reason for the enormous popularity of the Kalevala with the Finns, and Kalevipoeg with the Estonians. [...] Both epics traced the descent of the Finns and Estonians to Iron Age culture-communities, and thereby provided these dispossessed and subject peoples with a sense of their dignity through native ancestry and an ancient and heroic ethnic past.

---

26 By modernism, nationalism theory means the modernity of nationhood.
27 In another version of his Warwick Debates presentation, in *Nationalism*, Gellner clarifies the process he believes took place in Estonia: "A national culture was born, by the usual nineteenth-century methods (national theatre, museum, education)" (97).

Based on this answer, Smith apparently agrees that folk cultures as such do not constitute proper "parenthood" for modernity. However, "low" culture (folklore) can be turned into something resembling pre-modern "high" culture (an epic), which the Estonians and the Finns take careful trouble to do. Thereby Smith draws the conclusion for nationalism theory that the existence of parents and navels is relevant, and not purely ornamental—nations put in a lot of work to prove to themselves and to outsiders that they have them.

As indicated above, I, of course, agree with Smith that a viable modernity to a certain extent must draw upon such local features that are advantageous (or at least not blatantly disadvantageous) for modernization. However, the problem is that Smith, similarly to Gellner, views "modernity" as an outside force that sweeps national movements and nations into place, rather than studying it as something that itself can only be created through the interaction of particular people in their historical circumstances, whereas the latter can be very different.

In my argument, all people(s) have pre-modern history, whether or not they have pre-modern statehood, high culture or ethnic self-awareness, and an understanding of that history is crucial for understanding their models of modernity. Whether a modern nation develops relatively gradually out of a pre-modern ethnic community or is formed based on a hastily drawn colonial map, it in any case involves *humans*, who are, by definition, cultural beings always already socialized into certain institutions, practices and discourses concerning communication, work, family, power relations, spiritual life, etc. These cultural features do not all disappear overnight with modernization, but rather, many of them are, for better or for worse, transformed into intermittent or long-term features of a modern national society, if the latter should come into being and last.[28]

Smith, even talking of "low" cultures overwhelmingly concentrates on the more "epic" aspects of communal pre-modern inheritance (mythic narratives, heroes, festive rituals). Without denying their potential importance, I would also highlight the modern connections to, and modernizing transformations of, pre-modern "common sense" worldviews and everyday life patterns. Among the latter, the ones in currency immediately at the time of modernization are, in my analysis, more impactful than myths about the Iron Age.

Based on my mapping of the dominant discourses in Estonian literature relating to modernity, the following aspects of the pre-modern communities

---

28 This is not to say that new important features with no significant pre-modern pedigree cannot emerge during the modern period, e.g. government forms based on novel ideas concerning legitimation of power; new technologies (fast transport, telephone, internet) and related social interaction patterns.

of "Estonians" stand out as those most strongly feeding into Estonian modernity, impacting upon it at the period of its formation, or lastingly, even until the present day:

a) pre-modern presence of mutually understandable dialects; rudiments of a communication network and, since the early 18th century, relatively rapidly increasing literacy in mutually understandable dialects
b) currents in folklore, education and religious life that bridge pre-modernity and modernity
c) shared socioeconomic and political history: long-term experience of serfdom and peasant status, pre-occupation with land and agriculture; lack of pre-modern statehood or political autonomy as an ethnic group; specific regional identity within the Russian Empire due to the idea of Baltic autonomy sustained by the German-speaking elites
d) shared "significant others" (different in social standing and/or ethnoculturally): Baltic Germans, Russians, Finns, Latvians.

These factors promoted the conceptualization of certain pre-modern identities that differentiated the "Estonians" from adjacent cultures and conditioned their patterns of nation-building and modernization. Other important influences emerged later, but I will also repeatedly refer to the aspects of the "navel" sketched above in what remains of this chapter, as well as throughout the book.

The formation of Estonian modernity

In his *Social Preconditions of National Revival in Europe*, Miroslav Hroch elaborates a three-phase model depicting the formation of a number of small European nations, including Estonians. The national movements emerge in the conditions of economic modernization and the political weakening of the Old Regime. During Hroch's Phase A, scholars, often members of a politically dominating ethnic group in the territory, start to value and study the language, folklore, history, etc. of the dominated group (Hroch, *Social* 22). They are usually not interested in patriotic agitation, but rather motivated by "a patriotism of the Enlightenment type"—"affection for the region" and "thirst for knowledge" (23). However, this endows the subaltern forms of knowledge with some validation and status. In Phase B, scholarly research may well expand, but its main driving force is not interest in antiquities anymore, but the desire of a broadening group of activists mainly or entirely from the dominated group to persuade and mobilize people in the "national" interest. Phase C is characterized by widespread national consciousness and a mass national movement with a well-developed organizational structure extending over the whole territory the people inhabits. Hroch's model is not teleological: not only can the processes take place with different speed and timing, they can also be temporarily or permanently interrupted in any phase.

In the Estonian case, the beginning of Phase A can be placed at the end of the 18th and beginning of the 19th century. The first German intellectuals to acknowledge Estonian culture were more preoccupied with Latvians, but nevertheless left a lasting mark on the Estonian modern culture as well. Johann Gottfried Herder included Estonian folk songs in his publication *Voices of the Peoples in their Songs* (*Stimmen der Völker in Liedern*, 1787), thus both giving them a large audience and "consecrating" them for the international public (cf. Casanova). The liberal publicist Garlieb Helwig Merkel (1769–1850) is on par with Herder in terms of his impact on Estonian and Latvian modernizing thought. A pioneer for later Estonian and Latvian conceptualizations of history and change, he influenced it by providing in his *Latvians, Particularly in Livland, at the End of the Philosophical Century* (*Die Letten, vorzüglich in Liefland, am Ende des philosophischen Jahrhunderts,* 1796) romantic heroic images of Estonian and Latvian pre-Christian pasts. He also, in an unprecedentedly scathing way, criticized the ignoble treatment and savage institutions (serfdom) to which the local elite had subjected the former noble savages.

Yet, even more impactful than these inspiring narratives and images is *his general understanding of historical change*. For Merkel, influenced by Herder, the history of humankind as a whole is progressive, and yet the fates of particular cultures are cyclical, or even just twisting and turning (and the latter aspects of history interest him considerably more). Thus, the Estonians and Latvians may soon regenerate themselves and enjoy a new heyday—the Baltic nobility who think that the contemporary situation is inevitable are simply wrong. This model of history left a lasting impact on Estonian historiography (Undusk, "Kolm võimalust" 721-729) and discourses of modernity and nationhood generally. As we will see in the following chapters it also emerges as the dominant model for narrating change in Estonian literature: the breach with tradition and (un)predictability of the future is a central trope. In its semi-cyclicality it is at odds with the linear time model hegemonic in modernity. However, it offers an explanatory frame in which an arduous project of modernization can be enthusiastically supported as a progressive phase of rising from the ashes, and even disruptive violent events can be embalmed and (retroactively) made part of a larger continuity (cf. Krull 7). This narrative model works both on the individual and collective level. The related narrative of the destiny of the Estonian collective self can be described as a particular variant of the "phoenix rises from the ashes" myth of national self-explanation (Schöpflin, "The Functions" 32-33).

Further, during the first decades of the 19th century an increasing number of Baltic German literati, mostly serving as Lutheran clergy, became active in Estonia. Strongly influenced both by Enlightenment and Herderian ideas, they took to the study and advancement of the Estonian language and culture. The Pärnu pastor Johann Heinrich Rosenplänter (1782–1846) launched the first scholarly publication on Estonian, *Studies Towards Better Knowledge of the Estonian Language* (*Beiträge zur genauern Kentniss der ehstnischen Sprache*), which appeared in 1813–1832 in 22 volumes, counting all the prominent Estophiles, as well as the few existing educated Estonians, like Kristjan Jaak Peterson (1801–1822) among its contributors. In 1838, the Estonian Learned Society was founded, which, among many other things, became the institutional home for the creation of the national epic *Kalevipoeg*. The latter was accomplished by a somewhat new kind of Estophiles: Friedrich Robert Faehlmann (1798–1850) and Friedrich Reinhold Kreutzwald (1803–1882), who were university educated (in medicine) and primarily German-speaking, yet of former-serf parents and considered themselves Estonians. Faehlmann and Kreutzwald bridge Hroch's Phase A and Phase B in terms of their motivation for creating the epic as well. Initially they meant the epic as a monument to a disappearing culture, not a battle-cry for a newly regenerated (or imagined) one (Kreutzwald, "Preface" 293, 295; Undusk, "Eksistentsiaalne Kreutzwald"). *Kalevipoeg* was first published between 1857–1861 as a German-Estonian scholarly edition, but in 1862 an abridged version for the common reader followed.

Before moving to the development of patriotic agitation in Estonia (Hroch's Phase B), I wish to discuss in some detail another pre-modern force introduced to Estonians by Germans, because it is a significant, yet frequently under-emphasized factor in the formation of the Estonian modernity the way it did, as well as an enormously important impact on the Estonian thought-world and literature. This is the religious denomination of Moravian Brethren.[29] It first started to spread among Estonian and Latvian serfs, as well as among some Bal-

---

29 The denomination is also internationally known as the Bohemian Brethren; *Herrnhuter Brüdergemeinde*; the Moravian Church; *Unitas Fratrum*. The Estonian terms are *herrnhuutlased* and *vennastekogudus*.

tic nobility during the 1730s, running intertwined with, counter, and parallel to the concerns of the Estophiles and later to those of national activists. Historians of Estonia generally agree that while the earlier long influence of Christianity in Estonia cannot be denied, "it can nevertheless be said that it was the Moravian movement that truly awakened a great number of Estonians to spontaneous and enthusiastic acceptance of the Christian truths" (*Estonica*). Furthermore, it is to a large proportion the impact of the Moravian movement that the full Bible was published in North Estonian in 1739[30], and that the literacy rates reached two-thirds among adult Estonian peasants towards the end of the 18th century (reading only, writing rates are estimated to have been considerably lower) and became close to 90% by the 1850s (Raun, *Estonia* 54-55). From the 1730s onwards there is also an increasing number of Estonian-language literature, intended to enlighten the peasants, first written by German-speaking clergy (Vinkel, *Eesti* 17-19).

The Moravian Brethren denomination is a direct offshoot of the Hussites, followers of Jan Hus (1372-1415) in Bohemia. Founded as *Jednota bratrská* in 1457, the brethren officially seceded from the Church of Rome 1467, which makes them one of the earliest Protestant churches. An impactful Moravian brother who needs to be mentioned here is the educationalist and the first Moravian bishop John Amos Comenius (1592-1670), whose views strongly influenced Count Nicholas Ludwig von Zinzendorf (1700-1760), the re-founder of the church in the beginning of the 18th century and its introducer to the Baltics (Fahlbusch 649). Zinzendorf was an educated and widely travelled person, and a Pietist by upbringing. In 1722, he decided to grant some land to a group of religious refugee Moravian Brethren. He subsequently became deeply involved with them and under his leadership there developed a new religious, social, and political unit, which in its creed and praxis intertwined the older Moravian influences with early Lutheran and Pietist ones, also developing entirely new features influenced by the currents of the time and by Zinzendorf's personality. (Fahlbusch 649; Hillerbrand 864, 2079) Very briefly, the dominant features of the revived Moravian Church could be outlined as follows.

Unlike many other Protestants, the Moravian Church strongly focuses on Christ and his suffering. Every believer's personal relationship to Christ, his/her regeneration (analogous to the need to be "born again" taught by Pietists),

---

30 The New Testament had been published already in 1715 under the influence of the Pietist clergy. This had an important influence on the development of the Estonian language, but the Pietists attracted primarily the German-speaking clergy and nobility, not the peasants.

and justification by faith alone, are at the core of its creed (Hillerbrand 1310). Despite the Moravian emphasis on Christ's Passion, the message it derives from there is optimistic and hopeful. Differently from earlier Pietism, the believer's regeneration ought not to be "a process of guilt, pain, sin and distress, but a joyful apprehension of a loving father" (Gollin 146-147). The centrality of Christ's suffering derives from early Lutheranism (Hillerbrand 1491), but creates affinity with Greek Orthodoxy, with which the Moravians have liturgical similarities as well.[31]

On the one hand, an individualistic and introspective creed, on the other hand, the spirituality of the Moravian Church is strongly marked by the emphasis on neighbourly love, fellowship, and practical cooperation. The spirit behind the apparent duality is the perceived interrelationship between one's personal regeneration, and one's contribution to the continuation of God's plans in the world. The central conception is that if one is personally renewed through God's grace, one leads by personal example and works in service to mankind.

The Moravians' educationalist work, both in Germany and in their other settlements, including Estonia, relies on all the above-mentioned characteristics of the Moravian Church. It is in accordance with the idea expressed by Comenius that education as a means of personal salvation and a tool of God's work should be available to everyone: "not the children of the rich or of the powerful only, but of all alike, boys and girls, both noble and ignoble, rich and poor, in all cities and towns, villages and hamlets, should be sent to school" (Comenius). Their pedagogical methodology too follows the spirit of Comenius and that of Pietist educationalists like August Hermann Francke (1663-1727) who emphasize that education ought to rely on the thought and individual experience of the learner, rather than rote memorization, and that it ought to promote the building of a strong work ethic in the learner's life.

Thus the most basic Moravian schooling would seek to achieve literacy in a vernacular; certain knowledge of the scripture (drawing upon emotionally charged hymns, as well as the Bible itself); practical skills, like accomplishment in a craft. In addition to that the brethren consciously put special emphasis on promoting people's organizational and administrative skills, so that they could carry responsibilities in improving their religious and communal life.

---

31 Probably the best known among the Moravians' colorful liturgies is the Easter morning sunrise service, expressive of its spirituality (centrality of Christ and regeneration) as a whole. At Easter Sunday dawn congregations gather in graveyard and greet the rising of the sun with joyful choral singing and brass bands. According to Zinzendorf, the tradition began spontaneously, following the example of Greek Orthodox Church ("The Easter Morning Sunrise Service").

The Moravians supported lay priesthood (women not excluded) and sought to involve the members in the running of the congregation, including its intercongregational correspondence.

The Moravian mission reached the Baltics as early as 1729, Zinzendorf himself visited Estonia and Livonia in 1736 (Põldmäe 34-35). The movement won increasing popularity among the local serfs on whom the official Lutheran religion had sat very lightly (Võõbus 104, 110-118). The optimistic message of regeneration accompanied by affective music came shortly after the misery of the Great Northern War (1700–1721). The gospel was spread not by the clergy of the landlords, but rather by travelling craftsmen who quickly became fluent in the vernaculars, thus speaking to the Baltic serfs in their own language in two senses of the word. There is also considerable evidence that the Moravians' egalitarianism had its part in winning hearts and minds.

Active peasants could gain positions of some esteem and self-fulfilment in both the church and community. They served as lay preachers, organized events, exchanged information with other mission congregations as far away as Greenland or Suriname, wrote their Christian autobiographies and translated religious literature from German, sang in choirs and played in brass-bands. In addition, egalitarianism could also provide a rationale for social protest or upfront rebellion. The best-known early example of the latter is the charismatic Moravian lay preacher Tallima Paap and his followers who got in trouble with authorities in 1842 for arguing that the power of German overlords was from Satan and that the manorial lands should be divided between peasants in equal shares (Võõbus 106).

Although officially not separate from the Lutheran church, the spreading movement became very unpopular with mainstream Lutheran clergy and with a greater part of the nobility, who had it proscribed by the Czarist government from 1743. In 1764, the ban was lifted, and the movement enjoyed its greatest popularity during the first half of the 19th century, when it developed a well-organized network of prayer houses all over the region, as well as bred several mystical strands. In 1839, the number of members in Estonia and Livonia totalled 50,000 (*Estonica*). After that, increased pressure from the mainstream Lutheran church and, even more importantly, general secularization during the second half of the 19th century caused the decline of the Moravians (*Estonica*).

Spreading written culture, the Moravians are with justification held responsible for the decline of Estonian traditional folk culture from the turn of the 18th and 19th centuries. This included the loss of many semi-heathen customs which had been less affected by the official churches, and the destruction of numerous pre-Christian sacred sites. Yet, the historian Toivo Raun cautions that the influence of the brethren ought not to be overestimated—after all, even in their heyday the number of members did not exceed 10% of the population. "For all the importance of Pietism [i.e. Moravians], it should not be assumed that paganism disappeared among the peasantry" (Raun, *Estonia* 53).

Raun's point is undoubtedly true, yet it should be noted that the dissemination of Moravian discourses and practices through schooling, concerts, ceremonies, and social events was wide. Thus their impact extended far beyond the core group of devout believers, and they may well have influenced people syncretistically. Furthermore, whereas generally the Estophiles are mentioned as the main pioneers for the following Estonian national movement, it is also worth adding that Faehlmann and Kreutzwald, as well as the prominent leaders and ideologues of the Estonian national movement in Phase B, had all without exception family background among the Moravian brethren.[32] Although some of those modernizers became hostile or scornful towards Moravian sensibilities, or against church and religion in general, it is in itself not strange that families that encouraged book learning, music, and organizational skills should have bred future national activists. Finally, as nauseating as the brethren's contemporary enlightened Estophiles may often have found the emotionalism and "superstition" of the brethren, yet, with hindsight we ought not to be blind to the affinities between the two groups.

What Crowner and Christianson observe in *The Spirituality of German Awakening* rings true for the Estonian context as well. Even though there was often no love lost between the rationalist enlighteners and their contemporary religious revivalists,

> [t]he Awakened[33] were not as far removed from the Enlightenment as many believed. In their scepticism of traditional church structures, as well as in their organization of new initiatives, they shared a spirit of rational inquiry that does not simply accept the status quo. Like the leaders of the Enlightenment, the Awakened desired liberation from the strictures of the past and were optimistic about what could be achieved. Both camps espoused more individual autonomy, more personal responsibility, and a great sense of individual worth. The ecumenical spirit of the Awakening was also related,

---

32 I mean Johann Voldemar Jannsen (1819–1890), Jakob Hurt (1839–1907), Carl Robert Jakobson (1841–1882) and Jannsen's daughter Lydia Jannsen (Koidula) (1843–1886).
33 By "the Awakened" the authors refer to the followers of the Protestant revival churches like the Moravian Brethren.

if only indirectly, to the scientific method's dispassionate and unified view of the world and the Awakening's emphasis on the practice of faith and on the importance of experience corresponds to the Enlightenment's delight in empirical proof. (Crowner and Christianson 13-14)

In the case of Estonia there were three points in particular where the Estophile and the Moravian currents coincided or worked to the same modernizing effect. Firstly, in both cases the indigenous underclass acquired novel attention and respect, even if with different emphasis—in the case of Estophiles primarily directed towards folk *culture*, and in the case of Moravians towards the folk *people* (fellow human beings in Estonian incarnation). Secondly, high value was placed on the pursuit of formal education and on self-betterment in general. Thirdly, Garlieb Merkel's vision of cyclical-spiral historical change has an affinity to the Moravian emphasis on personal and communal rebirth and renewal. Both ways of thinking about history see it as a course of ruptures followed by regeneration and promote positive evaluation of historical change.

The Estophile and Moravian influences feed into and shape the period of national agitation (Hroch's Phase B) that took place roughly from the beginning of the 1860s to the beginning of 1880s. The immediately preceding changes in the economic and legal situation of the Estonian peasantry were an essential contributing factor. In a delayed move to modernize, between 1849-1856 the provincial Diets finally passed new agrarian laws, which allowed the peasants to start purchasing farms (for free market prices) in perpetuity, and thus laid the foundation for the gradual emergence of peasant landowners. The reformism of the early period of Alexander II's reign (1855-1881) made several changes possible. The network of the elementary village schools broadened and, furthermore, the schools were emancipated from the German pastors and moved under the administration of local governments instead. As discussed above, literacy was relatively widespread among Estonians already in the 18th century. However, for a long time there was little to read in the Estonian language. Only from the mid-19th century and especially the end of the 1850s, as censorship barriers temporarily liberalized, Estonian-speaking educators and activists started publishing increasing numbers of secular titles, many promoting Estonian cultural identity or addressing topical problems (Vinkel, *Eesti* 231-232; 266-300).

The year 1857 could well serve as a symbolic starting point for Phase B, because that year Johann Voldemar Jannsen founded the first Estonian-language weekly newspaper *Perno Postimees* and addressed its readers as "dear Estonian people" in the first issue. This was followed by Jannsen's second newspaper *Eesti*

Postimees 1863, which he edited together with his daughter Lydia Koidula. The paper discussed local and foreign events in an accessible style and devoted considerable space to fiction (see Chapter Two for a detailed account). Carl Robert Jakobson ran a rival paper, the more directly political *Sakala* 1878-1882. Both papers had a print number of about 5000 at the end of the 1870s and several hundred correspondents (Jansen, *Eestlane* 415-416).

Beginning in the 1860s, national activism in societies and associations became another widespread feature of Phase B in Estonian life. There were all-Estonian initiatives like the Estonian Alexander school movement, which strived to raise money and establish an Estonian-language secondary school; the Society of Estonian Literati; the Estonian Agricultural Association; six all-Estonian song festivals organized between 1869-1896. Those endeavors rested upon a network of hundreds of local societies and clubs, devoted to literature, music, drama, adult education, agriculture, temperance, etc. (Raun, *Estonia* 76) There were also salons of activists where topical cultural and political issues were discussed in private houses and sociable circumstances (Laar 343-354).

Opinions differ as to when exactly the activist national movement became a mass movement, passing over to what Hroch calls Phase C (Hroch, *Social* 80; Raun and Plakans, "The Estonian"). By the 1880s ethnic patriotism may have started to become an everyday value to share among different groups of Estonians, as opposed to being a ground for activist claims (Laar 131). However, during the 1880s the Czarist government also intensified Russification, in the endeavor to centralize and modernize the Empire, particularly concerned about Baltic Germans' possible orientation towards the strengthened Germany and the Germanization of Estonians and Latvians (*Estonica*). The centralized Russian nationalism meant, among other things, clamping down on Estonians' public expressions of national identity (publications, societies, mass events), and it is difficult to measure what people thought or did in small groups (Raun and Plakans "The Estonian"; Raun "Nineteenth-").

To track the emergence of the mass movement, Raun, following Walker Connor, suggests to "work backwards" from "an effective illustration of mass mobilization in the name of the nation" (Raun, "Nineteenth-" 135; Connor 99). For the Estonians, such a case is their organized mass participation in the political events of 1905. The 1905 revolution in Estonia was a call for political modernization, directed against the Old Regime both in terms of Czarist power and Baltic German privilege. The demands were made in national terms—the all-Estonian Congress demanded Estonian national autonomy (within Russia) with a strongly empowered national government which was to be elected by universal suffrage (Raun, *Estonia* 85; Raun "Nineteenth-" 135; Raun, "1905").

"Working backwards"—the revolution was preceded by the Estonianization of major cities, modernization of agriculture and beginnings of industrialization, as well as the appearance of daily newspapers and a new sharp rise in the number of bookshops and published titles. In 1905, Young Estonia emerged as a modernist art and literature group of major relevance, pressing for a more refined cultural life, as well as for a more developed common written language. It is perhaps telling that the slogan of the group was "Let us remain Estonians, but let us also become Europeans!"—the existing national identity was already a fact, now the challenge was to make it better, renew it. The Russification campaign, though painfully felt, had waned without much lasting effect (Raun, *Estonia* 67). If anything, Estonians had won ground from Baltic Germans, who had also lost rights with Russification, and had had many more of these to lose compared to Estonians. Learning Russian also opened new contacts, cultural avenues and "radical political ideas, which previously had been unknown" (Raun, *Estonia* 67). Metaphorically speaking, there had emerged a shadow modern society locked in the shell of the Old Regime, tapping at it in frustration. It is not so strange that in 1905 something cracked.

The revolution brought backlash, rather than change, yet it provided Estonians with a significant, albeit traumatic experience in political organization. Furthermore, the violence that had been involved intensified the hostility between Baltic Germans and Estonians to the point of no return. Thus in a major way it prepared the events of 1918-20, which led to the independent Estonian republic. Again, although the establishment of Estonian statehood was certainly not an inevitable outcome and would have been impossible without favorable international circumstances, neither was it a sudden or a rootless event. Indeed, the same ought to be repeated concerning the entire process that I have briefly sketched above—that of a pre-modern peasantry transforming into a modern society. The transformation was certainly relatively rapid, but only at a superficial glance looks like a birth *ex nihilo*. Estonian modernity did not lack pre-modern "parents", but rather had several different lineages feeding into it, not all of them routinely acknowledged. These include the folk poets and musicians, but also the Moravian converts; the Estophile linguists, but also the long line of land-obsessed peasants behind the agricultural modernizers, to name but a few important ones.

The power of communication

I am now going to discuss the mechanisms of national mass mobilization and the beginnings of the struggle for popular sovereignty in Estonia in more detail—an issue surveyed in more general terms in the introduction. There I concluded, following Hroch, that affinity of culture and values alone do not necessarily create a nation. The existence of features that the pre-modern group that became the Estonian nation did share, including widespread literacy and usable systems of communication, did not make the formation of a nation inevitable or necessary. Why, then, were the national activists in Estonia able to mobilize a mass national movement in a relatively short time, regardless of factors that should in a conventional view make nationhood unviable, such as low ethnic self-awareness, previous lack of access to political power and high culture, the absence of higher social strata, etc.?

Hroch argues that non-dominant ethnicities bred mass national movements in the circumstances where the ethnic lines of difference coincided with the lines of major socio-political confrontations, and where the national activists successfully expressed and addressed the crucial generally shared problems and aspirations. Research in social psychology shows that values and group dispositions are the two factors that most influence the formation of political opinions (Castells, especially 153). People are most likely to believe and support discourses and speakers which are in accordance with (some of) their pre-established values and frames of reference, even if the discourses contain novel material as well. New goals and strategies are accepted if they can be linked to existing beliefs and aspirations. I characterized the socio-cultural background and thought-world of the Estonian-speakers in the previous sub-chapter. To try to understand how the Estonian national agitation succeeded, I must now start with the consideration of who the activists were, what they wanted to achieve, what values motivated them, and what kind of discourses they used.

Generally, in cases where the potential "small nation" is part of a political unit dominated by a group of a different ethnicity, the national activists in Phase B largely come from *"the highest category of professional groups, which was as yet accessible to the members of oppressed nationality"* (Hroch, *Social* 181, Hroch's italics). Hroch stresses that, contrary to the stereotypical model of how nations ought to be formed, this need not be the bourgeoisie or the literati attacking the Old Regime, or any one particular class or group (180), as the "concrete possibility of social ascent" is very different at different places and times.

As for Estonians, their social mobility under the Old Regime was extremely low, at the low end even compared to Hroch's other "small nation" case studies. The tiny uppermost layer of the ethnic group (where the main ideologues of the national movement belonged to) were no higher than lower-middle class. Hroch's and Jansen's studies of the social background of the members of Phase B broader activist groups in Estonia show that these groups were overwhelmingly dominated by rural elementary school teachers and by peasants (Hroch, *Social* 78-79; Jansen qtd. in Hroch, *Social* 79, 199). Some urban professions, above all artisans, small shopkeepers and town council employees also played a noteworthy role, especially where urban initiatives, like the organization of song festivals was concerned (Hroch, *Social* 78-79). The contribution of university educated intellectuals or students was insignificant (Hroch, *Social* 80), simply because their number was minuscule during Phase B. Even the top leaders of the movement were all village-born (though some recently urbanized) with elementary school teacher, sacristan, or peasant fathers.[34] Only one of the top leaders who emerged in Phase B, Jakob Hurt, had university education (in theology), others had graduated from German-language secondary schools or seminars.

The lowly social composition of the patriots was, on the one hand, certainly a handicap. The activists would have aided their pursuit by higher levels of education, experience, wealth and social connections. On the other hand, many of the usual problems of decolonizing nationalisms did not arise in Estonia, exactly because the distance between "the people" and "the elite" was relatively small. The factor of Germanization did create some barriers—before the onset of Phase B almost all Estonians who managed upward mobility outside farming careers had become Germanized, and also in Phase B the better educated patriots' "high cultural" language was German, the language of their education. However, this does not seem to have created decisive communication problems.

Why and how did people from an ethnic group, which had had no access to political power since time immemorial become national activists? What values and beliefs motivated them? It is hard to make a quantitative study of personal motivations, but a few salient points have been highlighted by Mart Laar

---

34 Koidula is a partial exception, as her father Jannsen becomes an urban journalist, making Koidula a second-generation intellectual, though Jannsen too started out as a village teacher and a sacristan. It should be emphasized that although the social differences between Estonians look insignificant in international comparison, yet the lifestyle of the small urban petty bourgeoisie that moved in the German circles of their class and that of the rural peasantry were perceived as far removed from one another. Thus the national activists continuously passionately urged successful Estonians not to Germanize, but rather to show solidarity with their less privileged fellow-ethnics and use their achievement to advance the life of the whole people.

based on the self-explanations of the very first "awakeners" in their letters, diaries, memoirs, etc. (366-391). Knowledge of Herder's, Merkel's and Estophiles' thought, as well as of the development of national movements in other countries such as Germany, Finland and Latvia is a strong common nominator. This allowed one to draw pride and energy from a membership in an ethnic group and optimism for its future. Yet one needs to ask further what made Estonian patriotism inspirational for a Hurt, Jannsen or Koidula, as Germanization would also have been an option for them.

One reason emerges expressed in religious terms—there is a moral dilemma perceived in the enjoyment of social mobility and self-fulfilment, on the one hand, and the resulting pressure to violate the fourth commandment, on the other hand—to become alienated from one's origins and one's parents (Laar 372). Working for the national movement, perceived as serving one's people, helped to bridge that dilemma, and gave a boost to ambition. A second big motivator is a sense of injustice of the social order in the Baltics, drawing upon international comparison and mixed in varying degrees with personal bitterness against the Baltic Germans (Laar 376-377). As an increasing number of people became involved in the national movement, many report having been personally inspired by the earliest activists; a shared sociability and a sense of optimism and attainment were added to the previous factors of motivation. In the following, I will shortly describe the main discourse-clusters of the national movement that emerged during Phase B.

a) Hroch emphasizes the fact that the movement consistently and very concretely approached the problems relevant for the peasantry (*Social* 85). From the outset, major attention was turned to the modernization of agriculture, both in its political aspects (protest against the corvée system) and its know-how aspects. One of the most popular leaders of the movement, Jakobson, started to run an experimental farm and his politically radical newspaper *Sakala* devoted much space to agricultural issues. *Sakala* discussed methods and technology in a pragmatic manner, but also habitually referred to the unhappiness of a country where most of the land is in the hands of a small section of population. Jakobson brought up the example of the United States where the land was divided between free smallholders. (Jansen, *Carl Robert Jakobson* 111)[35]

---

35 The peasant background of Estonian modernizers played a crucial role in shaping it in a particular form, and its influence has not disappeared even today. The first Parliament of Estonia,

b) More broadly, the role of the Estonian peasants in history and in society was being defined anew. The activists proudly talked about the grand pre-Christian history of the Estonians (Jansen, *Eestlane* 390), but also emphasized the aspect of regeneration, that a new "age of dawn" had arrived.[36] It was regularly repeated that Estonians were no longer serfs, but free persons, human beings equal to the German nobility; since the late 1870s the demand for legal equality with Germans emerged more strongly. Being a free person, in this discourse, meant that one had not only the right but also the responsibility to be active in public life and to work for the public good (*rahva kasu*). It would not do to just wait for an outside savior, one had to be hard-working and enterprising, as there were so many ways to serve oneself and one's people—writing stories, preaching in church, starting a farm or a business, founding more Estonian societies. A dominant feature of the movement during Phase B was its optimism for the future, brimming with the sense that history was on its side.

c) Education was promoted as a remedy for anything, an almost limitless power in order to make the world better, more fulfilling and less unjust (Jansen, *Carl Robert Jakobson* 154-155), a guarantor of Estonian emancipation. One of the main ideologues of the movement, Jakob Hurt, turns the Baltic German belief in the unviability of small nations upside down, saying that though Estonians will not be great in might or power, if they persist they can certainly achieve "greatness of mind". For that, small nations have, if anything, an advantage, if only Estonians work hard and build up their own culture and educational system (qtd. in Laar 66). Literature was seen as a crucial force in broad-based cultural and social development, most of it being first written for publication in journalism or school textbooks. The aesthetics combined Romanticism with Enlightenment and Realism—romanticized folklore models, a cult of information and debates on topical social issues. The education question was also

---

elected by universal suffrage during the War of Independence (1919), immediately drafted a radical land reform, which divided almost all the manorial lands into smallholdings to be distributed equally. By common consent this act played a crucial role in making mass mobilization to the newly born republic's army a success. "The reform provided concrete value in the form of redistributed manorial lands, for which people were prepared to fight, even against a seemingly overpowering enemy" (*Estonica*). In Europe, the Estonian land reform was seen as too radical, almost on par with Bolshevism. It has also been said that it pushed the new republic's development in a particular agricultural direction (*Estonica*), diminishing the scope of further choice and decisions.

36 Cf. Carl Robert Jakobson: "Our ancient Estonian spirit will not let us rest before we have equal political rights with other ethnic groups in our country" (qtd. in Jansen, *Eestlane* 401).

foregrounded in the context of the modernization of agriculture and the need for knowledgeable and forward-looking agriculturalists.

d) Discussions of significant others as role models for nationhood and modernity have a very prominent place in the discourses of the national movement. In the beginning of Phase B, as it was throughout the early part of the century, Germany, but also in many ways the local Baltic German upper class, were acknowledged to be the main examples and objects of imitation. The Estonian activists openly expressed their admiration for German literature, journalism, music, and public associational life, and enthused their fellow-ethnics to follow the German example. The institution of Song Festivals, which achieved Estonian mass participation in the 19th century and is central for the Estonian national identity to this day, was originally borrowed from the Baltic Germans.[37] The newspaper *Die Gartenlaube* (1853-1876), later generally acknowledged as crucial in shaping German unified national identity (Belgum), was also staple reading among Estonian national activists.

However, already during the 1860s, sights were being turned increasingly from Germany to Finland. "Drawing upon the recent history of the Finnish national movement the Estonians found a strikingly successful example of a possible path towards modernity" (Raun, "Nineteenth-" 134). Finland was proclaimed as especially inspirational, because it existed not in Western Europe, but right there, next door to Estonians in the Russian Empire. Furthermore, the Finnish activists openly showed support and respect for the Estonian pursuit. To a lesser extent, Latvia functioned in a comparable role—it was more industrialized and prosperous than Estonia, and its national movement also frequently developed one step ahead of Estonia (Raun, "The Latvian"). As for Czarist Russia, it was represented as a framework for action, rather than as a source of examples. It is important to remember that for a long while (until the Young Estonia generation born in the 1880s) the Russian language skills of the activists were negligible. At the same time it seems that, even censorship is factored in, before the Russification phase most of the activists, like most Estonians in general, were genuinely loyal to the Czarist power, and hopeful for liberalizing reforms.

To sum up, the discussion of the fast mass mobilization of Estonians' national sentiment can be finished with a conclusion that it was so rapid because

---

37 The tradition of joint singing in folk culture and the Moravian music tradition are, of course, earlier cultural currents that feed into the song festivals, when they are adopted.

the activists' discourses were in accord with the population's background and thought patterns, and also with their indignations and aspirations. In this particular sense, the Estonian modernization in the 19th century was actually a comparatively rooted one. Tellingly, it was for its provincial narrow horizons and general country-bumpkin lack of sophistication that the modernist Young Estonia generation later came to criticize the model (see Chapter Four). The greatest change the 19th-century movement brought about in the population was exactly national *mobilization*. It persuaded large numbers of previously politically passive people that there was a realistic chance for their lives to be improved, that their input could truly make a difference, and that it was one's moral responsibility to serve the public good—public, in practice, being the public of Estonian fellow-ethnics. It is to the interaction between the ethnocultural and the civic aspects in the evolvement of Estonian nationhood that I will now turn.

Ethnocultural and civic nationhood

The discussion so far has shown that to a great extent the agenda of the Estonians' national movement did not concern their ethnicity as such, let alone their deep primeval Estonian soul, but instead their civic status in the Czarist Empire. Why are civic issues (legal equality, educational and economic reforms, access to political participation, etc.) addressed via a national patriotic movement in Estonia?

I want to raise this question because Estonian sociopolitical and cultural life of the second half of the 19th century has been viewed almost entirely through the prism of the development of Estonian ethnic identity, patriotism and nationhood. It is taken almost for granted by most Estonian scholars that ethnoculturalism is the primary reference point when explaining people's political mobilization and decisions at that time. Ea Jansen's *Eestlane*, however, usefully suggests an improvement on this perspective by adding the study of the development of civil society, both of ethnic Estonian and Baltic German publics. This is very much in accordance with my own approach in this book, which studies national mobilization as an aspect of modernization, rather than the other way round. This enables the consideration of the civic and ethnic aspects of Estonian nationhood, as well as its interrelationship with Baltic German identities.

Jansen's main interest is in the human dimension of historical processes. She uses the methodology of cultural history to investigate daily life, popular traditions and grassroots-level experience of participation in the public life of the Baltic provinces. She bases her account on Habermas's concepts of the "public" and the "public sphere", yet siding with those critics of Habermas who emphasize the existence of lower-class competing publics of peasants, workers, etc. alongside the bourgeois ones[38], and such defining values of associational life as mutual acceptance and respect, or shared sociability, alongside the Habermasian 'rationality' (*Eestlane* 19).

Jansen's account, which does not privilege ethnic patriotism over civic aspirations in the modernization processes, cannot but ask in all seriousness why Estonians and Baltic Germans did not develop a common public sphere. Modern nationhood means equalizing redistribution of power across different social groups and strata, but members of non-dominant ethnic groups do not always pursue their rights via politically engaged national movements. Hroch gives the 19th-century examples of the Welsh in Great Britain and the Bretons in France, where sociopolitical conflicts did, to a degree, coincide with ethnocultural lines, but where national movements nevertheless did not find a mass following ("From National Movement" 83, 87-88). Instead, the central conflicts could be more efficiently addressed in a civic framework and through party politics. However, this option can be found only in systems relatively open to negotiating power across society. It is not available in autocratic systems, including the territories under French or British *colonial* rule, where political discourses available for free use are very limited and, furthermore, civic oppression is often based exactly on ethnic group-membership. In the Baltic provinces of the Czarist Empire, social and political modernization, which would have favored the low-strata indigenous people numerically in majority remained off the negotiation table.

Estonians and Baltic Germans had several central cultural features in common. While much of historical literature on both sides highlights contrasts and otherness, there is no question that the histories of the ethnic groups in the area are entangled and their life-worlds were interdependent. Furthermore, since the first half of the 19th century Baltic Germans had developed a vibrant civil society (scholarly societies and associations, salons, clubs, charity organizations, ever more influential professional associations and press), which included both aristocrats and literati and within its boundaries "valued the principles of equality and tolerance" (Jansen, *Eestlane* 505). These were the organizational structures that Estonians during the second half of the 19th century followed and adapted for their circumstances.

---

38 Habermas has accepted this criticism and modified his views (Habermas 14-21).

However, besides the language barrier (which, considering international examples may not have proved decisive), the fundamental reason that kept Baltic Germans and Estonians apart was the barrier of status in the Old Regime sense. The German elites were socially so far away from Estonians that a common public sphere was hardly conceptualizable for them. This is not to say that Estonians and German elites did not meet physically or that they were not socioeconomically interdependent. A large German landowner could well do business with an Estonian farmer at the end of the 19th century, the two could even be on friendly terms. However, this large landowner would certainly not, let us say, invite said Estonian smallholder for a coffee in the drawing room of his manor. (Jansen, *Eestlane* 459)

Histories of Estonia habitually refer to the "long Middle Ages" in the Baltic provinces; by the same token, one could in connection with Germans talk about a subsequent "long Enlightenment". This is in the sense that though various liberal ideas concerning Estonians and Latvians were often discussed in Baltic governmental institutions, almost no one would advocate allowing these lower orders to be part of the discussions concerning them. For the estate mentality of the Baltic Germans, peasants in their traditional role could be viewed with benevolence, but upwardly mobile Estonian or Latvian "mimic men" became an object of scorn and/or fear. The Russification campaign of the Czarist regime came as a terrifying threat against Baltic German identity and did not push the Germans towards seeking a united front with Estonians and Latvians, but largely the other way round: to the clamping of the more liberal German opinions and to the rigid defence of the Baltic "special order" at its most conservative.

Thus, it can be concluded that modernization and redistribution of power to include the low-strata majority populations were no more on the negotiation table with the Baltic Germans than they were with the Czarist regime. If the Estonians wanted to modernize at all they had no option but to do it themselves, in their own mode, against the grain of the Old Regime. There the national movement played the role of establishing Estonian public life, condensed cultural power and constructed shared meaning, based on which claims for land reform, universal suffrage, autonomy and statehood were later made. One should be wary, however, of making the process sound too calculated or rational. Estonian discourses of modernity are shaped by a contradictory and fluid mix of reactions towards the Baltic-German other—esteem; fascination; sense of inferiority; ressentiment; pride of being the better modernizers more "in keeping with the times"; amazed indignation.

In order to investigate more deeply the above-mentioned nexus, I think it is worthwhile to consider the ethnocultural and civic aspects of Estonian modernity in the theoretical framework of Nationalism Studies, where the consequences of the civic versus ethnic origins of the building of different nationhoods has been a long-standing topic. I will digress a little sketching that framework, as it allows a perspective the relevance of which is not limited to the 19th- to early-20th- century Estonia considered immediately above but concerns the development of Estonia's modernity as a whole and has not lost its actuality today.

The best-known formulation of the problematics comes from Hans Kohn's *The Idea of Nationalism* (1944) who contrasts "Western" (civic) nationalism with the "Eastern" (ethnic) one. This differentiation has been echoed by influential scholars ever since. Western nationalism is seen as individual-centered, cosmopolitan, rational, liberal and forward-looking, whereas Eastern nationalism is collectivistic, irrationally past-oriented, xenophobic and illiberal with its valorization of "common language, blood and soil" (Montserrat Guibernau qtd. in Brown 56) at the expense of individual rights and welfare. This difference is tracked back to the "reactive" origins of the Eastern latecomer modernities. It is argued that while Western nations were generated in legitimate existing states which gradually established popular sovereignty, Eastern nations grew out of conflicts with the established political systems. Therefore, they are prone to breed elites who feel threatened by and *ressentiment* (Liah Greenfeld's term) towards other national groups, as well as insecure populations vulnerable to authoritarian and xenophobic propaganda.

The Australian nationalism scholar David Brown subjects the civic-versus-ethnic approach to thorough analysis and constructive criticism. He argues that contrary to received wisdom there is no necessary civic-liberal—ethnocultural-illiberal correlation.[39] There are illiberal nationalisms which are civic, e.g. Suharto in Indonesia, or, most famously, Jacobin nationalism in France; and there are predominantly ethnocultural nationalisms which are liberal, like the Welsh or Slovene ones (Brown 56). Secondly, it is not only ethnocultural (or illiberal) nationalisms that are "reactive"—it would be hard to find a nationalism developing completely self-sufficiently, not defining "us" against "them". However, nationalisms may be reactive against different forces—external threat, in-

---

39 By liberalism, Brown does not mean a specific political persuasion, neither of my time of writing or J.S. Mill's period, but a more general idea broadly including the rule of law, human rights, and basic collective rights of minorities.

ternal authoritarian ruler, colonial overrule, which can influence their formation in very variable ways.

Perhaps Brown's most important point concerns the protean nature of nations on the liberal-illiberal scale—and this regardless of their mix of civic or ethnocultural, "Eastern" or "Western" characteristics. Whereas Kohn's approach implies that the nations' natures are fixed at their origins, Brown argues that nationalisms can have more or less (il)liberal phases, as well as liberal and illiberal proponents, quoting for example. the three completely different Irish "revivals" (68). Brown agrees with previous scholars that it is often a sense of insecurity or inferiority, a sense of being under a threat that leads to illiberal forms of nationalism. By the same token, a sense of self-worth, agency and optimism tend to translate into liberal forms. It is one aspect of the equation concerning to what degree the threat to insecurity is realistically there. Yet it is also important how "the other and thence the self are depicted" by different political leaders and opinion-makers in a given situation, the "visions" and "political goals" they express, and, most of all, what sort of ideas and narratives resonate with wide sections of the people (67). If the nationalisms "do not develop their identities primarily in relation to threatening others" (67), but instead are able to pursue other means of resolving the situation, setting their political goals in a legitimacy-oriented value system, they are very likely to regenerate in a liberal form.

Against this background, let me return to the Estonian case. 19th- and early-20th-century Estonian national activists' understanding of nationhood was generally ethnocultural—for them, a nation was a group of people with a shared history, language, traditions, as well as a national psychology, features of appearance etc. (cf. Laar 66). Simultaneously, as elaborated above, their outlook and agenda were liberal—it is their interest as well as their belief that all national groups, as well as all individuals ought to have equal legal and civic rights and equal basic economic opportunities. Statehood was not considered a necessary condition for national/ethnocultural development; even up to 1918, leading Estonian figures continued thinking in terms of autonomy within a reformed Czarist Empire/Russia. On the other hand, major indignation and polemic confronts the internationally spreading idea favored by Baltic Germans that there are "historyless" nations incapable of high culture or self-rule.

There emerges at this point an interesting and consequential twist in terms of nationalism theory: Greenfeld's *ressentiment* was not at all felt towards any early modernizers, but, quite the opposite, towards the anti-modernization Baltic Germans. The *ressentiment* came from the sense that, unlike Estonians, Baltic Germans had enjoyed a proper history, a glorious one, unjustly at the expense of indigenous subjects. However, even more importantly, *ressentiment* was fed by the situation that Baltic Germans felt entitled to continue this history to eternity, as if the French Revolution, Merkel, or Finland did not matter at all. Thus, on the one hand, Estonians did worry about constructing a respectable pre-modern history for themselves. They certainly made the Herderian argument concerning the sacrosanctity and equal intrinsic worth of all cultures a central one for both their external legitimization and internal mobilization. Yet, it ought to be remembered, to paraphrase Hans Kohn, that the Estonian national movement also most persistently appealed to exactly the Western liberal ideas for its justification and *for its differentiation from Baltic Germans*. It was exactly the universal standards of political equality and freedom for peoples and for individuals that the ideologues of the Estonian national movement extolled in defence of their case.

Attention to the civic-ethnocultural dynamics is essential for understanding the way in which the decolonization processes evolved and Estonian modernity developed in the framework of statehood. The concerns and ideals discussed above had the utmost impact, even if practical issues, topical pressures and contemporary international situation undoubtedly played a determining role as well.

The Estonian Republic

I have argued thus far that one of the most defining factors impacting the formation of Estonian modernity was the fact that the ethnic-linguistic lines of difference coincided with the lines of socio-political and economic oppression and antagonism. When the independent Estonian state was established in the aftermath of the First World War, the colonial situation suddenly ended and decolonization was to begin with the Estonian state power in the lead.

The Estonian patriots who only a couple of years previously had set minority autonomy within the reformed Russian state as their highest aim found themselves in the position of a very dominant ethnic majority (about 88% of the whole population). However, ethnic Russians and ethnic Germans formed the largest minorities, with their looming mother states (recent enemies in war and fast emerging new military powers) nearby. By the time the Estonian state came into being, Estonians' outlook and aspirations can be fairly described as modern. Nevertheless, the change that took place with decolonization was immense in terms of the new sociopolitical structures and options for social mobility and realisation of different life-trajectories.

One of the most important reference points for understanding these transformations is the Land Reform of 1919, which was undertaken with the decision of the Constituent Assembly during the War of Independence. It would be misleading to understand it purely as a pragmatic economic move. It was also a development of the discourses and ideals of the 19th century and before, an enormously significant political and socio-cultural topos, not far short of the capture of the Holy Grail. Great numbers of people saw it as offering them a concrete personal stake in the newborn republic worth risking one's life for, and arguably nothing else could have had the same effect.

At the end of the Czarist period 58% of the land, including the most profitable areas, had belonged to 1149 large estates, the majority owned by Baltic Germans. With the reform, most of the estate lands were expropriated and 55,104 new farms created. Thus thousands of land-hungry Estonians became not only citizens of a democratic state, but simultaneously a large proportion also established themselves as rural middle class, as propertied smallholders. From the socioeconomic aspect, what developed was similar to other Baltic states and Scandinavian countries, an expansive network of small dairy and meat cooperatives (already started before the war), which provided marketing, credit, insurance and know-how for its members. It should also be noted that it was the mix of market economy with state interventionism that kept the property and status security of the farmers stable throughout the interwar period, however much difficulty some of them faced (Parming, especially 36-37). This was the political will supported by broad sections of Estonian society.

Estonia's population stayed predominantly rural. In 1922, 75% of the entire Estonian population lived in the countryside, and in 1939, the percentage was still 67.2 (Raun, *Estonia* 131). However, the numbers of the urban middle class also increased: the realization of statehood produced thousands of newly available positions in the government structures, education, professions, private enterprises, etc. Tartu University was opened to Estonian-speaking students and adopted Estonian as its primary language of study and a new Tallinn Technical Institute was established in 1918.

The accelerated embourgeoisement of the Estonian society equally rapidly impacted on its political views. Before the land reform the majority of Estonians had supported left radical and left liberal parties. The Left had been the main anti-Old-Regime force in the Czarist Russia, and, after all, a truly transformative egalitarian reform was exactly what most Estonians wanted at that point. However, the Bolsheviks lost ground quickly as they turned out to stand not only against Estonian independence, but also the land reform. The first State

Assembly elections in 1920 witnessed a further big swing towards the center and the center-right. From then on, the center-right agrarian parties continued to dominate during the whole constitutional period. It was not only that more people voted for those parties, also the left parties themselves could be said to have drifted towards center-right together with most of the population.

In terms of the land reform, the Labor Party's idea that land should be leased to the settlers by the state, rather than privately owned, turned out to be generally unpopular. On the other hand, the settlers accepted the originally conservative proposition that moderate compensation ought to be paid to the (mainly Baltic German) expropriated estate owners. Altogether, as ethnicity and class were bound up so strongly and in such a specific way in Estonia, the rightward turn of Estonians went along with an increase rather than decrease in their acceptance of their former lords as a national minority.

Kari Alenius, the Finnish scholar of inter-ethnic relations in 1920s Estonia has perceptively noted how the historical concurrence of ethnic and political-socioeconomic barriers brought about a situation where two almost contradictory forces simultaneously acted upon the Estonians' political vision of a fair and decent social order ("Under the Conflicting"). On the one hand, there was the long-time and strongly internalized Herderian ideal that the ethnic groups ought to have the right to self-determination and opportunities provided to develop their culture. In the immediate aftermath of the First World War this for a short while also received decisive international backing, most prominently by the principles announced by the US president Woodrow Wilson, which were partially adopted by the League of Nations. On the other hand, there was the —equally long-time—sense of social injustice relating to the Russian, and especially the Baltic German, overlords, and the concern that these were seeking to restore their hegemony and playing the minority card only as a move in the power game. This view often drew upon international left-wing ideals, according to which it was economic fairness that mattered and which found that social, not ethnic, equality ought to be the first point of reference in political decision-making. From that perspective it was hardly justifiable that anyone should have special prerogatives based on ethnicity, which the rest of the society had to pay for.

The debate becomes most pronounced in the negotiations of the Law on Cultural Autonomy for National Minorities, in which Estonian and minority groups interacted and certain individual Estonian and Baltic German partisans and opinion-makers played a decisive role. The discussions started as early as 1918 and after fierce arguments, quite a few stand-stills, and an extremely careful crafting, the law was finally passed by the parliament in February of 1925.

The primary inspiration for the law came from the works of the Austro-Marxists Otto Bauer (1881–1938) and Karl Renner (1870–1950) who created the model for non-territorial cultural autonomy in the attempt to reconcile the ideals of social democracy with the pressing concerns with nationality in the Austro-Hungarian Empire at the turn of the 19th and 20th century. The idea was developed and disseminated in Czarist Russia by Vladimir Medem (1879–1923) and his socialist Jewish Labour Bund, as well as by the liberal Russian Constitutional Democratic Party. Furthermore, the Estonian version of the model was influenced by the views of the German-American classical liberal political theorist and jurist Francis (Franz) Lieber (1800–1872).[40] Lieber's notions of 'self-government' and 'institutions' as the safeguards of stable liberal state order had a considerable impact on the political views of the future Estonian statesman Konstantin Päts (1874–1956) who had translated Lieber's *On Civil Liberty and Self-Government* (1853) into Estonian during his post-1905 exile (Päts, *Rahwawabadus*). Indeed, in Estonian the autonomy law is literally called the Law of Cultural Self-Government (*kultuuromavalitsuse seadus*).

Once the law was in place, the internal ethnic relations remained stable throughout the otherwise turbulent inter-war period and did not figure as a prominent concern either for Estonians or for the minority groups (cf. Kasekamp, *A History* 118; Smith; Tchassovskaia). There were other much more pressing matters on the agenda: international political insecurity, economic crises, constitutional conflicts, and in-group identity-building—all viewed from the perspective of a society perceiving its own speed of modernization dizzying. Yet I agree with the British scholar Martyn Housden that "[i]n a number of ways, the principles enshrined in [the Cultural Autonomy] law were integral to the construction of the independent Estonian state" (228). In this connection it is also noteworthy that while both the law and its implementation throughout the inter-war period have been generally praised as an exemplar of tolerance and liberality (Kasekamp, *A History* 118), the two most important masterminds and dogged partisans of the law, the Agrarian Party leader and future Estonian President Konstantin Päts and the Baltic German MP Werner Hasselblatt, during the 1930s went on to have political careers not very compatible with the above values. Hasselblatt went to Germany and joined the National Socialists; in 1934 Päts took power through a *coup d'état* and democracy was never fully re-

---

40 Internationally, Lieber is today probably best known for the so-called Lieber Code from 1863 that laid the foundations for the Geneva Conventions. Lieber created it as instructions for soldiers' behaviour during the American Civil War and it was signed by President Abraham Lincoln.

established under his presidency. While it is arguable that the persons as well as their political environment simply changed from the 1920s to the 1930s, there are also continuities in their political ideas.

Before turning to the Cultural Autonomy law in more detail, it is helpful shortly to map the politico-juridical situation in which the law was imagined and introduced. Estonia was declared an independent democratic republic on the 24th of February 1918 by the "manifesto to the peoples of Estonia". The manifesto announced that "[a]ll citizens of the Republic of Estonia, irrespective of their religion, ethnic origin, and political views, shall enjoy equal protection under the law and courts of justice of the Republic". The manifesto also declared that all ethnic minorities[41] within the Estonian citizenry shall be guaranteed the right to establish their "cultural autonomy" ("Declaration of Independence").

The first Estonian citizenship law (November 1918) created a citizenry from zero, as, of course, there had never been an Estonian state before. Combining *ius soli* with the conception of "originating from Estonia" the law proclaimed everybody, regardless of their ethnicity or faith, Estonian citizens, if they fulfilled all three following conditions:

> 1) were permanently residing on the territory of the Republic of Estonia on the day the Resolution came into force; 2) had been subjects of the Russian State prior to the 24th of February 1918; 3) originated from the territory of Estonia or were entered in the parish registers held in the territory of Estonia" (qtd. in Rohtmets, "Birth of a State" 291).[42]

The Constituent Assembly, elected during wartime, had a center-left majority and without much public debate crafted the first Estonian Constitution drawing upon American, French, Swiss and Weimar models. Estonia gained a very egalitarian political system, with proportional representation, strong elements of direct democracy, and, most unusually, with no head of state and the executive branch of government fully responsible to the legislative one. This solution won over the constitutional vision of the conservative right, most prominently advocated by Konstantin Päts. Päts criticized the Estonian system calling it an essential monarchy—even if the monarch might have 100 heads instead of one

---

41 Germans, Jews, Russians and Swedes are specifically mentioned.
42 The majority of the population in Estonia met these requirements. Most frequently problematic was the third clause, however, § 2 specified that people with "vital interests" (property, business, job) in Estonia could naturalize through a special simplified procedure. (Rohtmets, *Eesti* 24)

(Päts, "Parlamentaarse vabariigi riigipea" 274). Here, as well as in his other favorite cause, the Cultural Autonomy Law, Päts was inspired by his political ideals at the time. These related to the examples of classical Anglo-American political liberalism in general, particularly as processed by their continental interpreters Alexis de Tocqueville and especially the latter's friend and intellectual ally Franz Lieber, mentioned above.

In his *On Civil Liberty and Self-Government*, Lieber time and again warns against the "continental" idea that universal suffrage and "power of the people" in itself be thought to bring about a society of true "civil liberty" (e.g. 18). Instead, Lieber emphasizes the importance of the balance of powers, protection of both the individual and the minorities, as well as widespread and "self-reliant", while also institutionalized and law-bound self-government by different sections of society. As Theodore Woolsey's introduction puts it, Lieber's *On Civil Liberty* "teaches that there is no safe liberty but one [...] which by institutions of local self-government educates the whole people" (Woolsey 10).

In his *Modernity as Experience and Interpretation* (2008), Peter Wagner argues for the need to uncover and award proper status to the political tradition of "non-individualist liberalism", making Tocqueville his main 19th-century example of it (24-38). This tradition, differently from the individual-autonomy centered liberalism hegemonic today, proceeds from the idea of collective autonomy and collective self-government in a liberal democratic society (Wagner, *Modernity as Experience* 33-35). There the polity has to make a fundamental dual commitment: both to guaranteeing "extended spaces of individual liberty" *and* to the solidarity of the individuals (38). Indeed, this tradition sees solidarity and collectively built institutions in practice as the only way to combine individual liberty with democracy, and indeed, the only way to guarantee individual rights in practice, rather than only in the abstract.

It is also understandable why Päts would have found exactly Lieber most relevant and relatable within the political tradition that inspired him. Alan Grimes's *American Political Thought* characterizes Lieber as follows:

> Lieber skilfully synthesized the English emphasis on civil liberty and the importance of local political institutions, with the German emphasis on nationalism. Thus Lieber's nationalism was built upon decentralized institutions which in turn helped protect the civil rights of the citizens. It was, Lieber believed, the happy combination of local institutions and national purpose which protected and fostered civil liberty in a modern nation state. (283)

The 1925 Estonian Cultural Autonomy Law granted the ethnic minority groups who had more than 3000 Estonian citizen members residing in Estonia the right to establish non-territorial cultural self-governments. Such authorities, if in existence, had the competency to establish schools in their minority language(s),[43] as well as other minority cultural institutions and activities that they deemed necessary. In practice, the German and the Jewish communities in Estonia made use of the framework of the law; the Swedes and the Russians, who mostly lived in geographically compact communities, continued to work through local self-government institutions, where they had the majority.

As noted above, the law was first advocated by the center-right, with Päts as the main champion among the Estonians. The critics from the center and center-left persistently expressed their fear that the law would give minorities the possibility to establish themselves as a state within a state and that the endeavor ought to be interpreted as a Baltic German revisionist attempt to restore their pre-eminent position, threatening the Estonian state order (Smith 218).

It is fair to say that some of the German proponents of the law did see it as a "new vessel" to be filled with a lot of the "old wine" (Housden 238). Päts's enthusiasm for minorities' self-government probably exuded at least partly from the same source as his general interest in forms of social organization more "organic" and communal than his contemporary party politics. The latter—increasingly—saw as overly materialistic and self-seeking bargaining, lacking broader vision. However, a defining principle of the cultural autonomy law, and one that is distinctly "new wine", is the respective weight it accords the individual in relation to the collective.

In contrast to the more familiar territorial models of ethnic autonomy, the Renner and Bauer model adopted in Estonia rests on the 'personality principle'. The cultural self-governments of an ethnic minority formed a unitary association, and it was not relevant where or among whom one resided in order to be a member. Each citizen was *to determine* his/her ethnicity when s/he reached the voting age of 20 years. If the representatives of a minority wanted to establish cultural autonomy, they firstly had to enrol at least 50% of the citizens who had entered the relevant ethnicity in their passport onto a national register. A minimum of 50% of the enrolled members of the group then had to pass a vote on whether they wanted to implement cultural autonomy. If the answer was at least two-thirds "yes", they could proceed to elect their governing bodies. These hurdles were to ascertain deliberate political will on the part of the

---

[43] The six Jewish schools taught in Russian, Hebrew and Yiddish.

minority citizens, avoiding individuals being automatically subjected to collective identities, or the self-government being hijacked by self-appointed spokespeople. (For a detailed account see Smith 215-216.)

The cultural autonomy law can also be called characteristic of the Estonian state order in that it adapts the Renner and Bauer model, structuring the institutions of minority cultural autonomies, though non-territorial, according to the principles of *the existing local self-governments*. This change had symbolic force beyond good practical applicability. In his many speeches in defence of the law Päts frequently emphasizes that the organs of minority cultural autonomy are not associations only working in particular group interests but are rather organs of the Estonian state. They are, according to Päts, exactly the kind of structures—self-reliant but law-bound—that liberal government thrives upon (e.g. "Põhiseaduse" 141; "Vähemusrahvuste"). Päts stresses, on the one hand, that the law would promote the loyalty of the minorities by protecting—as is just and noble—their communal Herderian development, and, on the other, echoes classical liberal values of self-reliance, and responsible interaction. These two strategies together help persuade his audience.

The inter-war Estonian state-builders, like their precursors, the modellers of minority autonomy and the personality principle, sought to negotiate between different individualist and collectivist ideas to envisage a well-functioning and just modern society in their particular historical situation. Like many "latecomer" modernizers, in terms of ethnicity they proceeded in a circumstance different from the "normal" homogenized modern states of Western Europe. Whereas for the Western political opinion such a state was the norm, and by the mid-1920s the League of Nations saw the eventual peaceful assimilation of minorities as the only option worth promoting (Hiden and Smith 388), this was unacceptable in Estonia with its minorities of strong identities and self-consciousness.

Furthermore, if Bauer and Renner tolerated ethnic loyalties, in Estonia these loyalties were positively affirmed by not only conservatives like Päts, but also people of different political persuasions. Up until as late as 1917 Estonians had been working with the Bauer and Renner model *in reference to themselves* within a hoped-for reformed Russia. The Cultural Autonomy Law debate is very aware of this legacy and of independent state-builders' obligations to stand by their long-time principles (Aun), if sometimes quite grudgingly, as the records of the parliamentary debates testify. In David Brown's terms, cultural autonomy was an early multicultural solution of a particular kind, combining civic and ethnocultural elements (56), and it is not by coincidence that the interest for the model has revived since the 1990s (e.g. Nimni; Smith; cf. Hiden and Smith 398-399).

What separates the democratic Päts of the 1920s of the authoritarian Päts of the late 1930s is not so much a sea change of his vision of the ideal Estonian state, but the collapse of his ideals of parliamentary democracy and democratic procedure. In Jüri Adams's account, Päts' initial strong allegiance to democracy fades by 1933:

> we [then] see a man with a very sceptical outlook towards the lottery of elections. Also, he regards the party representatives at the parliament disdainfully, often impatiently: the narrow stratum-based interests they represent, their lack of a wider or longer perspective, not to mention their scholarship and erudition being inferior to his (19).

It is probably right to conclude that it is both Päts' personal sense of resentment, and his genuine fear of the "tyranny of the majority" supporting the paramilitary Veterans League that, ironically, turned him into a minor tyrant from 1934.[44] Päts's "paternalistic" authoritarian regime apparently met no considerable resistance. To the anxious society, he seemed a strong guardian of political stability, and he was also lucky to have his takeover coincide with the beginning of the new upward turn in the economy. Under Päts's rule, industrialization accelerated, offering new and better chances for prosperity and upward mobility to the urban dwellers across the class spectrum (Parming 62-63). However, as the acceptance of the regime was predicated on a sense of threat, the political resistance would probably have expanded, had the international situation resolved differently and, indeed, some scholars argue that there was considerably more subdued resentment of the dictatorship than usually assumed (Turtola *Kindral*; Turtola *President*).

The period was a "Silent Era" for state-level political debate and initiative, or far-reaching intellectual criticism. One repercussion was that the difficult decisions in international politics, including the possibility of resistance to the Soviet Union were taken entirely behind doors, ignoring or misleading wider audiences to the last minute. Yet, as testified in contemporary personal documents and later memoirs, for many the "Silent era" was an active, vocal and fulfilling

---

44 The Central League of the Veterans of the War of Independence was a nationalist anti-parliamentary and anti-socialist organization that criticized what it saw as the liberal decadence and corruption of the Estonian state order. For a while the movement was popular with a large section of the society. In 1934, it looked like they were going to win the elections, curb parliamentary powers and institute a much stronger presidency. However, before the elections, Päts interfered and declared a state of emergency, justifying the move with the need to save Estonian democracy from fascism. (Kasekamp, *A History* 109-110)

period on the personal and local level, not only concerning individual self-betterment but also in terms of communal initiative and enterprise. It could be said that, in a way, people did exactly what they knew best since the Moravian times: organized themselves in groups and along networks while they did not control the top level government.

The self-image that Estonians emerged with as a nation, and that Estonian literature both reflected and reproduced, centrally involved the figure of a hard-working farmer sometimes successful in his struggle (the dominant 19th-century model), often also destroyed by economic hardship and political domination (early-20th-century critical realism) (cf. Kaskla 301). After the independence and the land reform, the discourses transformed into perceptions/representations of Estonia as a country of small hard-working self-bettering farmsteads, cooperative yet self-reliant systems. This not only literally, but also symbolically: the country is guided by farming values, run through institutions rather like neat hard-working farms, and, furthermore, the Estonian state is itself not unlike a relatively large farmstead (Kõresaar, *Elu* 50-52), with Päts as the master of the household.

Such an approach is not specific to agrarian or right-wing political ideologies: the vocabulary pervades the discussions of Estonian life in general, and clearly resonates widely and strongly. In 1923, Päts argued his case for a thrifty state budget using the metonymy of hard-working poor homesteaders and evoking the topos of a new, swampy-but-cherished farm (Päts, "Riigieelarve" 213-214).[45] A few years later, the same topoi and mentalities were philosophized about in *Truth and Justice*, the literary masterpiece by Päts's future political critic Tammsaare. Later still, a large number of memoirs set in the inter-war period employed the same themes, and also self-reflectively mentioned Tammsaare's *Truth and Justice* as a kind of a master-text which expressed their own childhood memories, only "much better" (Kõresaar, *Elu* 61).

The topos of the farmstead is often evoked as a carrier of continuity and sustainability of values, but there is also a perception of increasing urbanization, and, even more importantly, that change is a feature of rural as well as urban

---

45 "Look, gentlemen, the new state is also like a swampy field where we have to struggle on steadily step by step [...] I know there are a lot of homesteaders who go on their plot of land with the hope of [building up a household like others have, or better] and work there tirelessly. [...] The steady, peaceful and companionable work that we all carry out together is the proof that though the Russian Authorities considered this swampy piece of earth of such minor significance, we love it beyond expression, and that through working with united strength we are going to turn it into our blossoming Estonian state, which will have no cause for embarrassment among other states." (Päts, "Riigieelarve" 213-214)

life. The sense of change is expressed, for instance, in the discourses of *tõusik* (parvenu), the concept appearing in the Estonian language first in 1910 (Haug 309). The *tõusik* is mostly depicted as a profoundly negative figure, "an other within". He is the adversary of the hard-working farmer, an ideological descendant of the old-time manor house overseer; a dubious city slicker; manifestos appear against the parvenu as the uncultured, unethical materialist destroying art and thought in the country (Haug).

Yet, as some authors observe: all Estonians, in fact, *must* be parvenus, social climbers: what else could they do or be in their situation? Both economic and cultural climbing is natural and inevitable (Tuglas, "A.H. Tammsaare" 61-62). The Finnish-Estonian modernist author Aino Kallas famously describes Estonia as a "parvenu-society" (16), a nervy, disoriented one, engaged in an all-too-rapid rootless progress. On the one hand, the country is still crude and materialistic, "literally as if its physical hunger has not been quite satisfied [it] presently has a strong appetite, uncontrollable greed, good instinct for accumulating money" (16). On the other hand, it is so alert, so highly-strung and sensitive that it comes to remind one of a very old culture, a refined and decadent one (17). Such perceptions are not confined to the beginning of the republic: "the present time we often call a period of transition," writes Tammsaare in 1937 ("Vaim ja võim" 212).

Frequently, the sense of change, excitability, sped-up time was specifically related to urbanity and its new experiences: crowds, trams, cars, factories, banks, cinemas, cafés, restaurants, offices, telephones, etc. The Estonian cities of the inter-war period were, of course, modest compared to some metropoles, yet they clearly did not seem so from the perspective of a newly arrived rural. However, as Tuglas, one of the Young Estonians, observes already in 1912:

> maybe it is even somewhat less important that our cities grow, and more important that the city mentality, urban way of thinking, urban psychology is penetrating the countryside through the press, mass education, politics, and all the ideas of the modern time. This mental urbanization that in Western Europe has to a great extent already taken place is happening at our place too—whether it makes us feel proud, happy, or sad about the loss of the poetry of the past. Together with former dress, housing and agricultural tools the village will lose a lot of its mental independence and worldview which distinguished it from the city beforehand. ("Kirjanduslik" 96)

The memoirs of the inter-war period tend to represent the period as far more "rooted" and secure than other sources would indicate. However, the reason is not just the idealization of childhood and/or the vigor of nationalist indoctrination of the late-1930s culture and school-education (cf. Kõresaar, *Elu* 62-64). Rather, versions of the public discourse were so strongly integrated by a large proportion of Estonians who received their education during the inter-war period because these resonated with them to a relatively high degree. During their school years they experienced "a relatively high correspondence between the private and public worlds", which was then "contrasted with the experience [of the German and Soviet occupations] that followed" (Kõresaar, *Elu* 62). As the above discussions of the farmstead topos attest, the agrarian sociopolitical ideal of an independent farmer who owned the land that he tilled and thus became a committed master of both the land and the country (Eellend 45) was close to many Estonians' worldview. So was the socially and economically inflected idea of citizenship that to a great degree related it to labour, ownership and responsible inter-action in practical matters (Eellend 48)—which must have made Päts's top-level "paternalistic" authoritarianism less of an issue for many.[46] Of course, had the Estonian state survived, the inter-war period would probably have been remembered in a considerably different manner.

The Soviet model of modernity and its failure

The Soviet takeover of Estonia marked the beginning of a new phase of accelerated modernization, now of a qualitatively different type than experienced in the inter-war period. Estonia was rapidly integrated into the Soviet project of industrialization centralized in Moscow, which concentrated on the extraction of natural resources and privileged heavy and military-related industry. In 1947–1952, Estonian agriculture was collectivized under Stalinist coercion, which contributed to fast urbanization, while the type of agrarian path of modernization discussed in the previous subchapter was proclaimed reactionary and exploitative.

---

46 According to Eellend these agrarian ideals were characteristic of the inter-war Eastern Europe more generally, but their power and popularity was not the same in every country (36). The attitude of these agrarians towards the possession of land, however, could mostly be contrasted to that of agrarian socialists (e.g. in 19th-century Russia) who thought that land had such essential value that it could not be individually owned (45), as well as to that of liberal capitalists who judged land property purely in terms of profit potential. The inter-war Eastern European agrarians generally promoted "a third way" of political and economic modernization, falling between liberalism and socialism, e.g. combining ideals of self-government and responsible inter-action with those of unalienated labor and communal solidarity. Agrarian thought as a whole is associated with societies in a rapid phase of modernization and industrialization (37), striving to carry on "farmer virtues" in changing circumstances.

On the one hand, the Soviet urbanization and industrialization, as well as many other Soviet initiatives of modernization (secularization; mass education, communication and health systems; electrification and union-wide transport routes) paralleled those that proceeded in the West, and most probably would have continued in Estonia if it had remained independent. Indeed, the original Marxist-Leninist vision foresaw exactly a powerful catch-up modernization broadly of the Western type, which would then surpass the West and open "a new historic path that the Western world would follow" (Carrère d'Encausse 45).

On the other hand, what was distinctly different and defining about the Soviet model of modernity was that the modernization was carried out in an authoritarian state, with merged a mutually enforcing management of politics, economy and legal order. That is, it was governed by a single-party political regime with a distinctive ideology, running a centralized state economy, backed by a regime-dependent security police. The post-WWII arms race intensified the development of the Soviet Union into an externally oriented "garrison state" (Zaslavsky 76) which enhanced the militarized concept of rule internally.

The system that fed not only great quantities of raw materials, but also massive human "resources" into its machinery enabled, for a while, an impressive efficiency of reforms, rapid infrastructural modernization and economic growth. Already in the 1960s, however, the economy started to stagnate. The population had been pushed to the limits of what could be achieved through coercion. When the revolutionary drive eased and concessions were made, these were generally geared towards cementing deals with various groups in the society (blue-collar workers, creative people, technological elites, indigenous administrators in non-Russian "republics", etc.) trading stability and some self-actualization/consumption opportunity in exchange for obedience. However, before Gorbachev initiated reforms in the 1980s, there was never enough space for impactful off-mainstream initiative that could have resulted in truly new innovative paths. The potential to renew the coercive pressure was there until the end of the Soviet period and the security police and central control remained.

Yet it is also important to avoid collapsing the totalitarian rule of high Stalinism with the totalizing system of the Khrushchev and post-Khrushchev periods. There were very important differences between the various phases of the Soviet rule on the everyday human level. In Estonia, as elsewhere, the Stalinist repressions rooted out great numbers of people who had been active in Estonian cultural and social life: deported, killed, made to flee to the West or to the forest, simply banned from the public sphere. Among those banished were also the early Estonian communists and collaborators who almost without exception were purged from politics, accused of bourgeois nationalism, deficient class consciousness, or other similar infringements (Zubkova 217-230). Thus the terror kept the majority of the population alienated from the Soviet rule and collaboration was in the majority of cases more inspired by schemes of survival than by ideals. From the "thaw" period following Khrushchev's denunciation of Stalin, however, one can talk about a certain internalization and adaptation of some modern Soviet ideals, to detect the beginnings of an *Estonian* version of Soviet modernity.

The suppression of the Hungarian Revolution of 1956 had demonstrated that the West would do nothing to interfere in the Eastern European situation, that the Third World War was not likely to happen soon, and that Soviet power was there to stay. On the other hand, a lot of Estonians developed the disposition that the worst ordeals were not likely to repeat and that there was a possibility to craft a better future for oneself and for the country within the Soviet structure. There was also a new generation growing up after the war that did not have strong personal memories of the inter-war republic. Many people who were young in the 1960s remember the atmosphere as filling up with novel promise and dreams of major human achievement, perhaps best symbolized by the fascination with space flight as a literal vision of the human pursuit of the stars, an image of a realized utopia.

The 1960s saw an explosive modernizing drive in Estonian literature, especially poetry. This was aided by the partially restored possibility to establish contacts with Western authors, including Estonian exiles, to translate and to communicate. The blacklist of entirely banned writers shortened and some impactful authors returned from Siberia or from internal banishment. Some of the new poetry reconnected with the pre-Soviet currents that the imposition of the socialist-realist poetics had cut short, much of it also strove for technical and axiological innovation. *Vers libre*, surrealist and unconventional futurist modes, as well as expressions of political protest and proclamation of individualist humanist values struggled with censorship and faced the disapproval of some established critics, but for about ten years reached the audience relatively freely. The creative boom was accompanied by widespread reader interest for the new poetry during that period (Velsker, "Nüüdiskirjandus" 414). It is also interesting to note that while most poets of this literary wave belonged to the post-war generation, even the works of the 1920s-born authors who returned from long sentences in Siberia (Jaan Kross, Artur Alliksaar) carry a defiant, experimental, but ultimately upbeat mood of the time, not unlike that of their younger colleagues.

However, from the second half of 1960s the outlook became more disenchanted *even before* the failure of the Czechoslovak transformation of 1968 crushed the political hopes: already in 1966 one talks about the "inflation of poetry". The suppression of the Prague Spring (in which some Estonian officers and conscripts in the Soviet army also participated) indicated beyond doubt that despite some pleasant creative freedoms the principles of the system were the same and it could not be reformed from within. At the same time, much of the most outspoken and poignant, as well as formally novel poetry of the period was written in exactly 1968–1974 (some of it officially published only from the *glasnost* period of the late 1980s). At that time poetry also started to adopt from and mingle with folk song on the one hand, and, on the other, with the newly evolving youth culture and various forms of socially involved pop music, especially rock music. Thus the public sphere of singing in Estonia did not remain confined to the choir and folk music cultures, but found new avenues of development in the pop scene, where it, similar to the earlier joint singing traditions, promoted a close relationship between song and poetry: songs are often composed based on existing poetry and lyrics created specifically to be sung can end up published as poetry. From the later 1970s, the symbiosis of punk rock and underground punk poetry developed as another example of this pattern.

From the retrospective of the end-of-the-1980s reform period (*perestroika*), the 1970s have become known as the period of "stagnation", dominated by the increasingly aging and conservative *nomenklatura* both in Estonia and in the Soviet Union more generally. The exile Estonian political theorist Rein Taagepera has pertinently characterized the rule at the time as "softening without liberalization" (97). What emerged was a degree of space that could then be filled with far greater diversity of lifestyles than before the "thaw", which promoted the emergence of hybridities. These were not sanctioned officially, but they could be tolerated if they remained within an undefined margin. At the same time, the margin was discretionary and often created uncertainty and confusion. Thus, though direct state violence was much diminished compared to the Stalinist period, habits of self-censorship and mutual scrutiny gathered growth (Kharkhordin 279-280; Shelley 42). The Soviet principle of collective guilt (a collective could be held accountable for its member's transgressions) placed an additional social and moral pressure on the individual to stay within the bounds of the permitted and to treat with caution those who did not.[47]

---

47 Alexei Yurchak, interviewing "the last Soviet generation" in Russia, records expressions of dislike of and unease about trouble-makers rocking the boat: "[The dissenting colleague] refused

If the 1960s had inspired inventive present-oriented poetry in the Estonian literature, the 1970s and early 1980s are dominated by historical prose. The most prominent are Jaan Kross's widely read novels that methodically construct a story of Estonian modernity in the interplay with different political circumstances. While in the previous periods the popular historical prose had mostly dramatized heroic battles or uprisings (for example by Lydia Koidula, discussed in Chapter Two), Kross presents multiple-perspective discussions of the individuals' dilemmas related to admissible rules of compromise under an oppressive social order: the possibilities and limits of individual agency; the relationships between moral integrity, responsibility for the welfare others, and strive towards creative self-realization. His protagonists, usually based on exceptional and high-achieving persons of Estonian history, are confused and unheroic when faced with their difficult choices, yet remain capable of guilt, critical self-analysis, and altruistic behaviour. The pre-*glasnost* Kross's narratives do not directly touch upon his contemporary Estonian system or the Second World War, but they could be given allegorical interpretations which his contemporary readers were often prone to do.[48]

The post-Stalinist relaxation of rules, such as it was, was to a great extent encouraged by the realization that further economic and military advancement required a competent technical intelligentsia that could explore alternatives not completely confined by the ideological straitjacket. This shift, which was gradual and at times contradictory, meant that certain fields, especially in the natural and applied sciences, but sometimes even aspects of economy, were no longer regarded as "bourgeois" and therefore off limits. Importantly for later *perestroika* period developments, in the 1970s Estonia was already selected by Gosplan, the central economic planning agency in the Soviet Union, to be the laboratory for experimenting with decentralized profit-oriented economic strategies. To an extent, Estonia was picked because of its small size, partly because of its comparatively high level of agriculture, the field in which the experiments were begun. The idea of profit-oriented production where the managers were given relative

---

to pay the Komsomol dues, in his words, 'out of moral principle' [...] What he was doing was not just silly and useless but could actually cause problems for others" (107). While Yurchak's account is not fully transferable to Estonia, such attitudes could probably be met throughout the Soviet bloc.

48 Jaan Kross himself says he has "never wanted to write transparent, sterile allegories. If at all, then a real, psychologically sufficiently rich and alive historical novel" that could "offer opportunities for socially critical interpretations" ("Kirjanikuna" 237). Jaan Kross's most influential stagnation period novel *The Czar's Madman* (1978) and its reception will be further discussed in Chapter Three.

autonomy to achieve targets was influenced by the liberal economic ideas in the West generally banned in the Soviet Union at the time (Darden 127).

Several people involved in the Soviet period economic experiments went on to have decisive positions shaping Estonian politics and economy after the country regained independence. The experience of working with elements of market economy and the opportunities to study economic thought in Finland fed into the 1987 proposal "Self-Managed Estonia" ("Isemajandav Eesti") by a group of Estonian economic and social thinkers. Their particular programme of market-oriented reforms predicated on *economic* autonomy from the rest of the Soviet Union was never materialized in this form. Yet the proposal played a paramount role as a persuasive refutation of the argument that Estonia was too small and weak to survive in the contemporary global world independently of the Soviet Union. Thus the phrase "Self-Managed Estonia" became a catchy political banner (IME, the chosen acronym for "Isemajandav Eesti", also means "miracle" in Estonian), and at a relatively early stage simultaneously launched sober discussions on planning the organization of a future autonomous/independent Estonian state.

In broader generalization it can be said that the Soviet sphere as a whole evolved towards an ever-greater complexity of uneven modernization, even while the central power structures of the political-economic order remained inflexible and stagnated. It is no exaggeration to suggest that the Soviet Union eventually collapsed under the weight of this contradiction. Gorbachev's reforms sought to bridge this gap, but could not do so, as the sub-systems were too divergent. Many Estonians saw viable alternatives in an idealized West and/or in an equally idealized inter-war Estonian past.

Soviet (Post)colonialism?

Discussing the Soviet period of history, it is fundamental to ask what the most useful categories and paradigms would be to foster its analysis in the global framework, rather than as a wholly idiosyncratic phenomenon. Since the 1960s political activists and scholars in different disciplines have raised the question of how useful or appropriate it would be to consider the Soviet takeover of the Baltic states as a form of colonialism, or, more generally, whether it would make sense to discuss the Soviet Union as a colonial empire (Annus, "The Problem" 21-24). Yet, the Soviet dimension was not immediately included in discussions either during the post-WWII extensive decolonization of overseas colonies, or when the Postcolonial Studies became an established academic discipline in Western academia in the 1980s. This has the following interrelated reasons.

However different the varied strands of postcolonial thought may be (the *Négritude* movement, the outgrowths of and reactions to the Commonwealth Studies, critique of Orientalism inspired by Edward Said, etc.) all treat "Europe" as their opposite pole, and as a result conflate and homogenize their concept of "Europe" to fit the European/postcolonial binary opposition. This conflation makes Eastern Europe invisible as a separate category. Additionally, many of the early postcolonial critics were Marxists and presented their case as a critique of Western capitalist imperialism (Annus, "The Problem" 24). Furthermore, though the imposition of the Soviet power followed various patterns in different localities,[49] in the Estonian case (and in a number of others) it was a takeover of an established modern nation state geographically close to the metropole, with a population of the same skin color, and with the educational level and material living standards higher than its own. At a superficial glance, none of this corresponds to the established model of what colonialism looks like: Western European "civilizing" colonialism of the overseas "Other".

Furthermore, in Russia and elsewhere there are many critics who argue against the applicability of the Postcolonial Studies for the reason that in the Soviet Union there was no typical colonial contrast between a wealthy and liberal center and a destitute and oppressed periphery, where cardinally different sociopolitical and economic orders would rule (Buckler). The totalitarian Soviet Union incorporated its newly seized territories within the mother state boundaries and the same rules applied to everyone: large numbers of Russian people suffered coercive collectivization, state terrorism or religious persecution similar to Estonians, Lithuanians or Moldavians. Indeed, the Baltic states retained higher living standards than most of Russia throughout the Soviet period and for a while (1970s), so did the Central Asian and the Caucasian republics, the latter subsidized from the center (Zaslavsky 87-88).

As said above, this book sides with those scholars who argue that the Postcolonial Studies ought to analyse imperial structures and ideologies in a greater variation than it has done so far. Generating interpretative models to include the Soviet sphere in the global Postcolonial Studies would allow a broader perspective and more commensurate analysis. Despite all the differences between

---

49 Western scholars generally agree that the Czarist and USSR period takeover of Central Asia is largely compatible with the established understanding of colonialism (Annus, "The Problem" 27; Carey and Raciborski 200).

the Soviet and Western European empires (which are, of course, important and will be further discussed below), the Soviet rule over the non-Russian territories still corresponds to the generally recognized definitions of colonialism. Gayatri Spivak, for one, in her answer to the questionnaire about the appropriateness of postcolonial terminology in Soviet Studies by *Ulbandus*, the Slavic Review journal of Columbia University, confirms: "When an *alien nation-state* establishes itself as ruler, impressing its own laws and systems of education and rearranging the mode of production for its own economic benefit, "colonizer" and "colonized" can be used" ("Empire" 5, my italics). David Moore argues that the Baltic schema where the initial military conquest is followed by the colonizing regime's exploitation of local resources and promotion of colonial settlement in the subjugated area is broadly analogous with the similar process in sub-Saharan Africa:

> Indigenous governments are replaced with puppet control or outright rule. African education is revamped to privilege the colonizer's language, and histories and curricula are rewritten from the imperium's perspective. Autochthonous religious traditions are suppressed in the colonial zone, idols are destroyed, and alternative religions and nonreligious ideologies are promoted. The colonized areas of Africa become economic fiefs. Little or no 'natural' trade is allowed between the colonies and economies external to the colonizer's network. Economic production is undertaken on a command basis and is geared to the dominant power's interest rather than to local needs. Local currencies, if they exist, are only convertible to the metropolitan specie. Agriculture becomes mass monoculture, and environmental degradation follows. In the human realm, African dissidents' voices are heard most clearly only in exile, though accession to exile is difficult. Oppositional energies are therefore channelled through forms including mimicry, satire, parody, and jokes. (114)

However, Epp Annus makes a persuasive case that it would be more reasonable to term the initial violent takeover of the politically sovereign Baltic republics (including the deportations, guerrilla warfare, the 1950–51 purge of the local Estonian communist from the upper power structures, etc.) "occupation" and not "colonization", exactly for the reason that the situation concerns one modern sovereign state subjugating another ("The Problem" 35-36). Yet, from the latter half of fifties "the period of occupation nevertheless developed into a period of colonial rule, as the modes of resistance [typical of shorter period occupied territories] turned into a hybrid coexistence with the new power" (Annus, "The Problem" 37). In the categories of international law, the situation can be classified as occupation followed by illegal annexation (Mälksoo). In terms of ground-level culture and power relations, however, there developed typically colonial forms of colonizer-colonized interaction, collaboration and complicity, mutual fears and desires, and, as described above, new modes to imagine the future of the country.

Of course, the coercive reshaping of the earlier socioeconomic and cultural order could also be called, as it often has been done, "Sovietization", equalizing the situation with what happened in the Russian territories. Yet it seems inadequate to ignore that outside Russia the military takeover and the coercive imposition of a new model of modernization took place under a *foreign* power and included the demotion in status of the local languages and the subordination of the local collective narratives of self to the Soviet grand narrative were the leading role was reserved for Russia. The perception of being colonized was enforced by the rapid demographic change with the arrival of Russian-speaking settlers: in Estonia the percentage of the "titular nation" dropped from over 90% in 1945 to 62% in 1989 (Kasekamp, *A History* 154). In the Baltics as well as in the other non-Russian "republics", Sovietization certainly had a Russian face.

In this connection, it is relevant to note that since its very beginning, Soviet nationality politics always uneasily negotiated the tension between territory-based hierarchical national federalism and russocentric unification. Lenin proclaimed the right of self-determination in contrast to what had been the Czarist "prison of peoples", yet with the understanding that the great socio-cultural revolution will soon give birth to the new Soviet man and the nations will disappear. Thus, for example, the Ukrainian ambitions of independence or the Central-Asian national Communists' organization around the idea of their special historical destiny building Islamic Communism received decisive counterblows when they were believed to derail the revolutionary cause (Carrère d'Encausse 41, 44). Differently from Lenin, Stalin saw nationhood as a permanent historical entity, based on the "real" categories of ethnicity and territory, and international relations as based on power struggle. Thus he considered it paramount to establish Russian domination over the other Soviet nations in order to to hold the formation together around a unified russocentric Soviet identity. He boosted ethnic Russian nationalism by promoting the propagandistic creation of a seamless narrative uniting the Soviet achievement and the victory in the Great Patriotic War with the pre-revolutionary greatness of Russia since times immemorial (see Brandenberger for a thorough account of the formation of Russian nationalism during the Stalinist period).

Thus Russia emerged in Soviet propaganda and in popular Russian consciousness as "the first among the equals" and "the elder brother" among the Soviet nations, "justified by its historical role and superior culture" (Carrère d'Encausse 50-51). The rest of the Soviet ethnic groups were also hierarchically systematized: they were assigned their officially recognized territories and organized administratively into an elaborate system of stratification, in which those with their own "republic" were on the highest rank (Zaslavsky 86). Individually, Soviet citizens inherited their nationality from their parents (or one of them, if it was a mixed marriage) and had it officially registered as an unchangeable classificator. The republics all had structurally identical paraphernalia resembling independent states (coats of arms, ministries, national operas, academies of sciences, etc.). On the one hand, these were puppet institutions entirely in the power of Moscow. On the other hand, the titular nations had certain privileges within their territories, such as established quotas for university places and for covetable administrative and managerial positions (though top political, security and militia posts were reserved for Russians), as well as some acceptance of the local languages as vehicles of high culture.

This "divide and rule" system kept the diverse empire in check in the short term, but in the long term contributed to ethnic solidarity and interethnic conflict in the mock republics. It beleaguered not only the titular nations who resented their collective lack of agency and were concerned about their national survival, but also the settlers who could feel betrayed by the center which had promoted their move to the periphery, but excluded them from certain republican networks. The post-Stalinist leaders did not seriously reform the system, maintaining its essential tensions. Khrushchev famously declared at the XXII Party congress that the Soviet nations had already acquired the socialist consciousness surpassing the national ones: they had already "converged" (*sblizhenie*) and were advancing the point of fusion to one nation (*sliyanie*). However, no massive violence and coercion was used to enable this desirable state to come into being. It was long hoped this would somehow happen on its own, based on the attractions of the Soviet dream and Russian culture. The 1979 population census in Estonia indicated it had not happened: only 24.2 % of Estonians acknowledged having a good knowledge of the Russian language—down from 29% in 1970 (Kiin, Ruutsoo and Tarand 14).

Victor Zaslavsky correctly observes that the Balts, as well as Moldova and Ukraine, rebelled in the late 1980s "based on a quest for self-assertion and identity, on a group's concern with ethnic survival and on a collective perception of collective self-interests, fuelled by aspirations of joining the world market" (90).

It is important to recognize that Estonians did often feel also *economically* oppressed by the Soviet state ("the Russians") even if the standard of living was higher than in most Russian regions. It is true that the Soviet economy did not aim to enrich the center at the expense of the periphery, and allocated funds for transfer payments to reduce the differences in economic modernization between the republics (Zaslavsky 87). However, from the Estonian point of view they were subsidizing economic failure elsewhere in the Soviet Union. What is even more important, the Estonians did not measure themselves only by the Soviet standards but also compared themselves to the Finns with whom they felt similar in culture and potential and blamed their stark inferiority in living standards on the Soviet rule. From the perspective of many Estonians, the USSR had a coercive economy where the center dictated the economic model, used the output according to its own alien rationality, plundered the local resources and kept the population in misery. The criticism of the Soviet command economy for its disregard of regional differences in culture and natural environment, its high pollutiveness, stifling of individual initiative, responsibility and hard work, and its essential inability to plan production without constantly creating shortages had a prominent place during the Singing Revolution decolonization movement in the Baltics.

In the context of Postcolonial Theory, it can be argued that the colonial center, faced with this contradiction between the complexity of society and the anti-innovative, inflexible quality of power, gradually lost the will to rule. In that sense, the end of the Soviet Union resembled the collapse of the other European colonial empires. The loss of will to rule both promoted and was itself promoted by the "hollowing out" of the Soviet official discourses, the hackneyed phrases becoming ever more alienated from people's lived experience. As Alexei Yurchak puts it in his anthropological exploration of mature socialism, *Everything Was Forever, Until It Was No More*: "The late Soviet world became a kind of "postmodern" universe where grounding in the real world was no longer possible, and where reality became reduced to discursive simulacra" (76). Yurchak, however, makes the case (based on the analysis of private documents from the Soviet period, as well as later interviews with the last Soviet generation in Russia) that though most of the "normal" people (i.e. neither *nomenklatura* nor dissidents) were alienated from the empty Soviet propaganda, they saw it as a necessary by-product of an essentially decent life.

Socialism, according to Yurchak, still offered the people a set of collective values (altruism, equality, community, creativity, work, education, etc.) to which they could sincerely subscribe (8), thus they were willing to go through the motions, so to speak, performing their role as a Soviet citizen, even if the motions had no substantive meaning. It is only with Gorbachev's externally provided "deconstruction" of the authoritative discourse that the whole ideological universe unravelled and transformed. Yurchak's book has been influential as it offers a very valuable critique of the approaches that view the Soviet system wholly in terms of binary oppositions like oppression/resistance, culture/counter-culture, public self/private self, truth/lies, morality/corruption, etc. In the Estonian context, for example, a similar perspective has supported studies into the ambiguous role of various Soviet institutions, such as trade unions or Komsomol that often became a site of non-official networks and formed an important part of the institutional base of the Singing Revolution. However, Yurchak's entirely functionalist over intentionalist explanation over why the Soviet Union collapsed does not seem justified. Concentrating on Russia, he overlooks the decolonizing agendas such as Solidarity in Poland or the nationalist movements in the Baltics. True, the center's loss of will to rule is a mainspring of a decolonizing moment, yet it is also important that the colony develops a will to adopt agency and to rule itself.

The case of the so-called "letter of 40" usefully complicates Yurchak's analysis and illustrates many of the characteristics of the Soviet colonial situation discussed above. This joint letter signed by forty respected Estonian intellectuals (scientists, creative people, leading administrators, etc.) was composed in October 1980 and sent for publication to the newspapers *Rahva Hääl* and *Sovetskaya Estoniya* in Estonia, and to *Pravda* in Moscow. None of the newspapers published the letter and the signatories were variously harassed by the authorities, though not imprisoned. The immediate trigger to write the letter was the case of the 1980 Estonian youth riots that started in reaction to the authorities cancelling a punk rock concert, but developed into protests against the Russification of the education system. The riots were harshly suppressed by militia, and there was no public discussion of the matter.

In a concerned matter-of-fact tone the letter criticized the Soviet economic and social policies, concentrating on explaining how the 1970s Russification campaign looked from the Estonian perspective and how gravely it damaged social and interethnic relations.[50] Quite contrary to Yurchak's account, the letter not only did not use the "authoritative" Soviet vocabulary, but directly identified its hollowness as a major source of the problems, and demanded a more substantive approach: "The tensions that exist in reality are further exacerbated

---

50 The text of the letter is available in Kiin, Ruutsoo and Tarand 3-7.

by the lack of correspondence between how things are and how they are said to be" (Kiin, Ruutsoo and Tarand 3); "an honest and deep analysis of the situation that has developed" has become "inevitable" (7).

The signatories' political perspectives included a range from idealistic communists to people with strong anti-Soviet views, yet all would presumably count as Yurchak's "normal" people, i.e., not *nomenklatura* or established dissidents. Interviewed by Sirje Kiin in 1988, they also expressed a varied scale of personal motivations as to why they signed and expectations of what the letter might achieve (Kiin, Ruutsoo and Tarand 39-56). Some sincerely hoped the letters could incite discussion and reforms; some wanted to record a protesting voice, even if to no avail; several said it was about not losing the trust of their children (the generation of the protestors). Yet there are also generalities: they all wanted public discussion, they were ready to claim agency and accept some personal risk, and they were ready to cooperate with other Estonians, even with those of hostile political views. The same seems to hold for many "normal" people who gained access of the letter, as it soon leaked and was spread in thousands of handwritten copies. For example, Kiin, Ruutsoo and Tarand report the words of a music school teacher who saw it as her pedagogical duty to read the letter to her students with whom she had discussed the situation in Estonia before: "if *they* [the forty signatories] had the courage to write it, I had to have the courage to make it public" (73, emphasis in the original).

The letter of forty can be seen as a deconstruction of the authoritative discourse in the Gorbachev mode Yurchak describes, and has, indeed, been described as part of the early 1980s "false start" to the Singing Revolution. On the other hand, it came from below rather than from above like *perestroika*, it fed upon ethnic networks, and, crucially, was received by an audience that was already considering possibilities of change, even if mostly hypothetically. If the "everything forever" perception did not fully hold in the Estonia of "mature socialism", neither was the *perestroika* period wholly perceived in terms of an unsurprising melting away of the previous reality. Rather, for many it was a tough ambitious struggle for freedom, historical justice and the Estonian cause (of course, these aims could be interpreted in very different ways). The speech given in 1988 by Edgar Savisaar, one of the leaders of the Singing Revolution, is high-flown, but broadly typical of the emotions of the time:

> This is not the first occasion that the Estonian people have dared to want the impossible, or what many saw as impossible. The first time it happened 120 years ago when almost no-one believed that the Estonian people would

awaken—and despite that we succeeded in becoming a cultural nation. The second time it was 70 years ago when nobody in the world believed in the birth of a sovereign Estonian state—yet it *was* born. Now the third time the occasion has arrived and again there are doubters who think that the bar has been raised too high. (13, emphasis in the original)

The above quote is also typical as an example of the logic and rhetoric of historical analogies, a sense of rupture and regeneration that played a major role during the process of decolonization. In the beginning of that process there was disagreement about whether to aim for autonomy within the Soviet Union or to bid for full independence (and later whether the republic ought to define itself as a new, "second republic", or claim legal continuity with the interwar period), yet all sides used the "phoenix rises from the ashes" model, even if the relationships between the different incarnations of the phoenix were heavily contested.

The rhetoric of historical regeneration/continuity as well as the direct impact of earlier models of socio-cultural condensation are very evident in the numerous popular rock, choir and folk songs that gave the Singing Revolution its name. A good example is "Dawn" ("Koit", words and music by Tõnis Mägi) that became the unofficial anthem of the Singing Revolution and 2009 was voted the favorite Estonian song of all times. It re-evokes the 19th-century trope of a new "age of dawn" that wins over the "age of darkness" and awakens the country, so that slaves can be reborn to freedom: "Again it's time to stand up straight/ and cast off slave robes,/so that in a flow of creativity everything created/could all together be born again.//It's dawn, a majestic blaze,/the victory of the light will awaken the country."

Like the 19th-century tropes themselves, the imagery of the song also harkens back to an even earlier, Christian, and particularly Moravian, vision of regeneration. This impression is reinforced by the music of the song which blends rock with jubilant hymnal music and starts with a call of trumpets. In fact, Mägi, the performer and author of "Dawn", was at the time involved with the political-religious anti-Soviet organization "Word of Life" ("Elu Sõna"). It emerged out of Baptist and Methodist circles, and its leaders have proclaimed its religious views closest to those of the Moravians (Saarsen). It had a strong influence on Mägi during the Singing Revolution, yet the inspirational power and lasting popularity of his songs show that the aesthetics resonates far wider than the minority of religious believers among Estonians.

Another example is the "Five Fatherland Songs" ("Viis isamaalist laulu", music by Alo Mattiisen, words by Jüri Leesment and Henno Käo), a contemporized folk rock re-writing of five 19th-century patriotic songs. The most popular of these, "Keeping the Beauty of the Fatherland" boosts the participants' sense of agency, proclaiming a vision of individual-collective relationship that could also be taken back to the Moravian period (the "you" is in singular everywhere): "if you believe in yourself, / then you will believe in the people / [...] then you will get a powerful spirit, / then you will get a better life // [...] if you believe in yourself, / [...] in sisters, brothers, / first of all in yourself, / first of all in yourself, / then you will get a better life." The song works best, of course, when sung by thousands of people simultaneously, heightening the perception that everyone's individual sense of agency is decisive for the empowerment of the collective.

While the political preoccupations manifested themselves directly in the patriotic songs, the literature during the Singing Revolution was not predominately "fatherlandish", but rather responded to the spirit of the time through an explosion of variety. Poets developed the interrupted themes of the 1960s and early 1970s or the interwar-period experimentalists, explored relativities with international postmodern and postcolonial currents, redefined the concern with ethnic identities in ethnofuturism, increased the interchange and syncretism between literature, music and performance arts even further than beforehand (Velsker, "Nüüdiskirjandus" 625). There were several nuanced novels written about the previously restricted historical topics, but much of the creative effort also went into publicist writing. Numerous new cultural-political journals, newspapers and magazines were created (importantly *Vikerkaar* in 1986, *Akadeemia* in 1989), some also with parallel editions in Russian (*Raduga* 1986), or by the Russian wing of the Popular Front movement (*Tartuskii Kur'er* 1989). It is important to note that the Singing Revolution did not work only (or even primarily) through mass rallies and joint singing, but also through continuous country-wide debates over issues like the economic future of Estonia; the Molotov-Ribbentrop pact and the status of the Soviet power under international law; the best strategies for pursuing Estonian interests (to liberate and taking cue from the *perestroika* or to restitute the interwar Estonian Republic). The experience of "the highest possible level of civic participation" (Lauristin and Vihalemm 7) has proved to have been strongly formative for the Estonians' political mentality and expectations.[51]

---

[51] This has parallels in other former Soviet bloc countries where the political turn was carried through with high levels of direct democracy (Isaac).

Post-independence Estonia through the postcolonial lens

This book argues that Postcolonial Studies can be helpful not only for analyzing Soviet Estonia, but also the Singing Revolution and the independent republic: more so than the framework of post-Soviet or transition studies. These tend to disregard the problems of nation-building (a state population must equal a nation without further ado) and generally simply assume a "reintegration" into the political and economic normativity of the West in the particular form it has taken at the end of the 20th and the beginning of the 21st century. Viewing the situation through the lens of Postcolonial Studies provides a better angle to analyze the role of nationalism (in the sense of national mobilization) in the 1980s popular anti-status-quo movements (they would be described as "decolonizing"), as well as a major proportion of their post-independence ramifications and discontents.

In Estonia itself, issues relating to competing (more ethnically or more civically accentuated) models of modern statehood are today habitually treated within the parameters of a mutual offensive between conservative nationalists (considered (proto)fascists by adversaries) and liberal cosmopolitans (self-colonizers and "red professors" according to the other side). I believe that it is useful to consider this deadlock also in the global and postcolonial framework, rather than solely in the context of Eastern European vs. Western values (as does Saarts, "Kahest"). The postcolonial perspective can provide a reflective intellectual space in which to examine the comparable post-Soviet processes without idealizing or demonizing them or taking for granted that they ought to fit a Western grid of normality.

I do not mean, of course, to explain the specificities of the post-Soviet Estonian society with some deep primeval cultural idiosyncrasies. Rather, the talk is of the very particular political-socio-cultural imprint left by the experience of triple colonization (Baltic German, Czarist Russian and Soviet) described in this chapter, native and imposed aspects of modernity, and struggles for political emancipation in shifting historical circumstances. These all shape the present-day Estonians' definitions of their collective self and influence their present political and socio-cultural imagination. The definitions in their turn are continuously internally contested by different actors and are not unchanging, but the modes of contest too are conditioned by previous history. One central focus in the post-Soviet nation-building is the role of the Soviet period settlers who sometimes come to be lumped together as "the colonizer" by Estonians, but who include a variety of people whose expectations, like those of Estonians, have been shaped by different experiences of modernization. Furthermore, they can have their own competing narratives about their part in the decolonization of Estonia and their share in the nation (e.g. Grigorjan and Rosenfeld on the Russian-speaking wing of the Popular Front in Estonia).

Here the postcolonial lens can help to foreground the problematics of collective *formation* in Estonia which theories of democracy tend not to address (Calhoun 80). As Calhoun points out, if one defines a political nation by its will to political self-determination, one needs to discuss who is included in or excluded from the self (96-97). This is also the case with politically and culturally "stable" nations with a long historical pedigree. However, the issue becomes much more foregrounded in a postcolonial situation. There the values, power mechanisms and even boundaries of the nation are typically under fierce contestation by a variety of stakeholders who have different social and cultural backgrounds, whose experience of the former empire was very different, and whose historical world-picture and political aspirations may be strongly at odds with one another.

Such a situation does not encourage re-imagining the national community in more inclusive terms although this is not impossible either. Whether or not such a reimagining is possible depends to a large extent on the public narratives that the population ("people") as a whole creates and endorses (cf. Brown above). Thinking in a global framework can help the Balts to acknowledge the objective difficulty of the challenge of nation formation in postcolonial circumstances. The "back and forth of historical grievances" (Yack, *Nationalism* 296) is almost a given of postcolonial history, yet one can also learn from international experience the high stakes involved in (not) being able to evolve the postcolonial nation-building successfully. Bernard Yack's tentative advice from the social psychological perspective suggests that thinking only in terms of "rights" (whether individual or group rights) can sometimes be counterproductive (239-244). Solutions could often be pursued more successfully when approaching the postcolonial grievances in terms of clashing wrongs, not clashing rights (295- 296). That is to say: in case of an entangled post-imperial history, such as the Soviet one, people (from ever new generations) find themselves in conundrums they did not themselves cause or choose, yet must bear the consequences of. Thinking in terms of multiple wrongs gives one the opportunity to acknowledge the injustice or misfortune suffered by another group, *without thereby delegitimating one's own claims* (296, my emphasis).

Placing Estonia in the global postcolonial context also brings out some internal connection-patterns not otherwise visible. The above-mentioned Estonian/Russian and liberal/conservative controversies inter-relate with the third major division in the country. That is between the so-called "first" and "second" Estonia, i.e. the relative winners and losers of the decolonization and reorganization of the economic sphere.[52] This third division is not a feature outside or cross-cutting Estonian national identity as the divisions of "class" might be thought to function. Instead, the post-Soviet Estonian national consciousness evolved strongly bound up with the worldview of neoliberalism, its value structure widely internalized as part of a shared national ethos, promoted by "top-down" state nationalism from the early 1990s (cf. Annist 108-109).

As always with "latecomers" there is an in-built tension between the need to resonate with the outside on the one hand, and with the inside on the other (cf. "Introduction" and Lauristin and Vihalemm). The early 1990s radical economic turn-around in Estonia for a long while helped to handle this issue. It founded a sphere of consensuality that could act as a balm regarding the hostilities in Estonia and pacified the foreign critics of Estonian citizenship policies that had left the Soviet period settlers without automatic citizenship in the independent republic. The Estonian elites carried out "shock therapy" economic reforms inspired by the theories of Milton Friedman and policies of Margaret Thatcher, extremely rapidly opening the economy to integrate it in the West.[53] Despite large segments of population strongly negatively affected, there was practically no debate or protest. Ethnic Estonians generally accepted personal hardship as a necessary sacrifice in order to escape the Russian sphere of influence and perceived continuing imperial ambitions, and Estonian Russians also welcomed the market and consumer society as a seemingly ethnicity-neutral sphere where they or their children could enjoy life in Estonia.

Neoliberalism, in the sense I use it here, is a form of liberalism with a strong concern for free capital movement and individual property rights that correspondingly de-emphasizes some other traditional liberal preoccupations, such as a culture of political debate, and equal opportunity. Neoliberalism assumes that markets will invariably return to a state of equilibrium and that thereby all will benefit from the market. It prescribes the role of the state as minimal:

---

52 The widespread notion of the "two Estonias" stems from the open letter of 26 Estonian social scholars published in the daily *Postimees*, 23rd of April 2001 (discussion in English by Lagerspetz and Vogt, "Estonia" 2004, especially 57-58). In the letter the expression primarily refers to the cleavage between the the political power elite and the general population. However, as shown by a poll conducted by the survey firm EMOR it quickly acquired more varied connotations, also understood as the rich and the poor, the elites and the marginalized, the advanced and the lagging, etc. (Saarts, "Kas teine Eesti").

53 It is illuminative that Estonian leaders of the time reminisce about their problems with the European Commission and even with the IMF who (unsuccessfully) tried to talk them into using at least some minimal measures to protect the local economic actors (Muuli 111, 251-252).

primarily to safeguard and, if they are lacking, to create, the free markets. Such a division of roles implies "relocation of power from political to market-economic processes" (Thorsen 16), both on the national and international level: economic processes appear as a natural phenomenon, not as an object of political debate and intervention. Thus if the democratic process interferes with neoliberal policy-making, it is right that "democracy ought to be sidestepped and replaced by the rule of experts" (16). Neoliberal national politicians also typically assume the role of market experts, as this expertise is seen as the key legitimation of political power.

Thus, one can see why the neoliberal ideology, on the one hand, seemed attractive in 1990s Estonia, as the exact negative mirror image of the Soviet Union where the state was large and intrusive, everything was politicized, and shopping was an unpleasant ordeal. On the other hand, the neoliberal outlook ran counter to the culture of nationwide debates and participatory democracy that had developed during the Singing Revolution. Consequently, even if there was no contestation of neoliberalism, disappointment in and alienation from "politics" (in the sense of party politics) followed already the first half of 1990s (Mikko Lagerspetz and Henri Vogt, "Estonia" 1998, 55). I will return to discuss the developments of these contradictions in 2010s Estonia after considering what particular illuminating potential the Postcolonial Studies may have for the matter (besides offering an appropriate framework to place the Estonian case into global perspective).

Much of Postcolonial Studies today, including its most canonical authors, are not very interested in the processes of national mobilization, decolonization or state-building. According to Simon Gikandi, the way Postcolonial Studies are constructed today by theorists like Homi Bhabha, there is not much between the texts of the colonial project and the postmodern migrant writers and intellectuals "writing back" to them. There is an "invisible space between colonialism and its transcendence, a nadir located somewhere between 1945 and 1975, which postcolonial theory seems unable to account for in significant ways" (Gikandi).

The strongest reason is probably that at the time that the Postcolonial Studies consolidated themselves in the 1980s and early 1990s, the hopeful period of anti-colonial Third-World nationalism had come to an end and had largely morphed into a disappointing, dictatorial and violent one. Furthermore, to a large extent the Postcolonial Studies developed in the wake of the so-called culturalist turn in critical theory and thus came to "view nationalism as a primarily cultural and epistemological, rather than socio-political, formation" (Chrisman 183). So in the works of leading postcolonial scholars, nationalism mostly appears as a failed historical project, exclusionary and inherently dominatory, and/or as a form of make-believe, a false consciousness, a rhetorical strategy. They almost exclusively deal with Western metropolitan nationhood in the need to be deconstructed by the very abstractly presented migrants at its margins (e.g. Bhabha, "DissemiNation"; "On Writing") or with top-down and nativist nationalism (e.g. Spivak, "Nationalism"). This limitation is probably also one of the reasons why the decolonization problems of the Soviet bloc for such a long time attracted so little attention in Postcolonial Studies.

Nevertheless, this culturalist, poststructuralist turn in Postcolonial Studies has enabled a more realistic understanding of the dynamics of colonial oppression (also pertinent for analysing the Soviet sphere). This dynamics is no longer understood as a straightforward clash between coercion and resistance or coercion and submission, but rather as an interplay of complicities, contradictions, temporal change, unintended consequences and extensive ramifications. The culturalist turn has also promoted proper scepticism concerning any easy idealization of national unity, including that presumed by decolonizing nationalists. The apotheosis of unity necessarily overrides the internal variety of groups and perspectives inside the nation, thus paradoxically promoting the hijacking of what was an endeavor of *collective* liberation by the agenda of some particular political elite.[54] Both of these aspects are, without doubt, directly relevant also for the analysis of the Soviet and post-independence situations in Estonia.

However, what is limiting in this paradigm is the lack of interest in decolonizing nationalisms and state-building attempts and in the groundedness and functioning of particular national endeavors in and through their historical institutions, discourses and practices. Indeed, the culturalist approach disregards the very historical role of nationalism in modernity: its acting as a reaction to a legitimation crisis in the way a society is ruled and a mobilizing force in the struggles towards popular sovereignty, factors discussed in this book above. In the 1980s and early 1990s it seemed to many Western leftist scholars, both in Postcolonial Studies and elsewhere, that nationalism was no longer relevant in the globalized world, and they predicted its immediate (and salutary) obsoleteness (Hobsbawm, especially 183).[55] Today some make a strong argument

---

54 These dangers were already pointed out by many decolonizing nationalists themselves, such as Cabral, Césaire or Fanon (Chrisman 188).
55 On the other hand, Suny in 1993 interprets his contemporary nationalism analogically to its role in the 19th century as "a form of self-defence. In a world chronically unevenly developed [...] those disadvantaged try to find their own way to modernity without falling prey to imperial subordination" (*The Revenge* 156).

for nations and international cooperation as a potentially beneficial resource to counter or at least buffer the global forces of neoliberal capitalism and neocolonialism (Calhoun, especially 17-26, 169-171), that is, to resist the present day's major crisis of power legitimation. Pheng Cheah, invoked by Gikandi in the work cited above, challenges Benedict Anderson's famous pronouncement of the philosophical poverty of nationalism (Anderson 5), Cheah opens up nationalism as a philosophical concept, developing closely intertwined with those of freedom, culture and self-realization (*Bildung*). Thus he "situates nationalism at the heart of the Western intellectual tradition," as Craig Calhoun remarks on the back cover blurb of the book.

Cheah's careful and detailed archeology of the affiliation between the 18th- and 19th-century German ideas of individual and collective self-realization on the one hand, and the liberal-universalist ideas of emancipation on the other is relevant for the Baltic field in its own right, considering the region's rootedness in Herderian thought. However, Cheah conducts this archeology in the first part of his book as an introduction to the second part's comparison between the European constellation of ideas and decolonizing national thought overseas. The latter he explores in journalistic writing, as well as in the post-independence *Bildungsromane* by the Indonesian author Praemoedya Ananta Toer and the Kenyan author Ngũgĩ wa Thiong'o. As did the 18th- and 19th-century Germans, these authors understand "culture" as a broad dynamic force incorporating various creative aspects of life, not only artistic but also political imagination. It is rooted in the everyday life and traditions of the people, yet it is dynamic and aligns with critical reason, appropriating European influences and turning them into something new (Cheah, *Spectral* 217, 286, 290). *Spectral Nationality* never mentions Homi Bhabha directly, but much of the work could be read as a dispute with Bhabha's take on nationhood. As I see it, Cheah's understanding of decolonizing nationalism as a kind of individual and collective self-realization deconstructs the divide of pedagogical (top-down, elite-governed) and performative (people's everyday ways of life) nationalism posited in Bhabha's "DissemiNation".

However, both Cheah's and Praemoedya's texts, in different ways, demonstrate that the very same forces that make popular emancipation possible (literacy, modern means of communication, organizations, etc.) enable oppression and domination in the hands of the colonial state, transnational economic forces, but also the postcolonial state (as the Indonesian experience shows only too well), or even the power structures of a formalized mass movement. In Cheah's terminology, modern organizational culture is a form of *techne*, a prosthesis that enables the life of a nation, but can also come to the service of instrumental reason (as opposed to critical reason) and, if so, becomes a mechanical force that destroys life.[56] Thus the institutions of the state provide protection for national culture, which legitimizes struggles for statehood, but the same institutions can equally constrict culture, binding it in statism that stultifies creativity. The purely instrumental aspect of the modern world outlook is in principle analogical to a stagnant feudal approach to the world: it is an oppressive force stifling *Bildung* and leading to a remythologization of the world "where enlightenment or technological progress itself revert to myth" (Cheah, *Spectral* 282). The almost seamless cooperation between the colonial state apparatus and the traditional Javanese aristocracy is one paradigmatic example of this affinity, the mechanistic market fundamentalism of the neoliberal order is another.

Cheah makes it clear that the problem is not entirely in Indonesian idiosyncrasies, but that to some degree all modern organizations—including national movements—are always contaminated by the same mechanisms which make their existence possible. Still, the unavoidable contamination need not be a reason for fatalism, or for the condemnation of the national project. Rather, it ought to be a reason for the awareness and guarded acceptance of the project's dangers and limitations. In the present world of globalized capitalism, a postcolonial nation-state is both dependent on and undermined by the *techne* of transnational forces (of which the state becomes an ally). However, the *techne* of popular national organization can enable resistance against total capitulation to these forces.

From the perspective of studying Baltic postcolonialism, there is the handicap of Cheah's relative indifference towards the question of destructive potential not only of modern organizations, but also of the communal aspect of nationhood[57], and the problems of collective formation in a postcolonial situation that may proceed from there. There is no reason to assume that the sense of lacking sovereignty and danger to the community always disappears with decolonization, as (perceived or realistic) foreign threat and/or indirect forms of

---

56 Cheah's notion of prosthesis grows out of his construction and rereading of the German philosophical lineage (Kant, Fichte, Hegel and Marx are considered in detail) that sets up organic life "as the paradigmatic metaphor for social organization and political life" (Cheah, *Spectral* 8).

57 According to Bernard Yack, modern nations are, firstly, one version of generic "communities". Community in that sense is a flexible form of social cooperation that is based on the universal human disposition to develop some sense of loyalty to and concern for other human beings with whom s/he shares something (*Nationalism* 4). The modern conceptualization of nationhood forms itself when the idea of the political "people" (with a right to sovereignty), emerges as embodied in the type of intergenerational communities that imagine themselves socially connected through some shared cultural heritage. (Yack, *Nationalism*, especially 113-19) These two aspects together make national loyalty a very strong, possibly explosive, form of attachment.

domination still remain. This breeds vibrant nationalism even after decolonization, which may enhance distrust and ungenerosity towards minorities, especially if, as in the Baltic case, the minorities are related to a colonial enemy estimated as continuously dangerous. However, despite the objective problems of the historical situation, as David Brown points out, much depends on the public discourses (and their resonance): whether the nation develops an identity primarily warped "in relation to threatening others" (67) or is able to pursue other means of coping with the problems and setting goals for itself.

Attempting to analyze this set of problems, the political scientist Tõnis Saarts ("Kahest") argues that in Estonia there are competing models of democracy—a more liberal civic model open to ethnic minorities and a more confrontational and closed "nationalist defence democracy". The latter became popularly wider spread following the 2007 Bronze Soldier conflict[58] and the 2008 Russia-Georgia war. At the same time, the nationalist model also carries the frustrations of the rapid subjection to "European" norms and values in the name of the wealth and security promised by EU membership.

It could be useful to supplement Saarts by identifying main strands of thinking about, or attitudes towards, nationhood in Estonia: nativist, popular, top-down, constitutional, and cosmopolitan.[59] These do not exclude one another and occur in overlapping and in various (also counter-intuitive) combinations in the case of different individuals and groups depending on the situation. It would be difficult to find one strand with consistent purity anywhere. Indeed, it can be observed that most members of Estonian society to an extent share the "popular" and the "constitutional" approach to nationhood or at least must recognize their normative status in the society.

---

58 In April 2007 the Estonian government abruptly relocated the only remaining Soviet "liberation" memorial in Tallinn ("the Bronze Soldier", officially first known as "Monument to the Liberators of Tallinn") from the city center to an outskirts military cemetery. It had been the location of many Russian-speaking Tallinners' celebration of the 9th of May and the decision was linked to some Russian and Estonian extremist' altercations at the monument. The removal was accompanied by a demonstration of mainly Russian-speaking defenders of the monument which turned into violent street riots. In protest against the Estonian governments' actions, the Estonian Embassy in Moscow was besieged by pro-Kremlin youth activists and the websites of Estonian government institutions, banks, newspapers, etc. were attacked from Russia. See Petersoo and Tamm; in English e.g. Ehala, "The Bronze Soldier"; Lagerspetz and Vogt, "Estonia" 2013, 57; 61-62. For an in-depth semiotic and discourse analysis of the construction of "the Bronze Night" by the Estonian media and public communication, see Selg, "A Political-Semiotic".

59 Kalev, Lumi, and Saarts that approaches Estonian national politics with a wider focus than ethnic vs. civic identity politics provides a more complex and fluid picture. It is broadly compatible with my own following account.

By constitutional I do not mean a "postnationalist" constitutional patriotism, but rather the symbolic weight of laws as an essential part of being the legitimate "masters of one's home". The central controversies in society are almost always fought around specific laws and in legal terms. The strong strands of popular activism and legalism supplement very different political and moral agendas. In recent decades one can mention the campaign against the plan to increase the share of Estonian as a language of instruction in the Russian-language schools; protests against the Anti-Counterfeiting Trade Agreement; the so-called Charter 12 initiative that condemned the corruption and top-down decision making of the government and led to the creation of the People's Assembly that proposes crowdsourced solutions to problems concerning political legitimacy; a campaign to call a referendum on the definition of marriage in Estonia, initiated by the Conservative People's Party of Estonia, part of the governing coalition at the time.

Seeing nationhood as not only based on popular sovereignty, but as a matter of popular activism and organization, and the preoccupation with legitimacy and legality as categories of much more than only pragmatic significance stem from the political experience of the decolonization period. The above ideas became very widely internalized as the natural way to pursue one's political aims and participate in the life of the nation. The vision of nationhood as properly popular runs in parallel with the top-down nationalism that also formed during the Singing Revolution and consolidated in the 1990s when the decisive economic and state-building reforms were ordained by the ruling elite (Lauristin and Vihalemm 8-11). Furthermore, both the economic creed of neoliberalism and the decolonization in the form of excluding the Soviet period settlers from the "people" of popular sovereignty were largely accepted by ethnic Estonians as fair and internalized as part of Estonian national values (Lauristin and Vihalemm 9-11).[60] The radicality and exceptionally fastidious implementation (Annist 118-119) of the neoliberal reforms that made Estonia the IMF's model

---

60 In 1991, Estonia proclaimed independence as the legal and historical successor to the inter-war period republic established in 1918. The 50 years of the Soviet republic were defined as a period of illegal occupation under international law; *de jure* there never was a Soviet Socialist Republic of Estonia. While the citizens of the inter-war period republic and their descendants received citizenship after the country regained independence, the Soviet period settlers have to apply for citizenship, passing a B1 exam (European Framework of Reference language levels) in the Estonian language, as well as an exam on the Estonian Constitution and Citizenship Act. From 2002, children of non-citizens younger than 15 and born after the 26th of February 1992 can obtain Estonian citizenship without passing exams, if their parents apply for it for them. In 2020 about 85% of the Estonian population had Estonian citizenship, about 6.5% Russian citizenship, and about about 5% were stateless.

pupil have an important postcolonial background. The memberships in WTO, NATO and EU were for many Estonians pursued not (only) as aims in themselves, but as an escape route from the economic and political sphere of influence of Russia, continuously perceived to have colonial ambitions (Lagerspetz and Vogt, "Estonia" 2004, 77).

The central governments had free hands to carry out the 1990s reform policies, as well as the extensive austerity measures after the 2008 economic crisis without a debate, causing no popular unrest or even much protest from the so-called second Estonia. Beside the Russian issue, the fact that the neoliberal rationale had established itself without viable alternatives, as something to be simply accepted, also played an important role (Thorhalsson and Kattel 91, 95-96). It was only after the worst of the economic crisis was over that large-scale popular activism re-emerged in the form of the initiatives mentioned above. It is significant that the activism frequently does not focus only on a particular policy in question, but questions the habit of top-down governing itself.[61] In the aftermath of this turn, income inequality that had been the highest in Europe according to the Gini index, also started dropping gradually from 2016 thanks to the measures of a national conservative/left-center government, and almost reached the European average in 2020.

Finally, we could consider looking at the controversy between "defensive" nativist and "civic" cosmopolitan nationalism from the same explanatory angle as the conflict of Estonians and Russians in *The Handful of Dust*. What Frank Furedi writes of contemporary liberal elites internationally is also often true of the cosmopolitan perspective in Estonia: "at a time when the cultural elites lack a coherent moral project, they often succeed in establishing a sense of moral authority by favorably contrasting their enlightened values with the prejudices of ordinary citizens" (162). In 2012 there was created the Conservative People's Party of Estonia (EKRE), described by different observers as right-wing populist, far-right or national conservative. Gathering voter support, it participated in the governing coalition of 2019-2021, embarrassing mainstream politicians with anti-gay and racist anti-immigration statements in the Estonian and international press.

---

61 In retrospect one can view the idiosyncratic 2010 Unified Estonia performance project by the NO99 theatre as the symbolic inception of this change. The theatre troupe attracted national attention when it created a fictional new political movement, Unified Estonia, through which it parodied and exposed the mechanisms of Estonian party politics for six weeks, inviting popular critical enquiry and participation.

In Pheng Cheah's view discussed above, popular nationalism offers protection against oppressive forces exactly because it promotes a creative relationship between individuals and the collective that enables cultural-political *Bildung*. Hard-line nativist nationalism, whether top-down or popular, that reduces Estonianness to a limited set of features and sees non-compliers as wrongdoers is not congruent with that creative role. At the same time, the rise of EKRE should be acknowledged as a symptom, not demonized without a proper analysis of the varied groups of population who vote for it. It is particularly problematic that the concerns that many people have about EU-induced new immigration have been ridiculed or classified as racism by the cosmopolitan-minded.

It is easy to ridicule concerns about immigration because (before Russia's war on Ukraine 2022 and the resulting waves of refugees) the immigration numbers were relatively low, and the Estonian state, aided by quickly mobilized volunteers, was quite successful in creating support and integration mechanisms. What was there to worry about? However, it would be more fruitful to address people's concerns in the context of Soviet-era colonial mass-immigration and, even more importantly, in that of the Estonians' awareness of the problems raised in connection with immigration elsewhere in Europe. The liberal discussion has entirely ignored the fact that people's opinions are influenced not only by their own direct experience, but also by their diverse sources of information in the globalized world.[62]

The combinations of popular, constitutional and cosmopolitan perspectives to nationalism (which could be summed up as "civic") do produce, in my view, some of the most productive and promising cultural and political endeavors in Estonia today. However, the popular strand in the combination often seems to fade in the face of people who do not fit the pattern and this narrows the field of engagement. Despite the rhetoric of inclusivity, ideal Estonian nationhood from the civic perspective probably still tends to be seen in terms of a community of principle, rather than one of solidarity and care.

---

62 In this connection it is important to emphasize the relatively strong general support to the *Ukrainian* refugees in Estonia, as well as in the other the Baltic states and in Poland. This should be seen, I argue, as a part of these countries' identification with Ukraine's efficient struggle against Russian imperialism. As we know, Russia justified its "special operation" not only by the duty to de-nazify Ukraine, but also by Ukrainians not being a separate nation, thus lacking the right to build their own modern statehood.

Coda

To conclude the chapter, I want to re-emphasize that Estonian discourses of modernity are to a large extent conditioned by the tension between the need to conform to the standards of earlier and/or more powerful modernizers, and the need to negotiate the *problématiques* of modernity (Wagner, *Modernity: Understanding* 74-76) in a manner resonant and legitimate in the often strenuous local historical circumstance. The repeated experience of colonization and the challenges of decolonization are of crucial significance. This postcolonial heritage has obvious dangers and disadvantages, but, I claim, it can potentially also provide useful cultural resources to deal with discontinuity and change.

In processing the experience of rapid change and sudden radical breaks from preceding life-worlds, three main interrelated temporal tropes dominate Estonian discursivity at its abstract level: "rupture", "rebirth" and (not quite the same as the latter) "return". The poet and cultural scholar Hasso Krull perceptively writes in 1996 of Estonian culture as a "culture of rupture": Estonians conceptualize their history as built on the repeating motif of ruptures, either negative (sudden loss of a good life) or positive one (bold tearing off from a bad life) (7). Seen as an "endless series of ruptures", Estonian history paradoxically acquires meaning and continuity, in which even the most destructive ruptures have a place (7). "Continuous ruptures create a continuity", says Krull, "continuity is created exactly by repetition of rupture" (7). In a more mythological tonality this could be also described as a series of deaths and regenerations, consonant with the "phoenix from the ashes" model. Krull's analysis also implies another relevant aspect of the Estonian regeneration-discourse—not only can the return/rebirth to the good life be emphasized as positive, but so can a rupture, an attempt to "make a complete break with the past", and to be born anew. These two discourses are often used intertwined and emphasis can vary.

The Finnish scholar Mikko Lagerspetz points to the discursive strategy of "return" that Estonia and other "postsocialist" countries used to legitimize their chosen paths of decolonization. Estonia's "return" to the inter-war republic enabled to define the Soviet period as a rupture to "normality" ("Postsocialism")[63], while it also left the Soviet period settlers out of the citizenry. During the 1990s, a narrative pattern of the "Soviet rupture" was also gradually adopted on the level of individual lives in the autobiographies by people who grew up in the

---

63 Soviet historiography, of course, had constructed the inter-war period as a rupture to normality, before the Russian historical territories returned to the motherland.

inter-war period (Kõresaar, *Elu* 107; Kõresaar, "Nostalgia" 764-765). However, while the principle of state continuity rests on the tropes of return and restitution, the imaginaries of change have been much more open-ended and ambitious than a return to the 1930s. Estonia's *tour-de-force* to be e-Estonia, leaping into digital democracy and education is one of the best known examples. The idealization of the inter-war period has today largely lost its role as a resource for future social and political projects, especially for the younger generations (Kõresaar, "Nostalgia" 763).

Illustrating the concluding points and prefacing the analysis in the next chapters, I will give two post-Soviet literary examples of how the discourses of rupture, return and newness typically exist side by side.

The poetic essay "Sermon at the Grave of a Schoolhouse" ("Kõne koolimaja haual") by the poet and author Viivi Luik (b.1946) dramatizes the narrator's drive through Viljandi county, historically an exceptionally wealthy agricultural heartland, now empty and deserted. Because of the prosperity of the area it severely suffered under Soviet repressions and the continuity with the pre-war period was destroyed (105). Luik conjures up a vision of the past glory of the interwar agricultural modernity: "large and wealthy Viljandi farmhouses" (105), "like fortresses" (106), "a part of Estonian culture [...] about which almost nothing is known anymore" (105).[64] In the old days the farms had not only tractors and telephones, beehives, orchards and fashionable landscape gardens, but also harpsichords in the drawing room, and book cupboards full of quality literature (106); "in summer children returned from Tartu University, the hammocks were put up, the coffee pot steamed..." (106).

Coming up to a deserted schoolhouse, however, the narrator is suddenly struck by an entirely different mood, a thrill of pleasure for the chance to shake free from the burden of the past and to start anew:

> This land has been so thoroughly and grandly deserted, the past things and places so deeply forgotten that all my previous talk seems narrow and limited. In front of this forgotten schoolhouse in the middle of thickets, on the ruins of a lost culture there rises the question: why not make the dearth a merit! [...] Maybe there is a magic flower growing among the weeds? Maybe there is too much tilled and cared-for land in the world already, maybe it is fortunate if a piece of land can breathe, grow bush and weeds as it feels like.

---

64 Luik remembers the area from the 1950s when the houses were already empty or used by the kolkhoz (105-106).

Maybe the world does not have a shortage of bountiful fertilized fields, but of rested soil [...] Maybe exactly here [...] there is hidden a freedom which we don't quite understand yet, but which will become ever more treasured. Maybe my talk about Occupied Estonia and lumpen vandalism is only a cliché, the usual spiteful, sullen whinging! (108) [...] This land will shake itself free again and again, here the fields have repeatedly grown into thickets and the number of people shrivelled [...] and all this has not mattered (109).

The changes in the landscape will bring with them a new way of making speeches, a new language, Luik says at the end of her essay: one that we do not know yet (109). While the essay questions the aptness of agricultural modernity for contemporary Estonia, it shapes Estonian history through the traditional "phoenix from the ashes" model. Her positive inclusion of the "ashes" stage of the cycle in the story enables her to tell it as one of regenerative dynamism and resilient continuity, rather than, say, one of random objectification by stronger powers. It is significant that not only the destructive past of the Soviet period, but also the interwar-period idyll evoked at the beginning of the essay must be in the final instance ruptured for the model to work. The anthropologist Rijk van Dijk describes this phenomenon with the term anti-nostalgia: "*not wishing to remember* a past", "wilfully disempowering the past" (157, emphasis in the original).[65] If the interwar period has lost its political role for the younger generation, scholars also note that rememberances of the Soviet period now mainly concentrate on humorous reminiscing about the absurdities of the stagnation years, whereas talk about political repressions is rare (Kõresaar, "Nostalgia" 766).

Andrus Kivirähk's (b. 1970) play *The Blue Carriage* ("Helesinine vagun"), a self-proclaimed "nostalgic comedy" concentrates on the memory culture of the Estonians born in the early 1970s. The title of the comedy refers to a ditty in a popular Soviet cartoon about Gena the Crocodile (1974), so the play inspired the moniker "Russian cartoon generation" (the age group who experienced the Soviet life-world as children and teenagers, but not as adults), now generally used. The play is a comedy of manners where a few representatives of that generation, now in their 30s, gather to a boozy birthday party of their classmate Indrek, and

---

65 Rick van Dijk's, Birgit Meyer's and Anthony Simpson's articles in *Memory and Postcolony* (ed. Richard Werbner) discuss the models of willful rupturing of memory in Malawi, Ghana and Zambia respectively. Although none of the cases parallels Estonia's exactly, these societies similarly struggle with postcolonial situations in multi-ethnic states employing a variety of discourses of "returning" to a past, as well as of making "a complete break with the past" (Meyer 182). It is interesting that in all the African cases discussed in the collection, the radical discourses of rupturing a past grow out of Christian movements that strongly emphasize believers' rebirth.

get their memories, values and jokes clashed against those of two other characters, born in 1940 and 1980 respectively. The different memory groups are in important respects entirely incapable of understanding or relating to one another, and a lot of confusion and conflict occurs. Yet paradoxically the comedy, though at places its humor is very dark, promotes a sense of togetherness in the audience who jointly laugh at the sense of radical discontinuity they know and recognize.[66]

In the symbolic final scene of the play one of the guests, Leopold (who had not seemed significantly stranger than most of the other characters), confesses that he actually comes from an alien planet destroyed in an explosion. It had been a fine place with three black suns, where the fish and the humanoids had flown in the air and the birds had lived underground in the warm blue sand. (Kivirähk, "Helesinine" 264-65) According to *The Blue Carriage* the past is not just another country, it is a different planet. One may nostalgically reminisce about it if one is lucky to find a sympathetic ear, but there is no return. The play ends with Leopold circling above the house tops and Indrek dancing alone to the cartoon song about the blue carriage rolling along:

> Slowly minutes are floating into distance
> Don't expect to see them again
> Maybe we are a bit sad about the past that is gone
> But the best is certainly ahead of us! (Kivirähk, "Helesinine" 267)

---

66 Kivirähk's humor will be further discussed in Chapter Four.

Chapter Two. Decolonizing Translations: Lydia Koidula's *The Last Inca of Peru* (*Perúama wiimne Inka*, 1866); *Martinique and Corsica* (*Martiiniko ja Korsika*, 1869); *Juudit, or the Last Maroons of Jamaica* (*Juudit, ehk Jamaika saare wiimsed Maroonlased*, 1870)

This chapter aims to explore the mechanisms of change in the thought-world of Estonian culture during the second half of the 19th century as the Estonian cultural community was emerging from the domination of the Baltic German upper class. This emergence is a concentrated example of a cultural turn-around, the speed and extent of which make it a relevant case study for the investigation of the typologies of postcolonial change more generally. How, then, did this change occur?

A central aspect of the development of the preliminary form of the modern Estonian culture is its working *on* and *against* German models, including both the local Baltic German ones, and those of Germany. It might be said the Estonians constructed themselves by imitating German precedents, while simultaneously re-shaping them, subverting, and supplementing them with other modern and pre-modern strands of thought and values. I want to propose that Estonian authors' prolific output of literary translations from German could be seen as an example, an extended figure (both a metaphor and a metonymy), for Estonia's process of decolonizing change overall. Thus I will draw upon the insights of translation studies both to analyse the texts mentioned in the chapter title, as well as to broaden this analysis to issues of discursive change and decolonization more generally.

I will approach the question of how change happened through three adaptations/translations into Estonian by one of the most important figures of the Estonian National Awakening, Lydia Koidula (1843–1886), briefly introduced in the previous chapter. In doing this I follow the perspective of the translation theories that emerged from the 1990s intertwined with Postcolonial Studies (importantly, Bassnett and Trivedi (ed.); Bhabha, *The Location* 212-235; Álvarez and Vidal (ed.); Tymoczko, *Translation in a Postcolonial Context*; Tymoczko, "Translation and Political Engagement"; Remael and Logie (ed.)). Thus, I emphasize that texts are not only made of language in the sense of the words on the page, but "in fact of culture, language being in effect a vehicle of the culture" (Trivedi). From that perspective any translation is not just an aesthetic-linguistic exercise, but rather part of the wider processes of cross-cultural discursive transfer, and of both inter- and intracultural negotiations of what counts as legitimate knowledge and power.

Next to that, however, my analysis also draws upon the methods developed in the Descriptive Translation Studies from the 1970s (e.g. Even-Zohar, *Papers*; Hermans, *The Manipulation*; Hermans, *Translation*; Toury, *Descriptive*; Toury, *In Search*), initially in response to prescriptive linguistic theories of translation. Their approach, though criticized for its lack of direct attention to matters of power and ideology (e. g. Tymoczko, "Translation and Political" 40), strongly emphasizes the socio-cultural embeddedment of all translation and in that anticipates the research agenda of the "cultural turn" mentioned above (cf. Chang 261). It provides a valuable set of tools that enables systematic close readings of translated texts in comparison to their source texts, in the manner that they are consistently culturally (and, if wished, politically) contextualized, yet simultaneously attentively analysed on the *textual* level. This helps to avoid the abstraction and sloganism for which some work in the more recent ideology-conscious current has been justly reproached (e.g. by Trivedi).

Typically for "young" literatures (Even-Zohar 23), 19th-century Estonian literature was dominated by translations or, more specifically, by *adaptations* that did not follow the source text closely but modified them as necessary to suit the local concerns and the translator's taste and agenda. Altogether, the understanding of intellectual property was different from the presently hegemonic one: copyright or plagiarism were no meaningful categories. Thus, the foreign (in majority German) stories were re-written and published in Estonian without mentioning the source title or author. The Estonian readers of their time did not know that they were reading adaptations from a foreign language, and more importantly, they would not have considered this a matter of relevance. Estonian adaptors often drew upon models in inexpensive books and periodicals circulating among lower layers of German society through travelling libraries and peddlers. These included sensationalist writings and political pamphlets that the authorities frowned upon. Another important source was so-called *Volksliteratur*: moralistic fiction by conservative clerical authors. Informational texts on a variety of topics were also popular, and so were religious tracts.

The particular individual examples for the Estonian works are hard to discover. Not only is the source not made directly clear and is often obscure, but the Estonian version can be far removed from the German one.[1] Koidula created over a hundred prose adaptations, but only about twenty-five per cent of the source materials have been deduced (Monticelli, Peiker and Mits 915). This chapter discusses three novellas in Koidula's adaptive *oeuvre* that are particularly significant in terms of understanding the 19th-century national movement and political modernization in Estonia. These texts were conceived on the upward curve of the movement when Koidula's writing turned openly political (Undla-Põldmäe, *Koidulauliku* 71). Furthermore, all the German models of these works are now known.[2] The identification of and comparison with the sources offer insight into Koidula's horizon of ideas, as well into her own political ethos and main concerns. *The Last Inca of Peru* (from here on *Inca*) is based on *Huaskar* (1861) by the Rhineland pastor and *Volksliteratur* writer W.O. Horn (1798–1867). An engaging storyteller of Christian humanist outlook, Horn was a favored source material for Koidula, for her father, and for several other Estonian adaptors of the time. The authors of the other two stories, Theodor Mügge (1802–1861) and Luise Mühlbach (1814–1873), however, are quite far removed from conservative clergy as they were supporters of the politically liberal and anti-imperial Young Germany movement.

The present analysis of Koidula's strategies will focus most extensively on *Inca* (and *Huaskar*). There close reading is needed to show how Koidula's small, but frequent and systematic alterations shape the story into new significance. *Martinique and Corsica/Kaiserin Josephine* and *Juudit/Eduard Montague* are discussed in the final shorter sub-chapters. Adapting Mügge, Koidula already has almost everything she wants and makes just a few—though remarkable—additions to make the fellow thinker's work express her own agenda more directly. As for *Martinique and Corsica*, only the first part of it was published due to censorship and the full version has not been found. However, it is clear that on this occasion Koidula makes especially extensive changes in comparison to the source, altering the central thematic focus, so this text is also important to include. At

---

1   For example, Koidula's *The Miller On the Stream and His Daughter-In-Law* (*Oja mölder ja ta minnia*, 1863) was discovered to be an adaptation of Ludwig Würdig's "At the Ditch Mill, or the Money and the Heart" ("Auf der Grabenmühle oder Geld und Herz", 1856) in 1932. The considerably altered and expanded story had been internationally praised and even translated back into German in Koidula's lifetime. The practice of anonymous appropriation of foreign sources gradually lost its legitimacy at the end of the 19th century.
2   *Inca*'s source was discovered by Aarne Vinkel in 1960 ("Mats"), the sources of *Juudit* and *Martinique and Corsica* by Krista Mits in 2018 (Monticelli, Peiker and Mits).

first sight all texts are, wholly or partly, set far away from the fermenting Estonian context of publication: in the New World, in the titular Peru, Jamaica and Martinique respectively.³ All three works dramatize popular insurrections against unfair oppressive rulers.

In *Inca*, the first protagonist the reader meets is the Spanish missionary Bartolomé de Las Casas who sails to Peru, feeling the calling to introduce Christianity to the natives. However, he finds it difficult to do so, as from the outset he witnesses the greed and cruelty of his compatriots. Fleeing Lima, Las Casas is joined by a sensitive young native called Halipa who saves his life. Halipa is a former slave of Francesco Pizarro's, the latter having been killed in the recent violent power struggle. Soon they meet another young Peruvian, Huaskar, who turns out to be the last descendant of the indigenous rulers and becomes another protagonist of the novella. Under Las Casas's influence Huaskar's initial fiercely anti-Spanish feelings disappear and he embraces the Christian humanist view of the world. However, after a violent Spanish attack on their village, Halipa disappears and is thought dead.

Exasperated, Las Casas travels back to Spain together with Huaskar, tells the Spanish Emperor, Charles V, about the Peruvian situation and receives his promise to put a stop to it. In Spain Huaskar also attends the University of Salamanca and falls in love with a Spanish noblewoman, Elvira. The feisty young lady later turns out to be the daughter of the next, law-abiding (though still condescending towards Peruvians) governor sent to Peru by Charles V. Back in Peru, Huaskar finds Halipa alive and repeatedly saves Elvira's and her father's life. When Elvira's father is ousted by yet another coup, Huaskar gathers Peruvian troops and leads them to a successful fight against the slave owners. Finally, he also gains Elvira's hand in marriage, and is named His Majesty's governor in Peru, thus enabling him to offer his compatriots good government while remaining loyal to the European sovereign.

At that point Horn's text ends. In Koidula's text, however, the happy end is followed by a second, contradictory ending/epilogue. There the reader is informed that the Inca population died out unable to bear the conditions of their slavery, and thus the importation of new slaves to America was launched, now black people from Africa. Yet finally the narrator expresses hope that President Lincoln's contemporary (19th-century) politics may bring a better life to black slaves as well.⁴

---

3   As we will see, much of *Martinique* is also set in revolutionary Paris.
4   Las Casas's visit to Peru and Huaskar's uprising are fictional. A few Incan "royals" who sided with the Spaniards were indeed recognized as part of the European system: Paullu Inca (1518–1549) got a coat of arms from Charles V in 1545 (Hunefeldt 39). However, the historical last in-

While the plots of the German and Estonian works mostly coincide (except for the ending) the Estonian text makes systematic small changes. It is important to note that not only the Estonian text, but the German novella too can be seen as a type of translation, as it transmits earlier thematic and formal patterns relating to the nexus of the New World. Since the beginning of colonization the topos of cross-continental encounter became (among other things) a *visionary* space in which both Europeans and colonials dramatized issues relating to the nature of humanity, relationship between self and other, natural law, domination and its legitimations, political change, and ideal forms of social organization. This tradition stretches from Bartolomé de Las Casas and Guamán Poma, defenders of native Americans' rights in the 16th century, to 18th-19th-century literature and philosophy working through the upheaval of modernization and formation of nations (Rousseau, Herder, Hegel, Chateaubriand, José de Alencar, James Fenimore Cooper, and many others). There are different sides to the nexus: it serves as a laboratory for contemplating changes to the status quo (both in exploratory and fearful ways), yet it can also evoke a nostalgic world of traditional manly virtue, or simply provide an escapist space of entertaining exoticism.

Koidula's translations constitute a new re-writing of this complex international tradition: they re-frame it in the Estonian context, so that it comes to present a range of new messages. As Bassnett and Lefevere put it: "all re-writings [...] reflect a certain ideology and poetics and as such manipulate literature to function in a given way" (vii). Koidula writes her texts in and for the literary and socio-cultural circumstance of their production: the National Awakening period Estonia. However, as the following analysis will show, the idea of "manipulation" ought not to be taken to mean that a re-writing can take total control over the manifold earlier material "usurped" and easily turn it into a unidirectional ideological tool. This is not so, as all texts are manifold, the different strands of thought in them do not simply accumulate, but may also clash, undermine, and destabilize one another (cf. Barthes, *Image–Music–Text* 146).

The internal heterogeneity of texts can be especially striking in the New World texts that necessarily carry the contradictions of the colonial ideology, blending discourses of civilization, modernization and the Christian mission

---

digenous monarchs of Peru, Manco Inca (1516–1544) and his son Túpac Amaru (1545–1572) lead *unsuccessful* rebellions against the Spaniards. Further, although the Incan population was almost annihilated, small parts of it survived retreating to remote neighborhoods. In the late 18th and 19th century the *Zeitgeist* inspired a strong neo-Incan revival among their descendants and several new unsuccessful uprisings took place. It is estimated there are about 3-4 million Quechua speaking people with Incan roots in Peru today, most of them subsistence farmers. (Hunefeldt)

with those of racism and apologetics of "unenlightened" pre-modern institutions like slavery. The re-writings by the colonized also tend to be shaped by multiple influences and motivations simultaneously: to imitate the colonizing power, to outperform it by its own criteria, condemn it, ignore it (in order to be authentic), etc. Homi K. Bhabha has approached this situation in terms of the "hybridity" of the postcolonial texts. The state can be both enabling, creating perspectives from which new cultural and political options can be imagined (Bhabha, *The Location* 219), yet also implies a sense of confusion, incomprehensibility, loss of control (213).

Both institutionally and discursively, Koidula's fiction adaptations are closely linked to the freshly developing Estonian-language journalism, which played a central role in the national movement. Koidula is one of the central ideologues of the awakening movement and stands at the foundations of Estonian national literature and culture with a multi-faceted body of work: intensely personal patriotic poetry,[5] popular comedy dramas (the first plays in the Estonian language), fiction, journalism, and organizational activities. Her life and formation as a creative personality are, on the one hand, very exceptional (even more so for a woman), but at the same time share many of the common elements experienced by her contemporary Estonian modernizers, and her writings pick up on and struggle with the central issues of her time.

Koidula's father, Johann Voldemar Jannsen, grew up in a peasant family and got an upward push in life thanks to a benevolent patron, a German-speaking pastor, who took interest in the talented boy. Koidula's mother, Emilie Jannsen (née Koch), was a daughter of a relatively well-to-do—thus probably at least partially Germanized—cheesemaker. It is speculated that in Koidula's early childhood both German and Estonian were spoken at home. However, she received her education entirely in German, finishing a prestigious secondary school, the Pärnu School for Girls, where she was deeply immersed in German literature and high culture. She spoke, and later consciously worked on her Estonian, yet German remained her best language. (Puhvel)

At the same time, in Koidula's case German skills and education did not merely mean a merger into the local German-speaking milieu. It also opened Koidula to influences beyond her immediate circles of association and outside the immediate grasp of imperial censorship, contributing to her formation into the

---

5   The poems are the most canonical part of Koidula's heritage. Some were already set to music in her lifetime and many have remained a popular part of the national canon, especially in the form of songs.

kind of author and activist that she did. Already as a secondary school student she became a regular reader of *Die Gartenlaube*, the modernizing cultural-political family magazine launched in the aftermath of the failed 1848 revolution to promote the liberal conception of German unification.[6] She knew the Young Germany movement and took major interest in the life and work of other radical patriotic poets, such as Hoffmann von Fallersleben and Friedrich Freiligrath (Undla-Põldmäe, *Koidulauliku* 14-15). Furthermore, probably the most important formative influence that came from her reading was the local Baltic German publicist Merkel and his fierce criticism of the situation in the Baltics that he compared to the colonial regimes outside Europe (cf. Chapter One).

A major side of Koidula's experience was, of course, her early absorption into newspaper work. Allowing one's name to appear in the press was considered improper for a woman in the local petty bourgeois circles of Koidula's time, thus most of her texts (including those considered here) were published under the name of her father.[7] Yet, despite the social constrictions placed on her due to her gender, her work demanded a good bearing in the current affairs of the time and she and her father built up a solid network of contacts among Estonian and foreign national activists.[8] Her newspaper work also put her in touch with a variety of Estonian-speaking readers. The newspapers the Jannsens published aimed to broaden the horizons of their peasant readers, relating domestic and foreign news in an approachable style, commending education, enterprise, temperance, and ethnic solidarity. A lot of their space was devoted to literature, mostly the kind of translated/adapted prose narratives discussed above, sequenced over several weeks.

Before moving on to the close comparative analysis of *Huaskar* and *Inca*, the following subchapter offers a broader exploration of the key discourses and tropes that get translated and re-translated in the Estonian adaptations and their sources, as well as of the Postcolonial Studies' notion of translation.

---

[6] On *Die Gartenlaube* see Belgum. Koidula's father, though politically much more careful and conservative than Koidula, was also influenced by *Die Gartenlaube* as a journalistic model. It can be supposed that it also served as a model for "popularizing the nation" (Belgum) and for public interaction even if in very different circumstances from the ones of *Die Gartenlaube* itself.
[7] Her *nom de plume*, Koidula, that she is known by today was given to her by the fellow national activist Carl Robert Jakobson: a poetic name that could be translated as 'of the dawn'. Koidula's legal name was Lydia Emilie Florentine Jannsen, becoming Michelson after marriage.
[8] Some of her relevant contacts were Carl Robert Jakobson, F.R. Kreutzwald, Jakob Hurt in Estonia, the Fennomans Yrjö-Koskinen (1830–1903) and Antti Almberg (1846–1909), and the Hungarian Finno-Ugrist and 1848-revolutionary Pál Hunfalvy (1810–1891).

Chapter Two. Decolonizing Translations

The value systems of German/Estonian New World stories: discourses of legitimation of power, history and change

The postcolonial aspects of translation

From mediaeval times until the last decades of the 20th century, the dominant European standpoint was to judge translation as inferior to the original—a copy secondary both in terms of chronology and authenticity. "Translation is the wandering existence of text in a perpetual exile," as J. Hillis Miller summarizes it (qtd. in Devy 182).[9] Proceeding from a similar primacy/secondariness thought scheme, (former) colonies have often been described as imitations of the Original by nature, alienated copies of their motherland (e.g. Naipaul's *Mimic Men*).

As the paradigm shift of the late 20th century placed the very idea of originality under radical scepticism, it is no wonder that the notion of translation as referring to forms of copying and reduplication has become a theme word *per excellence* referring to a whole field of meanings and perceptions. In the postmodernist parlance "translation" often does not indicate merely translating from one natural language to another; the etymologies of *translatio*, *traduction* or Übersetzung are figures for dynamics, movement, rearrangement. (Niranjana 8)

The Estonian word for "translate", "tõlkima", at first sight has an etymology with a very different logic, as it does not mean rearrangement like the equivalents straight from the Latin stem but is a loan of the Russian *tolkovat* (> Lat. loquor, locor, Eng. say, speak). It is considered likely, however, that the reason why the meaning of the word shifted from speaking to translating was that the *logos* was not used monologically but for political and trade negotiations (Karulis 438). Thus, it makes quite a useful metaphor to generate insights into texts (like those by Koidula and Horn) linked by a tense relationship of interpretative dialogue, and into their stories where characters repeatedly cross the stormy ocean to negotiate between Europe and the New World. The figure of negotiations is well-established in postcolonial thought and writing; some of the most important earlier lines of study relevant here are Mikhail Bakhtin's theories of dialogism and polyphony.

---

9   A partial exception are the modernists who generally see translation as an important way to experiment with language and form to revitalize a literary culture (Venuti 71). This relates to Even-Zohar's point that for literatures going through a turning point or crisis, translation is often of central importance (23-24). Modernist schools of literature could be said to have general affinity to "young literatures", as they want to make literature anew. I will return to this in Chapter Four.

Bakhtin expands on Saussurean linguistics, which distinguished between the systematic (langue) and the dynamic or communicative (parole) aspects of language. Bakhtin links parole to the social, historical and immediate context of an utterance. According to Bakhtin, any utterance is necessarily dialogical as it is always in some sense aimed at an addressee and is always connected to other discourses simultaneously existing in society; all utterances contain "alien speech" (e.g. *Dialogic* 279-80; *Speech* 91). Further, it should be stressed that for Bakhtin, "self" and "other" do not form a synthesis: as "I" cannot become homogenized, identity and existence as such mean dialogue and negotiations between different discourses (Bakhtin, *Problems*). The theory of dialogism in language has been transferred to the dialogical situation of colonialism by the postcolonialist thinker Homi K. Bhabha. Benefiting from the reception of Bakhtin in poststructuralist text analysis, in the 1980s and the1990s he transformed the study of colonialism by arguing against the earlier prevalent idea that the language of the colonizing power system establishes itself as totalizing and monolithic, in order to maximize its strength and self-legitimation. Bhabha holds that while the dominating discourse aims at monology, its seamless unity will always be an illusion. The end result of colonization will not be the "noisy command of colonialist authority" (Bhabha, *The Location* 112), but the emergence of a hybrid.

In contradiction to Naipaul's vision of "mimic men", Bhabha believes that the very same colonial structures that posit the colonized as a translator, a servant, a parrot, inevitably also imply his/her emancipation. When the allegedly solid and transparent messages and truths of the colonizing power are read, interpreted, translated and repeated in the colony, they are inevitably caught up in the general rules of textual dynamics. When the "universal" truths of European Christianity, Enlightenment and Humanism are thus proclaimed in the colonial situation, their internal contradictions, doubts and fragmentariness, or their applicability and rightness in a certain context only, become thereby highlighted and perceptible (*The Location* 115-116). The alienating cracks in the colonizer's texts create spaces for hybridity; the colonial repetitions of power-texts fluctuate between imitation and parody (*The Location* 86).

In postcolonial literary studies, Bhabha's theories have frequently been used to discuss the postcolonial re-writings and re-interpretations of European texts (e.g., Charlotte Brontë's *Jane Eyre*/Jean Rhys's *Wide Sargasso Sea*, Daniel Defoe's *Robinson Crusoe*/J. M. Coetzee's *Foe*) that, on the one hand, reprise the classic and, on the other hand, consciously aim to change its meaning—to relativize, highlight contradictions, add new voices. Bhabha's insights make it possible to see how these texts function as reading strategies, critical metatexts to which not only literary but also general cultural and political influence can be attributed. As he sees it, postcolonial fragmentedness creates "in-between spaces", where constantly changing and transforming new cultural identities—not determined by the "fixity of the past"—are being negotiated (*The Location* 219). At the same time, one dimension of living in-between is living "in the midst of incomprehensibility" (*The Location* 219).

Bhabha argues this with reference to Conrad's *Heart of Darkness* with its "Gothic" motifs that Bhabha considers generally characteristic of postcolonial literature (*The Location* 213; "Representation" 114-120). He first formulated the conception when analyzing Naipaul's *A House for Mr. Biswas*. On the one hand, Bhabha finds, Naipaul's novel is connected to the Great Tradition of British realism in the framework of which it had traditionally been read ("Representation" 114-115). On the other, the comparison with the Western tradition with its convinced proclamation of values of liberal humanism, individualism, universalism, progressivism, etc. remains very problematic. The narrator's lack of authority already does not fit; he repeatedly loses control over his yarn as the narrative's negotiations between Indian and European traditions create contradictions and aporias. The recurring tropes of *A House for Mr. Biswas* are doubles and other uncanny repetitions, strange diseases and madness, motifs of loss and lack. This is symptomatic of postcolonial writing as Bhabha sees it: noting these figures and forms allows better insight into postcoloniality than simply studying particular colonial themes or so-called local color in postcolonial texts.

It is with Bhabha's insights that the Koidula-Horn negotiations will be viewed here. As said above, Horn's text is itself an eclectic echoing of a great deal of European (anti-)colonial thought, synthesized into a seemingly seamless vessel of conservative Christian humanism. However, old and new cracks are revealed in this multi-layered heap of ideas and motifs when Koidula re-arranges the text. As her *Inca* makes full use of the possibilities for liberalist emancipatory negotiations that could be read into Horn's text, it also plunges into change as the in-between space, the place of incomprehensibility. Its vision of history holds both the claim for a long and heroic past, and a wish to be fully freed from the burden of pre-modernity, to start again as a New Adam or a New Eve. Its figure of the enslaved native uneasily combines the traits of the Rousseauian "noble savage" with its dark double "natural slave" motifs.

Slaves and savages

The concept of the noble savage is far older than the colonization of America, having already been used in Ancient Greek and Rome and in early Christianity. However, the idea-cluster re-emerged vigorously in 16th-century Spain during the stormy, extended dispute on the status of the natives of the newly "discovered" America. It seems that initially they were just declared ordinary subjects or vassals of the Spanish monarchs (Hanke 15-16). The heated dispute followed later, when some early colonists expressed the opinion that as the life-habits of the natives should be considered animalian and some rites (cannibalism) were apparently derived from the devil, they might not actually have a nature able to receive the word of God and be Christianized. And thus, were the natives quite human at all, if they lacked the two traits that separate human beings from the rest of creation: rationality and the ability to accept God's grace? (Robe 46-47; Honour 57)

Proceeding from these arguments, there was established a long tradition of applying Aristotle's conception of natural slavery to the American situation. According to that, nature may have destined one part of humankind to live a virtuous and intellectually challenging life as rulers and masters without doing any physical work, while another part was, by nature, meant to serve them as slaves (Hanke 13).[10] The most famous assailant of the application was the Dominican missionary in America, Bartolomé de Las Casas, the prototype for one of the protagonists of *Huaskar/Inca*. Las Casas attacked the doctrine in principle, claiming that all peoples were able to understand Christianity, and hence it was not justifiable to force it on them through violence or by enslavement. He also added, just in case, that the "Indians" were the total opposite of Aristotle's natural slaves anyway, as they had weak bodies but intelligent and noble minds (rather than sturdy bodies and minds incapable of deliberation). Though Las Casas achieved little in practice, there emerged a number of people both in Spain and elsewhere in Europe to defend the native Americans in theory; many idealized them into images of the virtuous and harmonious human being and likened them to the people of the Classical Age. Those ideal-

---

10 The first book of Aristotle's *Politics* argues that someone as different from other people as the body is from the soul or tame animals are from human beings would be a slave by nature. However, there are enslaved people who are only slaves by convention or law, not by nature. Some authors (e.g. Nichols 20-21) hold that Aristotle's complex argument does not necessarily show that he believed people with natural slave qualities exist in reality.

ized images became the repository for the later conception of the noble savage, customarily associated with the name of Rousseau (although he did not use the actual term).

However, the noble savage has always proved inseparable from his double, the natural slave (and vice-versa), the pair often forming uneasy, superficially "illogical" relationships. It is symbolic in the present context that it was precisely Las Casas, the protector of the "Indians", who is credited with the idea of bringing African slaves to America, to ease the lot of its natives and free them from hard physical labour. Whether he really made this proposal is not clear, but the attribution is interesting, and it is certainly a fact that no 16th-century documents protesting specifically against the enslavement of Africans have been found.

Further, it is noteworthy that the idea of the noble savage was most enthusiastically discussed during the second half of the 18th century, when the actual political question of America's natives had already lost topicality because of their almost total physical extinction. Hayden White offers a persuasive explanation: the preoccupation with the image had very little to do with the New World natives. It was not needed for symbolically redeeming the people in America but rather for discrediting the aristocracy at home, in Europe. The contradictory concept of the noble savage was a way for the rising bourgeoisie to undermine the idea of nobility as a birthright. It served as a subtle tool of discrediting political opponents precisely because the noble savage image continued to evoke its other side, the ignoble savage, the half beast who did not disappear from European thought even at the heyday of the noble savage cult, firmly holding its place in the apologetics of slavery (White 191-192).

White emphasizes that, like the aristocrats, the bourgeoisie also divided humankind into qualitatively different parts (193). They resented the inherited prerogatives of the nobles, yet "in general honoured the idea of a social hierarchy", though one based on talent and wealth rather than on birth (192). The homelier surrogate for the (ig)noble savage, the inferior social classes, were seen by the enlighteners alternately, and often simultaneously, as noble (the people, the future of the society, the repository of authentic values) or as ignoble (the rabble, the "dangerous classes"), depending on the context (193). In the chapter "On Savages" in his *Philosophy of History* Voltaire directly compares European rustics to non-European "savages" and finds the former infinitely coarser and lowlier (Ginzburg 17). This is, of course, intended as social criticism of the orders and circumstances responsible for the bestialization of the peasantry, yet it also abases its object of patronage.

Conceptions of colonial space and historical change

Congruent with the images of being populated by savages, American land itself emerged for Europeans as one that was wild and empty. From the earliest accounts of its discoverers, conquerors and colonizers, the prevalent vision was that of *tabula rasa*, a place that was still pure and could and should be covered with European writing. Despite the political events and great changes that took place in North America around 1800 and their very practical consequences, one can say that in the mainstream of European literary creativity, the romantic topos of America as an unpolluted land ready to make a better New World was overwhelmingly popular by that time. This was certainly true for German literature and hence for the America-image that informs the writing by Horn and is later re-interpreted by Koidula and her younger generation followers in Estonia.

Rousseau's views are of interest here because they are the concentration point of all kinds of earlier ideas of America, as well as being the most powerful, multifaceted, and paradoxical influence on discourses of the New World and exoticism in the 18th-19th centuries (and later). Afterwaves of certain aspects of Rousseauism are very obvious also in W.O. Horn's writing, toying as it does with exotic motifs. Rousseau's thought is profoundly radical in its implications. It does not critique only a particular power-structure, but the "alienated and alienating" modernizing society in general: if its members are to be saved, it must be reformed fundamentally. Rousseau's texts, such as *Émile* (1762) or *Discourse on the Origin and Basis of Inequality Among Men* (*Le Discours sur l'origine et les fondements de l'inégalité parmi les hommes,* 1755) refer to the original inhabitants of the New World in order to help the reader imagine a life not yet alienated.

The American savages and pure nature function as a conceptual basis for criticizing the prevalent values in Rousseau's contemporary Western Europe. The two aspects of Rousseau's doctrine—"noble savage" and "social reform"—have generated two divergent traditions for conceptualizing non-Europe in general and the Americas in particular. The noble savage *topoi* were sentimental "repositories of moral and physical virtues that European civilisation (identified with civilisation as such) had lost" (Wassermann 77) and did not have designs against any particular political orders. The "social reforms" type of argument, on the other hand, used the Americas as a conceptual laboratory to create new political arrangements. The two approaches found connection points with varying earlier lines of thought and differing support in various European countries. In Italy, for example, the Mexican and Peruvian natives were often typecast as the Ancients; not in the sense of people living in harmony with nature but to discuss various social forms and political systems (Scaglione 66), whereas in Germany the nostalgic vision of America prevailed. Even when German authors write of Northern America (which they, after the first states gain independence, mostly do), they often assume the idyllic qualities of South America (Jantz 310).

Rousseau was much read and imitated and so were Chautebriand and Saint-Pierre, the novelists dramatizing culture/nature conflicts into tragic American love stories. Defoe's *Robinson Crusoe* was translated into German in 1720 and found a number of followers, although Germans preferred to depict whole groups of people living in nature, rather than a single individual. When the geographer Alexander von Humboldt started to publish his travel-writing about both Americas in the nineteenth century, he was read in a framework familiar to the expectations of readers. (Jantz 324; Mayer 46)

The influence of British and French writing did not mean that the longing for a Golden Age in German literature was only a borrowed element. German fiction and travel writers did indeed borrow descriptions of landscapes and exotic stereotypes. However, the myth of an innocent paradise-like Golden Age in Western culture is far older than the 18th century, going back to the Ancient Greeks, and occurs very frequently in German writing long before Rousseau (Jantz). Furthermore, there is a very special feature in the relationship of the Germans to America. Although America came to mean land and living for vast numbers of German colonists, German literature keeps stressing Germans' unselfishness and lack of material interest towards the New World. As Germans were not among the conquerors of the Americas, for a long time it was only an object of study and meditation, a source of emotional and intellectual wisdom. In this respect they could see themselves as morally superior to the colonizer-nations like the British and the French, not to mention the Spaniards who had encountered all-European disapproval. The Enlightenment poet Christlob Mylius writes: "Open for me, America!/The treasures/That Cortes fled, that Raleigh didn't seek/ [...] Let me find—not Gold—no, God and Wisdom" (qtd. in Jantz 326).

The above account does not concern only the German America-concept but has wider bearing. At the turn of the 18th and 19th centuries German thought generally contrasts "Germanness" to the spirit of the French Enlightenment, the German contemplative philosophic mind and religiosity to foreign pragmatism, materialism and over-rationalization (Kemiläinen, especially 38-63 and 228-230). There was to be a great German historical mission, but emphatically a spiritual and moral one: a cultural, not a military world conquest. The Germans were not made to be great conquerors, they were made to be great couriers of culture (*Kulturträger*).[11] The belief in the great role of Germans as such lacked exact political content and could be filled in many ways.

A number of conservative nationalists (Adam Müller, later Friedrich Schlegel) shared the view that the peak of social development and Germans' greatest gift to humankind were their perfectly developed model of feudal society. At the same time there was a strong indigenous liberal tradition in Germany that welcomed the American and, initially, also the French Revolution. When soon repulsed by the violence of the latter, many liberal thinkers saw German culture with its special qualities as a transformative force that could achieve the aims of the French Revolution without bloodshed, as it did not rest on a set of abstract universalist ideals, but was both cosmopolitan in the real terms of world knowledge, and carried by a rich dynamism of a living historical people (*Volk*). "Reference to history and culture legitimized demands for greater political participation in the imagined national community" (Berger 44; cf. also Jusdanis, *The Necessary* 86-89), whereas these changes could again be envisioned in various terms, be they monarchical or republican. Both Koidula and Horn were writing in the force field of a variety of both liberal and conservative ideas of sociopolitical change, partly overlapping, partly separate.

As discussed in Chapter One, countering Russia's intensifying attempts to centralize and russify the empire, towards the end of the 19th century Baltic German identity was strongly conservative, as their self-legitimation based itself deterministically upon historical tradition. Baltic Germans saw themselves as an ancient historical organism or symbiosis unified by language, religion and an administrative system. In this connection history was understood as a formative force, but a legitimizing and sacralizing, rather than a progressively teleological one:

> The centuries-long overlordship of the Swedes in the Estonian region, the continuous supremacy of Poles in Livonia and all the horrors of war and violent politics that oppressed Courland under both monarchies were not able to inhibit the united development of these three lands that the deeply rooted national feeling had destined them to have; just as little could it bring down the institutions that they had taken over from their fathers as their

---

11 This anti-military, anti-conquest feeling was even in Germany not necessarily applied to "uncivilized" people by all authors. Wars against "wild" people could be justified in the interests of such peoples themselves, so that they could be brought in among the civilized nations. (Kemiläinen 271-272).

sacred inheritance (*The Livonian Privileges and their Confirmations* (*Die Livländischen Landesprivilegien und deren Confirmationen*, 1841), qtd. in Garve 83-84).

The role and destiny of Estonians and Latvians, the "ethnic fragments" in the Baltics (Garve 216), were likewise historically conditioned to remain linked to those of the Baltic Germans, their civilizing teachers, in a kind of a natural symbiosis. The perceived historical weakness of Estonians and Latvians or their cultural dependency on Germans did not necessarily mean that these groups ought not to feel ethnic pride or that they should be prevented from honoring and practicing their languages and folk traditions. On the contrary, by the second half of the 19th century Baltic German mainstream opinion was influenced enough by Herderian thought to believe that even the smallest ethnic groups had a place and mission in the world (cf. e.g. Garve). However, Baltic German opinion emphasized that all those roles had been sanctified by history, so they were now natural, and ought to remain unchanged. The pastor and scholar F. Luther formulates it in a typical way:

> The task of Estonians and Latvians is certainly not the pursuit of intellectual knowledge or skills. Their cultural mission is not there, it is in the field of practical activity. Long centuries have ripened them into an honorable peasant people whose hard work, serious mind and frugality can serve as an example to all other agricultural workers of the Russian state. Those men who really care about the welfare of their people should turn their eyes to that. (qtd. in Garve 221-222)

However, Baltic German thought also had its own, albeit relatively weak, liberal anti-determinist counter-current, propagated mostly by the few "bourgeois" literati who were neither aristocrats nor clerics. This current is most pronounced in the work of the 18th-century Herderian thinker mentioned above, Garlieb Helwig Merkel, who influenced Koidula profoundly. Merkel was born in the Latvian-speaking province of Livonia; his father was a clergyman yet had studied in Strasbourg and approved of Enlightenment thinkers such as Voltaire and Rousseau. Merkel, philosophically an anti-determinist advocate of sociopolitical change, held that the standing of different peoples was not predestined for ever, as the course of history was not straight and teleological, but forever turning and twisting. Like Herder, he was convinced that changes in the life of nations were inevitable and, indeed, that history might well be on the side of a group like Latvians or Estonians whose potential was still unrealized.

His best-known work *Latvians* (*Die Letten*, 1796) is strongly influenced by the ideas of the French Revolution: uncharacteristically for an Enlightenment thinker he warns that if the Rousseauist "social contract" with the oppressed Latvians remains unwritten, they may "document their rights with fire and sword and the despots' blood" (Merkel, *Die Letten* 11). However, he does not see the conflict as class-based, but rather as a struggle of colonized peoples/nations (*Völker*) against their foreign conquerors.[12] On the other hand, he does believe that if the landowners saw reason they could be in charge of the changes themselves, and furthermore, that the sovereign, the Russian Czar, would be the most appropriate figure to push the reforms in the region (cf. Plakans 148).

Much in the bourgeois spirit described by Hayden White, Merkel depicted the ancestors of the Baltic serfs as noble savages and those of their noble overlords as savage plunderers, thus discrediting the local aristocracy and taking the halo of inevitability from the contemporary situation (cf. Undusk, "Kolm" 723-729). Though the 13th-century crusaders cut down the ancient Estonians' holy groves, Merkel proclaims, these sprouted up and grew again, so the Estonians visiting them cannot but be reminded they are the "offspring of those free men who once so bravely resisted the barbarians" by whom they are now oppressed (Merkel, *Liiwimaa* 127). Even in their misery Estonians are empowered by their lively cultural tradition (Merkel, *Liiwimaa* 125-127), apparently like the other "belated" modernizers, Germans. However, the transformations in the peoples' characters constructed by Merkel are logical and continuous, rather than random. Thus he created impactful national stereotypes of Estonians and Latvians, indicating dotted lines between the former noble savages and their present incarnations, the numbed slaves: "In the vices of slaves, you can sense the virtues that would embellish them when free," he wrote (Merkel, *Liiwimaa* 124). The once gracious and merciful Latvians had now become weak and backboneless, he argued, and the once valorous and firm-spirited Estonians were now merely malevolent and dully obstinate. Both peoples, thus, still have the noble savage in them, but in a perverse disfigured form (Merkel, *Liiwimaa* 48, 123, 124).

Merkel's account of these malformations was undoubtedly meant as a charge against the Baltic-German nobility and food for thought for the wider German audience, Merkel's intended reading public. "Don't judge them [the peasants],

---

12 This approach has a long pedigree. Ulrike Plath points out that German travel writing on the Baltic provinces, such as. the influential accounts by Adam Olearius in the mid-17th century habitually describe the Baltic situation in terms of conquest, colonization, enslavement, ethnic feud and resistance. Thus they follow the models concerning overseas colonization of native peoples, rather than the ones concerning the discontents and unrest of German peasantry. (Plath 113)

judge those who have turned this people's character so deplorable", he advised (Merkel, *Liiwimaa* 124-125). However, as an unintended part of Merkel's legacy the new native literati and activists ardently drew upon his ideas and motifs to create their national narratives and discourses of resistance. Among other things they integrated Merkel's local version of the noble savage/natural slave topos. Thus the activists are prone to see the national self as if in uncanny mirror images where the figures of the noble savage and the dull slave time alternate, time merge into one. For the activist, the noble savage ancestor carries the modern promise of changing the world and liberating the slave, yet as the slave and the savage are not (entirely) separate, this is accompanied by the anxiety that full liberation from natural slavery is never possible.

Estonian New World literature

Koidula, like her Juudit and Huaskar, and a number of her contemporary Estonian activists, stood between two social worlds. She had a German education and belonged to the thin upper layers of her ethnic group. Even if her family was only recently urbanized petty bourgeoisie and historically not far from its peasant background, their lifestyle was already removed from that of most of her fellow-ethnics and rather resembled that of the local Germans of their class. It is noteworthy that time and again the Estonian national activists discuss their related identity and loyalty problematics in the imagery of the New World. Koidula's father, in a letter to the Finnish friend Yrjö-Koskinen, compares the history of Estonians to that of "Negro slaves" without education or justice, with Germans even presently regarding Estonians as "dogs", rather than humans (qtd. in Laar 376-377). Though bourgeois and primarily a German-speaker, it is the Estonians he calls "us".

Elsewhere, Jakobson employs the recent American Civil War not only for the usual implied stabs at the German "slaveholders". He writes: "During the four-year war in America, hundreds of thousands of people lost their lives. And why? So that their neighbors, the poor Negros, should become free. These people were prepared to die for the honor of their fatherland and for the freedom of the black Negro slaves. What have you done for the freedom of your Estonian brothers?" (qtd. in Vinkel, *Eesti* 288). Here, though slaves are kin, Jakobson interpellates the Estonian national patriot as a liberator ready to die for honor and freedom, rather than fully identifying with the slaves.

Thus when the noble savage/natural slave figure emerges in Koidula's fiction, the perspective is necessarily completely altered compared to that described by

White. Koidula also employs it to undermine the nobility, yet it is *not a figure of an outsider*, it is a figure with which the text primarily empathizes, for all its double-edgedness.

Historical topics are generally common in early Estonian popular fiction. This is typical of 19th-century tastes internationally, as well as the educative and often politically engaged agenda of the Estonian literati. Koidula's father Jannsen alone wrote around twenty historical tales, being especially fond of the topic of patriotic resistance during the Napoleonic wars. Also, the theme of slavery is an established one, with non-fictional as well as sentimental literary texts on the subject emerging in Estonian-language prose early on. The first is probably "Inkle and Jariko" (1782), a very pious version of the international Inkle and Yariko sujet of an Englishman selling his black/native American lover to slavery, by the Baltic German pastor Friedrich Wilhelm Willmann (Mits 74-75). However, during the 1860s-1870s Koidula initiated with her *Inca* and *Juudit* a stream of stories on anti-slavery resistance and slave revolutions set overwhelmingly in South America and the Caribbean. In contrast to the earlier slavery stories published in Estonian they are politically inflected and engage with topical debates in Estonia. Besides Koidula, the best-known among the many writers on these themes is Mats Kirsel (1825–1884), the author of *Slave Life* (*Orjaelu*, 1872) and *Siimon: The Life-Story of a Negro Slave in Brazil* (*Siimon. Ühe neegriorja elulugu Brasiilias*, 1876).

As mentioned above, a frequent source the 19th-century Estonian national activists used for their New World stories (and for their other works) is paradoxically *Volksliteratur*, which expresses disquiet with potential liberal political change emancipating the lower orders. The explanation for this can be that the German conservative clergymen and the Estonian mobilizers shared a sociologically similar target readership of peasants and artisans. Furthermore, both aimed at offering instruction in the form of entertainment, as the Enlightenment tradition prescribed (on Germany: Müller-Salget 97). However, the objectives of the instruction were quintessentially different. German clergymen authors of the genre consciously set themselves the task of defending traditional values and order (church, feudal system, patriarchal family) at a dangerous and confusing time, especially after the 1848 revolution. They wanted to produce suitable reading material for the rural lower orders "to fight what is new, alien and disturbing", as the pastor and writer Glaubrecht put it (qtd. in Müller-Salget 27).

Thus the Estonian adaptors engaged with the material in a particular way. Firstly, when one considers the whole corpus of *Volksliteratur*, it is evident that the New World and slave rebellion stories so popular with Estonians constituted a very small part of it (cf. Müller-Salget). Horn, a favorite for Estonian adaptations was altogether exceptional with his attraction for exotic settings, and occasional treatments of slavery and colonialism. Most of the German clergymen's works preferred a domestic German village or small-town setting and outsider figures, if any, tended to be presented in negative roles. Thus it can be said that the Estonian authors specifically singled out the space of the New World and the opportunities to debate political and socio-cultural change that it carried.

Further, the noble savage/natural slave nexus takes on a different meaning in the Estonian stories as the natives/slaves become protagonists through whose sociopsychological perspective the events and story-world are predominantly presented. Horn's native characters are stylized into noble savages (with subdued Whitean bourgeois satisfaction, it could be said) who in their melancholy, individualism and love of peaceful home-life also seem to enact the ideals of the middle classes themselves. Although his stories use the New World space as an accepted arena for occasionally provocative critique of some European ways as well as for the dramatization of exotic love affairs, it simultaneously remains a soothing space that permits conflicting ideas to co-exist and happy endings to come about.[13] While the topic of slave uprisings is not uncommon in German literature (though rare in the works meant for lower orders), the Estonian adaptations historicize and politicize it by various means, even adding direct references to the Estonian situation.

It is altogether typical for the Estonian adaptors to reshape the German version by embedding the fictional plot into a "documentary" historical one. Before the beginning of the main story, the reader is provided with the information of the historical proceedings leading up to the period in which the story is set; often the fictional conclusion is again followed by an "epilogue" relating the historical aftermath, sometimes connecting it to the topical affairs or questions of the present day. This is characteristic of all America-stories, even for those which are more entertainment-oriented than Koidula's or Kirsel's works. Historicizing tendencies are also eminent in literature about slavery and freedom-fighting set in the Old World (e.g. in Koidula's *Olesja* and Kirsel's *Gustav Wasa*). The New World-set historization, however, is of a notably different kind:

---

13 Here the axiology of Horn's work could be related to that of the popular (and for some notorious) dramatist August von Kotzebue (1761–1819). His Peruvian plays *The Virgin of the Sun* (*Die Sonnen-Jungfrau*, 1791) and *The Spaniards in Peru* (*Spanier in Peru*, 1796) may well have influenced Horn's *Huaskar* directly, as both present Las Casas in Peru where he historically never went and even the name of one fictional (i.e. without historical prototype) Spanish heroine (Elvira) overlaps. Of course, in Horn's *Volksliteratur* rendering the social and erotic friskiness remain infinitely more subdued.

the historical developments in the Americas and the Caribbean lend themselves to broader generalizations, they evolve on a higher plain of abstraction and expand to gigantic scales. The events described may well be very particular and taken from respectable history books, but they move towards the legendary.

Story and narration in *Huaskar/Inca*

Narrative situation and strategies of communication

In the final analysis, the *Huaskar* and *Inca* texts emerge as very different. Yet, *Huaskar* and *Inca* are telling the same story, and furthermore, both are signalling by various means that they are not just narrating a story but a story from history, that is, a "real" story backed up by other sources, trustworthy documents. Against this background one must ask: how do the works telling the same story become different? Where are the changes and what effect do they have on the overall meaning? The first answer I explore is in the communication strategies of the stories. The Estonian version is narrated differently and thus also invites a different reading. The appeal to the reader to approach the text in a certain way starts already on the "thresholds of interpretation"—from paratexts, that is, textual signals around the main text such as author's name, genre indicators, preface, advertisements and reviews of the work, etc. (Genette, *Paratexts*).[14] Paratexts can strongly influence how a work will be interpreted as they are the place where the author and other persons connected with its publishing locate the guidelines and instructions for the reader. Even if the instructions are ambivalent, dubious or can be proved false, they still constitute the author's/publishers' declaration of aims and their assumed responsibility to the reader.

So far as the immediate 19th-century reader was concerned, it was not Koidula but Koidula's father who was the author of *Inca*: the author's name given on the book's title page is Johann Jannsen. Underneath, added in brackets, are the words *Eesti Postimees*: the name of the newspaper Koidula and his father ran. Thus, whoever is believed to be the author, it is clear that s/he is presented not merely as an individual, but in connection with the institution of the newspaper. The note on the title page is not the only such paratextual indicator; the ad-

---

14 I use the narratological concepts and terminology in the vein of Gérard Genette (*Narrative Discourse*; *Narrative Discourse Revisited*; *Paratexts*) and semiotic concepts and terminology concerning cultural and literary space in the vein of Yuri M. Lotman ("O metayazike"; *Universe of the Mind*) and J.J. van Baak.

vertisements preceding the publication (Undla-Põldmäe, *Koidulauliku* 70) and its foreword also link the book to the newspaper. An important reason for stressing the relationship with the well-known newspaper was probably the need to launch an effective sales strategy, but an additional outcome is certainly also to encourage the reader to approach the story as one written by a journalist and if not as a journalistic text, then certainly in the journalistic context. Furthermore, the connections with *Eesti Postimees* are not limited to the paratext, but are continued in the beginning of the main body of the text, where the author and the narrator merge, as they describe the space of the story-world: "This city [Lima] is still the capital of Peru and the very same place were at Martinmas-time 1863 so many women were killed in a fire inside a Catholic church, which *Eesti Postimees* told us about in 1864" (Koidula, *Perúama* 11).

Huaskar, on the other hand, was first published in the calendar-almanac *The Spinning Room* (*Die Spinnstube*), edited by Horn himself. *The Spinning Room* may also be formally classified as a periodical, yet in fact the publication is far closer to the general tradition of publishing books of *Volksliteratur* type. This is indicated both by the subtitles of the issues that call them books (*Volksbuch*) and by the non-topical discourse of the prefaces. The overwhelming majority of those deal with moral concerns of a general nature (mercy as a Christian virtue, the commandment to respect one's elders, etc.) which do not vary in the course of years. The main generic influence on the prefaces appears to be the clerical sermon and not journalism.

In *Inca*'s case, there are also further features of narrative poetics that remind the Estonian reader of Koidula's contemporary journalism when reading the text. The model of this early journalism (practically invented by Koidula's father) is that the journalist chatters to the reader about foreign news, for instance, in the style of a better-informed fellow villager gossiping about local events. Or as the Estonian media-analyst, Juhan Peegel, formulates it: early Jannsenian journalism tries to diminish the distance between the reader, the journalist and the object of writing to the minimum both in time and space (289-292). *Inca* can be characterized in much the same way. The text is full of the narrator's rhetorical questions, "asides" and reminders to the reader, as well as of interventions into the story-space. For instance: "Reader, what would you have done if it had been you and not the missionary on that ship to hear the foul talk of these people [the Spanish colonists] in itself making clear what their aims in America were!" (Koidula, *Perúama* 13)[15] Or:

---

15 "Luggeja, mis sa olleksid üttelnud, kui sa missionäri assemel ühhes nendega laewa peal olleksid olnud ja kuulnud, kuida nende innimeste roppud sõnnad jubba tunnistasid, mis nemmad sinna otsima läksid!"

"Looking at that woman's face in our mind's eye we get the feeling that we have seen her somewhere already. But of course, she is the same as the one whom the Inca Huaskar addressed at the arena in the town of Madrid!" (Koidula, *Perúama* 66)[16]

This rhetorical strategy is very different from that of Horn's *Huaskar*, where the phrase "dear reader" only occurs a few times in the foreword and both the narrator and the narratee are strictly distant from the story-world.

The two narrators' positioning to their story in time differs in the same manner. *Huaskar* specifies the date of the events of the story (in the 16th century), but it does not give any references to the time of narrating: for all that the narrator is saying to the reader, it could be taking place at absolutely any time after the occurrence of the events retold. *Inca*, on the other hand, foregrounds the time of narrating expressly; it is explicitly dated, as well as referred to constantly via thematic linking (issues of slavery, colonialism, social class) and indications of overlaps and continuities between the story-time and the time of narrating. For example, the discussion of 16th-century slavery is connected to its continuation in the 19th century: "the Southern slaveholders started a rebellion which went on for 4 years [...] before it was suffocated this spring (1865)" (Koidula, *Perúama* 138-139).[17]

The links so created are not only chronological but also causal. African slaves were taken to America in the 16th century and four years before "this year", the American Civil War started (which, of course, *Eesti Postimees* had extensively reported on). From there, the timeline even moves on to the narrator's future: "Let's hope the Lord may give the poor blacks better days from now on" (Koidula, *Perúama* 139).[18]

The linkage of issues enables Koidula to make sweeping generalizations and hint at ironic similarities between the "savage" Spaniards and the "culture courier" Baltic German overlords: "Already 400 years ago this missionary was sensible enough to perceive what even in our time many a pious wise man doesn't want to know: that no one with a clear mind should be refused worldly education only because we may think they are of lower birth" (Koidula, *Perúama* 40).[19]

---

16 "Kui meie waimus selle naisterahwa silma watame, siis on meil, kui olleksime tedda kohhegil juba näinud. No muidugi, eks ta olle sesamma, kellega Inka Huaskar Madridi linna mänguplatsi peal kõnneles!"
17 "[...] tõstsid lõunapoolsed orjapiddajad mässamist, mis 4 aastat turis [...], enne kui tännawo kewwade (1865) lämmatud sai".
18 "Lodame nüüd, et Jummal waese Neegridele eddespiddi parremaid päiwi annab".
19 "Jubba 400 aasta eest olli sesinnane misionär ni mõistlik, ärratundma, mis meie aeal veel mitto wagga tarka ei tahha tunda: et kellegi terrase waimoga innimessele ilmliko tarkust ei pea keeldama üksi sepärrast, et temma ehk meie arwates allamast soust innimenne on".

In this manner, the historical story becomes a heavily contemporary one, inclusive of the most recent past and the writer's and reader's own experiences and concerns. Also the very beginning of *Inca* fortifies these parallels, although in a somewhat different way. The first chapter starts with the words: "I believe it can only bring pleasure if I tell you a story out of an old chronicle-book or annals that I myself have been reading with appreciation since my childhood" (Koidula, *Perúama* 4).[20] This certainly stresses that the story is not from the narrator's own experience but from another text—an other's text—and furthermore, that the text is an old one, about the past. But with the self-same sentence the narrator is also claiming personal knowledge and interest: it is the narrator's reading of the story that is the basis of the re-telling, the narrator's reading that is contemporary and continuing.

In short, telling a story about the colonization of America, Horn's *Huaskar* tells an old historical story from the 16th century whereas Koidula's *Inca* tells an old story from the 16th century that is still going on, is of direct concern to its writer and readers, and thus continuously re-read and re-written in the present.

Histoire and discours

We can gain a deeper insight into the differences between the narrative techniques of *Huaskar* and *Inca* in the light of the linguistic categories of Emile Benveniste, *histoire* and *discours*. When discussing French texts, Benveniste in *Problems of General Linguistics* differentiates between them as *histoire*-type and *discours*-type, according to the tense they use to express past events. There is the so-called literary or narrative past, *passé simple* (*histoire*), and the spoken-language *passé composé* (*discours*). Benveniste explains that with the passé simple there is no I-you (narrator-reader) relationship, it is the third person who is at the center of attention. In histoire-texts the speaker is erased as much as possible: "the events seem to relate themselves" (208). In *discours* the narrator-reader (or narrator-listener) relationship is flaunted, the narrator has "the intention of influencing the other in some way" (209).

Passé simple is seen in the same way by Roland Barthes. It is an abstract tense that does not so much refer to the pastness but merely to causality, the interconnectedness of the events, teleology. (Barthes, *Writing* 26-27). That makes it "the

---

20 "Ma mõtlen, egga se kellegile wastomeelt ei peaks ollema, kui ma wannast kronika= ehk aearamatust ühhe jutto kõnnelen, mis ma isse lapsepõlvest sadik hea melega ollen luggenud". According to Undla-Põldmäe, Koidula's sources on South American history were the popular German history writers Heinrich Dittmar and J. H. Campe (*Koidulauliku* 72).

ideal instrument for every construction of a world; it is the unreal time of cosmogonies, myths, History and Novels. [...] Behind the *passé simple* there always lurks a demiurge", an Author/Creator of the World of Truth, coherent in its self-sufficiency (Barthes, *Writing* 27). *Discours*, on the other hand, draws attention to the narrator and the particular circumstances of narration, thus destroying the self-evidence and closure of the created world. The fact that the events do not just happen but are presented by somebody—in a subjective interpretative form—is foregrounded. *Discours* is frequent in oral discourse, diaries, autobiographies and other first person narratives, as well as many journalistic genres. There the narrator can give ideological evaluations, comment on events, move back and forth in time, etc. It is probably not even important that *passé composé* is used throughout the narration; should some events be related in the *passé simple*, the reader would not lose awareness that a speaking subject is still present.

Although German and Estonian lack grammatical categories exactly equivalent to the French *passé composé* and *passé simple*[21], one can still differentiate text-types broadly corresponding to *histoire* and *discours*: (1) in the first type, the narrating instance aims at transparency and creating the idea that the story-world has a life totally its own and (2) in the second, the narrator makes references to his/her speech act and readership; discussing the circumstances of narrating is part of the story.

It is, of course, clear that when one uses the latter type for telling a historical story, it can undermine its "objectivity" for the reader: highlighting the communication act necessarily breaks the self-sufficient reality of the story-world and makes it obvious that the narrator is rendering a subjective version of the events. Yet, it would be misleading to assume that the *discours*-texts are not making any truth-claims. They are indeed also establishing a truth but the truth they are insisting on is not abstract and universal but personalized and particular.

Describing autobiography, a *discours*-genre *par excellence*, Philippe Lejeune uses the term "autobiographical space" to describe a certain effect of authenticity and three-dimensionality created by a first-person narrative in his opinion. The narrators of actual autobiographies, as all first-person narrators (and any *discours*-narrators, one might add), are perceived as expressing a certain subjective reality. Even if the reader detects obvious mistakes, gaps, or distorted interpretations in the narrations, these are accepted as certain additional aspects of the particular authentic speech act (Lejeune 214).

---

21 In the German case Harald Weinrich has drawn parallels with *Perfekt* and *Präteritum*.

The rhetoric of the *discours*-kind, with emphasis on the narrating instance and I-utterance, is frequent in writing categorized as postcolonial (Peiker, "An Account"). This is not to claim that there are specifically postcolonial topics or issues that particularly cause this kind of poetics. Rather, the question concerns wider issues of social and cultural communication: the *discours*-rhetoric seems to be able to function well as a strategy for challenging dominant axiomatics from a disadvantaged non-dominant position. Sometimes the best or the only way to re-open a discussion on "timeless", "universal" truths seems to be to drag them to the margins by subjective discourse, make them particular and present, thus persuading the audience that there are alternative "authentic" perspectives in addition to the dominant one, that different ways of thinking are imaginable.

Estonian historical fiction has practised *discours*-writing to a great extent, and it could be argued that during certain periods (the second half of the 19th century and the end of 1980s) even non-fiction history writing used its elements extensively.[22] It has certainly not always been a conscious rhetorical strategy, frequently informal texts like oral accounts, letters or memoirs have simply been the only extant sources of some historical event. Yet one can undoubtedly speak of a specific tradition of historical conceptualization—reading "old chronicle-books or annals", others' texts, and writing "out of" them from *a new subject position*. Koidula's *Inca* is an early example of this tradition.

The thought-worlds of *Huaskar* and *Inca*

As discussed above, the literary space of America itself was one heavily loaded with contradictory meanings and values long before either *Huaskar* or *Inca* were written. Furthermore, it is impossible to speak of America without implying Europe. The issue of America is never just the New World itself. America is the 'Other' of the Old World, its device for introspection, or its noble-savage critic.

A character embodying a critic of this kind dominates both *Huaskar* and *Inca*, articulating a good deal of their ideological discourses. Huaskar, the main character of the texts is the last descendant of Peruvian pagan royalty, whom Bartolomé de Las Casas converts to Christianity as a youngster. He and Las Casas

---

22 E.g. *Kodulugu* by Laar, Vahtre and Valk (1989) and the history account blended with personal and family experience in Taagepera's *Estonia: Return to Independence* (1993).

himself are commuters between their two worlds, who ponder and discuss both in the spirit of Christian humanism resembling that of the historical Las Casas. The narrators of both *Huaskar* and *Inca* too generally share this worldview to a degree and use it as a key for interpreting the problems they face. Yet their value structures and ideological messages also have intriguing differences, as do their ways of presenting and negotiating them.

Nobility, serfs and savages

Horn's *Huaskar* establishes its two main ideological camps early in the story: on the one hand, innocent and naturally noble Peruvians plus the true Christian Las Casas; on the other, Pizarro's bunch of blood-thirsty, gold-obsessed Spanish bravos (293). The narrator speaks of the Spanish colonizers as barbarians who were

> wilder and harsher [...] than the people they called wild, whom they sought with all coercive means to bend to the worship of the cross, but who as heathens and wild men, by their beliefs, could make no claim on the true rights of men (296)[23]

At the same time the narrator also occasionally refers to the natives as savages (e.g. 294). They are savages because they are still in the state of nature and immature. The Spanish colonizers, on the other hand, have grown savage, because they have lapsed from Christian civilization.

Yet *Huaskar*'s world cannot be described as generally anti-European or even as anti-Spanish or anti-Catholic. On the contrary, the young convert "prince" Huaskar, who used to denounce the whole Spanish nation, changes his mind in Spain. Many Spaniards are good and friendly (319), they have impressive religious ceremonies, wonderful churches and hymns (318). And, of course, Las Casas himself is a persuasive counter-example of a true Catholic Christian. It is he who connects with the noble savages and teaches them his religion as they, in their turn, help him to survive in the wild paradise of South America. In fact, the noble savages are remarkably open to Christianity and feel deeply grateful to its promoters. Las Casas' first native ally Halipa even feels thankful to the generally hated tyrannical Pizarro: "I owe him much, very much", he says, "above

---

23 "wilder und roher [...] als das Volk, das sie wild nannten, das sie mit allen Zwangsmitteln zu Verehrern des Kreuzes zu zwingen bemüht waren, das aber auch als Heiden und Wilde, nach ihrer Überzeugung, nicht Anspruch an Menschenrechte machen durfte"

all knowledge of the true God; now since my lord [Pizarro] is dead, I cannot be another's slave, for with him I was as free and cared for as a child." (305)[24]

Even Las Casas's own relations to all the natives other than Huaskar take the form of a friendly informal master-servant relationship. The Inca Huaskar is different in that he is a borderline figure. He is a child of nature with a European education, the native "crown prince" who at the end of the story is also granted a European title. As a borderliner he is also the one to enter into a symbolic marriage with a Spanish noblewoman. His beloved Elvira has been destined by her parents to marry her very close relative; God's will is, however, that she should form an extremely exogamous alliance with Huaskar and thus reconcile America and Europe, nature and civilization.

Like in *Huaskar*, judging the Christian morality of the Spanish colonizers plays a significant role in Koidula's *Inca* too, being presented in two different ways. In the first historical-introductory chapter there are commentaries, starkly reminiscent of Merkel both in their particular style of sarcasm and in their approach to history: "Were the Spaniards then bad? [...] But it was nothing less than Christianity they came to bring to America. The stupid folk just didn't want to understand that their lands and gold were all quite a cheap price to pay for that!!" (6)[25]

In the main body of the text the ideological function is largely carried by the characters Huaskar and Las Casas. Like in Horn's *Huaskar*, Las Casas's role is to comment on and interpret the activities and opinions of the colonizers and the colonized; in both texts he is also the bold witness who in determination points out the shocking American facts to Emperor Charles V as well as to the reader. Yet the ideological speeches of Las Casas of *Inca* are followed by a shadow that is lacking in *Huaskar*. The reader in *Inca* might well get the impression that a part of the missionary's ideological message is exactly that he stops ideologizing, even stops commenting and interpreting because he does not understand, does not know.

In *Inca* he is unable to answer Huaskar's seemingly naive questions about colonial policies and is reduced to contemplation without reply (Koidula, *Peruama* 47). In *Huaskar*, on the other hand, "Las Casas took endless trouble to explain

---

24 "ich verdanke ihm viel, sehr viel, und vor allem die Erkenntnis des wahren Gottes"; "nun da mein Herr [Pizarro] todt ist, mag ich keines Anderen Sklave werden, denn bei ihm war ich frei und gehalten wie ein Kind."
25 "Kas Spaniamehhed siis pahhad innimesed ollid? [...] Nad tullid jo ristiusko Amerikamale toma. Agga rummal rahwas ei tahtnud arro sada, et nende kulda ja maad selle eest ärra anda, jo üsna oddaw hind olli!!"

the situation to him [Huaskar]" (Horn 319). In *Inca*, Las Casas is staggered that the native Halipa saves his, a Spaniard's, life and "does not know at all" how to thank him (Koidula, *Perúama* 28). The Las Casas of *Huaskar* takes Halipa's behaviour for granted as one proper for a Christian and briefly says: "for having saved me, receive God's blessing and my thanks." (Horn, *Huaskar* 306)

The main story-lines in *Huaskar* and *Inca* end similarly. Thanks to Las Casas, the lovers are united and political justice established. Yet, as mentioned above, *Inca* includes a controversial epilogue (138) where it is said that actually it was Las Casas himself who suggested that black slaves from Africa be imported to America. He did not mean it badly, says the narrator, he just wanted to ease the lot of the native Americans: "Las Casas could not at the time understand what a horrible thing was being started" (Koidula, *Perúama* 138).[26]

Another change in the relations between Spaniards and "Indians" in *Inca* is that the savage/grown savage line of *Huaskar* is played down. The narrator never calls the Peruvians savages throughout the entire Estonian version; from the outset they are the "people enserfed". Further, "Spaniard" in many contexts becomes the signifier of a privileged social class. The notion of "serfdom" creates an allusion to the near-contemporary situation in Estonia. However, the impact of this change could be considered even wider. "Serf" is a historical and social word, rather than an embodiment of timeless and essential features like the *Huaskarian* concept of the noble savage; it is a word brought into usage by certain people in a certain timespace for certain reasons. Thus the enserfed situation of the natives need not be eternal. This line of ideology, developed by the narrator and passionately polemicized over by the characters, is entirely lacking in Horn's *Huaskar*.

The point is made in various ways. Las Casas's relationship to the natives is not that of master-servant but that of a foreign visitor to local hosts and guides (e.g. Koidula, *Perúama* 28). Halipa's declaration, quoted above, that after his lord Pizarro's death he could not be another's slave because specifically with his deceased master he had felt "free and cared for as a child" (Horn, *Huaskar* 305) is translated by the Estonian Halipa without any shadow of child-like gratitude: "Nobody will set a yoke of slavery on Halipa's head again or make me a slave! [...] in the midst of high mountains there will be enough deep and secret valleys where none of your cruel people have stepped yet" (27).[27]

---

26 "Las Kasas ei mõistnud sel aeal mitte mõttelda, mis hirmus assi sellega peale hakkas"
27 "Keegi ei pea Halipa pähhe enam orjaikket pannema egga mind pärrisorjaks teggema! [...] kõrge mäggede wahhel on meil ommeti weel süggawaid ja sallajaid orgusi, kus kegi teie kurja rahwa jalg ep ole käinud"

Yet the most cutting and complex discussions of the Peruvians as a slave people take place in the context of Huaskar's relations with the governor Nunez, the father of his beloved. Nunez of *Huaskar/Inca* is different from most of the Spaniards of the story: he is neither brutal nor greedy or sadistic. He respects law and order and he is polite to his inferiors. At the same time, he perceives the walls between social standings as something natural and eternal. Thus, the romance between his daughter Elvira and Huaskar is not just unacceptable to him, but above all a quite inconceivable anomaly. This situation is described both by *Inca* and *Huaskar*, yet the emphases are different.

In *Huaskar*, Nunez's main fault is his excessive orientation to the world outside. In his social pride and ambition, he destroys the natural patriarchal human relations of the little group of noble savages and true Christians in their idyllic paradise. *Inca*, on the other hand, is not interested in experimenting with closed systems; there the conflict between Nunez and Huaskar is dramatized as polemics over distinctions of class everywhere and anywhere and there are added paragraphs making the point in various related ways. Firstly, the idea of class and class pride becomes uncivilized and savage-like in a negative sense; class is dangerous but also ridiculous, old-fashioned: "[In Spain] class divisions and pride separate one human being from another so frantically [...] that it couldn't be crazier even with pagan Hindoo castes. [...] Fortunately, this old mould is beginning to bleach off more and more in the light of newer sun" (Koidula, *Perúama* 96).[28]

In the same vein, Koidula ironizes over the idea that any "serf" is by nature only an emotionless and ambitionless servant:

> as kind and grateful Nunez might otherwise have felt towards Huaskar—he never forgot his class and his name and Huaskar was nothing more in his eyes than just another Peruvian—his inferior and underling. How could he have forgiven the sin if such a Peruvian, his subordinate, or if he had wanted, his serf, had cast his eye on a noble Spanish girl [...]? Such an idea was so remote from him that he probably wouldn't have been surprised if he had seen Huaskar carrying Elvira in his arms; he would just have thought that he is doing it as a serf. Indeed, that is his duty to a high-born Spanish lady (Koidula, *Perúama* 87; see also 103, 108).[29]

---

28 "lahutavad seisuste vaheseinad ja uhkus ni meletumal wisil innimest innimesest [...] et assi Hindu pagganate kasti seltsides mitte hullem ei wõiks olla. [...] Õnneks hakkab se wanna hallitus uema päwa paiste all ikka ennam ja ennam ärraplekima".

29 "ni hea ja tännolik kui Nunez ka muido Huaskari wasto olli—omma seisust ja nimmi ei unnustanud temma ial ärra ja Huaskar ei olnud jo temma silmis muud middagi kui iggaüks mu Pe-

The third difference is most evident in the quarrel scene between Huaskar and Nunez over Huaskar's right to have a love relationship with Elvira (Horn 361-363; Koidula, *Perúama* 101-103). Both Huaskars stress that Huaskar is indeed also a nobleman, albeit from Peru, and equally that all Christians are equal in the eyes of God. But for *Inca's* Huaskar, high standing is not only trivial before God, but it is also something that may be voided at any moment in the complex course of history. The honor of social standing is, according to Huaskar, not something one can always retain; it changes under the pressure of external phenomena, in the turmoil of events, in history. *Inca's* (and only *Inca's*) Huaskar tells Nunez:

> Everyone remains just that, human, and if they are in trouble like you and me, then all their glory and standing is worth less than naught. [...] Your glory and position as the governor of Peru went just the same way as my parents' throne was destroyed and their sceptre broken! (Koidula, *Perúama* 102)[30]

Space, time and change

Huaskar's Las Casas is relieved when his ship is about to land in America: "soon he rejoiced to see the snow-covered and likewise leaf-green peaks of the Andes, as they stretched themselves across the glorious country" (296).[31]

Inca's Las Casas' reaction is totally different. Reaching the New World, he is already carrying the pain of its history with him: "Tears rose to Las Casas' eyes when he saw the high peaks of Peru, some covered with eternal snow, some decorated with green forests. What an amount of injustice had already been committed and suffered there!" (14)[32]

Huaskar also has a sense of injustice, but in its value system suffering in violent history is always juxtaposed to idylls in the almost timeless, closed spaces the novella creates. The key words characterizing the Las Casas of *Huaskar* are qui-

---

ruamees—temma allam ja kässoalune. Kuda wõis temma sedda pattu andeks anda, et niisuggune Peruamees ja temma allam, ehk, kui ta tahtis, ka temma pärrisorri, oma silma ühhe suurtsugu Spania tüttarlapse [...] peale julgeks tõsta? Se mõtte seisis temmalt ni kaugel, et wist immeks ep olleks pannud, kui ta Huaskarit olleks näinud Elwirat sülles kandwad; waid olleks mõttelnud: Sedda teeb ta kui pärrisorri. Se on jo temma kohhus Spania suurtsugu naesterahwa wasto".

30 "Iggaüks jääb seks, mis ta on, innimesseks, ja kui ta, nago teie ja minna, hädda sees on, siis ei maksa au ja seisus mitte musta küne all. [...] Teie, Perua mawallitseja, käest on au ja ammet kaddunud, nago minno wannemate troon lõhhutud ja nende wallitsuse kep katki murtud!"

31 "bald hatte er die Freude die schneebedeckten, mitunter auch grünebelaubten Gipfel der Cordillera de los Andes zu erblicken, wie sie sich hinziehen durch das herrliche Land"

32 "Las Kasal tõusis vesi silma, kui Peruama kõrged mäeringad, mis muist allalisse lumme, muist halja metsadega ehhitud, ta silma paistsid. Kui paljo üllekohhut olli seal jubba tehtud ja kannatud!"

etness, peace, and tranquillity. When he first decides to travel to Peru, his greatest concern is giving up his "peace and quiet" (Horn 295); having fled warring Lima to settle in the countryside he is looking for a "haven of peace". When he finally finds it "in enclosed isolation", there is created a simultaneously Christian and nobly savage space, in harmony with both God and Nature. Time becomes still, days "flow in uniform peace and quiet" (308-309). The characteristic activities of this space are prayer and walks in the fruitful natural environment. In this context the Peruvian hinterland is primarily a "lovely wilderness", full of "wonderful flowers" and countless fruits, birds and animals; the text is abundant in alien detail not explained to the reader and the exact meanings are indeed not important because all these names have one meaning—the exotic (308-309). The space of the countryside is directly contrasted with that of Lima where violent historical events are taking place. The fear of the threatening force of history is an integral part of the conceptualization of the idyll.

The thought-world of *The Last Inca of Peru* lacks this type of a paradise motif entirely; it takes history everywhere, starting from the title. While *Huaskar* begins in the same historical period as the one when its main events take place, *Inca*'s first chapter introduces the history of pre-conquest society. The Peruvians, it relates, had their own laws and customs, their own civilization, although not so developed in military arts as the European one. They had inner political struggles and conflicts over power (Koidula, *Perúama* 7-8). *Inca* creates a vision of a particular people who meet an evil fate after foreign conquest. Its sketch of history is stylized but nevertheless complex; its Peru never was a *tabula rasa*, never a paradise.

Neither is the Las Casas of *Inca* looking for a paradise; he has no hope of finding a "haven of peace". For him Peru is a landscape for activity—missionary trips, gathering herbs, etc. It is also a foreign space to be educated into both geographically and socially: "In that manner [walking] he got to know the land and the people and saw too how the injustice and greed for gold exhausted and pressured them" (34).[33] Hence, in *Inca* there is no existential juxtaposition between the spaces of the city and the wilderness. If there is any, it is expressed on the time axis: "One heard about those terrible things [that were happening in Lima] in the quiet valley of Las Casas as well but [...] one didn't see any of it *yet*" (33; my italics).[34] Everything is historical.

---

33 "Sel kombel õppis ta maad ja rahwast ikka ennam tundma ja näggi ka, kuidas üllekohhus ja kullaahnus neid kurnas ja pigistas".
34 "Neist hirmsaist asjust kuuldi küll ka Las Kasa waikses orgus, agga [...] neist ei nähtud seal weel midagi".

Strongly linked to their ideas of history are the divergent visions of Divine Providence and human fate in *Huaskar* and *Inca*. Opposing the next world to this one and asserting the vanity and transitoriness of worldly values is a traditional argument in Christian thought. In the post-1848 *Volksliteratur* by German Lutheran pastors, this world-perception is foregrounded, acquires new forms and meanings, and is so dominant that Klaus Müller-Salget's thorough study considers it the most fundamental ideological basis for the German popular literature of that time (210). Differently from the more familiar Protestant world outlook, the sense of crisis provokes a situation where "the authors are mostly not even satisfied with establishing a hierarchy of values, but instead construct an oppositional model, according to which the rejoicement in God and the rejoicement in the world exclude one another" (Müller-Salget 210).

The popular stories often present a character-ideologue like *Huaskar*'s Las Casas—a person spiritually withdrawn from the world who experiences various blows of fate and goes through terrible ordeals but always trusts God. This character functions as an interpretive center of the story who explains story events like sudden misfortunes or lucky coincidences as manifestations of the will of God. The two main models of interpretations are the Finger of God (Exodus 8, 19) and that God's thoughts are not our thoughts (Isaiah 55, 8). The first model operates on events that are positive or fortunate according to the values of the story, while the second accounts for "unjust" and inexplicable events. The Finger of God is often used for the final resolutions of a story; the second model never is, it always appears as the ordeal in the middle of the story and can be interpreted as the trial of the characters by God. Thus, God's will may be beyond understanding for the heroes in the middle of the story but by the end everything is rationalized and the Finger of God will indicate the solution and the meaning. (Müller-Salget 214-216)

The idea of God's ways being beyond understanding has influence on both *Huaskar*'s and *Inca*'s thread of narration and values, but otherwise we are dealing with different divinities. While the God of *Huaskar* is guiding a continuous and regular sequence of events that at times cannot be grasped in human terms, with *Inca*'s God one must be always ready for sudden changes and reversals. *Inca* never talks of trust in Divine Providence like *Huaskar* (Horn 304, 355, 366), but only about how one should try to retain dignity and strength of mind in a turmoil where all social certainties, standing, position, wealth or customary routine can become nothing at any moment. What cannot be lost are Christian values—piety of heart, grace, but also the humanist values of love, friendship and learning.

The God of *Inca* is a God of vague interpretability. He is rarely perceived to point his finger directly. For example, when the fugitives' hut is destroyed in the earthquake, the German Las Casas says: "It must seem to me as though the destruction were the sign of the Finger of the Heavens, that we seek a surer abode" (*Huaskar* 356).³⁵ The Estonian Las Casas says: "The Lord giveth, the Lord hath taken away. [...] Who knows what the punishment may be good for" (*Perúama* 92).³⁶

There is also another notable difference between *Huaskar*'s and *Inca*'s ideologies of fate. In *Huaskar* the principle of Divine Providence is part of an established and unquestioned tradition and rather an unemphasized ideological background; in *Inca* the fluctuation of the world is an issue constantly discussed, it is brought up in places where *Huaskar* does not mention it at all. The German version describes Pizarro's funeral as follows: "The body of the murdered man was carried into the church by Las Casas and one loyal retainer of Pizarro's; and only Las Casas and Halipa, a former servant, had the daring to bury the body of the unfortunate man" (Horn 304).³⁷

Inca says:

> This horribly grand and feared man who had made everybody tremble when alive was now not considered worthy of even a few spadesfuls of earth. So goes many a thing in this world and some people still do not notice. [...] Las Casas and the poor Peruvian serf were the only two people who were not afraid of the wrath of the new governor Almagro and said Our Lord's prayer at the grave of Prants Pitsarro, once grand and powerful, now disgraced and condemned by everybody.

> It is easy for God
> And he often makes it so
> That one who has been doing well
> Will fast become a miserable beggar

---

35 "Mir [...] will es vorkommen, als sei diese Zerstörung ein Fingerzeig des Himmels, dass wir uns einen sichereren Wohnort suchen"
36 "Issand on andnud, issand on võtnud! [...] Kes teab, mis peale see karistus hea võib olla".
37 "Von Las Casas und den treuen Bedienten Pizarro's wurde der Leichnam des Ermordeten in die Kirche getragen, und Las Casas und Halipa, ein gewesener Diener Pizarro's wagten es allein, den Leichnam des Unglücklichen zu bestatten"

> The same God can help
> To make a poor one rich in no time
> (Koidula, Perúama 24-25)[38]

This train of thought cannot be reduced to the "God's punishment" motif. In *Inca* the same kind of ideas (different from those in *Huaskar*) also relate to the far more ambivalent "rich man" Nunez (Koidula, *Perúama* 99, Horn 361; Koidula, *Perúama* 113, Horn 369) and as we saw above, also to Huaskar's parents (Koidula, *Perúama* 102).

The vagueness of God's will, the ideology of changes and turns of fate color both large and small history in *The Last Inca of Peru*. This coloring is distinctly modern and spells out that historical institutions and positions, the order of the things of the world are not eternal but ever and again in alteration. In such a thought-world, relations with the disappearing past (ancestors, principles of fathers, history) become problematic in themselves.

The curses and blessings of the elders

The two native American protagonists of *Huaskar* and *Inca*, Halipa and Huaskar, are both orphans, their parents and/or close relatives were killed by Spaniards. In that situation they are adopted by Las Casas. Considering that Huaskar's parents were killed by Las Casas's compatriots and that Halipa's father and Huaskar's first stepfather, the old Peruvian is depicted cursing all Spaniards on his death bed, the adoption marks a notable cultural turning point.

This point is present both in *Huaskar* and *Inca*, but it is modelled somewhat differently. In *Huaskar* the cultural cleavage is diminished into non-existence. Comforting Halipa after his father's death, Las Casas states that he will certainly meet his father again in Heaven as the old Peruvian was "noble and good" (Horn 311). Thus Halipa's father is brought into the Christian family tree; he will be a child of God in Heaven just like Las Casas himself, so it becomes natural for them to share the fatherhood of Halipa (and Huaskar) in a brotherly

---

38   Sedda hirmus suurt ja kardetawat meest, kelle eest elloaeal iggaüks wärrises, ei arwatud nüüd pärrast surma mitte pari labida täie mulla wäärt ollewad! Nenda on ni mitmed asjad mailmas ja mitmed innimessed ei panne sedda ommeti tähele. [...] Las Kasas ja se waene Perua pärrisorri ollid need kaks ainust innimest, kes ue mawallitseja Almagro wihha ei kartnud, ja endise wägewa ja sure, nüüd agga teutud ja keigest rahwast ärranetud Prants Pitsarro haua äres issa meie palwet tegid.
Kül Jummalal on kerge assi, / ja temma teeb ka saggedast, / Et se, kel hästi käinud kässi, / saab waeseks sandiks ussinasst. / Sesamma Jummal awwitab, / Et waene pea rikkaks saab

manner. It can be ignored that the Peruvian died hating and cursing the Christianizers: he is still a noble proto-Christian, who even "blesses" Halipa before his death (Horn 311).

The lines of the family-tree that are sketched in *Inca* are far more dotted. The worldview of Halipa's dying father is straightforward and presented very clearly: he asks Halipa to support and protect Huaskar, their last Inca, curses the Spaniards and wishes "a blessing of ancestors" to his own people (Koidula, *Perúama* 37). Las Casas' equally direct words of comfort say nothing to Halipa about heavenly re-union. Instead, he is practically demanding that Halipa deviate from his father's world, which is even more remarkable as Las Casas, differently from *Huaskar*'s version, in his mind recognizes all the accusations of the dying Peruvian as "pure truth" (Koidula, *Perúama* 37). He says to Halipa: "Look towards the Heaven, my son, there you have a better father than the one who is cold in front of us. What a mortal father can do, I have promised to do for you" (Koidula, *Perúama* 38).[39]

At that point Halipa brings Huaskar to Las Casas as well and spells out several aspects of the culture-shift ideology in *Inca*:

> My father, here is the last sprig of the tree in the shadow of which the land and people of Peru have lived and seen peaceful days for a long time. Accept him too as your child and teach him so that he may know Lord Jesus! He cannot [...] make you grand and rich thereby for the seat of glory of the Peruvian Incas has been overthrown, but he will love you as I and my brothers do (Koidula, *Perúama* 38).[40]

Individual love and the loyalty based on it are more relevant than duties that spring from birth or traditions. This is a repeated and foregrounded message in *Inca*, which is lacking in this emphatic form in *Huaskar*. The differences between the respective scenes showcasing questions of birth and ethnic belonging where Peruvians ask Huaskar to become their leader, are characteristic. In *Huaskar* the emphasis is on the "holy rights" of family-ties, in *Inca* it is on the

---

39 "Wata taewa pole, mo poeg, seal elab sul parrem issa, kui se, kes külmaks jänud meie ees seisab. Mis surrelik issa wõib tehha, sedda ollen ma sulle ka lubbanud".
40 "Mo issa, siin on se wiimne wõsso sest puust, kelle warjo al Perúama ja rahwas kaua on ellanud ja rahho päiwi näinud. Wõtta ka tedaomma lapseks wasto ja õppeta tedda Issandat Jesust tundma! sureks ja rikkaks ei wõi ta sind selle eest [...] teha, sest Perua Inkade aujärg on ümberlükkatud; agga ta saab sind armastama nago minna ja mo wennad".

choice whether to *love* one's own people or their enemies (Koidula, *Perúama* 117; Horn, *Huaskar* 379).

Differently from *Huaskar*, in *Inca*'s worldview social signs in general are perceived as negative, arbitrary, and despotic. The text appears to encourage the readers to try to eliminate these signals and diminish their importance as much as possible, almost like wanting to create a sign-free world. The description where Huaskar obtains the power symbols of the Incas covers almost a page in *Huaskar* and only gets a couple of puritanical lines in *Inca* (Koidula, *Perúama* 118; Horn, *Huaskar* 382-383). The social communication between Peruvians is described as less ceremonious and hierarchical by *Inca* than by *Huaskar*. And it is not only the signs connected with Peruvian tradition that wane and fade. When in *Huaskar*, Las Casas declares his names and family connections to pave his path to the emperor's court (Horn 320), then *Inca*'s worldview demands that this documentary detail be changed: Las Casas invades the finery of the court as a "poor monk" dressed in an "undecorated long rough coat" and a stranger to all (Koidula, *Perúama* 49).

Clinging to one's ancestors or to the traditional order of things is generally perceived as dangerous and/or ridiculous by *Inca*. An entirely negative conception used only in *Inca* and never in *Huaskar* is "suckled with mother's milk". Huaskar's initial deep hatred against all the Europeans has been "absorbed with mother's milk" (Koidula, *Perúama* 40)—but he is educated out of it. A parallel to Huaskar's hatred is the far more difficult case of Nunez's, used for broader generalizations:

> If we assume that Nunez's heart was softened by the pain the others now had to suffer, we are very much mistaken. [...] Rather we can learn here how difficult it is for people to forsake and deny that which they have considered true and firm since they were at their mother's breast (Horn 105).[41]

It is precisely the ancestors, especially those of Nunez, who constitute the immediate threat for Huaskar's and Elvira's love. "As far as I remember or have heard anything of the elders of my elders," Nunez says "—when has anyone in our family been involved in an abominable thing like that?" (Koidula, *Perúama* 101)[42]

---

41 "Kui arwame, et wallo, mis teiste peale langenud, Nunesse südant pehmeks tegi, siis eksime wägga. [...] Paljo ennem wõimme siit õppida, kui raske se innimestel on, sedda mahhajätta ja walleks piddada, mis nad jubba emma rinnust sadik tõeks ja kindlaks piddawad".
42 "Nikaua, kui minna omma wannemmate wannemmatest middagi ollen kuulnud ja mälletan.— mil on meie sugguseltsist kegi nisuggust jõledat tempu teinud".

Yet, Huaskar's elders of Peruvian "aristocracy" do also have a positive aspect in both texts. In *Huaskar* they serve as a proof of Huaskar's noble nature, in *Inca* rather as a proof that "a Peruvian" and "a serf" need not be synonyms. Both texts, interestingly, however, have to stress and to challenge the importance of Huaskar's royal parentage simultaneously, in the framework of one and the same line of ideology. "A poor Peruvian? [...] Huaskar is of the ancient kin of Peruvian Incas!" Elvira shouts indignantly and adds: "But even if he were a beggar's son—wouldn't he still be a human being like myself? [...] he has saved my life [...] Alonso is a high-born man, and my relative at that, why didn't he do what Huaskar did?" (Koidula, *Perúama* 101; Horn 362)[43] Only such a double argumentation can make the love of the young people legitimate—both the noble lineage of Huaskar and the proclamation of egalitarianism and humanism are needed.

Inca's New World is a world where one puts up with the loss of the past, to make (what is perceived as) the best of the present and the future. In *Inca*'s world Emperor Charles V declares to Huaskar from his position of authority: "What has been, has been [...] no one can undo things already done [...] but from now on things must change" (Koidula, *Perúama* 53).[44] The whole scene essential from *Inca*'s point of view is lacking in *Huaskar*.

In principle the same kind of difference between the forgettable past and relevant present/future is accepted by the Spanish colonists in *Inca*. They do not agree that Huaskar be killed as their fanatical leader demands: "'The Peruvian people will smash and grind us all in a mortar,' they said, 'if we dared to do that and kill their Inca *one more time*.'" (Koidula, *Perúama* 124, my italics).[45]

Yet there is also a certain sense of loss built in into the Brave New World. There are the glorious but deserted ancestors whom *Inca*'s emancipatory worldview cannot honestly incorporate in the new family tree, but also cannot quite forget. As the earlier Peruvian generations are presented as historical beings, rather than as shorthand for the ideals of noble savagery, there emerges a modern, perhaps in particular a belatedly modern, sense of a historical rift that is not there in *Huaskar*. There is the feeling that some things are gone so irrevocably that it would be meaningless even to try to return to them; the question can only be in replacing them somehow, in possible compensation mechanisms. It

---

43 "Üks vaene Peruamees? [...] Huaskar on Perua wanna inkade soust! Agga olleks ta sandi poeg, - kas ta sellepärrast innimenne ei olle naggo minnagi? [...] ta on mind surmast peastnud ... Alonso on jo suurtsugu mees, pealegi minno suggulane, miks ta ei teinud, mis Huaskar teggi?"

44 "'Mis olnud, on olnud [...] ja sündinud asjo ei wõi üksigi innimenne ennam sündimattaks tehha. [...] agga siit sadik peab assi teiseks minnema'".

45 "Purruks ja jahhuks," ütlesid nemmad, "sawad Peruarahwas meid keiki teggema, kui sedda julgeksime tehha ja weel ükskord nende Inkat ärratappa".

is exactly the notion of replacement that *Inca*'s Charles V and Las Casas are discussing: "I have found the last son of Atahualpa, the hapless Inca of Peru and have taught him Christianity," Las Casas says, "I have brought this young man to Spain, so that in replacement for his lost power and glory he could at least be educated as a Christian. But I am myself too poor to send him to the University of Salamanca and have him taught there—". "—May God be thanked" [...], Charles V quickly interrupts: "then I can still undo some of the great evil that has been done to his unknown, unfortunate family in my name!" (Koidula, *Perúama* 52).[46]

The power of knowledge

Both *Inca* and *Huaskar* support the value of education, emphasizing the development and self-fulfilment it generates and also the practical help it may provide. Generally, the Estonian text is content to repeat the German discussions closely or amplify their agenda further, but there are some aspects that appear only in *Inca*.

In the Estonian version, education is emphatically presented as a source of social and political strength and power. The Estonian Huaskar mainly agrees to go and study in Spain for the following reason: "education makes one tough and gives one power. This he had understood at home clearly. If the Peruvians had had the same knowledge as the Spaniards, they would probably still have been the free masters of their land"[47] (Koidula, *Perúama* 48; similar expressions 5, 8; there is no equivalent in Horn).

Secondly, the Estonian version is deeply preoccupied, even obsessed, with information and explanation, whereas in *Huaskar* almost the opposite is the case. As discussed above, the German text tends to emphasize the exoticism of activities and scenes of action. It seems that part of the intended charm of the story is that exotic plants, animals, and other realia are mentioned or enumerated without telling the reader anything about their appearance or nature, thereby achieving an atmosphere of exotic otherness. In the same way Spanish

---

46 "Ma ollen õnnetuma Perua Inka Atahualpa keige wimast poega üllesleidnud ja ristiusku tundma õppetanud, ma ollen seddasinnast noortmeest Spaniamaale kasa wõtnud, et ta siin omma kaddunud wäe ja au assemel ommeti ristiinnimese wisil õppetatud saaks. Minna ollen agga isseennesest liig waene, tedda salamanka surekoli peale sata ja õppetada lasta—" "—Jummal olgu tännatud," [...] "nattuke wõin ma siis ommeti sest surest kurjast heaks pöörda, mis minno nimel ta tundmatta õnnetuma sugguwõssale on tehtud!'"

47 "õpetus teeb kangeks ja annab wõimust. Sedda olli ta koddo selgeste näinud. Olleks Peruarahwal Spaniameeste tarkus käes olnud, siis olleksid nemmad wist praego weel omma ma pri perremehhed olnud."

life, manners and history are mostly left to the readers' imagination or to their assumed previous knowledge. While the narrator does offer some explanations (311, 320, 326, 352, 360) these are infrequent and limited in scope when compared to those in *Inca* (Koidula, *Perúama* 4, 7, 11, 12, 15, 18, 20, 31, 47, 48-49, 54, 56, 70, 86, 93, 96, 98, 99, 101-102). This creates the impression that knowledge and its mediation as such have considerable ideological significance in *Inca*, playing a role far greater than a simple need to provide the reader with relevant information. How else could we explain that even Huaskar's extremely dramatic and ideologically central monologue is ruthlessly interrupted by an encyclopaedic note by the narrator: "God has created all people and when he created them, there was not a single Spanish grandee (count or prince) among them!" (Koidula, *Perúama* 101-102).[48]

While *Huaskar's* narrator enjoys describing the otherness of the exotic, *Inca's* narrator draws upon the "domestic" space and sends the message that there is actually nothing much in the foreignness that the narrator/reader would not be able to understand or explain, even though the exotic may be part of the interest and excitement of the narrated story. Strange lands, the lands of otherness are not essential wonderlands, since for some (e.g. for Peruvians or Spaniards) they can be normal and natural spaces. It is knowledge and education—received, if possible, from the University of Salamanca but quite proficiently also from old chronicle books and contemporary newspapers—that renders the strange accessible. And this ability to learn about the foreign is a key to power and freedom, *Inca* seems to suggest.

The power of marriage

The relation to the Other is so important for the postcolonial sense of the world that the issues of Self—family and tradition—can only be thought of in the context of that relation. Thus it is quite natural that love between a man and a woman from different continents, from different Worlds, and the problematic wish that the society should give such love its recognition by allowing marriage is one of the repeating motifs of great symbolic weight in the postcolonial literature.

Discussing mainly works written from the 16th to the 18th centuries, Renata Wassermann points out that in New World literature the Self/Other relations

---

48 "Jummal on keik innimessed lonud, ja kui ta neid lõi, ep olnud weel mitte üht ainust Spania grandi (grahwi ehk würsti) nende seas!"

mean, to a great extent, relations on the boundary. Even the boundary between Culture and Nature can be perceived as very thin in this context (especially 69-154; see also Knellwolf 12). The exotic love affairs in works by Chautebriand or Bernardin de Saint-Pierre oscillate between two poles: extreme exogamy of an intercontinental marriage on the one hand, and on the other, extreme endogamy, protecting the racial purity of a group to the point of incest, the taboo of which lies on the boundary between Nature and Culture, according to Claude Lévi-Strauss.

Both of these fundamental metaphors of exotic literature carry their own hopes and fears. Exogamy is a way of making a conquest, of domesticating the Other and renewing the Self; yet, there is also the fear of dissolution, contamination of identity. Incest is an index of moral-free nature (as in Rousseau's influential *Discourse on the Origin and Basis of Inequality Among Men*), but not only of that, for it can also indicate the opposite: overculturation and deterioration, aristocratic decadence. Basically the same thought-mechanism is in function here as in the juxtaposition of natural savagery and the unnatural savagery through loss of civility.

The network of marriage motifs in *Huaskar* perfectly coincides with the structures pointed out by Wassermann, making it in this aspect similar to *Atala*, *Paul and Virginie*, *The Deerslayer*, and many other famous novels of exoticism. The governor Nunez, Elvira's father, destines her daughter to marry a nobleman whose parents are Elvira's paternal uncle and maternal aunt. Indeed, the relation is so close that the family has to request a special dispensation from the Pope, because the general rules in Spain would not allow a marital connection between such close relatives (Horn, *Huaskar* 342).

Marrying into one's close family is contrasted with marriage to Huaskar, the ultimate stranger. From the point of view of the traditional identity of the family, the union with a man from the New World would be an impossibility, an unthinkability even. What makes this marriage possible in *Huaskar* is that it is God's Will. From the Christian point of view, Huaskar and Elvira would be equals but even that is not the main point in Horn's *Huaskar*. God's Will primarily signifies that Huaskar's and Elvira's meeting and falling in love were meant to happen by the Higher Power; it is a miracle and thus ordinary human understanding of what is normal and natural can and, indeed, ought to be, suspended (see especially 329, 330). *Huaskar* spells out with great emphasis that the love of Huaskar and Elvira is not a mere "passing tremor of senses" (330) but the way of God.

Against that background it is rather noteworthy that in comparison to typical contemporary German *Volksliteratur*, but also in comparison to *Inca*, *Huas-*

kar's depiction of love is considerably more sensuous. Let us compare the characteristic scene were Huaskar cures Elvira from a potentially deadly snake bite in the midst of the primeval jungle. *Huaskar*:

> Then Elvira again opened her beautiful eyes and gazed at the young man with inexpressible tenderness and confusion, for her bare foot lay in his hand and she felt the warm lips of the young man upon it. [...] "Huaskar," lisped the maiden, "how can I repay you?" [...] "With your goodwill and remembering," he replied "and with that posy of flowers in your hand." Then she granted him the posy and a kiss burned her hand. (339)[49]

If we bear in mind the general conventions of exotic literature, it seems far from merely accidental that W.O. Horn was the only *Volkschriftsteller* of his time to use exotic settings and also the only one to be accused of sensuousness unsuitable for popular works by his contemporary critics (Müller-Salget 132, 145, 267). The link between lush and exuberant nature and "natural" love is a long-standing literary—and not only literary—convention; the erotics are motivated by the exotics; the exotic—the thicket of plants with unfamiliar names, the soft carpet of moss, the deadly dangerous rattle-snake itself—almost presumes the erotic. Yet at the same time, primeval nature is not the only or even the most dominant element in the rescue scene. The civilized romance etiquette, the bunch of flowers and the hand-kiss, are just as essential to it. For the culture that writes is not really concerned with a return to nature but with the titillating issue of the Culture/Nature boundary, that is, actually the culture itself (Knellwolf 10, 12). The noble/savage love discourse of *Huaskar* is one, relatively simplistic way of dramatizing this issue.

On the basis of the above scene alone it may seem exaggerated to stress the eroticism of *Huaskar* but if we compare it to *Inca*'s version which (at least when not subjected to a psychoanalytical reading) is an understated informative one, the difference is striking:

> Elvira's shoe and stocking were removed at the speed of lightning. The next moment the newcomer's lips were sucking the red wound. [...] The poison that had entered the blood was not to go any further, so the foot had to

---

49 "Da schlug Elvira wieder das schöne Auge auf und heftete es auf den Jüngling mit unaussprechlicher Zärtlichkeit und Verwirrung, denn ihr blosser Fuss lag in seiner Hand, und sie fühlte die warmen Lippen des Jünglings darauf. [...] 'Huaskar,' lispelte die Jungfrau, 'wie kann ich Euch lohnen?' [...] 'mit Eurem wohlwollenden Andenken!' erwiderte er, 'und mit diesem Blumenstrauss aus Eurer Hand!' Da reichte sie ihm den Strauss und ein Kuss brannte auf ihrer Hand."

be arranged higher than the body. [...] At that Elvira opened her eyes. [...] With a hot glance she caught Huaskar's eye. What she felt in her heart I do not know [...] "Huaskar," the girl said with tears in her eyes, "in what way can I thank you for that [...] ?" "If you sometimes remember me with kindness, that is the only and dearest thanks that I ask!" Then he bid farewell and disappeared among the trees like lightning (Koidula, *Inca* 70-71).[50]

It cannot at all be said that *Inca* is censoring the physicalities out in a Victorian manner. The body just acquires different meanings in its discourse: the snake-bitten foot is primarily an object of care and medical attention. These kinds of differences are deductible in the whole of the texts. The exotic and the erotic intertwine nowhere in *Inca* as they do in *Huaskar*. *Inca* also lacks the emphatic incest motif: there Alonso is just Elvira's cousin, the problem of the special marriage licence is not mentioned.

Why then does *Inca* exclude the basic characteristic motifs of exoticizing literature that *Huaskar* had easily included? The simple reason, to my mind, is that the strategic boundary in *Inca* lies in a different place from Horn's, J. F. Cooper's or Chautebriand's works: not between Culture and Nature but between two different cultures. Both cultures have their own history and civilization, the boundary is difficult to cross primarily for the reason that they are different in status; the question *Inca* dramatizes is the social one of class partitions and the possibilities of getting over them.

Huaskar's "God's Will" argumentation is relocated into this new context. In *Inca*'s value system, love is a proof of essential humanity destined by Higher Powers to overcome the arbitrary boundary created by social inequalities. Huaskar's love for Elvira cannot but show that the Peruvian is not a natural slave but someone who has emotions and ambitions of a dignified human being, and Elvira's return of his love signifies, among other things, her culture's recognition and appreciation of that fact. Eventually his love and marriage will also become the most efficient compensation mechanism of the story: to marry Elvira, Huaskar must be made a nobleman and the governor of his native land for Charles V.

---

50 "Nago wälk ollid Elwira king ja suk jallast maas. Teisel silmapilgul seisid wõera mokkad immedes punnase hawa peal. [...] Kihwt, mis werre sisse olli tunginud, ei tohtinud kaugemale minna. [...] Selle peale lõi Elwira silmad lahti. [...] Pallawalt tungis Huaskari silm kohkund tüttarlapse silma. Mis ta südda tundis, sedda ei tea minna üttelda [...] 'Huaskar,' ütles tüttarlaps silmawega, 'mil wisil wõin minna Teid selle eest tännada [...]?' 'Mõttelge mõnikord lahkeste minno peale, se on se ainus ja armsam tänno, mis ma selle eest pallun!' Selle peale terretas ta ja olli nago wälk pude wahhel kaddund."

Considering the above-quoted snakebite-love-scene, it is important to notice that it is not only much of the exotic erotics that disappear in the translation to Estonian, but also the indications of the European etiquette: the hand-kiss, the bunch of flowers. The social signs are similarly reduced to a minimum when the narrator describes the development of Elvira's and Huaskar's romance after they flee Lima and live in the midst of Peruvian nature. In fact, these sections introduce a stock space of exoticism literature used: that of paradise. This is the only part of the narrative where this *topos*, generally belonging to *Huaskar*'s value system, is used in *Inca*. It is, however, also relocated in a different context from that of the German version and acquires an entirely different significance.

In *Huaskar*, paradise is an anti-social space—the space where the little commune can live in the spirit of "patriarchal peace" undisturbed by the violent struggles surrounding them—thus still a social space. In *Inca*, on the other hand, it stands for the subjective paradise of Elvira's and Huaskar's love: "now blissful days came *for our young people*"; "the wood and the forest had become a paradise *for them both*" (85, my italics).[51] This space is only ever focused through the perspective of the lovers, and it only exists for them. The paradise-space of *Inca* is not emphatically exotic like in *Huaskar*, neither is it the journalistic-encyclopaedic space characteristic of most of the Estonian text. It is the spatial reflection of the new couple's emotional life and hence only contains for them signs connected to each other:

> Whatever Huaskar could read in Elvira's eyes he got for her even if it had cost his life. [...] And for Elvira the young man's love was present in every tree-leaf and when Huaskar was not at home every flower was nodding to her and saying: Huaskar sends his greetings! Elvira would pluck the flower, press it to her lips and say: "be thanked for passing it on!" Thus their hearts became ever more attached to each other every day[52] (86).

The subjectivity of Elvira's and Huaskar's space perception is further confirmed by the fact the rest of the characters in the same action space, Nunez, Halipa and Las Casas, do not think it a paradise at all. For them the worries of

---

51 "nüüd tullid meie norerahwale [...] õnsad päwad"; "mets ja laan olli mõllemile paradisiks sanud"
52 "Mis Huaskar ial Elwira silmast wõis ärratunda, sedda murretses ta temmal, ja kui se ka temma ello olleks maksnud. [...] Ja Elwirale paistis jälle noremehhe armastus igga pulehhe pealt wasto ja kui Huaskar koddo ei olnud, nikkutas igga õis peaga ja ütles: Huaskar sadab paljo terwist! Elwira noppis õit, surrus oma ulede wasto ja ütles: olle terwe tomast! Nenda kaswasid nende süddamed igga pääw ennam kokko"

coping with nature and the stress connected to the social events are continuously present, their time does not become still, their feelings are not reflected in space (86-88). In *Huaskar*, on the other hand, the circumstances of the "patriarchal peace" are the same for all characters, only the attitudes to it differ.

Thus "paradise" in *Inca* constitutes a mental space where the traditional signs of social partitions can be erased, where one can become the New Adam and New Eve. It is Elvira's and Huaskar's love that makes this space possible, and also the other way round, this space seems to be the condition of exogamous love in *Inca*'s thought-world. It is only superficially paradoxical that proceeding from this perception of love, *Inca*'s (but not *Huaskar*'s) Elvira and Huaskar speak of marriage as the only possible aim of their relationship right after their first proclamation of love (98). The New World utopia of *Inca* is still after all a social utopia, although one that in *Inca*'s thought-world can only be built on a ground cleansed of old signs.

Adapting a Fellow Spirit: Koidula's *Juudit* and Mügge's *Eduard Montague*

As pointed out at the beginning of the chapter, the realization of utopia is undermined by the second ending of *Inca*, which reports the obliteration of the natives and the introduction of black slaves from Africa at the suggestion of no other than Las Casas. An obvious explanation to this uncanny shift is that Koidula's engagement with Horn's text brought about a postcolonial genre conflict in her version. The literary logic of her source did not tally with Koidula's historical-political vision or with her journalistic mode of writing. Although Horn's *Huaskar* has a setting and subject matter that is unusual for its genre, yet its mode is sentimental and its *Biedermeier* thought-style results in a plot culminating in a clichéd ending. The traces of these features are also observable in *Inca*, despite the historicization and actualization strategies analysed above. The relationship between Theodor Mügge's *Eduard Montague* and *Juudit* is of a thoroughly different nature. Among the three stories discussed in this chapter, it is here that Koidula makes the least alterations. She shortens the novel and adds a few notable sections, yet it is mostly in the *choice* of Mügge's story for adaptation that we can see her own political agenda.

Mügge was a passionate political activist, a journalist and an extremely prolific author earning his living by his pen. As Cathrine Theodorsen puts it: "The general theme of all Mügge's work is the struggle for freedom against injustice and political oppression. His stories are about freedom fighters, oppositionals, revolts of minorities against colonial powers or authoritarian regimes" (361). Among others, he wrote at least two works on the Haitian Revolution (1791–1804): *The Chevalier* (1835) and *Toussaint* (1840). He was a characteristic representative of the ethnographic style in his fiction as well as in his travel writing. At the same time his foreign spaces tend to have a dark, abstruse atmosphere and the plots verge on the mystical and the fantastic. Mügge was frequently published in *Die Gartenlaube*, Koidula's favorite magazine discussed above. He also travelled in Scandinavia and repeatedly wrote both fiction and non-fiction on related topics. The novel *Erich Randal* (1850) about the Finnish resistance to the Russian conquest in 1808 and the novel *Afraja* (1854) on the plight of the Norwegian Sami are among his best-known works. Furthermore, Koidula was not the only Mügge enthusiast among Estonian national activists. For example, C. R. Jakobson sent a copy of *Erich Randal* to his fiancée in 1871, discussing the Estonian political situation in comparison to that in the novel and pointing out his own psychological kinship to the protagonist (Kahu, especially 14-15).

Eduard Montague shows a number of Mügge's typical characteristics. The features of postcolonial Gothic that make their appearance in *Inca* only through Koidula's re-writing are already prevalent in the novel's dark atmosphere, haunted characters and the elements of the mystical. It is also kindred to Koidula in its sympathy for the cause of the rebels, depicted as a just war, as well in its general liberal anti-imperialist views and its global perspective.

The novella is set in Jamaica in 1795, in the wake of the French Revolution. That year a group of Jamaican Maroons (escaped slaves residing in difficult-to-reach high mountain areas), fought the Second Maroon War against the Creole planters and against the British military—eventually unsuccessfully.[53] Part of the reference system of the novella is also the more widely known, geographically adjacent Haitian Revolution, which culminated in the abolition of slavery and the establishment of the world's first black republic. Furthermore, the Jamaican slave owners are also concerned about the developments in England where there is now high level critique of slave trade and talk about human rights. The Maroons are inspired by the international climate and ready to fight for their own freedom.

Intertwined with the account of the Maroons' war that follows historical sources, the fictional plot of the novella revolves around a racially complicated love intrigue. The female protagonist Juudit, though a striking-looking heiress, is known to be one-eighth black. In the racially sensitive world of the planters,

---

53 For a good historical account see Wilson.

this makes her social status and marriage perspectives problematic. In her compromised, ambivalent position in the community, she also develops an independent outlook and rebellious attitude considered inappropriate for a woman. Yet three men fall in love with Juudit: her pompous cousin John, a comic relief figure; the proud, audacious, intensely racist plantation owner William; and, most importantly for the story, Eevar, a young chieftain of the Maroons, black, and matching William in his pride, passion and resolution.[54]

The boundary between the whites and the blacks is not the only one in the novel. The Maroons are contrasted and compared with the enslaved blacks, Igbos, who work in the plantations and simultaneously look up to the Maroons and bitterly resent them for their freedom. From their side, in the peace treaty of 1738 the Maroons had agreed to a clause obliging them to return any runaway slaves to their masters. The whites also fall into two groups: the Creole planters, passionately proud of their patriarchal tradition and "benevolent" slave-owning culture, and the pragmatic, civil but *Realpolitik*-conscious metropolitan British military. In the beginning of the story, the peace treaty between the Maroons and the whites is in effect, but during the course of the novella tensions escalate and the Second Maroon War breaks out. At the end, goaded by William, the British military agrees to bring in pernicious bloodhounds. The Maroons are hunted down from the mountains and the survivors deported to North America. William, however, is killed, presumably by Juudit and Eevar in self-defence, and the lovers themselves disappear tracelessly: they are not found either dead or alive. Yet, "even today" (Koidula, *Juudit* 176), the black slaves tell the story as a legend and some claim they have heard the steps or glimpsed the figures of the lovers high up in the mountains.

Despite Koidula's closeness to her source, her re-writing with the introduction of her own Estonian political message still creates a genre-conflict. Chronologically, *Juudit* continues from the place where *Inca* left off, but poetically and ideologically it comes to repeat an analogous pattern with a similarly discrepant double ending.

Slaves and savages in Juudit *and* Eduard Montague

This time the natives are gone and have been replaced by the valorous Maroons and by the humbled, passive Igbo slaves, two groups that Juudit and Eevar fleet-

---

54 In the German version the main characters are called Judith, Ralf Williamson and Eduard Montague.

ingly hope to unite into one people. This remains only a dream, but the noble savage/natural slave tension is one of the main motors of the plot and generators of the rhetorical drive of the story:

> [The planters of Jamaica] wanted to be good slave masters, they wanted praise for that—but they wanted to be the masters until the end of time. They wanted to look after their slaves and protect them, [...] but may God save the soul of any black who dared to free oneself, to wish for more than for a good master! [...] And the Igbo Negroes put up with it. They sang on the fields during the daytime, in the evenings they danced in the middle of the coacoa bushes to the bagpipe [...] [T]hey picked the fruit of the palmtree, ate, drank—and cursed the Maroons to the bottom of earth as their masters had taught them to do, the Maroons who had in a contract promised to send the runaway slaves back from the mountains! [...] The white masters had succeeded in separating kin from kin, this was and remained their firmest control over their serfs! (*Juudit* 95-96; cf. Mügge 97, the last sentence is missing)[55]

Besides being embodied in the Igbos and Maroons, especially in Koidula's version the strain is also present in the split self-images of the main characters Eevar and Juudit themselves. Indeed, it could be said that the circuit of desire between the two is ignited on the tension of that split.

At the joint dinner with the Maroons, after a round of peace negotiations where William and Eevar quarrel and almost kill one another, Juudit comes to defend Eevar's pride behind his back. As Juudit's suitor John comments on Eevar's handsome looks and says he would like to have the African as a lackey, Juudit answers indignantly:

> This black proud man over there, no! [...] Never will he learn to bend and bootlick, to be servile or bend his back! I have heard him talk like a man

---

55 "Jamaika saarlased tahtsiwad head orjaperemehed olla, tahtsid endid kiita lasta selle eest, aga—peremehed tahtsiwad n'ad olla kuni päiwe lõppeni. Oma orje tahtsiwad n'ad kaitseda ja hoolitseda, selle eest pidi neid maailm kiitma, aga—häda ja wiletsust igale mustale, kes ennast julges wabatada, kes enam tahtis, kui head peremeest! [...] Ja Eboe-Neegrite sugu kannatas wälja. N'ad laulsiwad põllul pääwa aegu, tantsisiwad õhtate oma kakaopõõsastikude wahel tulede ääres torupilli järele ... korjasiwad palmipuu wilja, sõiwad, jõiwad—ja needsiwad Maroonlasi oma isandate õpetust mööda metsa ja laanetesse ära, Maroonlasi, kes lepingus oliwad lubanud põgenenud orjasi mägedest tagasi saata! [...] Walge isandatel oli korda läinud sugu sugust lahutada, see oli ja jäi neile kõige kindlamaks toeks oma pärisorjade juures!"

does, with firmness and rectitude, without fear, without boasting, saying what is true and just, like a king in front of paupers! With all your fortune you own nothing that would make him drop to a knee! (*Juudit* 52; Mügge 50-51)

Overhearing Juudit's raised voice, Koidula's Eevar at first spontaneously accepts the august portrait of a noble savage as being of him. "You are right! Right! You alone know my mind!", he would wish to shout to Juudit (53). Yet a moment later as he catches a sight of his black face in the dining room mirror, he turns his head away and covers his face with his hand. Because of his blackness Eevar initially sees himself as below consideration for Juudit, "the angel-like white lady" (*Juudit* 53).[56] Despite his fierce pride, blackness for him still equals "being born to a life of slavery and wretchedness" (*Juudit* 67; Mügge 69). Even for a rebel such as he, a personally free Maroon, blackness signifies being uneducated, crude, leading a poor, limited and joyless life. In an image repeated in several later texts of Estonian culture (e.g. Juhan Liiv's *The Shadow* (1894) discussed in Chapter Three), Koidula's Eevar later secretly wanders in darkness gazing towards the ball at the manor-house with its splendid lights, beautiful music, laughter, and people in glamorous dress (*Juudit* 67; Mügge 69).

However, admiring Eevar's beauty and dignity, Juudit gradually comes to perceive her own African origins in terms of noble savagery rather than shameful bad blood. As she sees it, quite apart from her one-eighth blackness she is treated like a slave anyway because of her womanhood. In the marriage bargaining between her uncle and the rivals for her hand, William and John, she finds she is traded "like a piece of goods" (*Juudit* 81; Mügge 85), a possession without any independent agency.

Eevar, to the contrary, sees Juudit not as a dependent lady but as a fellow spirit with a steady and firm mind similar to himself, a noble ally in the struggle for freedom. Whereas, in her childhood, Juudit had been enraged with her playmates when they mocked her dark complexion, towards the end of the book she flees to the mountains to live with Eevar outside of Christian marriage, wears traditional Maroon clothes and declares herself an African. Time and again, she symbolically turns the tables on her former kind, accusing them not only of racism, but also of servility, cowardice and beastly lack of decency

---

56 In Mügge's version the mirroring aspects are missing in this scene—Eevar is struck by Juudit as a heavenly lady to whose feet he would like to sink, he does not at this point see her as his soulmate, nor does he contemplate his blackness in the mirror. (51)

and honor in their dealings with the Maroons. Testifying that she was not kidnapped but joined the Maroons voluntarily, she says:

> In your smugness you counted and recorded every drop of blood in my veins, until my blood boiled over! You sneered at the yellow rings in my eye whites, as it spoke of my ancestors' black blood to you, didn't it? Only fear, only greed ever made you hide the mockery and condemnation at the bottom of your hearts! [...] Go, white servant folk, go crawl in front of your idols: I want to be blessed and happy regardless of all profit, wealth, and standing. (*Juudit* 143; *Eduard Montague* 146)[57]

She admires the beauty and dignity of Eevar's tribe and reminds him he comes from a lineage of chieftains (88). "How proud, beautiful and honest in his heart is this [...] unpolished child of nature," she thinks of Eevar, "and how shameless and cowardly are these tame animals dancing in the hall" (*Juudit* 73; Mügge 75). From his side, Eevar's political vision and his newly found determination to fight for racial equality and power-sharing are strongly inspired by his wish to be equal to Juudit, not a source of disappointment or embarrassment for her (*Juudit* 115, 120; Mügge 122-123).

From slaves and savages to an agent of history: the creation of a people

The works by Mügge and Koidula dramatize the controversies on Jamaica as complex. There are characters on different sides who are not overtly positive or negative, but rather overdetermined by their variety of loyalties and concerns. However, it is clear that the main authorial stance supports the cause of the Maroons. The reader is lead to the understanding that the imperial power and the local plantation owners are not doing their duty as fair rulers. The beautiful fertile lands of Jamaica are not shared with the blacks, they have no routes

---

57 "Teie kõrkus luges ja seletas enne seal all iga veretilka minu soonetes, et mo veri kuumas kees! Hirvitates vaatasite minu silmade kollakat ringi: eks ta teile ei tunnistanud minu esivanemate musta verd? Hirm üksi ajas teid, ahnus üksi sundis teie pilkamist ja põlastust sügava südame pohja tagasi! [...] Minge, valged sulased, minge ja roomage oma ebajumalate ees: mina tahan, kasust, varast, seisusest hoolimata, õnnis ja rõõmus olla."
The German version is broadly similar:
"Euer Hochmuth zählte einst die Blutstropfen in meinen Adern es rollte heiss darin! Ihn blicktet mit Hohn auf dem gelben Rand meiner Augen, und nur die Furcht hielt euch ab, oder die Habgier trieb euch an, mir nicht zu sagen, das Achtung oder Spott in euern falschen Herzen war [...] Ich werde glücklich sein [...] mit Dem vereint, der weisser und reiner ist, wie euer Gott und die Tausse eurer Priester euch jemals schaffen können." (146)

to power, to fair justice or to self-realization. Thus the slaves and the Maroons have no option but to unite forces, to take initiative and to fight for the betterment of their life.

But how to do that? How to empower, motivate or organize people whom their oppressors see as not quite human—as half-beasts (Koidula 41; Mügge 37) or as atrocious criminals outside normal ethical consideration (Koidula 104; Mügge 107)—and who have internalized the sense of inferiority in comparison to the whites? This is a question that is much more important for *Juudit* than for *Eduard Montague*. Koidula makes a number of adaptations to answer those questions and her lines of thought mainly relate to the questions of people's education, freedom and unity/solidarity.

Koidula's Eevar appeals to his god: "Why must all the good of all the honored life, all the educated life that counts in this world bear their [white] color?"[58] (68; the sentence not there in Mügge). Education, "stroking of the mind" (43; not there in Mügge), grants a person individual joy, self-confidence and freedom, but it is also related to collective political emancipation. The repeated thematic connection between education and freedom (similar to *Inca*) is especially vivid in Eevar's last conversation with Juudit. There Koidula has added to Mügge ideas and rhetoric typical of her writing and of the Estonian national movement generally (cf. e.g. Jansen *Carl* 154-155).

> "Our kin too has the strength to develop an independent educated cultural life; we too have the strength to work on ourselves and to make us equal to the boastful, prideful peoples who for all their grandeur have not had the generosity to do anything for *us*, for *our* good, for *our* freedom from the kindness of their hearts! They have treated us like they treat their horses and cattle: they have fed and stroked us for *their own* sake, but if we would rather starve to death in freedom than live on their piece of bread on their leash, they call us stubborn, they revile us to all the world, they summon "law and justice" to help them against us!" (170; not there in Mügge; emphasis in the original).[59]

---

58 "Miks peab kõik auusa, kõik haritud elu nende [valget] karva kandma, kui ta maksab maa peal?"
59 "Ka meie rahwasugu põu jõuab haritud, isewäelist waimuelu kaswatada; ka meie jõuame ise eneste kallal tööd teha, mis meid tõiste hoopleja, uhkete rahwaste wääriliseks tõstab, kes kõige selle suurustamisega siiski *meie* kasuks, *meie* wabaduseks lahkest meelest ei ole midagi raatsinud teha! Juudit, n'ad on teinud meitega nagu oma hobuste ja weistega: nad on meid silitanud ja söötnud *oma* pärast, ja kui meie enne wabaduses nälga tahame surra, kui kui nende köie otsa köidetud leiwatükist elada, siis sõimawad meid kangekaelseks, siis laimawad meid maailma ees, siis kutsuvad "õigust ja seadust" meie wasta appi!"

In connection with the topic of education and similarly to *Inca*, the unity of content and form should be remarked upon again. Although Mügge's version offers a lot of historical detail and analysis in the right key for Koidula, she still adds her typical "historical frame" to the story. While *Eduard Montague* starts *in medias res* and blends the extensive commentary on the world events mostly in the conversations between the characters, Koidula begins with an additional six-page essay and tells the reader in her journalistic style about the slave trade and the introduction of slavery in the Caribbean; the cultural and political history of the Jamaican Maroons; The French Revolution, the Touissant uprising and the creation of the Republic of Haiti (3-8).

The strong emphasis on the value of the unity of the people as the necessary basis to strive for freedom and development is also something that Koidula contributes and that is absent in this strong form in Mügge. While Mügge does introduce the topic of the enmity between the Maroons and the Igbos and the efforts to overcome it, it becomes a much more generalized point in Eevar's final conversation with Juudit. He rejoices that the Igbos are joining their Maroon "brothers":

> They have cut themselves off from the binds of the evil of the sly white folk. They have understood that only *unity* within a people makes a people strong, unity in the heart, unity in action! They are beginning to note that a people cannot achieve freedom, where the individuals cannot forsake their own good for the good of the *people*, where kin doesn't know to stand up for kin, when the wise ones cannot give way to even wiser ones, when the rightful ones cannot put their right at the feet of the people! (172; not there in Mügge; emphases in the original)[60]

The quoted passages immediately preceding the finale of the story make the Estonian version of the story confusing. The patriotic lovers' conversation is interrupted by William's sudden assault. The reader will not learn the conclusion of the prolonged fight episode, nor will most of the characters of the novella. Instead, after a narrative ellipsis, the Brits find the bloodhounds and William killed in a scene of carnage. The dead William is clutching Juudit's torn-out hair

---

60 Nemad on endid lahti löönud kawala walge rahwa õelusesidemeist: nad on aru saanud, et *ühendus* oma rahwaga üksi rahwast kangeks teeb, ühendus südames, ühendus tegudes! Nad hakkawad märkama, et see rahwas priiust ei teeni, kus üksikud ei oska oma kasu unustada *rahwa* kasu pärast, kus sugu ei moista sugu eest seista, kus targad ei oska targemate eest taganeda, kus õiged ei oska oma õigust rahwa õiguse jalge ette maha panna!

and rags of her dress and has a Maroon sword in his heart. The lovers will never be found, either dead or alive. In the final passages of the epilogue they become a folk legend in the minds of the Igbo slaves and in the aesthetics of the work.

In Mügge, this denouement could be considered satisfactory if we read it as a dark postcolonial novella of star-crossed lovers and fated passions—the bittersweet otherworldly end would be appropriate to the genre. However, it rings illogical against the background of the political ideas advanced by Eevar just before William appeared, as well as against his and Juudit's earlier statements that they will fight until the end and, if need be, die with their kin. If the couple indeed somehow died after killing William and the dogs, why were their bodies not found? If the couple escaped, as the reader is strongly encouraged to believe, why were they never seen again? How could they forsake their people for personal safety just after declaring patriotic unity and individual dedication to the good of the people the ultimate values? The attempted replacement of the slave/savage double with the idea of a people ends in a conundrum. The idea of a united people disappears and the noble savage gives up the liberation of the slaves, yet continues to haunt them.

Yet, the meaning of a story ought to be sought not only in the close reading/deconstruction of the text, but also in its reception and the horizon of expectations of its readers. As far as it is known, none of Koidula's readers complained about *Juudit*'s ending. Her Finnish friend Antti Almberg praises the psychologically complex characters of *Juudit*, but saves most of his enthusiasm for exactly the patriotic political discussion between Eevar and Juudit described above. "I wish that it [*Juudit*] should bring your people the benefit that you intended with it," he concludes his remarks to Koidula, without making any comment about the ending of the novella (Almberg 80).[61]

Legends can sometimes turn into identity-transforming and politically mobilizing mythic narratives for a collective (Schöpflin, "The Functions" 22). The enigmatic conclusion of *Juudit* can, among other things, call to mind the archetypal plot in which a hero departs from History to Myth but gives hope for his resurrection and return to save his people. The Estonian national epic *Kalevipoeg* that firstly appeared in popular edition in 1862 ends exactly with such a motif.[62]

---

61 Letter from 11 August 1871.
62 The last stanza of *Kalevipoeg* reads: But one day an age will dawn / when all spills, at both their ends, / will burst forth into flame; / and this stark fire will sever / the vise of stone from Kalevipoeg's hand. / Then the son of Kalev will come home / to bring his children happiness / and build Estonia's life anew (Kreutzwald 266).

From a Historical Romance to a Political Tale of Warning: Koidula's *Martinique and Corsica* and Mühlbach's *The Empress Josephine*

Luise Mühlbach (real name Clara Mundt) was a prolific author, highly popular not only in Germany but also in the United States in her time. She supported *Vormärz* ideas and married Theodor Mundt, an influential member of Young Germany and a friend of Theodor Mügge.[63] After 1850 Mühlbach mainly wrote in the genre of historical novel. These novels touch upon political issues, but their contemporary reader was primarily attracted by their emotional depiction of the (fictionalized) life affairs of prominent historical statesmen and -women. Mühlbach's take on the genre was thus quite different from that of Walter Scott whose protagonists are all fictitious, come from ordinary walks of life and have no exceptional capabilities. While Scott and his followers want to give a sideways "ordinary" glance at the grand figures and big processes of history, Mühlbach rather presents the private side of famous historical actors (usually rulers) and its impact on public life. The German scholar Hartmut Eggert emphasizes the chasm between the public and the private in Mühlbach's vision:

> In the backstage of the ceremonial public life and political events there opens [...] another world [...] This is the world where we can see "real" faces, "true" feelings and secret wishes. [...] But in the world where things are explained through private life the situations lose complexity and multifariousness, everything is reduced to simple structures and primary relationships. (136)

Mühlbach's own account of her agenda seems not entirely far from Koidula's aims. In the introduction to her *Old Fritz and the New Era* (*Alte Fritz und die neue Zeit*, 1867) Mühlbach says she wants to popularize history, share its riches hitherto accessible only for scholarly readers with everyone, bring it closer to the tumult of the present world (McClain and Kurth-Vogt: 929). However, among the three texts discussed in this chapter, Koidula changes Mühlbach's much more than the others. She focuses on different topics and creates an entirely different plot. Mühlbach dramatizes history by making historical figures private persons with universal human characteristics. Koidula is pri-

---

63 *Vormärz* refers to a period of German history that preceded the anti-feudalist and anti-autocratic 1848 March Revolution. It was a time when ideas of political liberalization and national sovereignty fermented in the states of the German Confederation.

marily concerned with the dynamics of historical processes with the emphasis on trying to understand the *collective* actors, including the potential role of a people in history.

In her 28 November 1873 letter to Almberg she says of *Martinique and Corsica* (again without mentioning any source material): "I have written a book about the first French Revolution" (*Koidula ja Almbergi kirjavahetus* 106). This indicates what aspect interested her in *Empress Josephine* and why she chose this novel for her rewriting. Josephine and Napoleon's love story is left to one side to communicate Koidula's take on the French Revolution, its reasons, consequences and larger lessons. The published part of *Martinique and Corsica* does not even get to the first meeting of the celebrity couple, the last event described is the discontented crowd's march on Versaille, 5 October 1789.

The ban on publishing the second half of the book was motivated exactly by its topical subject. As we know, Koidula's adaptation was written at the height of the Estonian national movement. While the faraway projection space of the New World enabled the sympathetic among the authorities to ignore the political implications if they wanted to, the French Revolution was much closer to home. Koidula's censor Mihhail Suigusaar, a fellow Estonian, explains to her in an apologetic letter: "it is such a time now that Republicans and Democrats are much feared and especially those among Estonians" (qtd. in Salupere 389).

Geography and History: Koidula's Adaptation Strategies

Koidula almost always changed the title when she adapted her sources, signalling the shift in the emphasis of the story. On this occasion the geographical names, of course, allude to Mühlbach's main characters: Josephine was born on Martinique and Napoleon on Corsica. However, the change of the title also creates a closer connection to the Estonian situation. Both Mühlbach and Koidula characterize the islands in terms of their being at the periphery of the French state. In Mühlbach this mainly has the role of adding exotic flavor to her main story. Koidula's version, on the other hand, adds a short overview of the history of both islands that is not there in the German novel. In the case of Corsica she specifically concentrates on its nationalist struggle against France.

Both authors talk about the educational inferiority of the peripheral islanders in comparison to the cultural center, Paris, but the topic is particularly developed by Koidula. Only *Martinique* emphasizes how Josephine "studied day and night" to become equal to the Parisian ladies and gentlemen (35). Thus, one aspect of Koidula's retelling is to make Napoleon's and Josephine's story a story about people from disadvantaged and small nations achieve emancipation and glory thanks to their extra effort. Similarly to Koidula's other New World adaptations, *Martinique and Corsica* also underlines the importance of the education for the slaves. While Mühlbach emphasizes teaching them the Catechism, in Koidula's version Josephine simply teaches the black children to read (Mühlbach 16-17; Koidula, *Martinique* 10). Like *Juudit*'s Jamaican Africans, the Martinique islanders offer the Estonian reader an opportunity to identify, and that not only in a universal humanist way but via direct social and historical parallels.

However, as mentioned above, the strategies of rewriting *Empress Josephine* are different from the previous adaptations discussed. Here Koidula restrucures the whole text in order to convey her ideas and concerns about historical change. On the one hand, *Martinique* metaphorically personifies history and seems to attribute it an agenda of its own (87), sometimes incomprehensible and beyond ordinary interference (3). On the other hand, the text is meticulous in trying to understand the particular social, political and intellectual reasons for historical events on the human level and to push the Estonian reader to draw lessons for the future. The first chapters add the history of the titular islands to the German version, plus short digressions on the US struggle for independence. The following ones go into a detailed discussion of French history leading up to the revolution: the disastrous reign of the Bourbon dynasty (Ch. 5); the situation in the city of Paris (Ch. 6); the ideas of the Enlightenment philosophers and their impact (Ch. 7). The descriptions of the carefree life of Marie Antoinette, the main thread of Mühlbach's narrative, are only blended in fragmentarily by Koidula. While Mühlbach highlights the personality of the queen, thus making it of major significance for the course of events, Koidula focuses on the financial and administrative problems in France and the irresponsible behaviour of the court. *Martinique*'s last published chapters are about the storming of the Bastille and the march to Versaille whereas the German version gives a much more detailed amount of the affair of the diamond necklace, the queen's suffering and Josephine's return to Martinique.

The extensive differences in comparison to Mühlbach's novel lead to the hypothesis that Koidula must have had additional sources for her historical deliberations. Indeed, our research discovered that Koidula's text strongly draws upon two books in her family library: Heinrich Dittmar's *World History for School and Homeschool* (*Die Weltgeschichte für den Schul- und Selbstunterricht*, 1859) and the third part of Friedrich Rösselt's *Textbook for Girls' Schools and Homeschool* (*Lehrbuch der Weltgeschichte für Töchterschulen und zum Privatunterricht*, 1858) (Monticelli, Peiker and Mits 931). Koidula characteristically rewrites the textbooks in her polemical and journalistic style and adds dramatic tension to the narrative. More importantly in this context, she again substantially changes the central focus. Dittmar concentrates on the established elite and on the National Assembly, Rösselt on the intrigues of the Duke of Orléans. Koidula's attention, on the other hand, is on the life world and expectations of the people and the role of the mutinous crowds during the revolution. These aspects are at the center of her historical analysis that she wants to communicate to her Estonian readers. It is significant that her account of the rebels in Paris is different from those of the New World slave uprisings in her *Inca* and *Juudit*. *Martinique* dramatizes the potential dark side of popular mobilization. The Paris cause goes disastrously wrong and ends in scenes of Gothic-style horror, as Koidula sees it.

A People Grown Savage

In *Martinique*'s analysis, the French Revolution has valid and understandable reasons, nevertheless the crowd's activity does not lead to a better social order, but to a disastrous cul-de-sac. How and why does that happen? could it be done more successfully? Koidula's account seems to ask.

Martinique first discusses the pre-revolution relationship between the rulers and the subjects. Ch. 5 that reconstructs the revolutionary situation emphasizes the enormous chasm between the Old Regime elite and the impoverished people. According to Koidula, (differently from Rösselt and Dittmar) the great "dividing wall" was established right after the death of Henri IV and just kept growing under the kings that followed him (45-46). She describes the misery of the "tortured [French] people" (49) in similar terms and with the same sarcastic rhetoric that she applied to the the New World cases of oppression in *Inca* and *Juudit*. For the elite, "God had created the people to pay the taxes, to honor and fear their rulers, even if the reward was just hunger and tattered rags for clothes" (46).[64] The court moved to Versaille "to spare them from hearing the screams of those chased and killed with sword, fire and blood" (49).[65]

However, in *Martinique* Koidula describes the conflict as turning into a terrifying savage rampage, devoid of meaningful human content (100-106). While she sees the chasm between the Old Regime rulers and the people as a just reason for the unrest in France, Koidula also finds fault with the inflammatory

---

64 "rahwas oliwad Jumalast loodud, maksusi maksma ja riigi ülemaid kartma ja auustama, olgu ka nälgend näo ja kaltsus hilpude eest"
65 "siis ei kuulnud ta nende kisendamist, keda mõek, tuli ja weri tagaajasiwad ja surmasiwad"

use of Enlightenment ideas as well as with the irresponsible leaders of the Paris crowds in action.

Martinique introduces the topic of the Enlightenment thinkers' impact translating Mühlbach's passage on young Napoleon's interest in "the intellectual work of the prominent men of the time" (Koidula 74). While Mühlbach merely lists the names of the authors whom Napoleon read and moves on to the story of his first love affair (156-157), Koidula skips the romance and instead goes into an extended discussion of Enlightenment ideas and their connection with the revolutionary initiative. The names in Koidula's list (Voltaire, Montesquieu, Rousseau, Diderot, D'Alembert) is different and more political than Mühlbach's (Voltaire, Rousseau, Corneille, Racine, Montaigne, Abbé Raynal). Altogether, Koidula emphasizes the directly political aspects in the ideas of the Enlighteners: "the limitation of the might and power of the monarch, the rights of the people instead of the inherited rights based on status, abolition of the deceitful powers of the clergy to distort the matters between the rulers, the church and the people" (75).[66] However, Koidula's own attitude is cautious and critical. Even if she considers the gist of the Enlightenment ideas to go in the right direction, she believes they became destructive because their reception did not go hand in hand with the political development of the nation:

> These teachings probably would not have done much harm to a state and a government that had been educating each other reciprocally for generations and reached the kind of emancipation of mind that can separate [...] the wheat from the chaff—to such a self-confident state they would have done a lot of good instead. (76, missing in Koidula's sources)[67]

In other words, the problem is not in the inflammatory ideas as such. It is rather, firstly, that the French lower classes lacked the capacity for critical thought and political experience to responsibly take their share in the governing of the state. Secondly, the ruling elites were equally lacking in political and moral maturity: instead of educating their people and promoting the development of a modern society, they only had their own status and short-sighted in-

---

66 "kuningliku wäe ja woimuse wähendust, rahwaõigust päritud seisuse-õiguse asemel, peteliku kirikuwäe kaotamist, moondamist poolitika, kiriku ja rahwa asjus"
67 "Ühe riigile ja tema walitsusele, kes põlwest põlwe iseennast wastastiku niisuguse waimuwabaduse poole oleks kaswatanud, kes wilja kestadest ... oleks osanud lahutada, niisuguse iseeneses kindla riigile ei oleks niisugused õpetused wast mitte wäga suurt kahjo saatnud, waid wäga palju head."

terests in mind. Again then, we are back to the idea of the necessity of a people becoming educated, knowledgeable and capable of critical thought—the same topics central to Koidula's earlier New World stories and to the discussions of the national activists in the Estonian context. If a people is not capable of organizing itself in a civilized manner and its rulers are morally bankrupt and blind to the changing world, then the Enlightenment ideas, Koidula thinks, will probably lead to a horrible disaster.

In comparison to *Inca* and *Juudit*, Koidula's pessimism and her concern for a popular uprising going wrong, is drastic. She describes the rebellious people at Bastille and Versailles as a "child entrusted with a sharp knife", so that the result can be nothing but "blood spilling" (102). As mentioned above, Koidula (in contrast to her sources) puts the rebels in the center, but her accounts of the crowd-led initiatives consistently describe the people involved as "uncoordinated mobs", "vagrants without features", "howling, screaming packs", "screaming packs of predatory animals", "blood-thirsty horrible street vagrants" etc. (100-106). Her history book sources do mention the bloodlust of the crowds gone wild, but they are very far from the repetitive and evocative descriptions in *Martinique* (cf. Rösselt 384; Dittmar 287). In her version Koidula clearly dramatizes the notion that it is not only the colonizers and aristocrats that behave in a brutal and savage manner. The *misérables* can also turn into "ignoble savages"—as was indicated by Garlieb Merkel in the case of Estonian and Latvian serfs.

This raises the question how the African Jamaicans and the native Americans differ from the outraged people of Paris for Koidula. Certainly, the issue is not only her condemnation of violence—she empathizes with the Maroons and the Peruvians when they take weapons to fight for their rights. We can speculate that one important distinction is the character of the conflicted parties. In France the conflict is between the French "themselves", tearing apart a potential budding modern nation. In the New World the Peruvians and the Jamaican Africans are differentiated from their oppressors by their history, culture, and language as well as by their class status and appearance. In the case of the Maroons, they are even geographically separated, having their own territory in the mountains. Thus, they are seen as colonized people who could well create their own separate nations if the colonizers refuse to share their power to govern.

However, there is more. Not only does *Martinique* depict the crowds in Paris as savage and immature and their established rulers as ignorant, despotic, and spoilt, the fault is also with the new leaders of the people who emerge during the struggle. They are not politically responsible persons, but rather "such men that lack any boundaries and limits"; they revel in the havoc they urge the crowds to bring about (82). On the other hand, Koidula's New World leaders in the earlier sections are dedicated and authoritative, with ideals and with depth to their political thinking. They stem from ancient ruling families of the colonized culture and are helped by the sympathetic and progressive-minded among the colonizing groups. In this combination they educate their communities towards becoming well-coordinated civilized peoples, capable of self-government. The leaders themselves also develop through the interaction and grow into their roles gradually. Thus, when these proto-nations fight for their rights, it is a just war, not a mindless bloodshed. As Koidula sees it, the opposite happens in Paris. The Paris crowds get no guidance, nor can they educate and organize themselves independently in the course of their struggle—thus the horror.

During the period Koidula was working parallelly on both *Juudit* and *Martinique* she was also organizing the first Estonian Song Festival (1869), mentioned in Chapter One, together with her father and other national activists. A comparison can be made here with her adaptations: the festival was inspired by the Baltic German Song Festivals and officially dedicated to the Czar, yet it was a statement of Estonian emancipation—the first time that Estonians openly dramatized their claim to be a people, rather than a peasant underclass or an ethnic fragment. About 16 000 people took part as choirs, brass bands, administrators, or audience, while the whole population was about 750 000 in the present-day Estonian area. We may assume that Koidula gave a lot of thought to the issues of popular mobilization and leaders' responsibility at that time. After the festival, the quality of the music was praised, but significantly the Baltic German accounts mainly express astonishment at the smooth coordination of the festival which unfolded without any confusion or security incidents (Salupere 145). This is understandable, "the country people" had never created a cultural event even close to that scale before. The organizers were jubilant and relieved. Due to her early death, Koidula did not have to take a stand on the 1905 revolution (see Chapter One) where both uncoordinated and coordinated violence pushed Estonia to a new phase of modernity.

* * *

Translation, adaptation and bricolage characterize Koidula's politically charged texts discussed in this chapter, and, as I argue, the 19th-century Estonian National Awakening culture more generally. Most of the sources of adaptation are in the German language, but it is important to note that the local Baltic German text pool was not that influential at all. The better educated activists' knowledge of the German language and culture enabled them to follow manifold political and cultural perspectives in Germany, and, through the German mediation, in the wider world in change. Koidula takes a mental leap to interpret this world for the Estonian National Awakening, considering both Europe and colonies, centers and peripheries. It is clear from the comparative analysis that Koidula's adaptations are not passive "parroting" copies of their examples—rather, the translator has an active relationship, sometimes a struggle, with them. She tries to assimilate them with mixed results—the source texts themselves are contradictory or politically reticent, and the Estonian ones also have to live not only with the censorship rules, but also "in the midst of incomprehensibility", unpredictability, unease.

As we will see, the central questions and the tropes discussed in this chapter will appear in new reincarnations in a number of works considered in the next ones. The discourses are by no means confined only to literature (the main reference point of this study), but the captivating plot lines, empathy-inspiring characters and figurative power that fictional works can offer do make them a major vehicle of sharing these discourses among wide audiences.

Chapter Three. *Bildung* in the Image of Modernity: Estonian Narratives of Formation, 1896–1993

This chapter will focus on the tropes, themes and plot trajectories employed in Estonian *Bildung*-narratives across time, focusing on five fictional works in particular. The analysis of the Estonian texts will be placed against the comparative foil of the classical Western European *Bildungsroman* (novel of formation) model on the one hand, and the postcolonial/belated modernity model on the other.[1]

The German concept of *Bildung* is much older than that of *Bildungsroman* and has a number of different connotations. It is rooted in the pre-modern ideas of the man carrying in his soul the image (*Bild*) of God, after whom he is fashioned and which he must nurture in himself. The concept acquires a variety of new associations and significance at the end of the 18th century in the thought of authors such as Herder, Goethe, Schiller, Wilhelm von Humboldt, broadly coming to designate a secular-humanist ideal of (self-)cultivation and (self-)formation. According to this theory, each human being carries an irreplaceable individuality, which, however, can and ought to be developed towards harmony and maturity only through enriching engagement with the diversity of the world. In the 19th century the idea of *Bildung* "dominated thinking about subject, subjectivity and subject formation" (Castle 30) in Western cultures and it has never quite lost this influence on the modern mind.

Furthermore, since the modern conception of *Bildung* in Herder's work, the idea of individual *Bildung* has been paralleled by that at the collective level: like

---

1 See "Introduction" for the discussion of the terms "postcolonial" and "belated modernity". Colonization and belatedness of modernization of a society in many cases coincide. Even where they do not, in either case the indigenous experience of modernization is strongly shaped by the pressured relationship to the earlier or more powerful models of modernity, be that the colonizers have imposed them by force, or local elites rapidly imported in the race to modernize, or both, or something in-between. As "postcolonial *Bildungsroman*" is an already established category I will stick to it with the assumption that it also relates to the experience of belatedness.

Chapter Three. Bildung in the Image of Modernity

each person, each culture or people (*Volk*) is also unique and unfolds in time through a distinctive *Bildung* process. On the one hand, Herder wanted to write "the universal history of the Bildung of the world" (qtd. in Boes, *Formative* 51), and "explicitly connected the concept of Bildung with an understanding of history as a universal and transformative current, a force that affects all of reality simultaneously and sweeps people, nations, and even the entire world into an unknown future" (Boes, *Formative* 51). On the other hand, this modern perception of history as dynamic is connected to the "emerging sense of the nation" and to the belief that that the ideals and drives of *Bildung* imprinted in different collectivities were not universal, but could be "almost infinitely varied" (Boes, *Formative* 52). These two aspects were not seen as contradictory: as Pheng Cheah points out, "[m]any German philosophers of national Bildung (e.g., Herder, Schiller, Humboldt, and Fichte) were also cosmopolitanists who saw the nation and its culture as the most effective actualization of universal ethical ideals" (*Spectral* 8).

The beginning of the *Bildungsroman* genre is commonly retrospectively dated to J. W. Goethe's 1795 novel *Wilhelm Meister's Apprenticeship* (*Wilhelm Meisters Lehrjahre*, 1795-1796). In his *Life of Schleiermacher* (*Das Leben Schleiermachers*, 1870) Wilhelm Dilthey famously conceptualized Goethe's text as the archetypal *Bildungsroman* and talked about other novels of similar characteristics as the "Wilhelm Meister school" (Hardin xiv). In *Experience and Poetry* (*Das Erlebnis und die Dichtung*, 1906) Dilthey further explains that in a *Bildungsroman* "[a] regulated development within the life of the individual is observed, each of its stages has its own intrinsic value and is at the same time the basis for a higher stage. The dissonances and conflicts of life appear as the necessary growth points through which the individual must pass on his way to maturity and harmony" (qtd. in Redfield 40). Since the 1960s, a number of critics and theorists have studied Goethe's *Wilhelm Meister* and other classical *Bildungsromane* as individual literary texts and convincingly underlined their intricate poetics that would allow more complex and less teleological readings of novels traditionally included in the genre (e.g. Boes *Formative* further discussed below and Saariluoma, *Erzählstruktur*). However, this has not refuted the widespread international reception of the classical *Bildungsroman* as an exemplary literary paradigm of the changes of the 18th and 19th centuries and the ideological currents of the Enlightenment and Romanticism period.

As Tobias Boes, a comparative scholar of the genre points out, the term *Bildungsroman*, though extraordinarily proliferant and productive in literary studies internationally, is also a highly vexed and therefore often disorienting one (Boes, "Modernist" 230). Some scholars support a restrictive usage, reserving the term only for works showing a specific aesthetic ideology, usually associated with German-language literature and/or the 18th-19th-century period in European literature (Boes, "Modernist" 230-232). However, especially since the 1980s and 1990s with the blossoming of Feminist and Postcolonial Studies, the definition of *Bildungsroman* has expanded to include coming-of-age narratives that sometimes "bear only cursory resemblance to nineteenth-century European models" (Boes, "Modernist" 231).

It is not my intention to engage in the normative debates on the appropriate genre nominator or taxonomy in this case. Rather, my approach specifically builds upon Franco Moretti's idea in *The Way of the World* that the body of works that depict the *Bildung* of their protagonists can fruitfully be studied as a "'symbolic form' of modernity" (5). Moretti casts *Bildungsroman* as a genre that narrativizes, explains and domesticates historical changes and problems relating to modernity and modernization by shaping the experience of becoming modern into a particular model. That is, the story of the social and spiritual maturation of a young individual, youth being the emblematic trope for modernizing change. The *Bildungsroman* genre, so Moretti, relies on the construction of the concept of youth as an apprenticeship, at the end of which the protagonist of the novel is to find his or her (traditionally usually his) place as a fully-formed citizen of a modern society and of modern history. Boes criticizes Moretti for essentializing the meaning of *Bildungsroman*: he takes Moretti's "symbolic form" to mean a signifier that simply reflects/represents a material social order, so that *Bildungsroman* becomes an allegory of the historical world, rather than a performative voice there (*Formative* 22-24; 31). While Moretti's use is perhaps in places open to that reading, I employ "symbolic form" in line with Ernst Cassirer (the source of Moretti's term) who sees symbolic forms as historically conditioned but dynamic tools of meaning-making through which human beings organize, articulate and (re)construct their worlds of experience (see e.g. Cassirer 221).

Secondly, I proceed from the idea that narratives of formation in the postcolonial world do relate to the Western *Bildungsroman* tradition (even if in many cases indirectly and remotely), and that they have become widespread and significant outside Western Europe exactly as a tool for addressing the problematics of modernity. As elaborated in Chapter One, Pheng Cheah analyzes the correspondences between the 18th-19th-century German thought of *Bildung* and the decolonizing narratives of "spectral" nationality in the postcolonial world. Maria Helena Lima observes: "*Bildungsroman*, a literary form that seems to have outlived its usefulness and become virtually defunct in the European context" has assumed "a new and viable identity 'overseas'" (14). The poetics of the postcolonial *Bildungsroman*, although greatly varied, generally differs from the forms that developed in Western Europe. Different postcolonial cultures, which (at least initially) found themselves at the more or less painful receiving end of Western modernity have often produced *Bildungsromane* which deal with exactly *that* experience of modernity, modernity perceived as alien and imposed.

Thus I use comparative genre studies as a broad framework of heuristic relevance in order to analyze the specific ways particular texts central to the Estonian cultural tradition have emplotted and troped modernizing change through the stories of the life and *Bildung* of their individual protagonists. It also interests me how each of these texts has been received and interpreted in the wider socio-cultural sphere during different historical periods. The aim is to enable new insight into the reception and cultural working-through of a postcolonial and belated rapid modernization.

In their thematic content, and even more in their plot structure, Estonian narratives of *Bildung* central in the culture closely resemble those in the postcolonial world. Thus I will discuss four of the selected five Estonian *Bildung*-narratives (Juhan Liiv's *The Shadow* (*Vari*, 1894); Silvia Rannamaa's two-part *Kadri* (1959) and *Stepmother* (*Kasuema*, 1963); Jaan Kross's *The Czar's Madman*; (*Keisri hull*, 1978); Tõnu Õnnepalu's *Border State* (*Piiririik*, 1993)) in the postcolonial scheme. This enables me to foreground how the development trajectory and the rites of passage of a protagonist are modelled: how and why s/he fails to perform the process of social integration in the manner of a classical *Bildungsroman* protagonist.

As a second move, however, I would also like to pursue the question, in the context of narratives of *Bildung*, whether there are ways of "overcoming" postcolonialism: are there postcolonial *Bildung*-narratives that construct recognizably *local* patterns of modern socialization, i.e. a local model of modernity and of ways for an individual to "survive" it? To this purpose, the last section of the chapter breaks with the chronology to take up Tammsaare's independence-period novel *Truth and Justice* (*Tõde ja õigus*, 1926–1933). I will discuss it as a "post-postcolonial" *Bildungsroman*: a work rooted in postcolonial poetics and axiology but in its last volume also transcending it.

The Western European *Bildungsroman*

The Western European *Bildungsroman* plot goes back to the topos of initiation into adulthood, as it exists in some form in all cultures. However, it also specifically responds to the modernizing sociopolitical change, the striving for nation-building and the perceptions of time and historicity that emerged at the end of the 18th and the beginning of the 19th century. Mikhail Bakhtin has famously claimed that a true *Bildungsroman* produces in its protagonist "an image of *man growing* in *national-historical time*" (*Speech Genres* 25). His individual path of coming-of-age emplots the formation of a modern autonomous person, but it also has wider social significance: he

> emerges along with the world and he reflects the historical emergence of the world itself. He is no longer within an epoch, but on the border between two epochs, at the transition point from one another. The transition is accomplished in him and through him. [...] The organizing force held by the future is therefore extremely great here—and this is not, of course, the private biographical future, but the historical future. (*Speech Genres* 23; Bakhtin's italics)

The ideal-typical plot associated with the traditional Western European *Bildungsroman* would be that the young protagonist leaves home, frequently with a conflict between generations involved; he goes into the wider world, often travels from province to metropole, there he goes through a pattern of experiences, develops and matures as an individual, and is then either reconciled with society, or at least consolidates his attitude towards it (Nyatetu-Waigwa 1; Buckley 18). The two poles that determine the plot and the moral of the *Bildungsroman* genre are the self and the collective, the two factors the dynamics between which is radically altered with the coming of modernity. The *Bildungsroman* approaches and re-negotiates the specifically modern dilemmas between personal autonomy and membership in a collective, between liberty and happiness, between innovation and socio-cultural reproduction, dramatizing them as the dynamics between the protagonist's desire for individuation and self-fulfillment and his duty of socialization; his youthful restlessness and his drive towards maturity and eventual re-integration in the social order around him. (cf. Moretti, *The Way*, especially 15-16, 23-24)

In our context it is important to remember Franco Moretti's emphasis on what is quintessentially modern about the *Bildungsroman*: it is not enough for the protagonist simply to accept his society and follow its "'standards of normality'" (Moretti, *The Way* 16). His acceptance and integration must be perceived as voluntary and satisfying: "it is not enough for modern bourgeois society simply to subdue the drives that oppose the standards of 'normality'. It is also necessary that as a 'free individual', not as a fearful subject, but as a convinced citizen, one perceives the social norms as one's own" (16). "It is not enough that the social order is 'legal'; it must also appear *symbolically legitimate*" (16, Moretti's italics). The finale and the outcome of a classical *Bildungsroman* is the "happiness" of the protagonist, typically in the context of concluding with a marriage—an obviously suitable trope for a circumstance where a modern free individual willingly limits his own freedom, symbolically "a 'pact' between the individual and the world" (22). "From the late eighteenth century on," observes Moretti, "marriage becomes the model for a new type of *social contract*: one no longer sealed by forces located outside of the individual (such as status), but founded on a sense of 'individual obligation'" (22, Moretti's italics).

Furthermore, the symbolic function of marriage is confirmed by the *Bildungsroman* marriages frequently being bourgeois-aristocracy *"mésalliances"*, which are eventually accepted by both families. As they (re)create harmony between the classes, these unions prove that "the French revolution could have been avoided" (*The Way* 64), that a modern social symbiosis can function based on a pact of free will and mutual understanding. Despite its obvious socio-cultural symbolism, the marriage trope is also indicative of *Bildungsroman*'s focus through and preoccupation with the personalized, with the individual and the everyday, at the expense of a wider political vision. The grand historical changes are domesticated and brought down to human size.

In Tobias Boes's argument the striving towards individual and social/national harmony in the classical Western *Bildungsromane* should be seen more fruitfully as performative and didactic rather than unambivalently teleologically realized in individual works (as Moretti's readings seem to imply). Boes cites in his support Karl Morgenstern (1770–1852), a professor at Tartu (then Dorpat) University in today's Estonia, then part of Czarist Russia. Morgenstern coined the term *Bildungsroman* in 1812, long before Dilthey's (independent) influential formulations quoted above, also mainly in response to Goethe's *Wilhelm Meister*.[2] According to Morgenstern, "[w]e may call a novel a Bildungsroman first and foremost on account of its content, because it represents the development of the hero in its beginning and progress *to a certain stage of* completion, but also, second, because this depiction promotes the development of the reader to a greater extent than any other kind of novel" (qtd. in Boes, *Formative* 27, my emphasis). Morgenstern celebrates *Wilhelm Meister* for "presenting German life, German thought and the

---

2 Morgenstern published on his theory of *Bildungsroman* in 1820 in the Tartu journal *Inländisches Museum* and in the serial publication connected to it, *Neues Museum der teutschen Provinzen Russlands*. However, his work did not gain wide currency and remained unknown for later *Bildungsroman* studies until it was rediscovered by Fritz Martini in 1961.

morals of our time through its hero, its scenery and development" (qtd. in Boes, *Formative* 2-3) long before there is a German nation state.

However, whether one reads Western *Bildungsromane* as "revealing" or—confidently and convincingly—"constructing" a vision of modern national culture/state becomes a matter of nuance in comparison to the postcolonial model (as will be shown in the next subchapter). The Diltheyan and the Morgensternian versions of critical tradition seem to share a fairly similar sense of historical progress, consensual social integration as an ideal (even if not realized) and cultural self-integrity. Boes himself, even if his readings add complexity to the discussion, echoes Bakhtin by saying that "the Bildungsroman is a genre connected more than any other to the rise of modern nationalism" (*Formative* 3)—having in mind the works, their critical reception, and general cultural relevance.

Nonetheless, before turning to the non-Western-European models of the genre, it is important to note that the Western European *Bildungsroman* ought not to be viewed as a unified category either, but rather as one ramified both in national-cultural lines as well as temporally. Moretti's *The Way of the World* compares and contrasts the development of the German, English and French models through the late 18th and the 19th century. Most authors agree that whereas the classical German tradition lays special emphasis on the inner self-cultivation of the protagonist, its French and English followers are more interested in scrutinizing the socialization and social mobility of the hero in his historical world (Castle 7, 12). Furthermore, a number of Western modernist *Bildungsromane* can also resemble, in some aspects, the postcolonial model as they reassess and cast doubt upon the idea of the maturing subject and/or the possibilities of the protagonist's harmonious socialization in a world of accelerating globalization through expansive imperialism 1880–1920 (Castle; Esty).[3]

However, Castle's study *Reading the Modernist Bildungsroman* also convincingly argues in the context of English and Irish modernisms that the European modernist authors harken back to the "Goethean and Humboldtian ideals of aesthetico-spiritual Bildung" in order to criticize the socio-cultural as well as aesthetic challenges of their time (47). The variety of *Bildung* developed by German thinkers such as Goethe, Schiller and Humboldt, though many ways transformed, is "one of the chief motivating forces in the modernist Bildungsroman" (Castle

---

3   19th-century Western novels too are influenced by the tension between the ideologies of colonialism and nationalism although not to the same extent (Esty 50). What Boes describes in *Formative Fictions* as moments of "vernacular cosmopolitanism" disturbing the national form could in many cases (including Morgenstern's work) also be read in my terms as locally inflected *imperial* relationships in conflict with rising nationalism.

63), constituting a set of ideals to which the modernist authors' contemporary form of modernity, perceived as one heading down a wrong track, could be contrasted. Thus for the purposes of this book it is fruitful to distinguish between the Western and postcolonial models as analytic types, even if they emplot inter-related processes, share genealogical roots and structural parallels, and one can easily point out intermediate or ambivalent cases.[4]

The Postcolonial *Bildungsroman*

"Bypassing Rue Descartes", a *"Bildungsgedicht"* ("poem of formation") by the Lithuanian-Polish poet Czesław Miłosz (1911–2004) serves as a good introduction into the non-Western *Bildung*-narrative poetics, as it offers in a condensed form the trajectory and a number of the key motifs and concerns that many novels deal with in a more ramified manner and bring to various different kinds of resolutions.

> *Bypassing* Rue Descartes
> I descended towards the Seine, shy, a traveller,
> A young barbarian just come to the capital of the world.
>
> We were many, from Jassy and Koloshvar, Wilno and Bucharest,
> Saigon and Marakesh,
> Ashamed to remember the customs of our homes,
> About which nobody here should ever be told:
> The clapping for servants, barefoot girls hurry in,
> Dividing food with incantations,
> Choral prayers recited by masters and household together.
>
> I had left the cloudy provinces behind,
> I entered the universal, dazzled and desiring.
>
> Soon enough, many from Jassy and Koloshvar or Saigon or Marrakesh
> Were killed because they wanted to abolish the customs of their homes.

---

4 The ambivalent position of James Joyce's writings, including the modernist *Bildungsroman The Portrait of an Artist as a Young Man* (1916) has been explored in *Semicolonial Joyce* (ed. Attridge and Howes), as well as by Castle and Esty.

Soon enough, their peers were seizing power
In order to kill in the name of the universal beautiful ideas.

Meanwhile, the city behaved in accordance with its nature,
Rustling with throaty laughter in the dark,
Baking long breads and pouring wine into clay pitchers,
Buying fish, lemons and garlic at street markets,
Indifferent as it was to honour and shame and greatness and glory,
Because that had been done and transformed itself
Into monuments representing who knows whom,
Into arias hardly audible and into turns of speech.

Again I lean on the rough granite of the embankment,
As if I had returned from travels through the underworlds
And suddenly saw in the light of the reeling wheel of the seasons
Where empires have fallen and those once living are now dead.

There is no capital of the world, neither here nor anywhere else,
The abolished customs are restored to their small fame,
And I know the time of human generations is not like the time of earth.

As to my heavy sins, I remember one most vividly:
How, one day, walking a forest path along a stream,
I pushed a rock down onto a water snake coiled in the grass.

And what I have met with in life was the just punishment
Which reaches, sooner or later, everyone who breaks a taboo.

(Miłosz 8, translated by Renata Gorczynski and Robert Hass)

This is in many ways a traditional *Bildungsroman* story of a young man leaving the periphery and going to the metropole, dazzling as a perfect ideal of universal modernity. In this case, however, it is not just a journey to a metropole, it is a journey to a foreign metropole. The foreignness of the "universality" is not easy to ignore, the empowering 'necessary illusion'—that becoming an adult in modern society is in some sense a coherent cumulative journey—is lacking. Adapting to the alien world is thus not projected as growth in terms of one's previously received values; it is not an evolution but a total caesura or a revolution. The protagonist could not possibly return to his/her home and father as a legitimate innovative reformer. If one is to return as an agent of change one must go back as a revolutionary—which is what the metonymic symbolism of the geographical names in the poem implies.

As it is, the final part of the poem proclaims disillusionment with the universalist project—with the idea that there is "a capital of the world", one single place where modernity, maturity and full personhood can be reached. It counterposes a different worldview—understanding of the world as one of multiple centers of moral worth. Paris itself is particularized, seen not as a capital of universalism but as a rather self-absorbed place of baguettes and lemons. Yet, the comfort of proclaiming a relativist world-order is thoroughly tainted by the sense of guilt and loss condensed in the motif of the harmed water-snake. It should be added that in his collection of lectures *Witness of Poetry* Miłosz discusses what is from his point of view a frequent misreading of the poem: the broken taboo the text refers to, is not the Christian taboo against killing, but rather the Lithuanian taboo against harming water-snakes who are considered "creatures of the Sun" (22). Thus the poem enacts what it is talking about, embodying local knowledge of the sacred that may remain unintelligible for the dominant tradition.

It is important to note that the bitterness of the poem goes far beyond disappointment in French ideas. The sacralized values of the protagonist's home culture have been violated and he finds himself in a world that is broken beyond repair. The ideals and the disappointments do not merge into a synthesis, there is no conclusion of 'the hero returns sadder but wiser' type, and the narrative remains haunted by figures conveying a sense of fragmentation, guilt, loss, and possibly an undercurrent of anger. Miłosz's poem is typical of the postcolonial/belated *Bildung*-narratives, in that it conveys the great psychological stress of living without the ability to construct a coherent self, resulting in feelings of immaturity, incompleteness, and impotence in dealing with what appears to be an equally fluid world. If the Western European *Bildungsroman*, despite its ambiguities, is widely perceived as "uncovering" or at least performatively constructing a concealed order or wholeness of life, Miłosz's Eastern European narrative registers a journey towards such an order (perceived as existing "elsewhere"), but then with a second move directly restates scepticism about the possibility or even desirability of achieving it.

It is this trajectory that Eastern European and non-European postcolonial *Bildung*-narratives share. The awareness of this analogy is made quite explicit in *Bypassing Rue Descartes*, as it mentions Saigon and Marrakesh in the same breath as Wilno (Vilnius) and Bucharest. The similarity of this journey to, for example, V.S. Naipaul's *Mimic Men* (1967) or Derek Walcott's *Omeros* (1990)—to mention two widely-known works in the English language—is obvious, although in the latter cases the metropole is London rather than Paris.

The permutations which the poetics of *Bildungsroman* has taken in non-European postcolonial cultures have been studied by a number of authors (e.g. Nyatetu-Waigwa 1996; Lopez 2001; Byrne 2007; Hoagland 2019). In addition to the structure and motifs described in connection with Miłosz's poem, a principal difference with the Western model that emerges in these studies, is that the protagonist of a postcolonial *Bildungsroman* is rarely concentrated on seeking his/her individual vocation in life. This is not for the reason that the focus is not on the human particularity: similar to Western *Bildungsromane*, the postcolonial versions do work through the personal and the everyday. However, postcolonial *Bildungsromane* tend to be far more explicitly political (in the direct sense of thematizing issues of power structures and government) in their themes than the traditional model. In their worlds, the spheres of everyday and personal life cannot but be explicitly linked to the position and fate of the protagonists' identity collective(s). Studying Irish, Scottish and early US-American *Bildungsromane*, Shannon states that in them the "characters transition into *political* adulthood", and through the characters' stories the novels are able to "try out various forms of national identity by investigating different avenues of subject formation" (Shannon 18, my italics).

However, it is important to re-emphasize that in many, even most, postcolonial *Bildungsromane*, the avenues for the development of and transition to adulthood, political or otherwise, may not be manifold, and the available few usually turn out to be far from "symbolically legitimate" in Moretti's sense (*The Way*, 16). Wangari wa Nyatetu-Waigwa's and Alfred Lopez's studies of postcolonial *Bildungsromane* from different time periods and locations demonstrate that a finished *Bildung* is often impossible as the heroes seek their identities in milieus that deny the protagonist not only a legitimate but even a legal path towards self-cultivation or citizenship, or which lack stability and consistency, being unredeemably split between contrasting sets of values, or in constant flux and change.

Nyatetu-Waigwa's ground-breaking work on three French-language African *Bildungsromane* draws upon anthropological theories to describe her cases of study as "novels of liminality", as they feature heroes who enter the phase of initiation, but get blocked there and do not emerge as mature adults or citizens during the course of the novel. Lopez discusses Jamaican and South African novels where the racially split worlds are reflected by the variously split minds of

Chapter Three. Bildung in the Image of Modernity

the protagonists. Significantly, like many other postcolonial novels these draw upon the marriage/romance trope, which, however, is re-written as accounts of broken relationships, of illicit loves and twisted desires across racial lines: the "social contract" remains unsigned and *"mésalliances"* impossible.[5]

It is also important to note that for the postcolonial *Bildungsroman* both the marriage trope and the symbolism of child/parent dynamics are equally central in modelling the protagonist's trials, decisions and possibilities relating to his/her socio-cultural inheritance on the one hand, and socio-cultural reproduction on the other. Generational discontinuity is an issue in the *Bildungsroman* genre as a whole, but like in "Bypassing Rue Descartes", in the splintered plots of the postcolonial *Bildungsroman* the cultural cleavage between the childhood home and (the currently legitimate form of) modernity is often presented as all but irredeemable. As also seen in Koidula's stories considered in Chapter Two, filiation in the postcolonial *Bildungsroman* is not a natural given. Rather, it is, like marriage, a kind of social pact consciously or half-consciously made. Through it the novel can enquire, if and from whom the protagonist has the moral right to "inherit", whether the existing social order and mentality allow this, and what kind of legacies the protagonist her/himself wants to claim or is prepared to accept. Of the five Estonian *Bildungsroman* protagonists considered in this chapter only one is brought up by both of his/her biological parents, four are orphans and/or abandoned children, brought up by people other than the parents. "The figure of the orphan holds a pivotal place in the history of the 19th-century European bildungsroman," observes Eleanor Byrne. "[T]he literary form of the bildungsroman has been appropriated widely by postcolonial writers, but [little] attention has been paid to rewritings of adoption as a central trope in this literary form".

In the English *Bildungsroman* the frequent orphan and foundling protagonists typically reach a happy finale in the "recognition-inheritance pattern" (Moretti, *The Way* 205), whereby they are not only restored their money and titles, but also "their very identity" "as *people endowed with rights*" (205, Moretti's italics), usually by means of an order-restoring judicial procedure of the English court system. In postcolonial *Bildung*, on the other hand, the same status figures open up ways of narrativizing and exploring issues of "unstable origins" and different "discourses of nation" (Byrne).

---

5   On the same kind of recurrent marriage motif in Estonian literature see Undusk, "Abielu" (in Estonian) or Undusk, "Die Ehe" (in German).

Estonian *Bildung*-narratives and the postcolonial model

Juhan Liiv's *The Shadow* (1894); Silvia Rannamaa's two-part *Kadri* (1959) and *Stepmother* (1963); Jaan Kross's *The Czar's Madman* (1978); Tõnu Õnnepalu's *Border State* (1993) are all united by a variety of motifs and themes. There is a shared perception that the recognized legitimate trajectory to adulthood is alien and presupposes estrangement from "home". None of the protagonists is brought up by both of their birth parents, and all involve problems with parenthood, in terms of ancestry and/or descendants. None of the protagonists ends up in a happy "social pact" of a marriage or another comparable relationship. What is more, the fragmentation and ruptures of the protagonists' life-paths clearly result, to a significant extent, from social and political counter-agencies rather than from purely personal ones.

There is also a family resemblance in the way these works, varied in time as they are, conceptualize and rationalize this life-experience: even if one manages to construct a "story of life" of some coherence, it is a record of stressful negotiations through many particularized small narratives, rather than a discovery or construction of a larger complete one. The topic of how to turn a fragmented and conflicted experience into a coherent worldview or a sense-making continuous narrative is, to a greater or lesser extent, an issue in all of the novels viewed in this sub-chapter, only one of which, *The Shadow*, is not narrated by the protagonist. All of these four novels I consider to generally follow the postcolonial model, even if they do it in different ways.

Juhan Liiv's The Shadow

The author of *The Shadow*, Juhan Liiv (1864–1913), has currently the greatest significance in the Estonian literary tradition as the creator of a highly original, non-romantic, yet very intense and personal patriotic and nature poetry. Though ignored at first, his poetry was hailed by the modernizing Young Estonia movement already in Liiv's lifetime as part of their own artistic lineage. The literary scholar Jüri Talvet compares Liiv's significance for Estonian culture with that which "Federico Garcia Lorca and T. S. Eliot have for modern culture created, respectively, in Spanish and English" (Talvet 29). In the context of Estonian culture, Liiv was also "an iconic national bard", the literary theorist Tiina Kirss writes, "incarnated as an archetypal 'other', a mad poet whose peasant roots, poverty and isolation due to recurrent psychiatric illness seemed to underscore the tragic view of Estonian history" ("Interstitial" 393).

Among Liiv's prose works the novella *The Shadow* is the longest, completed immediately before Liiv's mental health dramatically deteriorated. *The Shadow* soon became, and presently is, compulsory reading in Estonian secondary schools, while several later canonical Estonian prose authors, including A. H. Tammsaare, have acknowledged its impact on them (Vinkel, "Juhan Liiv" 114; Väljataga 1886). Although set historically in the 1830s and 1840s, it is clearly autobiographical and concerned with Liiv's contemporary social and political problems and sensitivities.

The protagonist of the novella, Villu, a talented and sensitive *corvée* peasant child, starts his life among the parish poor, but then becomes a protégé and pupil of the enlightened son of the local Murumäe manor, Hugo, and of his even more liberal-minded and empathy-filled fiancée Helene. Towards the end of the novella Villu is a young man, a promising poet, and about to continue with formal schooling in town. He is filled with ardor to become an educated man and an author, with the double motivation to serve his folk and to prove that, despite his origins, he can be worthy of the respect of his German patrons. However, Villu's dreams are suddenly aborted: once when the young nobility is away, Villu attempts to plead for a group of peasants, accused of damaging the manor's crops, and Hugo's father, the irascible old lord of the manor orders Villu to be flogged together with the rest of the group. As a result, Villu becomes mentally ill and never recovers.

Villu's *Bildung*-trajectory is, in a literal sense, very limited, even non-existent, when compared to the typical structure of the traditional Western *Bildungsroman*. As a true *Bildungsroman* protagonist, Villu fantasizes about foreign countries, seas and ships, faraway cities, Southern lands, mysterious names he has heard: Riga, Moscow, France, Egypt (38, 39). Yet, in reality, his *Bildung* only takes him as far as the manor-house, even his journey to the closest urban center remains an unrealized plan. However, the journey, crossing of spatial boundaries as part of *Bildung*, is central in the novella exactly in its absence and non-realization, as the sense of spatial narrowness, claustrophobic lack of horizon, shaded vision, both directly and metaphorically, are main themes of the work.[6] As a small child, Villu listens to the roar of the large Lake Peipus nearby, shaded from the view by the forest, and becomes obsessed with the desire to see the lake, "if only the forest were not in the way" (26)—a phrase that he later compulsively repeats in his insanity (81).

---

6   *Vari*, the title of the novella in Estonian, means both "shadow" and "shade".

Significantly in our context, Villu is not fully Estonian by blood. His father is a Dane, a head forester, working for a Baltic German manor in Estonia, while his mother Marie is a sensitive and talented Estonian peasant much like Villu himself. The Danish gentleman does not perceive a serious barrier between himself and Marie because in Denmark "peasantry is considered no worse than any other status" and a lord of the manor and educated peasants, he says, can associate with each other as best friends (28). However, as things are in Estonia, Villu's broken-hearted mother dies in childbirth, having been left by her lover after the lord of the manor dismisses him due to their love affair, and Villu starts his life as an illegitimate child and an orphan. In an English *Bildungsroman*, that opening might be expected to lead to the protagonist's slow but sure reclaim of the paternal side of his heritage. In *The Shadow*, however, the father never reappears in person, and the whole topic is all but dropped by the novella.[7] Instead, Villu enters a new set of family relations and emotional ties that symbolically map his life options.

He is initially brought up by his Estonian grandmother (the grand*father* dies of grief and shame), a significant literary type later repeating in the genealogy of many Estonian *Bildungsroman* protagonists, including those of *Kadri* and *Border State*. On the one hand, the centrality of a grandmother instead of parents strongly highlights the rupture in the family tree and in society (the ruptures always have to do with collective life, they are never purely personal). On the other, she is also an uneasy point of continuation. She undergoes all the suffering, hardship and social turmoil allotted to the rest of the family, yet she is the one who survives and helps the child survive. Stoical, reserved, often harsh, she is far from being either an Earth-mother or a patriotic teacher. Indeed, her simple pragmatism and common sense are frequently in contrast to the sensitive protagonist, with his/her intellectual drives and emotional longings possibly inherited from the tragically destroyed parent(s). Yet, for better or for worse, the grandmother is the protagonist's first emotional affiliation and his/her first link to Estonians as a group.

In *The Shadow* the function of the grandmother, who also dies when Villu is still young, is partially transferred to his adoptive family, the relatively affluent peasant household of the Kuuse farm. In time their relationship with Villu de-

---

[7] The symbolism of the scandal and shame of the relationship with Villu's Estonian mother is later echoed in Liiv's well-known poem 'Like a Secret Mistress', where the unacceptable mistress is Estonia itself: "Like a secret mistress, / my dear homeland, / you are not to be/mentioned in public. // When sometimes in secret/my thoughts go to you: / then they condemn it / the whole world is conflicted." (Meel 101)

velops to the point where the stepparents would leave their farm to him rather than to their own son who has gone into service at the manor and, they suspect, has lost interest in farm work. Under the juridical order of the time it is the manor that owns the farm in the last instance, but the offer of heirdom symbolically marks Villu as part of the family and offers a legitimate life-path for self-betterment. Villu does not accept the offer because he has decided to study in town to become an author. Yet, as he plans his departure, his pondering upon his peasant fellow-ethnics prompts him to make a special visit to his adoptive parents. The meeting confirms their family relationship most emphatically. "You have been as dear to us as our own son", says the mother. Villu answers: "Mother—father! You are my only parents, you alone, I do not know of any others!" (75)

Villu's dreams of his future mix with his trust for and appreciation of his chosen family in a way that make their characteristics become metaphorized into those of the people of "the farm" in general—in clear juxtaposition to "head foresters" like his birth-father:

> The love of his stepparents—so good! The future so attractive! [...] He wants to try to get on in life—oh how he wants to study! These people love him there, where he just came from. There is not that much said in words, but this manner, these serious faces, these good, frank, honest eyes! If a word does pass their lips, then it comes from the heart, speaks the same language as the eyes, whereas the people at the manor, the scribes, the head foresters, the lords themselves, are completely different. [...] Yes, there is such a curious difference between the farm and the manor. Here it is so simple and quiet, there everything is splendid and loud, cold, uncaring. (76)

However, Villu's attitude towards the manor is highly charged with very mixed feelings. The manor is alien, confusing, mean, yet it inspires him to admire and to dream; it evokes attraction and even tenderness as well as angry pride.

In a symbolic childhood scene Villu is spell-bound by Beethoven, played on the piano at a birthday party at the manor, attended by young ladies magically dressed in all white.[8] The irony is that Villu happens to hear the music or be at the manor only because he was taken there to be punished for catching a hare in the manor's forest. The narrator addresses Villu and muses that, in its insen-

---

8   There is a very similar scene in Koidula's *Juudit*. There it is the young Maroon Eevar who longingly looks towards the manor and listens to the music played there (Chapter Two).

sitivity towards the young man's need for Bethoven, the manor is also suffering from impaired vision, just as Villu is: "They have the habit of considering themselves better than you; they cannot see that your heart is moved in the same way as theirs, because they too have a shade in front of their eyes" (45). The two sides are both caught in the same deadlock and mirror each other in their disability.[9]

Villu's thoughts of his stepparents quoted above soon drift to his "dear benefactor" Hugo and then, as a daydream, to his patron's fiancée, whose eyes remind him of his Lake Peipus. He imagines Helene as an inhabitant of fairy tale palaces, but also as one of a roomy white house, "in every way similar to his own home"—before he reminds himself of the uncrossable distance between himself and "them" (76-77).

There is a special bond between Villu and Helene, which, however, remains vague and dreamy, implied rather than discussed, throughout the novella. Helene admires Villu's poems and she is one who clearly sees that his "heart is moved by the same things" as her own. Villu regards Helene with respect and wonderment, rather in contrast to her fiancé's patronizing and more conventional opinions about women's role and interests in society. Hugo also notices with concern that Helene has for a while been cool towards his propositions to finalize their union (68), although the reader never learns with any clarity what caused Helene's lack of enthusiasm, or, indeed, whether Hugo's worries were at all grounded.

As Villu is shaken from his daydreams by Helene herself, in a paraphrase of the traditional *Bildungsroman* resolution in *mésalliance* happiness, the two talk about their individual slim prospects of achieving it. Helene says that "the former *corvée*", as Villu had called himself, has every chance to become happy, and Villu answers: "Oh his happiness will never, ever be [...] He can just earn esteem—and every other possible thing, but not happiness" (77). No, you go, write more poetry and become a famous man, help your people, Helene urges: "You not—you ought not to be unhappy! You are not barred by the walls between the stands—I am, Villu!" (78). Helene's social standing and her gender make her, if anything, even less free than Villu to make the *Bildungsroman* choices concerning either vocation or spouse.

---

9   The attention paid to the psychological perspective of the Baltic Germans is characteristic of *The Shadow*. In his insightful article "Orja teadvus valguses ja varjus" ("Slave Mind in Shadow and in Light") Märt Väljataga discusses the significance and techniques of empathic representation of different minds and viewpoints in *The Shadow*. Liiv is the first Estonian author extensively using free indirect discourse, a technique generally associated with the emergence of the realist novel in Europe and with the modern understanding of the "interior human" (Väljataga).

Helene had sought Villu out in order to warn him against the anger of the old lord, but the intense meeting with the lady has exactly the opposite effect on him: electrified, he storms off to interfere on behalf of the peasants about to be punished.

Although Villu's tragedy affects Helene with a life-threatening fever, she recovers and during the few epilogue-like last pages of the novella the "correct" pair is brought together: Helene and Hugo marry and have children. They begin to run the manor according to Hugo's enlightened ideas: peasant schools, opportunity to buy the farms from the manor, idyllic relations all round. The old lord repents and even befriends Villu's adoptive parents. Soviet criticism has pointed out *The Shadow*'s naïve belief in enlightened feudals as a progressive force (Vinkel, "Juhan Liiv" 110), but the finale rather impresses one as bitter and possibly ironic. Villu loses his agency and is written out of any genealogy of modernizing reform; the changes at Murumäe are represented as an exception not followed by nobility elsewhere (80).

It is significant that Villu's tragedy of insanity is caused by his desire for light and *Bildung*, misplaced in a situation of barbaric feudal violence. While the novella clearly criticizes the feudal institutions, it may be said that violent dark forces are also indicated as the momentum of Villu's drive.

As a very young child, Villu wanders into the same forest that blocks his view of the Lake Peipus. He is dangerously bitten by a wolf and has a strange dreamlike impression of having seen a glimpse of Peipus (23). This is the origin of Villu's longing for faraway places and his desire for light and openness out of "the shadow", as well as the trigger of his poetic creativity, where the dark forest is a repeating motif (69, 70).

Is Villu to be seen as a doomed hero, destroyed not only by socio-political forces, but also by the darkness in himself? It should be noted here that Jungian psychoanalysis associates the wolf with the "shadow" side of the self (Casement 100). Like the Jungian notion of shadow itself, the archetypal significance of a wolf is, in many different cultures, bipolar: the wolf symbolizes the wild and the instinctive, both negatively as the destructive and the unreasonable, as well as in the aspects of free spirit, courage and passionate creativity (De Vries 615-617; Estes, especially 35-37). The Hungarian poet Sándor Petőfi (1823-1849), a few of whose texts Liiv translated, has twin poems 'The Song of the Dogs' and 'The Song of the Wolves' which interestingly parallel and may help to illuminate *The Shadow*.[10]

---

10 "A kutyák dala"; "A farkasok dala". I am grateful to György Schöpflin for drawing my attention to the poems and for providing the English translations.

The dogs sing of their pleasant safe life, eating the remnants off the master's table. Sometimes, true, "the whip cracks", but this is a minor discomfort to put up with, they say:

> And once his anger has passed
> our master calls us again
> and we are happy to lick
> his lordly feet.

The wolves, however, sing:

> We are cold and we are hungry
> our sides are shot through,
> every misery is ours...
> but we are free.

There is no doubt who the national romantic Petőfi thinks is in the right, whereas the proto-existentialist Liiv surprises us with his empathy for both the dog and the wolf in all his characters' minds, including those of the masters. At the end of the day, one is left with a disillusioned conclusion that a hungry, cold and persecuted wolf is not really much freer than a dog, but becomes a prisoner of, if nothing else, the destructive aspect of his own wolfness. For *The Shadow*, the heroic romantic choice is a non-choice.

Soviet period Bildungsromane

Silvia Rannamaa's (1918-2007) Kadri dilogy and Jaan Kross's (1920-2007) *The Czar's Madman* were written during the Khrushchev and Brezhnev era respectively and are also very different in terms of their temporal setting, the figure of the protagonist, and their intended audience. Yet they have a notable family resemblance. Both approach the *Bildungsroman* issues of social and cultural identity through a central thematic concentration on, and strong symbolic highlighting of, the problematics of family, filiation and (dis)continuity between parents and children. Both are narrated by the protagonist in diary form, and present writing and reading as avenues of forming and cherishing individual and private identities.

Silvia Rannamaa's *Kadri* and *Stepmother*

Silvia Rannamaa's small *oeuvre* is almost entirely focused on writing about and for children and young people, *Kadri* (1959) and *Stepmother* (1963), being her early and most important works. These share the protagonist Kadri Jalakas as well as a number of other central characters. Kadri is 13-14 years old during the main timeline of the first part and 16-18 in the second. The books, published in the beginning of the Thaw period of the Cold War and set about the same time (Kadri must have been born around 1943–1944) became immediately popular among young readers, but were also appreciated by adults.[11] Especially *Stepmother*, with its realistic set of colorful characters and exciting intrigues at a mixed-gender boarding school, presented by the sensitive and witty narrator, was a cult reading for Estonian teenage girls from the 1960s to the early 1990s. In 1985 an influential socially critical film *Well, Come On, Smile* (*Naerata ometi*, Dirs. Leida Laius and Arvo Iho) was made based on *Stepmother*, re-set at an orphanage in the 1980s. Today too the books remain relevant, both parts having been re-issued four times since the collapse of the Soviet Union. There have been several theater versions, the most recent one (2022) in the form of a musical. Despite the cross-generational centrality of the Kadri phenomenon for the popular consciousness in Estonia, the books have received little academic literary analysis.[12]

At the time of their first publication, the Kadri books strongly stood out against the prevalent poetics of the Stalinist socialist realism. The latter demanded depicting "life in its revolutionary development" which meant the duty to depict not only the future but also the present as bright and cheerful, and to contrast these with the darkness of the capitalist past, thus resulting in a strongly idealized picture of the historical situation the readers were currently experiencing (Epner, "Proosa ja draama" 378). Furthermore, the literary characters had to be created as "social subjects", i.e. their qualities determined by their class position alone, thus clamping down on the depiction of psychological development (378-379), as well as on nuanced engagement with human socialization and individual-collective relationships. As Reet Krusten points out in her

---

11 Some Soviet era critics argue that the topics and literary qualities of the novels make them relevant to adults as well—and in certain respects especially to adults (Krusten 509; Kalda). Rannamaa relates in an interview that right after *Stepmother*'s publication she once went up to a huge queue in the hope of having chanced upon oranges or some other goods in short supply, only to find that it was her own novel that the people were queueing for (Tali).

12 Reet Krusten's short article "Silvia Rannamaa ja Kadri Jalakas täna" ("Silvia Rannamaa and Kadri Jalakas Today", 1978) offers the most analytical account of the poetics and reception of the Kadri novels.

1978 article, Rannamaa's books are very different: they are psychological novels, principally focused on "the story of Kadri's internal development" (509). They present the characters and their surroundings in a non-idealized manner and involve the reader in a "wide range of emotions" (Krusten 512).

Rannamaa herself explains that she simply lacked the skills to approximate the officially prescribed model more closely, even if she did want to get published and thus tried to follow the demanded blueprint to some degree (Rannamaa "Kohtumine").[13] Having grown up with books like Jean Webster's *Daddy-Long-Legs*, Francis Burnett's *The Secret Garden*, and Louisa May Alcott's *Little Women* as her favorites, both their aesthetics and their moral outlook were engrained in her (Rannamaa "Kohtumine"). Even if the "girl book" genre was officially banned in the Soviet Union from the 1930s for catering to the petty bourgeoisie, the Kadri books became possible with the beginning of the Thaw and the supportive editor-in-chief, aided by the obscurity of the Estonian language and the relative marginality of children's literature (Jaaksoo, personal interview).[14]

Nevertheless, the dilogy is also a product of its time in the sense of presenting a number of discourses and topoi of the era: Pioneer and Komsomol meetings, a Comrades' Court, meditations about the proper code of honor of a young Communist, etc. Of all the texts considered in this book it is probably Rannamaa's novels that are to the greatest extent moulded by outward pressure. This did not only mean direct state censorship,[15] but also guidance and editing by the publishers, as well as the author's internalized sense of self-censorship. However, Rannamaa has said that though the end result was a compromise "in the things that mattered most" to her, she had got her way ("Kohtumine"). She also declined suggestions in the late 1980s to recreate the "uncensored" versions of her texts: she thought they worked best as genuine products of their time (Tali).

---

13 Sirje Olesk discusses this as a more general phenomenon: during high Stalinism the rules on what a socialist realist novel was to be like were so complicated that even those who tried hard to write a correct one were condemned for the many mistakes they had made (Olesk, "Kirjanduse võimalused kodumaal" 351).

14 Jaaksoo (b. 1945) is a publisher, a scholar of children's and youth literature, and was a personal acquaintance of Rannamaa. Jaaksoo points out that elsewhere in the Soviet bloc too the interpretation of the ban was fluid, even if formally it was never lifted (personal interview). One could draw a certain parallel with the film *Well, Come on, Smile* (1985) based on *Stepmother* that participated in the 1987 Berlinale film festival in the children's and youth film category, winning the UNICEF prize. The film expert Joachim-Hans Schlegel later remarked in reference to that occasion: "What tends to be forgotten in today's analyses of film history [...] is the fact that an essential impetus for the unvarnished portrayal of the problems in Soviet society [...] came from children's and youth films" (Berlin International Film Festival).

15 The first edition of *Kadri* bears the stamp of the censor's office, but by the time *Stepmother* was published children's literature did not have to go through there anymore.

The texts probably reflect both the direct external influence and the author's own ambiguous engagement with the different discourses, ideals and ambitions of the post-Stalinist Soviet period.

Quietly and for a present day Estonian reader occasionally perplexingly, Kadri's diary incorporates the ambivalences and opaque spots of the era. A text-immanent reading could also analyze this in terms of the narrative focus: the reader gets his/her whole information through the young protagonist trying to find her bearings and her place in the family and in the society. A number of ethical questions that she faces remain without a conclusive answer.[16] At the same time, in its own way the dilogy does not lack the didactic aspect associated with the *Bildungsroman* genre: as I will argue below, some of its messages are presented strongly and unambivalently. Inviting the readers to empathize with the life lessons of Kadri and her schoolmates, it socializes them into a particular moral thought-world.

Kadri's diary entries date from the mid-1950s to 1961 when Gagarin flies to space (the event is discussed in the epilogue of *Stepmother*).[17] She starts her account of her entire "sorry life" (9) while lying in hospital after having been run over by a car. The diary is the only place she can confide her unhappiness, she feels; at the same time the writing also functions as a screen of privacy to pull between herself and the curiosity of the other patients in the ward. Kadri begins thus:

> I have always read and heard that in our land the children are happy, that the children have a carefree childhood. I agree with that when I think of Anne Puust or any other classmate of mine. The only thing I don't understand: if I too live in the same happy land, why am I so unspeakably unhappy? (7)

On the first pages Kadri pours out her misery of not having parents, of living in poverty in a damp cellar flat with her strained and often harsh grandmother, of having no friends. She is mocked or ignored at school: other children look down on her because of her drab appearance, lack of social skills and poor study results. Kadri's words strikingly contradict one of the most dominant Soviet discourses throughout its existence: that of the happy Soviet childhood and of children as, in Stalin's words, the only privileged class in the country. The children were projected as a "prototype" (Balina and Dobrenko xviii)

---

16 The narrative gaps and deficient moral transparency were pointed out as flaws by some contemporary reviewers (e.g. Välipõllu 572); Krusten too considers Kadri's disinclination to express moral disapproval exaggerated (511).
17 There are no actual dates in the diary, the entries are marked by weekdays (e.g. *On Saturday*).

for the whole young Soviet state, thus their happiness was not a practical goal, but "a legitimating sacred value. The state's ability to guarantee happiness to children was [...] a key instance of the country's status as a kind of earthly paradise" (Kelly 9). Thus, as Kelly observes, "it became difficult from the mid-1930s to address in print cases of childhood unhappiness within the Soviet Union itself" (7). Even if there was, of course, statistical evidence of poverty and abuse of children, officially "unhappiness was the lot of children and adults abroad [...] and in Russia before 1917" (Kelly 7).

The presentation of Kadri's initial situation, however, more resembles the classical orphan-*Bildungsromane* (e.g. *Jane Eyre* and Rannamaa's childhood favorite *Daddy-Long-Legs*), or Liiv's *Shadow* discussed above, than the happy-Soviet-childhood model, even if the details of Kadri's misfortune are very much specific to its time and place. It emerges that her father had disappeared during the Second World War, never returning: something the grandmother refuses to talk about (7). Kadri's mother had died just after the war when Kadri was very young: ostensibly of angina, but it is later suggested also of a broken heart over her husband (91). The family home had been burnt down in the war, so they ended up in the cellar flat. Kadri feels out of place in life, her sense of inadequacy enforced by the chidings of her grandmother: the grandmother loves her but is worried about her future because of her clumsiness and ill health. Kadri finds solace in fairy tales and adventure stories, imagining herself to be someone different, a person who will reach a happy finale following the "recognition-inheritance pattern": an Ugly Duckling, a bewitched royal, most often the beautiful Swan-Princess in Pushkin's *The Tale of Tsar Saltan*.

A character in a realist novel, Kadri meets her "fairy godmother" at the hospital in the person of a fellow patient, a novelist called Elsa Sarap. Aunt Elsa (as Kadri calls her older friend) breaks through her shell of self-pity and encourages her talents, making her better equipped to interact with the world and develop herself. Thus the hospital becomes the first site of Kadri's *Bildung*. Aunt Elsa can be seen as the most important didactic voice in the novel: her ideals, which Kadri further interprets and aspires towards, color the whole dilogy. Though having a crippled leg herself, Aunt Elsa's credo is "everyone is the maker [original: 'smith'] of his/her fortune": not in the sense that a capable person can control his/her fate and make it a fortunate one, but rather that any circumstance of life, even a serious misfortune, can be "forged" in qualitatively different ways. Corresponding with Kadri when the girl is transferred to recover at a sanatorium, Aunt Elsa writes:

There are plenty of people who lament when they lose a little finger: now everything is finished, life is over. They may cry over the missing finger until they are too old to work with the nine that they have. It is the psychology of such people that is handicapped. [...] Should a grouch like that find ten roubles, s/he will be positively unhappy that s/he didn't find twenty. S/he does not give a thought to the person who lost the money. [...] You see, Kadri, it is not worthwhile to be the cause of one's own unhappiness [in such a way] [...] Everything depends on one's attitude and perspective... [...] Always and everywhere try to see the natural good, even when the good is temporarily latent or hidden. Always fight for the good to prevail. (Rannamaa, *Kadri* 39-40)

Significantly, Aunt Elsa is also an enthusiast of modern science and the opportunities it can give people to improve their lives. At her initiative, Kadri is shown to a medical professor who can diagnose her with an eye disability that turns out to be the cause of many of her health and learning problems, and she then undergoes a successful state-of-the-art operation. This is a symbolic moment in Kadri's life: Aunt Elsa helped her to see life and its potential clearer in more sense than one (119).

As Kadri thrives, going back to school, working hard at her studies and making good friends, a further event changes her life: her father turns out to be alive and comes to find her. It emerges that "the turmoil of the war" (91) had taken him to the West, he had lived in Sweden for a while, but had now returned to settle in Soviet Estonia, and had a job in a factory.[18] Kadri's grandmother who blames him for her daughter's death is to a degree reconciled with him, even if they never become a family unit. At the end of the first part of the diary Kadri and the grandmother move into a one-room fifth-floor flat in a new house built by Kadri's father and his workmates.

As in many other *Bildungsromane* (both Western and postcolonial), the living spaces and the aspiration towards a true home play a central and symbolically important role for the protagonist's life-path. During the initial part of *Kadri* the cellar flat is depicted as an "anti-home" (Lotman, *The Universe* 185), a prison to which the bewitched princess does not belong and that she wants to escape.

---

18 The fictional topos of an honest Estonian exile disenchanted with the West was not an unknown one, although in real life a naïve returnee would have been imprisoned. The manner the scenario is depicted in the novel, it more resembles the return of the deportees during the same period (after Stalin's death). I am grateful to Andres Jaaksoo and the historian Linda Kaljundi for their comments on this matter.

However, it is part of her formation that she learns to understand and appreciate her tenacious grandmother and feels she "would not leave her even to go to a king's palace" (93). She is overjoyed about the new modern flat with its "windows right into the sky" (106). Yet she reconsiders her initial judgement that there is nothing in the cellar flat that is good enough to take into the new one (107): she recreates their existing furniture by repainting it and builds bookshelves from old butter boxes.

The contemporary reviewer Välipõllu specifically criticizes the finale of *Kadri* for equating happiness with a cozy home and material possessions "like in a Christmas story of former times" (572). Kadri emphasizes how much she "loves beautiful things" (118), though this pleasure is related to making and individualizing them, "being quite a bit of an inventor" (108). Both at the end of *Kadri* and later once again in *Stepmother*, Kadri does not so much acquire a home or reach a home, but makes it from the same supplies that had been part of a space seen as anti-home. Inspired by Aunt Elsa's credo that one can forge one's own fortune, she comments on her furniture project in *Kadri*: "we shouldn't only see in things how ugly they are now, but also how beautiful they can be made" (108).

By the late 1950s, official Soviet discourses had also started to give more space to individual needs: in Estonia, the journal *Art and Home* (*Kunst ja Kodu*) was initiated in 1958, with an aim to give handy advice for the increasing population who, like Kadri, was expecting to move into a tiny new apartment. In the broader context of the Kadri novels and the life philosophy offered by Aunt Elsa, however, Kadri's desire to repair damage and to turn ugliness into beauty cannot be entirely reduced to either petty bourgeois longings or to a blueprint of how to deal with the Soviet shortage economy in an efficient manner. The tropes related to homemaking carry into the depiction of human relationships, of inter-generational problems and of the social fabric in general, with great symbolic power.

In this connection, it is interesting to note the differences relating to the furnishing of the flat between the first edition of Kadri in 1959 and the later editions. All editions feature the character of Aunt Elsa's mother, a strict and somewhat snobbish former schoolteacher most at home in the inter-war period, with whom Elsa has a strained relationship. In the first edition, Elsa also possesses a brother, a wealthy exile in Canada whom the mother seems to value more than Elsa, thus increasing Kadri's dislike of the lady (70). At the end of the first edition of *Kadri*, however, Elsa's mother also shows a different side of her, as she unexpectedly gifts the protagonist with a family treasure as her housewarming present—the writing desk that both Elsa and her brother had used as children. "Sit behind it with your back straight and study well like my children did. May you be happy in your new home!" she writes to Kadri (161).

The first edition also elaborates on the peasant clothes chest, only briefly mentioned in the later versions, that Kadri's granny moves to the new house (166). When asked about it by Elsa, the grandmother says it is a 150-year-old dowry chest, made by an ancestor as a wedding present for his daughter, decorated with burnt ornaments, and anointed with lucky blessings. Kadri muses in her diary that this may be where their old house spirit (*päkapikk*) lives. Thus, whereas the later editions of *Kadri* are more future-oriented, with the main emphasis on Kadri's creativity, the 1959 version makes a bigger symbolic effort to house different and possible clashing strands (positive memories of the interwar period, the awkward issue of the Estonian diaspora in the West) of Estonian history under the roof of the new tiny Soviet flat.

The novel comes to present home (and life) improvement as precarious, neither inevitable nor indelible. Kadri's cozy home life at the end of the first part of the novel does not last for long: *Stepmother* starts in a changed situation. The grandmother has died after a long illness; the father has married Gina, a glamorous young woman with whom Kadri, still mourning her grandmother, does not get along. When Gina becomes pregnant, Kadri volunteers to leave the small flat for a boarding school. The title can be seen as a multi-referential one: *Stepmother* refers not only to Gina but also to the boarding school: a body providing a home for children and young people from variously difficult, broken, poor, or disabled families.

While the dilogy is the story of Kadri's development, her *Bildung* and problems of socialization, this story is to a great extent told through the descriptions and tropes of inter-generational relationships. Though the domestic tragedies and their impact on the children, as well as their wit and resilience, are depicted very realistically and specifically in *Stepmother*[19], the boarding school students and their dysfunctional families can also be interpreted as a comment on the society at large. This interpretation is strongly foregrounded by the directly sociocritical 1985 film based on the novel, but it is also a recurring topic for Rannamaa to discuss the relationship between cross-generational heritage and social ills. In her essayistic memoirs *Since Tender Age* (*Maast madalast*, 1990) she goes so far as to talk about the "frighteningly many mutations" that the difficult history of foreign oppression has caused among Estonians across centuries, making

---

19 Rannamaa actually stayed at the Pukavere boarding school near the town of Rakvere, sharing the sleeping quarters with the female students, in order to do research for the book ("Kohtumine").

many of them "drunkards, slow-witted, suicides, handicapped in various ways already in the mother's womb", as well as putting their family relations under strain as secrets had to be kept even from one's closest family (62-63).

The figure of Kadri's father Ülo is an odd presence in the novel. It is specified he was a radio-telegrapher on a ship during WWII (Rannamaa, *Kadri* 97), but Kadri (or the reader) never learns exactly what he did in the West, how he got there, or how he arranged his return. It is also ambiguous whether the reasons he left his wife and young child without making any contact were fully to do with the political situation, or if it was also connected to personal relationships. The opaqueness that puzzles the teenage narrator parallels the silence about wartime secrets and betrayals that many of the book's initial readers would have experienced in their own families.

At the end of the day it is her "outwardly rugged, but dutiful and fair" peasant-rooted grandmother, called Kadri like the narrator, whom she considers the only person in the world she had felt entirely at home with (125). However, it is part of Kadri's maturation process to learn to live with the uncertainty and lack of immediacy in her relationship with her father. She does not condemn her father, and neither does the novel: neither he nor Gina is in any way punished by the plot, as it would happen in a socialist realist work. Furthermore, even if Gina comes across as insensitive and conceited in Kadri's account, Kadri's very sympathetically presented boyfriend Urmas (whose own father is a violent alcoholic, so he helps the mother to take care of the younger siblings) reproves her for not making a more wholehearted effort to solve her problems with Gina (142-143). As Kadri rejoices at the birth of her little sister, she promises herself to "forget all unpleasantness that has happened with the stepmother" (154).

At the same time, the primary school age girls at the boarding school who she talks to and plays with become no less important to her: she feels she has "more sisters than the little one at home" (190). Kadri, in her own turn, develops into an inspiring and eye-opening Aunt Elsa figure for the deprived children, two of whom emerge as fully-fledged "round" characters in the novel. The boarding school which initially had been a barely tolerable anti-home gradually becomes the main locus of Kadri's attachments and relationships. By the final third of the book she confesses that when on holiday at the family home she feels "homesickness for the boarding school"; "for the independence, opportunities and mates there" (258). Symbolically, at that point the previously bleak dormitory is redecorated and creatively "interior designed" in a joint effort of older and younger girls to make a real home (258-262).

Significantly, towards the end of the novel these developments are interrupted by an out-of-the-blue tragedy. Kadri's schoolmate Enrico is critically injured in a fight with escaped prisoners while he bravely saves Kadri from their attack. Enrico had already been introduced in the first part of the dilogy as a mean bully in his childhood, also from a family of alcoholics. Once Kadri meets him again at the boarding school he has acquired a good name, yet makes Kadri the object of his taunts. It turns out, however, that Enrico is in love with her; during their long conversations at the hospital a number of misconceptions are refuted, and both Kadri and the reader see the "temporarily latent" good (cf. 40) in him. There is every encouragement to make the reader believe that Enrico is going to recover, yet one day Kadri is unexpectedly informed by the nurse that he is dead. It emerges that Enrico's unstable mother had come to visit him, smoking in the ward. Afterwards Enrico had collapsed and died trying to open the window, too embarrassed to ask for help.

In her authorial preface to later editions, Rannamaa reveals that readers often ask her why she let Enrico die (Autori 375). It makes her glad every time they say they feel sorry for him, she writes: "one must feel sorry for a human being! That was the main reason for Enrico's death". One should not forget, she explains, even when young, that we don't necessarily have "a thousand years to get to know one another [...] The more seriously we relate to the main issues in life, the more right and reasons we will have to laugh and be happy" (Rannamaa, Autori 375). As indicated above, despite the Kadri novels' ambiguity and detachment in some aspects, they do send a strong didactic message about the duty to care for human lives and the belief in individuals' ability and responsibility to make their own and others' fortunes better, even if in an unstable environment. Reet Krusten perceptively points out that the widely read books themselves became a kind of a "collectively shared Aunt Elsa" (509): a wise mentor who comforts and encourages the readers.

The novel ends with Kadri holding her little ward Sass as she comforts her in their dimly lit dormitory, both grieving over Enrico's death. She writes: "Something akin to a smile flickered through me this morning, even if I would have wanted to howl with pain. It was love that awakened it in me and I realized with clarity how life was starting to give me its first conscious tasks" (371). In the first two editions of *Stepmother* (1963 and 1965) this wistful-serene ending is taken further in hopefulness by an epilogue-like final section in the novel, set about one year after the previous entry in the diary quoted above.

This section is mainly dedicated to Yuri Gagarin's space flight, celebrated by Kadri as a symbolic event. She writes jubilantly: "A human being, my compatriot, built a second floor on top of the low ceiling of our home. So spacious that it can accommodate the light of the whole universe!" (Rannamaa, *Kasuema* 273). Sass now wants to become a cosmonaut and Kadri believes she has just the right spirit for it: "we'll sure have to bring her back to Earth by force to avoid her scampering off to some other galaxy in her hyper-eagerness" (273). At the end of the epilogue Kadri's childhood boyfriend Urmas also reappears in the plot and the finale resembles the traditional model of the *Bildungsroman* in which the protagonist voluntarily integrates into his/her society:

> Urmas [...] takes my hand and we run together. I am breathless with happiness and would like to start doing great things right away. [...] Again Gagarin comes to my mind and his conversation with the Earth and quite unexpectedly four simple words of it in which I suddenly discover the whole great meaning of life: I CONTINUE THE FLIGHT!" (284-285, capitals in the original)[20]

However, in the further five editions of *Stepmother* the epilogue is dropped, so there is no happy couple, Gagarin or family/social integration. According to Andres Jaaksoo, both the epilogue and its removal in the later editions were entirely Rannamaa's own decisions, the reasons for which he never directly asked. He considered it obvious that by the 1970s the previous decade's enthusiasm for Soviet modernity seemed too much "of its time" (personal interview). Thus in these editions the tragic relationship with Enrico and his death carry a much greater weight in the plot. The happiness theme typical for *Bildungsromane* is also introduced before the dropped epilogue and thus remains in the post-Thaw editions. However, the post-Thaw version does not resemble the traditional *Bildungsroman*'s marital happiness model anymore: Kadri gives a silent vow to her dead beau Enrico that she will "fight for happiness and not only for [her] own" (Rannamaa, *Kadri* 370-371). "I want to fight so there would be fewer blind chances and nobody would hurt a child," she writes (371).

The world of "the parents" seems too full of hurt, insecurity and unfairness to recreate its models of family/society[21] and, without the Gagarin trope, the idea of a new era also remains colorless and unconvincing. This social-critical inter-

---

20 There is no direct *mésalliance* or exogamy involved in the solution, but the trope is approximated by the domination of the "Space Prince" (Rannamaa, *Kasuema* 274) Gagarin in the epilogue.
21 It is interesting to note that Aunt Elsa too has a strained and ambivalent relationship with her domineering mother, the underlying complexities of which Kadri or the readers do not really learn. Furthermore, Elsa is single and has no children.

pretation of *Stepmother* is amplified by the film version in 1985 and even more so by the film's reception. If in the novel the boarding school staff, though not idealized, is presented sympathetically, the reviews of *Well, Come On, Smile* liken its orphanage setting to the psychiatric hospital in *One Flew Over The Cuckoo's Nest* (Laasik). However, even if the film is a much darker work than the novel, its ultimate message is the same: it is the protagonist's care for—someone else's—children that brings a flicker of a smile on her face in the final scene, indicating that there will be a new beginning after the tragic rupture.

Jaan Kross's *The Czar's Madman*

Next to A. H. Tammsaare, Kross is generally seen as the second most impactful fiction writer for Estonian culture, his work being not only at the core of the Estonian literary canon but also Estonians' self-consciousness, "the Estonian myth" (Veidemann, "Jaan Kross"). Raised in an educated middle-class family in Tallinn, as a young man he was first arrested during the German occupation for six months (1944), then in 1946 by the Soviet authorities who imprisoned him first in Tallinn and from 1947 to 1951 in forced labour camps in the Komi area. After two more years as a deportee in Siberia, he was released during the Khrushchev period Thaw in 1954. He went on to achieve a successful career as an author in the Soviet Union (his works were published in large print runs, in 1977 he was named a People's Writer of the Estonian SSR, and was frequently nominated for the Nobel Prize), then together with many other cultural figures actively contributed to the Singing Revolution and, for a short period after independence (1992–1993), served as a member of the new Estonian parliament.

Literary scholars and media have often described him as a "witness" to 20th-century Estonian history, with a mission to relate the silenced stories of his era, whether directly or indirectly (Laanes, "Tunnistaja"). As briefly discussed in Chapter One, Kross started as an innovative modernist poet, but is best known in Estonia and internationally by his historical fiction that engages with Estonian history from the 16th to the 21st century, combining careful historical research with absorbing storytelling and psychological and philosophical depth. His protagonists (mostly Estonians, sometimes Baltic Germans) find themselves in the role of in-betweeners, exceptional or peripheral figures in their society, trying to be bigger than their hemmed-in historical circumstance, making compromises with the established structures with mixed results.

The Czar's Madman is widely considered one of Kross's most successful works, his most influential novel, both in Estonia and abroad. It has been translated into 24 languages (as of 2021), frequently republished in Estonian and twice staged in theater. Written some twenty years later than Rannamaa's *Kadri*, the book is set broadly at the same time and place as Liiv's *The Shadow*—in the Estonian countryside during the first half of the 19th century. Furthermore, like Liiv's text, though historically set, it is a personal and contemporary vision of the author's time and space, in this case Brezhnev-period Soviet Estonia.

As noted in Chapter One, it was important for Kross to emphasize that his works should be seen as complex texts in the literary sense rather than political allegories with neatly establishable critical references to topical politics. Nevertheless, it would have been hard to read *The Czar's Madman* in stagnation-period Estonia without thinking of the contemporary abuse of psychiatry as a political tool to label dissidence as psychopathology, enabling to confine and "treat" the non-conformers in mental hospitals, thus discrediting them for the wider public, and often truly destroying their mental health. The literary scholar Jaan Undusk (who was also Kross's son-in-law) writes that Kross himself also considered *The Czar's Madman* a politically outspoken, "even dissident" novel (Undusk, "Eesti lugu: Jaan Kross"), and according to contemporaries the citizen courage and sense of responsibility evoked by the book helped to inspire "the letter of forty" and the Singing Revolution later (Kisseljova 328; Allik).

On the other hand, Undusk has argued that in all Estonian literature, and possibly in world literature, Kross is the author most persistently interested in *Bildung*, in the possibilities of a human personality for development and self-realization—this preoccupation being so overwhelming that even his keen interest in the Estonian national story and politics is subordinated to that. Undusk nevertheless describes the two aspects, the collective and the individual, as inseparably related for Kross's mind-set. A liberal, nourishing sociopolitical environment is very important for full personal self-realization, but if it is lacking, the individual can still become a personality (even if a "compromised" one) by striving towards (re)creating such an environment:

> [p]ersonalities were there before the Estonian Republic and will be there when it once ends. Because otherwise there cannot come a new Estonian Republic. [...] Nothing in this world is eternal [...] But we must be ready: not only for that someday [the Estonian state] will fall to ashes, but also for the task of building it up again then. And in this sense personality is prior and more crucial than the Estonian Republic. (Undusk, "Isiksusest")

It is interesting to note that critics often disagree to what degree Kross's *oeuvre* could be considered realist, modernist or postmodernist—Undusk refers to a kinship between Kross's and Thomas Mann's work and this comparison is well justified in this respect too.

Jakob Mättik, the narrator and protagonist of *The Czar's Madman* is depicting his life in terms of the typical *Bildungsroman* oppositions elaborated in this chapter—personal autonomy and membership in a collective; liberty and happiness; legitimacy or illegitimacy of the existing social order; and the moral choices in integrating into it. At first sight, however, the *Bildungsroman* aspects of the novel may not be obvious as the Estonian narrator Jakob does not focus, so it seems, on his own life story, but instead relates the events of someone else's, that of his "mad" brother-in-law Timotheus von Bock, the Baltic German nobleman who scandalously marries Jakob's sister Eeva, an Estonian peasant girl. Soon after, Timotheus sends a memorandum to his boyhood friend Czar Alexander condemning his political rule, thereby honoring his one-time oath to the Czar always to tell him his true opinion. In consequence, he is promptly imprisoned by the Czar for nine years.[22] Jakob starts his secret diary in 1827 when Timo returns from incarceration, explaining: "I decided to keep a journal because I have found myself entangled in affairs so unusual that any thoughtful person, compelled to witness them by circumstance, would feel an urge to record his observations"(1).

Yet gradually, one becomes aware that the diarist, positioned as a witness-narrator and retelling dramatic events primarily for the reason that they happen to take place in his proximity, is largely pre-occupied with his own story after all. Or to be more exact, Jakob comes to narrativize, analyze and develop his own story, his formation and identity exactly through his endeavor to understand von Bock, and most importantly through the process of his critical engagement with von Bock's memorandum to the Czar, which he accidentally finds in a secret hiding place and then copies and comments upon in his journal.[23]

---

22 Timotheus Eberhard von Bock (1787-1836), Eeva (later Katharina) von Bock (1799-1862) and many other characters in the book are historical figures.
23 There have been different critical views on who is the protagonist of the novel, Timo or Jakob (or both). I agree with Eneken Laanes that "[t]he parallelism between von Bock's and Mättik's stories is the central structural and thematic principle in *The Czar's Madman*" and also with her statement, important in the present context, that through his narrating activity Mättik "undergoes changes as a character—previously without a job, lacking clear ethnic or class identity, Mättik becomes an Estonian and a Bourgeois" (219). Both characters are central for the novel, but whereas we meet Timo as a broadly ready-made figure, Jakob is undergoing formation.

It is crucial to the novel that Jakob's narrative of his *Bildung* begins as someone else's story. Jakob initially strongly feels his own lack of story, a lack of self. The diary first takes the reader to the time when von Bock proposes marriage to Jakob's sister and thereupon for four years sends her to the household of the Estonian pastor Masing to be instructed in "good manners, foreign languages and book learning" (9). It is as a spontaneous afterthought that von Bock decides that it would be easier for Eeva if Jakob went with his sister to become "an educated person" like her (11). Nobody asked for Jakob's consent, he reminiscences; "Eeva's departure was not postponed by one minute" for his benefit, "no such allowances were made in Timotheus's grand life plan" (11). The symbolic start of Jakob's life in an ambivalent social space and with ambivalent feelings sounded in his ears like the ringing of "church bells, two church bells, to be exact, one of them deep and slow, ding-dong, *treas-on, treason* against everything Eeva was sacrificing by her rise in the world; the other, high and quick, ding-ding-ding, *what a gift, what a gift, what a gift!*" (11).

If the traditional ethos of *Bildung* takes it for granted that every human being carries a self, an irreplaceable individuality—something that ought to be, as the next step, maturized and realized through diverse experience, but which in itself is a given—Jakob feels that he has a good deal of diverse experiences, yet lacks an individual personality. He does not have any position or role in the world, whether in the private or public sphere; he does not know what or who he is. Having acquired "the rudiments of draftsmanship and surveying" (15) and "the book learning of a lyceum graduate", as well "a good deal of worldly wisdom and judgement of character", he does not "know how to apply any of it" (18). As a former-serf half-educated Estonian kinsman of Baltic German gentry, he is a weird anomaly in the rigid estate society, someone most convenient simply to ignore.

In his late thirties, he is single, has no proper vocational application and nothing much to do. He continues to live at the von Bock Võisiku mansion and to depend for his livelihood on his debt-ridden sister and brother-in-law. He is not accepted among the gentry and in his turn considers them alien for himself, yet he feels almost equally uncomfortable relating to Estonian peasants ("I instantly feel I have been too familiar, or too fatuous, or too supercilious, or inappropriate in some other way" (74)), including his peasant parents at the Paluka farm.[24] On the first pages of the novel, Jakob also insists he does not love

---

24 Jakob explains his feelings: "once Eeva and Timo make good their escape in September [...] there will be nothing to keep me at Võisiku [...] Without them, I would be worse than a stranger. And so I would be at Paluka—well, perhaps not to the same degree, but precisely for that reason, much more painfully aware of it" (202).

Chapter Three. Bildung in the Image of Modernity

his sister who had been too eager to "leap into the unknown" and dragged him into it too (4). He does claim that Eeva and he trust each other, but then immediately contradicts himself, saying he did not ask his sister an important question, fearing to be fobbed off "with a lie", like "a stranger" (4).

Jakob's rootlessness in the estate society is only one reason for his constant outsider-observer position and lack of a personal story. Another, perhaps more subtly expressed one is his only half-conscious but persistent fear that any identity that he would develop, any life he would choose to care about would be soiled by the state, by powers that in him, differently from Timo, instinctively inspire repulsion and withdrawal for fear of contamination rather than rebellion. Jakob falls in love with Iette Laming, daughter of the steward of the Võisiku mansion and wishes to marry her, yet he abandons her immediately when he learns that Iette's father is a government spy, planted on the household, even though Iette protests her innocence and begs him to save her from having to stay with her father (66). Reminding himself that no father necessarily taints a daughter, Jakob still immediately realizes:

> time and again suspicion would descend upon me, so no matter how carefully I would lock my door, it would still remain open, because it would be impossible to close, and my floor would be covered by the muddy footprints left by a stranger... my own wife (65).

The secret diary that Jakob decides to keep becomes his most intimate possession, the embodiment of his "own" life, a counterbalance to his sense of dislocation and non-belonging, as well as a symbolic locked space not to be muddied by strangers. His obsessive preoccupation with hiding the diary, even before there is any clear reason for it, once again seems to have more to do with his overwhelming fear of contamination and intrusion of privacy than with an objective threat. Yet the diary becomes a vehicle for a truly engaged dialogue with the world for Jakob, literally a site for incorporation of the other, as he gradually copies Timo's memorandum, interspersed with his own comments. The latter are first shocked, almost comically annoyed with Timo's "madness" boldly to criticize the Czar, then ever more empathetic, analytical and intellectually acute. It is not by coincidence that Jakob discovers the memorandum at the same place that he had chosen for hiding his diary—there is a clear parallelism between the two texts, one standing for Timo's personality and understanding of the truth, the other for Jakob's.

On the one hand, Jakob comes to admit to himself that most of what Timo says about the Czarist state is not lunacy, but quite the other way round, it expresses the greatest lucidity from his point of view as well. On the other hand, he is critical and sarcastic in his comments on Timo's spirit of Baltic German Christian chivalry, and his (for Jakob) unbelievably naïve and patronizing attitude towards the Estonian peasantry. Jakob is astonished by "the appalling flaws in [Timo's] knowledge of the world" and "[by] the absurd belief, hard to reconcile with his education and experience, that the lord of an estate could somehow gain the *love* of his peasants" (115, emphasis in the original). However, the intellectual and emotional duel with Timo on the pages of his diary also brings Jakob closer to the nobleman than ever before, to the point that he admits: "[i]n his own life, at least, my brother-in-law managed to build a bridge across that chasm [between peasants and gentry]" (116). "And if I admit that to be true," he writes on, "I also have to admit that this achievement, however fragile (yet undeniable), is a seed of truth in the midst of all his fantasies [...] Laughable, of course, but in a certain way, *impossible to crush*" (116, emphasis in the original).

Thus Jakob's formation seems to be drifting toward its end, when almost exactly in the middle of his diary/the novel he realizes three important points within one entry. He concludes that Timo is not mad (181) and comes to a critical, yet charitable attitude towards his enlightened-aristocratic worldview; he discusses at length the nearby Rõika mirrorworks as a bourgeois entrepreneurial undertaking (184-188), tying this to the appeal in Timo's memorandum for creating a third estate in Russia, as well as to Jakob's own socio-cultural identity problems; third, he meets a new love interest, Anna Klaassen, a widow of an assistant master at the same Rõika mirrorworks. From there on Jakob's life takes a completely different turn—he woos and marries Anna, gets his first larger orders as a land surveyor, and the couple buys their own house in Põltsamaa township.

However, this does fall short of the traditional harmony at the end of a *Bildungsroman*. Half a novel is still to come, and there is a dark side to Jakob's emancipation and progress in the world. All through his relationship with Anna, Jakob is plagued by impressions, visions and dreams, seeing Anna as a double of Iette (219, 259-260, 267). After their marriage, he finally comes to admit to himself that his wife's subtle uncanny similarity to the woman whom he rejected, but still loves, is the reason why he was attracted to Anna in the first place (268-269). The resemblance between Iette and Anna receives a rational explanation. On her deathbed, Anna's mother confesses to Jakob that Anna too is a daughter, albeit an illegitimate daughter, of Iette's father Laming, the Czarist spy (297). The sense of shame relating to the realization that despite his sacrifice of his love he has still, as he sees it, ended up contaminated by Laming, poisons Jakob life. At the end of the day, he feels, he has neither integrity nor love. In his perception, he has betrayed Timo and Eeva by marrying their tormentor's daughter, as well as Iette and Anna. When his son who would have been born on Timo's birthday is strangled by his umbilical cord, he thinks of the sins of the father being revisited upon his children and compares his son's death with Judas Iscariot's suicide by hanging (287).

In addition to Iette, Jakob's dreams connected to his love-life include Czar Alexander and Iette's father Laming who merge into one.[25] Right after his break-up scene with Iette, Jakob in his frustration destroys the portrait of Peter I on his mantelpiece. He writes in his diary: "I stamped on it [...], ground my heel into the imperial visage, heard metal grate against stone. I grabbed the mantel and pushed against it in order to give my boot more weight. I remember groaning: *'Damn, damn—damned—oppression'*" (67, italics in the original). This scene is repeated in a later nightmare of Jakob, where Iette comes to visit him, pulls out of her cloth bundle not an almond cake, like she had once done in real life, but instead the head of Czar Alexander ("perhaps made of plaster of Paris—but dripping blood from its neck" (119)), commenting: "Look, Jakob, my father is dead now. So there is nothing to keep you from me", and lets her clothes fall off (119-120).

Maire Jaanus has written persuasively of Timo's "intense identificatory and mirroring relationship" with Alexander, even while it turns into a sadistic "master-slave relationship" in the prison (321), as well as of Timo's long-lasting belief in the Czar as "his own ideal ego" (322). Indeed, it is in itself significant that Timo addresses his memorandum intimately to his boyhood friend rather than more civically to the Livonian diet, as he had first intended. Jakob's attitude towards the Czar is very different from Timo's. Realizing that Timo is not mad, Jakob expresses himself characteristically in this connection, "I arrived at a strange conclusion: the conviction that everything that Timo wrote [in his memorandum] was nothing but the truth, as it was known to many, if not all. *The only thing incorrect was what he did with it*" (185, my italics).

While Timo retains a close identification with the Czar, Jakob's identification is *with* Timo *against* the Czar, most clearly exemplified in another of his dreams in which he is confused as to whether it is himself or Timo who will be crucified by Laming (and by extension Alexander) (259). Towards the end of his diary, Jakob twice calls Timo his Mephistopheles (300, 329) who, intentionally or

---

25   In the non-dream existence Timo pretends to take Laming for Czar Alexander, hoping to convince the informer he is truly mad, and Laming who does fall for it in his turn pretends to be Alexander, hoping to coax Timo into telling him the truth as Timo had sworn always to tell the truth to the Czar.

not, helped him become "a human being" (329), which in this context seems to stand for a modern individual. Jakob remains of the opinion that Timo's good intentions and noble plans caused almost nothing but ill fortune and suffering (212). However, while he sees Timo's fate as tragic, he considers his own life simply pointless, when he stands at the end of it (346).

The Czar's Madman's attack against dictatorial regimes was probably the most important aspect of the novel for many of its contemporary Estonian readers who understood the analogy between 1970s Soviet Union and the Czarist regime that Timotheus von Bock fights in the novel. In our context, the novel is also a study of the Estonian individual and collective modernization experience, both during the "long Enlightenment" with the Baltic Germans and during the Soviet phase of modernization, where individual emancipation and progress do take place, but not without "contamination" by the system. If Timo's memorandum expresses strong identity and principles springing from its author's Enlightenment values, Christian faith and confidence of status, Jakob's diary is, as its fictional afterword puts it, rather a "chaotic welter of questions", "a house of mirrors" (350) in more than one sense.

Intimate and private as Jakob's journal is for him, at the end of his life he uncharacteristically trusts it to Jüri/Georg von Bock, Eeva's and Timo's son although the latter has made his peace with the new Czar Nicholas and has embarked on a successful career in the Czar's navy, seeing it as an honourable way to clear the family name. Jakob and Timo both became unhappy with their children (Jakob also had a daughter with Anna) who, for different reasons, did not seem like their true heirs. Yet Jakob concludes at the end of his journal:

> If Jüri destroys my journal, there is no hope for the world.
> If he keeps it, there is hope for the world.
> It is a very good thing that I won't know what he'll do.
> It gives me a chance to hope even when there may be no hope. (341)

The reader does not learn what Jüri does with the difficult, inconsistent house of mirrors that Jakob's diary is, whether he reads it through, and if so, what he thinks of it. The only thing the reader knows is that it has not been destroyed and that it has been passed on to them.[26]

---

26 Actually, the Soviet period readers also knew that the Russian Czarist Empire too did not last forever, but fell to ashes one day. Ljubov Kisseljova calls this knowledge "an additional optimistic subtext" of the novel, as pessimistic as the book might impress one text-immanently (328).

Emil Tode's Border State

In contrast to the novels discussed in the previous sub-chapters, *Border State* (1993) was published and written in the Estonian Republic, two years after its regaining of independence. Emil Tode is a pseudonym used by the author Tõnu Õnnepalu (b. 1962). Previously known as a poet, translator and critic, *Border State* was his first novel, emerging as a major event in post-independence cultural life. Probably the most discussed literary text of the 1990s, it continues to produce new readings in the 21st century, republished in 2003, 2009, and 2015. Reminiscing in a later interview, Õnnepalu explains why the novel was published under a pseudonym: "I didn't want that it would somehow fall into the row of the already existing and wished the book would appear as if out of the blue" (Õnnepalu, "Kohaloleku"). Literary scholars and critics have repeatedly emphasized that a novel like that would have been impossible to write any time earlier than it was (Laak 137). Indeed, as a cultural phenomenon it is seen to be ahead of its time, creating a shock and simultaneously opening a new era in Estonian literature in terms of its form as well as themes and worldview.

What then was so different about *Border State* and, on the other hand, how does it compare, when we do place it in a line, with that of earlier Estonian *Bildungsromane*? On an important, if obvious, level the plot space and the field of vision are much broader there. The main character is a translator on an EU scholarship to translate French poetry, and his *Bildung*-trajectory takes him from Estonia to the chrestomatic metropole, Paris, now an end-of-20th-century consumer capitalist globalized city where one can meet people from all continents. He also stays with his Franco-German boyfriend in Amsterdam, considers travelling to Portugal and falls in love with an American, the letters to whom constitute the novel's text. Furthermore, this internationalization of the field of attachments echoed in the rapid international reception of the novel, unprecedented for a work of Estonian literature. It won the Baltic Assembly Prize for Literature in 1994 and came out in Finnish even before that. There soon followed translations into the Scandinavian and the Baltic languages, then into Dutch, Russian, Italian, Hungarian, German, French, Spanish, Turkish, English, Hebrew, Slovenian, Albanian, Chinese and Macedonian.

As was acknowledged by its first international reception, this was one of the earliest literary works to critically probe and try to make sense of the changes that had come into being as the result of the end of the Cold War (cf. Tuumalu). The novel does not support the widely accepted political discourse of the 1990s, which claimed that Eastern Europe can and must "return to the West", whether that return would be imagined as a complicated transformation (the EU point of view), or a natural homecoming to normality due to one's intrinsic "Europeanness" (Lagerspetz "Postsocialism"). The fall of the Berlin Wall created serious problems of identity and agency because one could not blame "the system" or "the Empire of Evil" anymore, one had "to take responsibility oneself", as Õnnepalu commented on his book at the Leipzig Book Fair upon the publication of the novel in German (Õnnepalu, "Piiririigis" B3). For many on both sides of the Iron Curtain, this development meant the end of their familiar, predictable world. Even further, getting to know the West could mean a powerful disappointment for an Eastern European such as his (autobiographical) main character:

> The crumbling of the Berlin Wall revealed primarily that that there is no *other world*. There never was. That despite the different systems the whole time we have been living in the same world, that the East and the West were only two different and differently flawed realizations of the same utopia. (Õnnepalu, "Piiririigis" B3, emphasis in the original)

The narrator of *Border State*, alienated both from his Eastern past and Western present, feels he is travelling on the boundary line between different worlds that people create, marginal or downright invisible to all sides. His imagery is fragmented, blending motifs of Parisian urbanity, Soviet industrial buildings, natural landscapes, and pre-modern and early modern rurality. The reader does not know how much of the account "really happened", nor is the reader always sure when the narrator is being ironic and flippant or deadly earnest. The fact that the story is narrated by a man rather than a woman, or the details of the narrator's exact origins also remain implicit, only hinted at: evocative details and figures point to Estonia, but he refers to it only as "a forgotten country" (Õnnepalu, *Border State* 1), "Eastern Europe" (2), "up North as they say here" (4), "the country from which I came" (66). Yet, despite the desire to escape pre-given identities, the nameless Eastern European homeland returns in sudden memories or Proustian sensory associations, dominating the narrator's dreams and nightmares. It also seems that this semi-repressed baggage of memories and feelings is behind the murder at the center of the plot, the main character's (perhaps purely figurative, perhaps not) killing of his doting but condescending and patronizing Western lover Franz.

Complex, many-layered, even hermetic in form, and thematically thought-provoking, the interpretation of and reactions to the novel over time have been varied, occasionally antithetical. While the Estonian reception often refers to *Border State* as a "European novel" (Undusk, "Eesti lugu"), its main character is frequently cynical about and finally entirely disillusioned with the promise of European consumerist society, which he describes as dead and mummified.[27] Further, while the novel undermines the "return to Europe" rhetoric, in doing so it also undercuts the dominant line of Estonian *ethnic nationalism* at the time. The desire to identify as European was a collective one. It is strongly related to the dream of shaking off the Soviet legacy, associated with lack of freedom, closed borders and material misery, and of "returning" to the pre-colonial Estonian Republic, associated with a prosperous economy and political agency as a sovereign modern state (cf. Chapter One).

Moreover, as Undusk points out, while the narrator's vivid sensory memory baggage of (implicit) Estonia is conceptually central in the novel, his "true Estonia is not a state or a people", but rather nature, conveyed in his emotional recollections of landscapes ("Eesti lugu"). The narrator is "almost a Noble Savage", "the embodiment [...] of the urge to hide in the undergrowth away from every suspicious and certain-to-be-corrupt organization, the state included" (Undusk, "Eesti lugu"). While suspicion towards official institutions is a feature often represented in Estonian literature, it contrasts with the mood of the early 1990s when the thought-style of the Singing Revolution still persisted and was expected by many to be carried on in the newly independent state.

Undusk also compares *Border State* to Juhan Liiv's *The Shadow*. Despite the postmodern metropolitan setting of *Border State*, according to Undusk, the situations and basic spiritual journeys of the two main characters are alike. I will discuss the important differences between the works in this aspect below—yet, no doubt, Undusk is in many ways right. Both protagonists admire and long for the cultivated, sophisticated beauty of the manor-house/Europe. They get a chance to pursue their *Bildung* with material means provided by the object of their admiration, with the aim that they could cultivate themselves in order to integrate into it (though not be equal)[28]. Yet, both end up tormented by and disillusioned with the former embodiment of ideals.

---

27 It is also possible to read the novel as the confessions of an unreliable narrator, a person overwhelmed and unbalanced by his sudden immersion in the Western lifestyle (e.g. the reader blog "Kiiksu lugemisblogi"; Lehiste). In that case the novel's target of criticism is not the inequality and consumerism of Paris, but the narrator's inability to participate in consumer capitalism in a proper manner; his lack of cultivation. Nevertheless, in that case too he remains an outsider in Europe.
28 The Border State's protagonist gets a grant to translate French poetry "within the framework of East European cultural integration" (Õnnepalu, *Border State* 33).

As Villu had the longing to see beyond the forest, *Border State*'s narrator associates France with the splendor of the sun that he longs to follow. "I yearned for sunshine," he writes to Angelo, "that brought me to this town, where so much of the world's beauty and wealth is gathered" (3). As a young boy he had dreamt of fleeing to Paris, escaping the squalid closure of home ("an apartment in the prefabricated apartment house which stank of Grandmother's medicines because no windows could be opened to let in air" (32)). His dream is that one day he "would walk along the boulevards, would sit in cafés, would smile at people who would smile at [him]", would admire the original artworks he only sees as copies presently. In contrast to the world of sunshine, the home "up North" is gloomy, dark and cold. It is also "in another century" in comparison to the West (1), or even from a different order entirely, "the world of plants", so that he feels curiosity to experience "what it is like to be human, to live like a human being" (70).

Border State's tropology also resembles *The Shadow* and other *Bildungsromane* analyzed above in the depiction of a ruptured family tree, full of uncertainties, and the strained or absent relationships between children and parents. The protagonist grows up with a woman he calls Grandmother, a tough survivor peasant woman familiar from Liiv's and Rannamaa's texts. In this novel she is a former deportee returned from Siberia who, even after many years back in Estonia, retains the experience in her body and "never [takes] her kerchief off in [a] train or unbutton[s] her coat, even though the compartment may have been warm" and keeps a bundle with food and medicines firmly in her lap for the whole trip (90). She instils her own ingrained memories of violence and hardship in the protagonist on both a verbal and bodily level: she has a fixed repertoire of stories of her life in Siberia that she keeps narrating over and over, indignant whenever he switches off in his thoughts, ready to punish him with her Singer sewing machine belt (54-55).[29]

The protagonist is not sure of his family tree. He seems to have infrequent contact with his mother, and his father is never mentioned. The Grandmother is actually a step-grandmother; she had brought the protagonist's mother back from Siberia, according to one version as the daughter of her lover by another woman who had died. "Mother was actually Polish or something like that," the protagonist tells Angelo, "[n]o one knew exactly, and Grandmother never talked about it" (Õnnepalu, *Border State* 47). The Grandmother becomes for him

---

29 The Singer sewing machine figures as a symbol of survival in many memoirs of deportation, as it often enabled Estonian women to make a living with their sewing skills (Laanes, *Lepitamatud* 269).

the embodiment of the materially and intellectually limited life he detests. He tries to escape her and "to do everything just the opposite from what Grandmother taught" (48) him—he reads books, delights in art and aesthetic beauty, learns foreign languages, dreams of travelling. Yet, the memories of his times with the now deceased woman, sometimes hurtful, sometimes ironic, humorous and even affectionate, as well as other memories of homeland saturate his whole narration. They intrude and intertwine with his experience of the Western metropoles, making unambivalent identification with the latter impossible (cf. Laanes, "Confession" 149).

A major important difference in comparison with Liiv's *The Shadow* is, however, that there is no equivalent to the Kuuse family in Tode's novel—parent figures coming close to symbolizing the idea of 'one's folk' more generally, 'a people' one wants to work for or with, or of that of a collective inheritance worth receiving. The *Border State*'s protagonist perceives his memories of his home and step-grandmother, although they are inseparable of the socio-cultural experience shared by Estonians collectively, in a very personal and subjective dimension, often involuntary, as sensual associations beyond his control. His past that he is processing is part of larger postcolonial history, yet the transformation that he seeks is an individual one, enabled by his trusting romantic relationship with Angelo who accepts his self-narration in his own terms, outside customary collective identifications (nationality, gender).[30]

This stands in symbolic contrast to his previous significant love relationship with a country pastor in Estonia. While romantic love and religious spirituality had been related to one another for the protagonist, he sees no value in the cultural-political role that the church adopts in the national movement for decolonization, as an antidote to Soviet-period prescribed atheism and as an attempt to "return" to the ways of the previous period of independence. "His fussing over youths who were studying to be confirmed, his blessing of flags, everything seemed hilarious to me," he relates to Angelo. "Suddenly he reminded me of an old woman who was airing all sorts of old rags that ought to have been burned much earlier" (Õnnepalu, *Border State* 74). These collective solemnities belong to the previous century, "discarded as trash long ago" (74). Now, as he quips elsewhere, "all countries have become imaginary deserts of ruins where crowds of nomads roam from one attraction to the other, sweeping over continents" (5).[31]

---

30 See Laanes's *Lepitamatud* 229-287 and "Confession" for an in-depth analysis of the self-transformation of the protagonist in his narration and its dependence on the figure of Angelo as the listener.
31 Here and in quotations below I have modified the translation to render the original more closely.

An important dimension of the protagonist's education about the ways of the world is his engagement with French consumer culture. As indicated above, besides belatedness, political repression, and the instability of family origins, another dominant theme in his vivid memory pictures is the material unsophistication of the Soviet world—"the gray houses with the peeling stucco" (7); "the suffocating stench of an indoor privy" (2); the bleak streetscapes with "fat women in polyester dresses, string bags for shopping in hand" "marching toward the trolley stop with determined faces" (62), or "stern women in heavy overcoats" queueing for Hungarian or Polish apples in the winter cold (54). *Border State* perceptively probes the cluster of meanings relating to identity, self-cultivation and labor in connection with consumer culture and, more generally, implies that the (re)production or rejection of certain humanly meaningful patterns of life can only happen through various kinds of human engagement with the non-human (natural or manufactured) world. It is from the aspect of consumption, rather than from that of political struggles that the protagonist keenly observes the possible dynamics between an individual's aspirations, and his or her opportunities to integrate into the modern (social and physical) world.

In his *Consumer Culture and Modernity*, the British sociologist Don Slater convincingly argues against the idea that everyday consumption is somehow a trivial matter:

> [T]he great issue about the consumer culture is the way it connects the central questions about how we should or want to live with questions how society is organized—and so at the level of everyday life: the material and symbolic structure of the places we live in and how we live in them; the food we eat and the clothes we wear; the scarcities and inequities we suffer (3).

"Consumer culture" in Slater's sense primarily means a particular kind of culture of consumption, the one that has developed as part of market society since the seventeenth century. The dynamic of wide consumer demand for fashion and changing taste for "the new" comes into being with the transition to modern society (Slater 19). Some, like Jean Jacques Rousseau in his *Discourse on Inequality* (1755) would find that this makes the wants of a modern consumer somehow automatically inauthentic. However, beyond the bare minimum for just staying alive (hardly a baseline for assessing what is an authentic need) human material "needs" are always partly socio-culturally constructed: in every age and society one needs certain material objects that enable one to enact and sustain one's membership in society. Under the Old Regime, fashionable, display-oriented consumption was the privilege of the upper strata, and not principally because of others' poverty but because of the fixity and rigidity of the prescriptions as to who was allowed to consume what. When Villu, in Liiv's *Shadow*, is apprehended for poaching a hare, this is in punishment for violating the nobility's sole right to hunt, not simply for stealing food.

In the liberal mind, modern market economy is associated with social democratization and increase of individual liberty to make choices, including consumer choices. Significantly, as Slater points out, the word commerce originally meant not only economic exchange, but the free exchange of ideas, conversation, etc. by various members of the society in the public sphere (23). In much the same vein in the late Soviet period Eastern Europe, certainly in Estonia, "consumer sovereignty" was often seen as "the mundane realization of civic freedom" and liberation "from various Soviet constraints" (Keller 13) not compatible with proper modernity. The Estonian sociologist Margit Keller argues that Western import items and other goods in short supply were, in a certain sense, individual status symbols, enabling to display "distinction" in the midst of forced Soviet homogeneity, but they were also symbolically associated with collective aspirations like national independence, westernization and "a general striving for what was deemed as the 'good life'" (19).[32]

Keller's research shows that by the mid-1990s, with the development of the local shopping scene, Estonians' attitudes towards shopping and consumption became even more differentiated and ambivalent—a development that Õnnepalu's novel foreshadows. There is resentment by many who feel excluded by the new scarcity, now not of goods, but of money, and there is criticism of the vulgarity and silliness of conspicuous consumption ("showing off"). There are also expressions of sincere pleasure in the choice of attainable goods or even just in the novelty entertainment of looking around in large glamorous shopping centers, such as the Finnish-owned Stockmann that opened in Tallinn in 1996, notwithstanding the lack of means to buy much. Being fairly democrat-

---

32 Zygmunt Bauman argues in *Intimations of Postmodernity* (1994) that the absence of consumer freedom, the Soviet economy's inability to provide a variety of goods to satisfy people's individualized desires (influenced by the West), was a major reason for the collapse of the Soviet system. Other authors (e.g. Gronow) have countered that Soviet patterns of consumption and coping with scarcity were relying heavily on conformity and mutuality of favors, so the desire for diversity could not have been the reason for the collapse (overview in Keller 32-33). Based on Keller's research and my own experience I agree with Keller's conclusion that the studies, like Gronow's, that concentrate on Russia and on the Stalinist period are not a useful indicator about the situation in Estonia, "the Soviet West", and that Bauman's account better agrees with the sociological research conducted on the values and practices of consumption in Soviet and decolonizing Estonia.

ically accessible, these shopping centers serve as schools of capitalist consumerism, teaching timely and appropriate tastes and lifestyle to the population at large, in disregard of their immediate purchasing power—an educative role reminiscent of that attributed to large department stores in the metropoles of the 19th century.[33] Furthermore, with the further "maturation" of the Estonian consumer experience, there emerges critique of the local lack of sophistication in terms of classy atmosphere, competent service and quality craftsmanship of goods, often with reference made to the longer and more refined tradition in the West with which Estonians still have to catch up (Keller 30).

In the Paris of the early 1990s, Õnnepalu's protagonist often takes great trouble to style himself as a Westerner, and he likes to present himself as Swedish, not to be typecast and prejudged as an Eastern European. He does not want to be associated with the kind of people who "buy themselves some horrible outfits on the Boulevard Saint-Michel and then prance about in them as if in seventh heaven" (27), with their lack of taste in consumption, and thus presumed lack of cultivation, as well as poverty and greed. He is acutely conscious that the "right" style is not just about money, it is about the right kind of knowledge and cultivation. "Even if they got hold of some Arabian oil sheik or some old émigré Russian Jewish lady," he writes, "who would dress them from head to toe in Versace or Rabanne clothes, I'd still recognize them, because they wouldn't know how to wear these clothes. Something would always give them away! Me as well." (27-28)

His feelings about this truth are ambivalent—while he is taken by the sophistication and masterfulness of Paris consumption practices, he is also repelled by what he sees as their hypocrisy and alienation from the rest of the world. Noting an "unbelievably stylish, á la 1960s" young couple taking pleasure shopping at a "terribly expensive" antiques store, he comments: "The man in his dark-framed glasses looked exactly like some innocent philosophy instructor from the Sorbonne, leaning toward Maoism but secretly enjoying the pleasures of life" (43). It makes him feel really happy that he is separated by a "billion miles" from people like that and that for them he is "as distant as the Yugoslav war refugee [...] crouching with her child by the column on the street" (43).

---

33 Michael B. Miller writes about the *Bon Marché* department stores in France (prototype to the setting of Zola's *Au Bonheur des Dames* (1883)): "The Bon Marché came to serve essentially the same role as the Republican school system, at least for those of middle-class means or middle-class aspirations [...] becoming a kind of cultural primer. The Bon Marché showed people how they should dress, how they should furnish their homes, and how they should spend their leisure time. [...] It illustrated how successful people or people who wished to be successful or on their way to being successful lived their lives" (Miller 183).

Chapter Three. Bildung in the Image of Modernity

Reminiscent of Slater and Keller, the protagonist also makes a strong connection between people consuming "right", with "distinction"[34], and being self-confident about their "rights" in the society, free from Soviet-type humiliations and constraints. However, he depicts this self-confidence with some cynicism, as rather self-righteous, even cruel, and at the same time potentially very naïve, too sure that the world will never change, at least not in terms of the—consumerist—pleasures they enjoy. An occasion at the Gare du Nord railway station, where Parisians aggressively protest against a cashier closing for lunch, even if the break is lawful and pre-scheduled, provokes the following reverie by him:

> People here are simply used to feeling that they have rights. I can't help it, but to me it seems very strange. I myself wouldn't mind at all belonging to these righteous ones, to be able to fill my shopping cart at the Auchan supermarket once a week with mountains of bottles of mineral water, heaps of toilet-paper rolls, detergent, pâtés, cheeses, and bran breads, to berate the cashier at the Gare du Nord. But it's probably too late for me to start now. It would be pointless at this juncture. I don't think my rights would last for very long, and will even theirs last forever? (15)

The protagonist's relationship with Western society is embodied in his destructive affair with his older lover Franz. The name can be seen as a metonymic pun: when the protagonist first mentions Franz in a conversation with Angelo, the latter mishears it as "France".[35] He is characterized by the protagonist much in the same terms as the hypothetical consumerist-Maoist Sorbonne professor discussed above. A philosophy professor, proclaiming leftist ideals of the end of 1960s, he at the same time owns inherited stocks in a business that makes warplanes (84). He enjoys an elegant lifestyle, largely ignorant of the world not immediately around him: for example, he is first incredulous, then sexually aroused when he hears that the protagonist had lived in "primitive" conditions without running water (71-72).

Franz's work at the university is shown up as deeply alienated, although the protagonist does not use Marxist language. Franz works diligently and consci-

---

34 Pierre Bourdieu's research demonstrates that people's tastes in consumption (of arts, but also of clothes, food, cosmetics, etc.) are not individual but culturally conditioned and a part of status competition. The "right" taste distinguishes one as part of an in-group, and also gives one "distinction" in the sense of social standing (*Distinction*).
35 Laanes *Lepitamatud* (264) and Laanes "Confession" (147) also point out the parallel with Milan Kundera's character Franz, a Swiss university professor, and his strained relationship with Sabina, his Czech refugee lover, in *The Unbearable Lightness of Being* (1984).

entiously reading and teaching ideas of radical philosophers, yet the sole rationale of it seems to be that he should earn a large salary and give the students the sort of cultivation that helps them "get on in life" as well (20, 34). Franz claims to envy the protagonist because he comes from a country "where history is being made on a daily basis" and "something real is happening" (75). However, when the latter is not enthusiastic about staying in France and rather considers returning home, it completely contradicts Franz's understanding of "the order of the world" (93) and what sane people must want. He reacts with violent incomprehension, shaking his boyfriend by shoulders, shouting: "But you're crazy! No normal person would refuse what I'm offering you and crave back there… there…there!" (92) lost for words to label the other's homeland.

Upon that the protagonist (as he relates to Angelo) gives Franz a fatal dose of heart medicine in his gin and tonic—thus literally killing the *mésalliance* with Western Europe offered to him in Franz's terms. For long before that Franz has been associated with deadliness and death, Franz's elegant pampered body reminding the narrator of a mummy of a young pharaoh they had seen in Louvre (20). In Franz's spotless kitchen, behind the veneer of neatly packaged consumer goods, aestheticism and functionality, he perceives "chaos that lay beneath those surfaces" only waiting to be exposed: "dirty cracks covering the walls, mud and blood bursting from the pipes, […] the decomposed head of a corpse stinking up the refrigerator!" (8-9). While for Rannamaa's Kadri, in the drabness of the 1950s beautiful things had been empowering and educating, enhancing Kadri's creativity and sense of agency, the protagonist of *Border State* feels the need to point to the alienation and ugliness behind the rich pleasures of variety, cosmopolitanism and self-invention that 1990s consumer capitalism offers.[36]

It is significant that Õnnepalu's protagonist does not associate his contemporary West with progress and development as the ideals of modernity and *Bildung* would presume; the change that seems to be happening merely consists of the repetition of the same. He writes about a group of his "countrymen", again

---

36 The historical sociology of Colin Campbell (1989) links the mentality of the modern consumer culture to the Romantic ideals of imaginative desiring and longing, sensibility, developing or re-creating oneself—the ideals of *Bildung* with their roots in Protestant religion, Pietism in particular. For early Marx too, capitalism is progressive, insofar as it can produce material culture for developing humans who are "rich in needs": the refinement of human self-expression and richly differentiated self-development depends on the progress and cosmopolitanism of material culture (qtd. in Slater 104). The problem is just that in capitalism, so Marx, humans are distanced and alienated from the material culture that they see as "commodities", unable to recognize them as products of human labor, as externalizations of human subjectivity (Slater 104-105). Human labor screened out, "the connection—and the control over the connection—between the transformation of objects and the transformation of ourselves" is lost (Slater 104).

Chapter Three. Bildung in the Image of Modernity

tastelessly dressed, whom he observes staring at the window displays of a famous department store, bound to be stuck there—like himself—because "if you've ever stood in front of those windows, you may pretend that you're above it all, but you'll stay there forever" (68). The parallel vision, noted on the same train of thought are prostitutes on Rue Saint-Denise, standing "absolutely still", making one deal after another with a succession of varied clients, then returning to the standing position, "a challenge, an insult to any idea of time passing, to any idea at all" (68-69).

As noted above, *Border State*'s sense of the end of history has a pre-apocalyptic undercurrent and does not share the optimism of its near-contemporary *The End of History and the Last Man* (1992) by Fukuyama, which sees the triumph of Western democracy and capitalism in the Cold War as, on the whole, a *happy* end point of human history. Rather, considering the tropes above, the novel's take on its contemporary history seems to have something in common with Hartmut Rosa's bleak description of postmodern change as superficial: it amounts to a succession of many new things, deals, interactions and so on that do not, however, change the underlying deeper system, thus making history come to a "hyperaccelerated standstill" where meaningful sociopolitical choices or change are no longer possible. While Rosa fears and warns that this speeding might result in a catastrophe, the protagonist seems to have accepted that the chaos beneath the surface will indeed soon burst, exposing the naïvety of the trust in the stable world that Westerners, in his view, hold despite the popularity of postmodern philosophers.[37]

The two reveries above are followed by a recurrent motif of *Border State*, here emerging as a counter-trope to the visions of flawed modernity and repetitive time with no change: the closest that *Border State* comes to a positive project. This is a *mémoire involontaire* of a wild landscape, this time a forest clearing with a deserted log farmhouse, the roof already leaking, soon to be overgrown. Predating Viivi Luik's "A Sermon at the Grave of the Schoolhouse" discussed at the end of Chapter One, *Border State* proposes a related vision of regeneration: soon the walls "would fall prey to the grass"; "young green blades" "pushing up through the earth": a "terrifying hymn to life [...] rising deafeningly through the previous year's thatch" (69).

The memory is triggered in an empty quiet church in Paris, with the smell of being long uninhabited that the farmhouse had also had. Both places are deserted, yet they emerge as sunlit and serene, with the promise of resurrection. In

---

37 Rosa's ideas are discussed in the "Introduction" of this book.

an earlier episode the narrator says he would want to be grass, belong to plant life that, simple in needs, will outlive humans and their ambitions. However, the wild landscapes of *Border State* are all strongly culturally coded, besides evoking the axiology of regeneration both in its general Christian and more particularly Estonian dimensions, the narrator's descriptions of nature also allude to, and once directly quote, the nature poetry of Juhan Liiv. Despite its cosmopolitan setting and the rejection of the central discourses of Estonian nationalism contemporary with it, *Border State* is, culturally, a deeply Estonian book, in certain nuances incomprehensible without the knowledge of its Estonian intertexts.

This Estonian dimension, however, is about individually inflected political-cultural experience and identity, not about collective political imagination. When receiving the Baltic Assembly Prize, the author of the book said: "I want to write books that create additional freedom, books that don't define our identities, but open them up endlessly" (qtd. in Laak 143). The protagonist of *Border State* enacts this creation of additional freedom and opening up of a personal identity through his transformative testimony to Angelo. At the end of it he is unbound by the defining identity narratives of his time, leaving his position "standing on the border" between East and West, starting "on the actual road to recovery" (96-97), on to new discoveries that he does not relate to Angelo anymore (99). This suggests moving beyond and away from this relationship as well, in *Bildungsroman* terms resisting the idea of a social contract that a romantic commitment would symbolize.

Eneken Laanes proposes that the narrator's liminal position "can best be understood through Homi K. Bhabha's notion of the 'third space' that 'displaces the histories that constitute it, and sets up new structures of authority, new political initiatives, which are inadequately understood through received wisdom'" (Bhabha qtd. in Laanes, "Confession" 151). Yet, a reading implying collective political creativity can, in my mind, only be sustained if one reads the main character as metaphorically also standing for his country. The author of the novel has suggested the opposite: that, rather, the country's liminal position metaphorically stands for the individuals' duty to move beyond borders and open up identities outside such structures of authority and collective political activity that Bhabha talks about, new or otherwise. Upon the occasion of the German translation of his novel he praises the title it has been given: *Im Grenzland* ("in the border area"). This is more exact, because the protagonist is not really narrating about the "province eternally passing from one hand to another, the symbol of Eastern Europe" he "claims to come from" but rather "about the border state he is in, everywhere and always", about "the boundaries in our heads"—

necessary for human thinking, yet at the same time always to be surpassed, to be "liberated from" (qtd. in Laak 133-134). Now that the Cold War "barbed wires" have been removed, "everyone everywhere can make choices and is forced to make choices".

Read in this way, the protagonist apparently makes his choice for individualism, post-materialism, spirituality and endless becoming, thus "privatizing" the remedy for the social and political malaise the novel dramatizes. Comparing the "make-believe", not-really-existent quality of his present life to the virtuality of the money he takes from bank machines (56-57), he embarks on his road of recovery alone, there are no shared systems and, indeed, no other people. He does not believe there is a "symbolically legitimate social order" for him to join, because the former Europe of *poleis* is now subjected to transnational economic forces and has itself become akin to a colony. It is exactly because of his experience of Soviet colonialism that he sees it with faster insight than the good citizens naturalized in the world of Auchan supermarkets. However, differently from the protagonists of the previously analyzed novels he does not have ambitions or hopes to change this. He feels that liberal capitalism does give him the freedom to opt out on his own terms—the kind of freedom not there for most people in the world.

Anton Hansen Tammsaare's *Truth and Justice*: A post-postcolonial Bildungsroman?[38]

Since its publication, Anton Hansen Tammsaare's *Truth and Justice* (1926-33) has had a highly canonical position in Estonian culture, one close to that of a national epic. A weighty socio-historical novel, which in five volumes covers Estonian history from the 1870s to the beginning of 1930s, it is generally considered the most resonant and formative work of fiction in terms of Estonian history and self-image. The history of its reception in criticism, subsequent fiction, film and drama, the proliferation of its themes, tropes and images in different areas of Estonian "high" and "popular" culture would certainly deserve a separate monograph. Furthermore, while telling the particular story of Estonian modernization in a mainly realist narrative vein, it is simultaneously a universally oriented philosophical exploration of the laws and paradoxes of history and human existence.

---

38 A version of this subchapter has been published as Peiker, "A.H. Tammsaare's".

Although the critical tradition has not considered *Truth and Justice* from a genre perspective or highlighted the *Bildungsroman* characteristics of the novel, the central thread of the book, both in terms of its plot and its axiology, is the formation of the main character Indrek through his childhood and school years to mature adulthood. It is both a strongly autobiographical novel, drawing upon the author's upbringing and life experience, and a philosophical one about the human experience of history and modernization. In this respect, Mikhail Bakhtin's characterization of the early Western *Bildungsroman* discussed above, perfectly fits Tammsaare's novel and Indrek's role in it as the *Bildungsroman* protagonist:

> [he] *emerges along with the world* and he reflects the historical emergence of the world itself. He is no longer within an epoch, but on the border between two epochs, at the transition point from one another. The transition is accomplished in him and through him. [...] The organizing force held by the future is therefore extremely great here—and this is not, of course, the private biographical future, but the historical future. (*Speech Genres* 23, Bakhtin's emphasis)

Up to a point Indrek's life develops in a typical postcolonial *Bildungsroman* plot pattern. The sensitive and talented protagonist is born and grows up at a punishingly hardworking Vargamäe farm, in turn-of-the-19th-century rural Estonia. He moves to town (first Tartu, then Tallinn) to seek formal schooling, which he eventually is unable to complete because of a combination of psychological, economic and political problems, but which leads him to lose his belief in God and to a great extent his spiritual ties to the world of his childhood in general. He becomes involved in the 1905 revolution, which ends tragically both in the personal and the political dimensions.

The novel skips the War of Independence (1918–20) and the establishment of the independent Republic of Estonia. Instead, it next takes the form of the family novel, intertwining the story of the collapse of Indrek's marriage with those of the crumbling of traditional morality and family values and the collapse of the economy at the end of the 1920s. Indrek's marriage not only fails, but ends with Indrek on trial for attempted murder, having shot at his wife Karin, and with the death of his wife in a traffic accident immediately thereafter. Part of the distrust between Indrek and Karin stems from Indrek secretly hiding an underground communist, a friend from the 1905 revolution, although he believes in the communist agenda no more than he cares for the unethical *noveaux riches* of his wife's family. In the final volume Indrek returns home to his father in the countryside not as the success the father had hoped his talented son would become, but a ruined, guilt-ridden and hopeless man. Although he has two children with Karin, he feels unfit to bring them up and leaves them in the care of his parents-in-law.

As in a typical postcolonial novel, Indrek participates in the violent and demoralizing events of history in a mundane, everyday way in the sense that they are an unavoidable part of Indrek's ongoing struggle of life and personal development. However, in what follows I want to show that *Truth and Justice* considerably differs from the postcolonial model of the *Bildungsroman*, including its versions in Estonia discussed above. The main difference is that it ultimately provides a model for domesticating historical change relating to modernity and establishing a bridge (or an illusion of a bridge, depending on interpretation) between tradition and modernity specifically in the Estonian context.[39] How does that happen?

The most important answer to the question is closely bound up with the ways *Truth and Justice* constructs time, and emplots its story time. The linear progressive "real historical time", the hegemonic type of time in modernity (Bakhtin, *Speech Genres* 25) dominates the narrative course, but it is partly paralleled and partly replaced by other perceptions of time, continuity, and change, which embed new meaning, and come to carry significant functions in the novel. The resulting narrative does not ignore the sense of discontinuity and alienation in the postcolonial and rapidly modernizing Estonian society, yet shapes it into a particular "usable history", which is not entirely congruous with the Western linear and progressivist model, but is easily combinable and compatible with it.

The best starting point to approach Tammsaare's different conceptions of time is to note Johann Wolfgang Goethe's and Fyodor Dostoevsky's influence on his work. Both the critical tradition dealing with Tammsaare's *oeuvre*, as well as Tammsaare himself, have emphasized the central impact of these authors with good reason (e.g. Grišakova; Teder; Treier, *Tammsaare ja tema*; Treier, *Tammsaare elust*). In the case of *Truth and Justice*, another core intertextual reference point is Oswald Spengler's *The Decline of the West* (1923) (Treier, *Tammsaare ja tema* 66-68), which in its turn links its account of world history to Goethe through its central notion of Western culture as "Faustian": individualistic, striving to master infinite space and, through that, time and mortality. When Bakhtin outlines his notion of "real historical time", in which "man emerges *along with the*

---

39 On Tammsaare's earlier phase of engagement with modernity and modernism, see Mirjam Hinrikus's discussion of his so-called "university novellas" ("Spleen").

world" (*Speech Genres* 23, Bakhtin's emphasis), he uses Goethe as his central illustrating example. Goethe is essential because of his way of seeing time in space, his "ability to read in everything *signs that show time in its course*" (*Speech Genres* 25, Bakhtin's emphasis).[40]

In *Truth and Justice* not only are the layers of the past embodied in space, but particularly in the first volume, space is also overripe with plans for the future, embodying Indrek's father's Faustian investment in history-as-progress and his desire to control space. At the beginning of the pentalogy, the father, Andres, has just bought a large but swampy holding, with the dream of draining the wetlands in order to establish a successful farm that his sons would inherit and develop further. As he and his newly wed wife Krõõt approach the farm for the first time and almost drown in their small cart, Andres comforts Krõõt with a very concretely spatialized vision of the future:

> It will not remain like that forever. We will make the trenches deeper, the road higher and smoother. At the bottom we will place junipers and fir branches, on top field stones and gravel. [...] In a few years we shall be able to go through here even in a two-horse cart (Tammsaare, *Tõde ja õigus I* 8).

And later the narrator says of Andres:

> As a matter of fact, when Andres bought the Eespere farm at Vargamäe he had not at all taken into account its present value, he had only been constantly pondering what could be made of it, what value could be given to the land through work. Thus the young owner didn't do anything else during his present survey-trip than plan and scheme, trying to look ahead in his mind to see how the ground of earth will change, what will the small birch, dumpy pine-tree and stunted fir become like when so and so many trenches have been dug in this and in that direction. (*Tõde ja õigus I* 14)

Significantly, Andres's plans to change his land are rooted in the past, and in the Baltic German past at that. He is following the example of an once successful land-amelioration project by a German landowner, noticed by Andres when travelling about in search for a farm to buy. Achieving what the baron

---

40 Goethe's innovations in the poetics of time have been noted and discussed since his contemporary period until today (Steinby and Schmidt (ed.)). The present argument limits itself to the aspects highlighted by Bakhtin, mainly based on *The Italian Journey* and *Wilhelm Meister's Apprenticeship* among Goethe's works.

had achieved, even if he does not have "the people of a whole parish to order about" is far more than simply a commercial aim for Andres, it has value in itself, so that he would not end up living his life merely like "a fly on a heap of shit" (*Tõde ja õigus I* 14-15). This is his Faustian endeavor.[41]

Anneli Kõvamees has elaborated on the centrality of both the past and the future in *Truth and Justice*, at the expense of attention to the moment at hand (Kõvamees). As time passes, the characters' desires for a better future are accompanied alternately by remorse and by nostalgia for the past. When Indrek and his brothers Ants and Andres are growing up, every field, nook and cranny at Vargamäe is connected to the older children's stories of what fun they had had at those places when they were small—but not anymore. Life and life environment are constantly changing, and even the successful endeavors for progress become part of a worn-out past, without one even noticing:

> When his first child with Mari had been born, it seemed to Andres as if his life was starting anew. Yet everything was old at Vargamäe. Even the new rooms were not that new anymore and no-one came to look at them as an object of curiosity anymore, because there were farms in the neighbourhood, which had even newer, larger and better-lit rooms than the ones that Andres had at Vargamäe—that was how quickly time whirled by and life changed (*Tõde ja õigus I* 237).

The decisions and sacrifices made in the name of future ambitions are transformed many times into guilt-ridden memories of the past. These too, in *Truth and Justice*, are often depicted as physically incised in the landscape, things and bodies, inheritable by the next generation, and becoming part of continuous history. In this regard Indrek's genealogy, his relationship to his parents and their history, is central for his *Bildung*, his "emergence along with the world".

Indrek's mother Mari is first introduced as a young, cheerful and hard-working servant girl on Andres's farm who in a while marries Juss, a crippled cottager on Andres's land. When Andres's first wife dies in childbirth, he blames himself for killing the sensitive and physically delicate Krõõt by his relentless demand for hard work, as well as by several births in succession, to fulfil his desire for a son and heir. Mari makes a deathbed-promise to Krõõt to look after

---

41 "A marsh stretching / Along those mountains / contaminates what's been / reclaimed so far; / to drain that stagnant pool / as well / would be a crowning last / achievement" (Goethe, *Faust* 2053 (end of part II)).

her children. As she spends ever more time with Andres, her husband Juss, desperate, attempts to kill Andres and commits suicide by hanging himself on a fir-tree. Mari and Andres marry and have Indrek as their first child. Yet Mari never gets over the guilt of Juss's death, as she tortures herself with the idea that she had secretly coveted not only Andres but also his farm and status even before Juss died. Indrek, whom Mari in her own mind calls a child of sin, is a sickly and delicate boy, resembling in character and appearance neither Mari nor Andres, but Andres's first wife Krõõt.

Indrek inherits his parents' sense of guilt for sacrificing the weaker members of the household to their own ambitions to progress in life.[42] As a boy, Indrek accidentally throws a stone at his mother, actually having aimed at his brother, who had angered him. Thus, he causes a lifelong injury to his mother and, as they both believe, her terminal illness, as well as his own lasting guilt. It was "Juss's stone", her punishment, that Indrek had thrown, Mari tells Indrek, suffering unbearable physical pain on her deathbed. It was a piece of one of the large fieldstones that her husband Andres detonated, using as burning material the fir-tree on which Juss hanged himself. Ostensibly he carried out the detonation to better the land, but actually his aim was to banish his own guilt by getting rid of the tree. "[I]f Juss had not hanged himself, the stones may have been left there and not been blown up at all," Mari says (*Tõde ja õigus III* 221). Indrek is the product, and also the heir, of his parents' progress and their guilt, thus Mari can ask him to give her a fatal dose of medicine to end her agony (*Tõde ja õigus III* 253-254). In the same line of reasoning she answers Indrek's pleading to have mercy and absolve him from this task with the words: "There is no mercy at Vargamäe, at Vargamäe one must do as necessary" (254).

The quoted key scene is not only a good example of the perception of history in the novel that Bakhtin describes as Goethean, but also of how *Truth and Justice*, at its crucial moments, combines linear and progressive "Goethean time" with a very different kind of time, one Bakhtin has famously described as a characteristic feature of the poetics of Dostoevsky. In order to understand the significance of "Dostoevskian time" in Mari's death scene, Dostoevsky's views on history and modernity first must be discussed.

---

42 The symbolism of the character names in *Truth and Justice* is a helpful layer of information here, although it should not be taken one-dimensionally or simplistically: Krõõt is the Estonian version of Margaret, or Gretchen, Juss is the short form of Joosep (Joseph), and Mari is the Estonian version of Mary (allusion possibly both to Virgin Mary and to Mary Magdalen). Andres (Andrew; "manly") can well be seen as a figure resembling Adam, Jehovah and Faust, but it is his son Indrek who is made to bear the Estonian version of Faust's first name, Heinrich.

The presence of Dostoevskian time in a *Bildungsroman* is itself noteworthy, considering Franco Moretti's specific emphasis that Dostoevsky, not by chance, never wrote a *Bildungsroman*. He could not have done, as his "ethico-metaphysical" thinking, which according to Moretti is characteristic of much of Russian literature, is incompatible with this secular Western genre. (*The Way* 247, note 1)[43]

What exactly might Moretti mean by "ethico-metaphysical thinking", a concept he does not elaborate? As theological studies of Dostoevsky point out, for him sacred history is not detached from secular history (Kroeker and Ward 85-93). In his works, the divine is constantly present in *this* world, and to find happiness, humans must be receptive to it, and act and think as much as possible in accordance with it. Central for the human ability to perceive the divine is Christ's command to love another as one's own self; this is the central and most important force that enables one to escape modern individualist isolation and to be open both to the collective and to the transcendental. For Dostoevsky, there is a sharp and unresolvable contradiction between the secular idea of progress and the idea of happiness. This is so both from the viewpoint of those who are asked to suffer as the "raw material" for achieving the progressivist goal, happiness in the future, and from the viewpoint of those people in the future, who must then base their happiness on their neighbors' suffering in the past (Kroeker and Ward 71-72). Progressivist thinking is wrong, and harmfully so, as it places the moral absolute in history and perfectibility, rather than in love and in God. Thus, for Dostoevsky, the whole *Bildungsroman* model of development towards true happiness would be faulty and misplaced in principle.

In accordance with this worldview, in Dostoevsky's poetics the form and function of time are at odds with Goethe's. Bakhtin contrasts them as follows:

> An artist such as Goethe [...] gravitates organically toward an evolving sequence. He strives to perceive all existing contradictions as various stages of some unified development; in every manifestation of the present he strives to glimpse a trace of the past, a peak of the present-day or the tendency of the future; and as a consequence, nothing for him is arranged along a single extensive plane. Such in any case was the basic tendency of his mode for viewing and understanding the world.
>
> In contrast to Goethe, Dostoevsky attempted to perceive the very stages themselves in their *simultaneity*, to *juxtapose* and to *counterpose* them dramat-

---

[43] Dostoevsky's novel *The Adolescent* could in my opinion well be considered an idiosyncratic *Bildungsroman*, but it definitely does not fit Moretti's concept of the genre.

ically, and not to stretch them in an evolving sequence. For him, to get one's bearings in the world meant to conceive all its content as simultaneous and *to guess at their interrelationships in the cross section of a single moment.* (*Problems* 28, Bakhtin's emphasis.)

Slobodanka Vladiv further describes the plot of a Dostoevskian novel as consisting not of a story, but of ""a-historical", allegorical scenes or tableaux". The suspension of realistic psychological motivation in character relationships and character movements on the plot level results in the impression that all of Dostoevsky's novels are "giant allegories or modern prose versions of morality plays". (Vladiv 158-159) Dostoevsky's events typically do not evolve, but follow one another unpredictably, improbably, against the characters' and readers' expectations; they are absurd in the way incidents in detective plots are, before one learns the hidden connections, the truth (cf. Lotman, *Universe* 164-166). Dostoevsky's plots are driven by the twin forces of scandals and of miracles, says Juri Lotman, "and the formal expression of the link between episodes is the little word 'suddenly'" (*Universe* 164; see also Slonimsky).

In Tammsaare's *Truth and Justice*, the protagonist, on the one hand, clearly evolves in historical time, carrying and developing his own and his parents' past into a future. Furthermore, he is deeply invested in history-as-progress: he wants political change, justice, personal happiness and strives towards these ideals. On the other hand, throughout the novel, history is mostly a source of loss, doubt, guilt and disillusionment for him, and it could be said that what positively grounds both him and the novel as a whole, are Indrek's rare but regularly returning "ethico-metaphysical" experiences, which can well be said to take the form of "a-historical" "allegorical scenes or tableaux", "modern prose versions of morality plays" (Vladiv 158-159).

These experiences always relate to circumstances when Indrek "suddenly", impulsively, unexpectedly even to himself, feels and does something that is contrary to his rationalist values, and instead inspired by love towards one's neighbor, unselfish and self-sacrificing. The experiences are as if outside linear history, yet on the other hand, as we will see, they will come to have a profound bearing on history, as they help to bring about Indrek's renewal, salvation and happiness at the end of the novel—in "real historical time".

One of the most significant examples, illuminating the interaction of linear historical time and the simultaneous ethico-metaphysical time, happens at the end of Volume II, set during Indrek's schooling in Tartu. Indrek is expelled from school when he writes an article for the school newspaper named *Truth*,

Chapter Three. Bildung in the Image of Modernity

arguing that God does not exist, and steadfastly refuses to renounce his views. At home, irritated by his landlady's mention of "God's will", Indrek spitefully re-iterates there is "no heaven and hell, only stars and emptiness" (*Tõde ja õigus II* 400-401). This can be seen as an absolute, universalist and thus ahistorical standpoint in itself, but it does not function like that for Indrek, who goes on to elaborate the historical and spatialized relevance of his truth most clearly: '"Elsewhere in the world this has been known for a long time, because there is more education and truthfulness there, only we here in Russia have been left behind the times. When all people become educated, then nobody will believe in God anymore." (402) What Indrek is complaining about is that Estonia, as part of Czarist Russia, is part of a spatially localized backward time, a time not *standardized* in line with true modernity (see Giddens 17-21).

At that point, Tiina, the little invalid child of the landlady, who adores Indrek and has been asking him to marry her when she grows up, starts sobbing in desperate grief in the next room, and Indrek remembers the child's firm trust that God's angels will heal her and make her able to walk one day. Looking at Tiina, Indrek "suddenly grasped everything": he has a simultaneous vision of his mother being hit by his stone, and of Tiina, both crying, both suffering. As a result of that, Indrek cannot but "give up his self" (402). He falls to his knees, his eyes in tears, and swears to the disbelieving Tiina that he had lied: "It is absolutely certain that you will get well, because God lives and he will send his angels. He will send a whole legion, so that if one doesn't know how to heal you, there is another one who does" (403). To convince Tiina, he further swears in the name of Christ that he will not marry anyone else, he will wait for her to grow up and get well, and he will marry her, exactly as she had asked. Tiina then stands up for the first time; this is the beginning of her healing process. Indrek's oath is in the direct sense completely untruthful: he does not believe in Christ (incidentally, neither did the atheist Tammsaare), and he immediately forgets his promise to marry Tiina. However, the forgotten promise becomes a prophecy. The reverberations of this scene where Indrek, in a sense, acted *like* Christ, continue to impact on the trajectory of his life.[44]

Another similar, central example is the death-scene of Indrek's mother at the end of the third volume, partially described above. At first, Indrek agrees to his mother's plea to give her an overdose for the very reason that Mari gives:

---

44 I emphasize Tammsaare's secular attitudes, yet it is also worthwhile to note Dipesh Chakrabarty's insightful reminder that "gods and spirits are not dependent on human beliefs for their own existence; what brings them to presence are our practices" (111).

Vargamäe is a place where mercy is not a recognized concept. He agrees "in full knowledge to commit an enormous evil" (*Tõde ja õigus III* 254) because he had thrown the stone and the logic of cause and effect obligates him to ease Mari's suffering. However, while telling his mother his reason for complying, Indrek suddenly notices that his words and his thoughts do not coincide. Counterposed to his causal reasoning, Indrek again experiences a sudden simultaneous vision of "half the world", "as if he was making an account of all his life" (254). At the same moment, his mother's plea also changes. She does not talk about a lack of mercy and doing what is necessary, but answers Indrek: "Do it if you love me!" (255). Confirming his love for his mother, Indrek again, similarly to the previously described scene with Tiina, suddenly "grasps" what is important: how immensely he loves his mother and how much having caused her pain has always oppressed him. "Then it is all good, Indrek", says the mother with "strange serenity", "because Vargamäe needs love more than the avoidance of evil." (255)

The two scenes described above clearly have an affinity to Ivan Karamazov's famous query into the ideal of modern progress in Dostoevsky's *The Brothers Karamazov*:

> imagine that you yourself are building the edifice of human destiny with the object of making people happy in the finale [...] but for that you must inevitably and unavoidably torture just one tiny creature [...] and raise your edifice on the foundation of her unrequited tears—would you agree to be the architect on such conditions? (245; cf. Grišakova 80)

The experiences of ethico-metaphysical time, conceiving everything simultaneously, rather than causally and progressively, makes Indrek get his "bearings in the world" differently from usual, and consequently to act in contradiction to his prevalent values, placing love for one's neighbor and the avoidance of the suffering of "just one tiny creature" higher than Enlightened truth or morality.[45] However, it is important to reemphasize that, in contradiction to Dostoevsky, the ethico-metaphysical aspect in Tammsaare seems to have less to do with man and God, and more with man and man, individual and collective. It is an attempt to de-instrumentalize human relationships, to place the concept of love for one's neighbor in the framework of modernity, even in the frame-

---

45 See also Epp Annus's poignant discussion of Indrek's "sudden avalanches of memory pictures", "heap-moments", and their epiphanic nature. (*Kuidas* 293-296)

work of an uneven modernization process—something that according to Dostoevsky one really cannot do.

This is certainly how the Estonian reception has reacted to the "morality play" scenes in *Truth and Justice*. One recent example is the author and critic Jan Kaus's interpretation of the scene of healing Tiina, with its emphasis on Indrek's firm atheism, and at the same time his profound human connection to Tiina, which enables Indrek to grasp his lack of right "to rob Tiina of her truth [...] however ridiculous it may seem in the light of Indrek's own truth" (Kaus 25). Moreover, the critic Jaanus Kulli's review in the popular newspaper Õhtuleht, in which he praises the dramatization of the second volume by the director Elmo Nüganen, places the mystical overtones of the healing scene in the context of the national story in *Truth and Justice*, mentioning both in the same breath: the play is true to Tammsaare, yet personal and new; it is, among other things, "about being an Estonian and remaining an Estonian, or about that that the belief in oneself and the belief in one's neighbor can work miracles" (Kulli) .[46]

Simultaneous time is outside public progressive history in *Truth and Justice*, yet it carries public socio-cultural meanings and impacts on progressive history. As simultaneity converges time, space and people into concentrated moments, it creates a link connecting progressive history with the third important mode of time construction in the novel, that is, cyclical time—the underlying "Estonian" mode to process historical turmoil with its full Merkelian significance and power.

The cyclical perspective on history in the novel has been pointed out both by Tammsaare himself and by literary critics, usually with references to the ideas of Oswald Spengler's *The Decline of the West* (*Der Untergang des Abendlandes*, 1918-1922) as an intertext for *Truth and Justice*. Tammsaare wrote an essay "Spengler's *The Decline of the West*" ("Spengleri Õhtumaa allakäigust") immediately before starting *Truth and Justice* and sometimes presented Spenglerian lines of thought commenting upon it, most famously in a letter to an Estonian journalist in the USA, Andres Pranspill (Tammsaare, *"Tõest ja õigusest"*). In this connection, the critical tradition has often emphasized Spenglerian pessimism, melancholy and spirit of resignation expressed, in particular, in the final volume of *Truth and Justice*

---

[46] Tammsaare himself writes in his essay "On Salvation" ("Lunastusest"): "A creative author can but guide a person to himself/herself, like Socrates did. [...] A person ought to be told: you have no other savior but yourself, whether you strive for a heavenly paradise or for an earthly one." Note the interesting relationship here between the personal and the inter-personal, individualistic and didactic: one ought to first of all trust in oneself, but it is a cultural concern that one ought to be guided to do so; the issue is not solely personal or existential. See also Chapter One.

(e.g. Treier, *Tammsaare ja tema* 66-67; Macura, "Epopöa lõpp" 182-183; for an opposite view more in agreement with my own, see Siimisker 180-181).

In my analysis, however, neither the letter to Pranspill nor the fifth volume of *Truth and Justice* where the cyclical perception of time becomes most explicit in the novel, ought to be interpreted as carrying pessimistic or apocalyptic overtones. Or, if so, perhaps only in the original Greek meaning of apocalyptic as "revealing," or "uncovering". Read in its entirety, *Truth and Justice* is not lamenting the decline of the Western or any other world. Rather, it considers the rise and fall of individual cultures not only inevitable and natural, but also the source of desirable renewal in the world whereby his Estonian characters gain more than they lose. What Tammsaare's novel absorbs from Spengler's worldview is exactly the aspect Spengler shares with the vision of history that the 19th-century Estonian national activists took from Herder and Merkel. Though primarily based on cyclicality, this Estonian worldview is compatible and well combinable with the modern belief in progressive change and improvement. As discussed in Chapter One, the Estonian activists were fascinated and encouraged, not depressed, by the idea that history was cyclical (or twisting and turning), hence making it possible for the losers of the history of mankind to shake off what had *seemed* their destined lot and start afresh.

Tammsaare has, with justification, said that the fifth volume of *Truth and Justice* is about "resignation, reconciliation" (qtd. in Macura, "Epopöa lõpp" 183); it can also be said to be about renewal and transformation. Indrek's sad "postcolonial" return home is not the end but only the very beginning of the volume, where he unexpectedly takes over the central and incomplete endeavor of his father, the draining of the swamps.

To understand the significance of Indrek's endeavor, it is further relevant to note that Dostoevsky also has a model of cyclical history, in some ways more akin to Tammsaare than Spengler: Dostoevsky thinks in terms of prophesies and their fulfilments—the old coming into being again, albeit with a difference. This is strongly connected with Dostoevsky's belief in the divine being immanent in the world: the sacred prophesies of the old are relevant and perceptible *now*, if one is open to them, and one becomes open to them, first and foremost, through the love of one's neighbor.

The crucial difference between Dostoevsky's and Tammsaare's models of historical cyclicity is that for Dostoevsky, modernity and modern rationalist and individualist views of the world cannot but be hostile and damaging to one's openness to the sacred. *Truth and Justice*, on the other hand, does not single modernity out as something so radically different from the rest of the history of humankind as to make it either all-powerful or all-irredeemable. Instead, it becomes yet another cycle of renewal and of fulfilment of prophesies. If one inserts such a twist and does not exclude modernity as an exception in the order of history, it is clear that the Dostoevskian prophetic model might actually serve as a very handy one in order to create symbolic continuity between modernity and tradition, or rapidly changing phases of modernity—between generations.

At the start of the fifth volume, Andres, similarly to Indrek, is a very disappointed man. It does not comfort him that the farm that he had started is prosperous: his life-work with the swamps is overgrown and has been forgotten; all his sons have left, and the place is run by his businessman son-in-law, a commercially astute man, who has no interest in expensive and potentially ruinous utopian projects. Andres's misery only increases when Indrek, who was once his pride and who was supposed to be engaged in finer things than farmwork, returns home as a failure and, in a state of remorse and despair, asks, in an echo of Dostoevsky's *Crime and Punishment*, to be allowed to do "forced labor" at the farm (*Tõde ja õigus* V 14).

Andres's feelings change when Indrek, first just to please his father, chooses the swamps as his particular form of punishment—and becomes ever more personally and passionately invested in achieving success. What had started as Dostoevskian forced labor rapidly develops into Andres's and Indrek's joint Faustian work, seen by Indrek not only as redemptive (although that meaning remains there too), but also as productive and progressive.

Significantly, Indrek discovers that his chosen endeavor demands not only an input of heavy physical labor but, even more crucially, the successful persuasion of dozens of sceptical neighborhood farmers to join forces in order to write a collective application for state financing to have the local river deepened. "For my father and for my godfather this idea remained only an idea", Indrek says in his speech at the farmers' meeting. At the time of their youth, he argues, people had no help or authority, but now with independence "the state—it is us. Who can hinder us if we really want something?" (*Tõde ja õigus* V 82). Moreover, Indrek also calls the War of Independence a time when "our fathers' spirit was alive in us" (83), an inspiring example the swamp-draining project should follow.

Here it is important to emphasize that *Truth and Justice*, like Tammsaare's work in general, is on the whole very far from flaming patriotism and remarkably critical towards the young Estonian state. Indeed, reviews of *Truth and Justice* routinely point out that Tammsaare left the War of Independence, one of the few stereotypically heroic pages in Estonia's history, out of his pentalogy, preferring to elaborate on the corruption of the 1920s (Macura, "Tragöödia" 175-176; Treier, *Tammsaare ja tema* 98). Whatever Indrek-as-character's motivation for his patriotic comments on the war and the resulting independent republic, in the structure of the novel as a whole they suddenly posit a worldview according to which the modern Estonian state does not take the sons away from their fathers but, on the contrary, it enables them as modern citizens ("the state—it is us") to fulfil their fathers' dreams on a new level and through more successful means. What is more, through his success Indrek himself overcomes his earlier all-encompassing pessimism, caused by the failings of the new state and his fellow citizens. When it turns out that some people in the collective project freeload on the prestige and material benefits of the protagonists' efforts, Indrek comforts Andres claiming that it does not really matter: it is the achievement of their "great thing" that is important; they only ought to laugh at the vanity and greed of those who know no better (*Tõde ja õigus* V 362-363).

It is true that whatever there exists between Andres and Indrek, father and son, is clearly more a renewal of beginning than a true continuity. Andres contemplates that he understands Indrek, his heart or mind, less than he would understand "a wild animal", "a hare in the forest" (*Tõde ja õigus* V 323); only when discussing their project together does he feel he is talking "not only to a human being, but his son, his child, who has learned from him, taken his guidance" (324). When the government officials finally arrive to measure the river in order to deepen it, Indrek carries Andres, weak with illness, on his back to see it. While Andres in his mind praises the kindness of God for having given him such a son, Indrek, on the other hand, suddenly silently falls into a pessimistic reverie. He reflects:

> He is carrying his frail father, and his father had carried him when he was still weak. That means—the stronger is carrying the weaker one. But it is constantly the other way round in the world: the weaker one carries the stronger one. This is true of individuals, social strata, peoples and races, and this is considered culture. (365)

Culture is parasitical and cruel: the progress of humankind demands ever more oppression of the weak by the stronger (365). Indrek does not stop to consider what it might mean that he is actually undermining this "way of the world" by (both literally and metaphorically) carrying his father. However, the symbolic point is elaborated for the reader when Andres dies the same evening and, carrying his father's fragile dead body, Indrek for the first time over many years is suddenly reminded of the fragile body of the child Tiina whom he had once held while renouncing his cosmogonic truths.[47]

Shortly afterwards Indrek learns what some readers may have guessed already two volumes earlier: that he had known adult Tiina for years without having recognized her, and that she had never stopped loving him, or lost her belief that he would one day fulfil his promise.[48] It is at this point, at the completion of his project, that Indrek is able to consciously recognize and accept Tiina's constancy and love, and she becomes part of the Western *Bildungsroman*-type happy finale, in its emplotment not too far from the Goethean model. Like Goethe's Wilhelm Meister, on the final pages of the novel Tiina and Indrek talk about happiness having been born. At the same time, the end of the novel also represents an emphatic structural repetition/opposition. On the first page of the novel Andres and his first wife had walked up the road towards the Vargamäe farm, and on the final page Indrek and the city girl Tiina walk the same way in the opposite direction, in order to go and live in the city.[49] The effect of repetition increases and that of opposition weakens if we consider that the dynamic of the movement is actually the same both times: away from a home, which is not a home anymore, towards a home, which is not a home yet.

*   *   *

What differentiates *Truth and Justice* from the postcolonial/belated *Bildungsroman* model, and in some respects brings it closer to the classical one, is the protagonist's eventual ability both to accept his parents' inheritance, with all the accompanying inconveniences, and to transform it into something new and different, his own consciously modern identity. Against the Dostoevskian background, it is paradoxically the protagonist's ability to inspire and value the trust of the "tiny creatures" of humankind that reconciles him to modern history and society. The novel is, in a way, a symbolic attempt to create a new model of modernity influenced but not determined by the colonial past, which borrows from different worldviews, experiences, and ideologies of modernity, questioning and

---

47   Furthermore, Indrek is not the only one of Andres's children carrying his body. On a more materialistic note of cyclical return with a difference characteristic of Tammsaare, Andres's dead body comes to be driven across the same causeway he had once promised to Krõõt, but failed to dry (*Tõde ja õigus I* 8)—and driven not in a mere two-horse cart, but in a large, modern car owned by another of his sons, a well-to-do rural businessman (*Tõde ja õigus V* 372). On depictions of rural modernization in the fifth volume of *Truth and Justice* see also Annus, "Tõe ja õiguse".
48   It is again helpful to note the symbolism of names: the name Tiina, similarly to Kristi (Indrek's early girlfriend killed in the 1905 revolution) is a version of Christina—a Christian.
49   It is interesting to note that here the *"mésalliance"* is intra-ethnic: a love story between the Estonian farm and the Estonian city.

reconceptualizing them at the same time. It builds on and reworks existing patterns in the Estonian cultural thought-world, and many later texts draw upon it as they attempt to rationalize and integrate change both in its painful and in its hopeful aspects. *Truth and Justice* is a complex, multidimensional novel, yet at one level it grants the reader an almost seamless narrative that makes Estonian modernization meaningful by placing it in the cosmic patterns of change. Thus, the modern text acquires a myth-like undercurrent.

Chapter Four. Self-Colonizing Translations? The Modernist Language Renewal Project of the Young Estonia Movement (1905-1915), and Andrus Kivirähk's *The Man Who Spoke Snakish* (Mees, kes teadis ussisõnu, 2007)

The final chapter of the book will take up the discourses of language and literature among the Estonian discourses of modernization. As discussed above, literature, especially prose, has been dominant over the visual arts and music in the Estonian canon, and central for cultural memory and nation-building. This, of course, is not unique to Estonia. Literature, made from the material of a specific vernacular, has been often described as a strong force for condensing national culture, for imagining a nation (Anderson). However, whereas in many cases the role of literature is balanced by that of religious ritual or other arts, in the Estonian case verbality is hegemonic. Thus it is illuminating to note the differing perceptions of what (the national) language ought to be like and ought to be for, and to follow the debates over tradition, continuity and change that are held in reference to language.

One of the two foci in this chapter will be the case of the early 20th century Young Estonia movement and its project to "renew" the Estonian language, centrally executed through Young Estonia's extensive translation activity from a variety of European languages. I will consider how Young Estonia saw itself, and how it figures in the eyes of its changing reception in Estonia, both in their time and ours, more than a hundred years later. In the latter connection I will involve in the discussion Andrus Kivirähk's novel *The Man Who Spoke Snakish*, a darkly humorous historical fantasy featuring the last human speaker of a dying language as its main character. The novel was published in 2007 during the period of intensive debates concerning the Young Estonia movement following its jubilee in 2005, immediately before the exacerbation of the controversy relating to the relocation of the "Bronze Soldier" (see Chapter One) memorial and the beginning of the global economic crisis.

Chapter Four. Self-Colonizing Translations

The Man Who Spoke Snakish, as well as Kivirähk's earlier novel *The Old Barny* (*Rehepapp*, 2000) are among the most sold Estonian novels in the 21st century. Kivirähk (b. 1970) studied journalism at the University of Tartu, and now works as a columnist for the daily *Eesti Päevaleht*. He is a prolific author who creates in a great variety of genres: besides novels and journalistic pieces, also short stories, plays, screenplays, TV-shows, and the kind of children's works which are read or watched both by children and adults. His texts have been turned into animated cartoons and board games, the popular characters appear as toys and decorate schoolchildren's notebooks. Next to his popular success, Estonian professional critics also consider him among the most appreciated contemporary authors. Early on, he earned the only half-joking title of the "grand young man of the Estonian theatre" and his novels are an established part of the literature curricula of schools and universities. References to his character types and expressive coinages appear as shorthand in public debate, and it is not unusual to find his texts quoted in scholarly works dealing not with literature but with history, politics or anthropology.

The long-held centrality of Kivirähk's oeuvre in Estonian culture is in contrast with its being mostly unknown outside of Estonia, with the exception of Latvia, until at least 2013. The issue here is probably not simply the limited international circulation of Estonian literature as a "small national literature" (Casanova) in general. Even the expert English translator of Estonian literature Eric Dickens, who translated Kross and Tammsaare among others, admits that he considers it essentially impossible to make accessible to the average Briton the folkloric grotesque happenings, the burlesque humor and the Estonia-specific concerns of *The Old Barny*. Furthermore, he confesses that even he himself is not "on the same wavelength" as the novel (Dickens).

Interestingly, when *The Man Who Spoke Snakish* was published in French in 2013, it met with unexpected critical and commercial success largely thanks to the persistence of its enthusiastic translator Jean-Paul Minaudier. Contemplating Kivirähk's reception in France, Triinu Tamm, a specialist of Francophone literature and a French-Estonian cultural mediator, observes that Kivirähk's kind of humor is not the kind that generally makes the French laugh. Based on French readers' and critics' comments she speculates that it is the combination of wild, exotic fantasy, and the preoccupation with a rather familiar sense of existential despair that draws the fans: "I suspect that the French may be taking Snakish as standing for the French language," she concludes her review.[1]

---

[1] *The Man Who Spoke Snakish* won *Le Grand Prix de l'Imaginaire* in the foreign novel category in 2014. Nils C. Ahl calls it "probably one of the best contemporary novels about loneliness" in his review in *Le Monde*.

Following the French success, the novel was published in English in 2015, and the reviews also primarily see it as a well-plotted, anxious "reactionary fantasy" (Illingworth) engaging with the precariousness of the world (*Kirkus Reviews*). It has presently (2021) been translated into twelve languages.

As for Kivirähk's humor, Daniele Monticelli, the Italian translator of Kivirähk's comedy play *Estonian Funeral* (*Eesti Matus*, 2002) which was requested for a reading at a theatre festival, was also certain that the play would not make Italian audiences roar with laughter like Estonian ones (Monticelli, personal communication). Most Italians, Monticelli explained, would simply fail to see the joke in a character's deadpan relation of the horrors of deportation in Siberia. No translation could carry over how a passage like that parodies Estonians' post-Soviet reappraisal of history in its different institutionalized and popular aspects to which local audiences can react to on many levels and often ambivalently. Playful fun is simultaneously poked at the national victimhood discourses as well as the coexistent ones of collective self-admiration that often accompany stories of suffering when these are taken to attest to the Estonian grit and resilience rather than to defeat and loss of agency. It is definitely not the deportations or the deported themselves that the Estonian audience sees as the target of the joke—this is clear from the fact that very few seem to consider Kivirähk's humor of this kind strongly offensive. However, one can speculate that it is essential to Kivirähk's appeal that he approaches the most traumatic and difficult topics but does so from such an angle that the audience/readership feels safe to laugh.

Exploring the mechanisms of Kivirähk's humor and its reception, it is useful to draw upon the sociologist, and a scholar of ethnic humor, Christie Davies. According to Davies, minority groups (and other marginalized or dominated groups) generally tend to tell more jokes about the failings and absurdities of their own group than about their "other(s)", and also judge these jokes to be the funniest. This kind of self-deprecating Jewish humor has often been noted as exceptional, but in fact it is characteristic of many other disparate non-hegemonic groups: African-Americans, the Irish in England and Israeli Arabs, to name but a few. This ought not to be considered masochistic self-hatred or uncritical integration of a dominant group's negative attitudes as has been haphazardly claimed, Davies argues. Rather, self-deprecating ethnic humor is a very ambiguous mechanism that cannot be reduced to one clear meaning or function.

Humor can be a playful way to dramatize the relativity-conscious, self-aware relationship to the world that is almost inevitable for non-hegemonic groups not "snuggly trapped in their own normality" like the majorities (Davies 191).

It can help to face real and serious political and cultural insecurities in a non-threatening theatrical manner. It can certainly be a form of self-criticism and self-irony, but it can at the same time function as self-affirmation and reinforcement of the sense of community, even collective self-congratulation. The source of the self-deprecating ethnic humor is also an essential factor. Confirming Davies, the humor researcher Srdjan Vucetic points out that sharing and laughing at self-derogatory jokes, including bitter war jokes is common among Bosnians, but that they find similar humor offensive when coming from Serbs or Croats.

Kivirähk's most popular work tends to deal with aspects in Estonian history widely considered sacrosanct, tragic or discomforting. It expertly taps into stereotypes and symbolic cultural topoi but is not satisfied with superficial mocking of obsessions and received ideas. Rather, he shows history as an abundance of paradoxes and ambivalence, as carnevalesque. A prolific reader in a number of fields of Estonian culture, the author creates parodic halls of mirrors where the familiar and intimate shapes get exaggerated and distorted, turned upside down and inside out, absurdly or fantastically combined without becoming unrecognizable. Thus they are also opened up from unexpected angles, provoke laughter and potentially also new insight and sentiment.

Kivirähk's early *Memoirs of Ivan Orav, or the Past as Azure Mountains* (*Ivan Orava mälestused ehk Minevik kui helesinised mäed*, 1995) burlesques the discourses of the idyll of interbellum Estonia and the myth of the indefatigable Estonian anti-Soviet resistance.[2] *The Old Barny, or November* (*Rehepapp ehk November*, 2000), set in a phantasmagoric 19th-century Estonia, turns the tables on the topoi of 'the honest Estonian' and of the seven-hundred-year suffering under the Baltic Germans. The German overlords are not up to much against the endlessly thieving and tricking Estonians, characterized by callousness, colossal material greed, and an amazing mix of narrow-mindedness and ingenious cunning. Nevertheless, it is still the Estonian characters who see themselves as the wronged party, robbed of their true history and status, thus with a perpetual right for material recompensation.

Differently from *Ivan Orav* and *The Old Barny* where the audiences perceive the laughter as predominantly liberating, the *Man Who Spoke Snakish* has been

---

2   The book begins thus: "Before the time the card-carrying snakes and murderous highwaymen cut up Estonia and drove their pike into our flesh, there blossomed happiness in the Land of Mary. There was the Estonian Republic. There won't be many left though who lived at that time and remember the silver and golden days when the sounds of a violin carried from the Moon every night and even birch trees bore apples. That is why I will tell you a couple of words about that time."

interpreted more darkly. Its plot concerns a group of people who voluntarily give up their traditional lifestyle to imitate foreigners considered more "developed" and forsake their unique knowledge of the Snake language in preference of German and Latin. Linda Kaljundi argues that for all its many layers and strands the novel's central morale appears very simple to summarize: "abandoning one's original nature and healthy common sense for the mindless aping of foreigners cannot but lead to decay".

If Kivirähk's earlier humorous characters had been engaged in the "parodying mimicry" of the colonizer, not fully aware of where the boundary between imitation and mockery lies (Hennoste "Postkolonialism ja Eesti"), Leemet, the protagonist of *The Man Who Spoke Snakish* is different. He derides those who mimic the colonizer and try to bully/educate their peers to do the same. Leemet's humor is not light-hearted and his own life story on the losing side probably does not strike most Estonian readers as an easy laughing matter. Leemet is bitter about a phenomenon that the linguist and literary critic Tiit Hennoste termed "self-colonization" 2003: people mimicking an authoritative alien culture not (primarily) out of self-gain, but out of a patriotic desire to "develop" one's "backward" culture ("Postkolonialism ja Eesti"). Some years later Hennoste used the concept of self-colonization for an extended reinterpretation of the role of the Young Estonia movement in Estonian culture ("Noor-Eesti kui lõpetamata"; "Noor-Eesti enesekoloniseerimisprojekt").

It is difficult to define or characterize Young Estonia in a few words exactly because, as we will see more thoroughly below, its features and significance have been and remain a matter of debate. In short, I see it as a modernist movement in literature and (secondarily) in other arts with wide socio-cultural ambitions.[3] I argue that it is crucial not to analyze Young Estonia as an isolated phenomenon, but to consider it in the comparative context of international literary and cultural modernist currents that developed in the 1880s-1920s, in response to the challenges of the period that social scholars (such as Hartmut Rosa, see "Introduction") describe as one of the two most rapid phases of socio-political and economic modernization until now. Literary modernists seek linguistic and formal innovation, proceeding from the perception that the world is changing so radically that existing formulas are inadequate to process the new experience (Eysteinsson 22-26). Young Estonia could be said to bear a specific family resem-

---

3   The main website on Young Estonia run by the Estonian Literary Museum says: "Young Estonia can also be considered an aggressive cultural political movement, the aim of which was to change Estonian society" (*Noor-Eesti 100*).

blance to movements such as Young Finland, Young Poland, or, Nyugat (West) in Hungary, where the struggle for cultural renewal and new means of expression was intertwined with a frustration with sociopolitical dependence, "backwardness", and a desire for reform.

Young Estonia's high period of activity was 1905–1915 and it was driven by young authors and literati who met and associated mostly in the town of Tartu. Making waves in Estonia by promoting form-conscious art and educated specialist art-criticism, the movement was interested mostly in antimimetic and linguistically inventive forms. Although it made some effort to know and educate its audience about varied aspects of their contemporary international scene, their greatest attachment always was to *fin de siècle* and symbolism (Baudelaire, Verlaine, Verhaeren, Rimbaud, Maeterlinck, D'Annunzio, Poe). Nowadays it is often remarked that, compared to their acknowledged importance for Estonian literature, it is notable that Young Estonians produced relatively few original works, both in volume and in terms of their share in the national canon (Olesk and Laak 8; Hasselblatt, "Sajand").

True, some short stories by Friedebert Tuglas and poems by Gustav Suits and Villem Grünthal-Ridala are taught at school and are widely known. Recently there is also a rise in the scholarly interest for Tuglas's artist novel *Felix Ormusson* and Johannes Aavik's novella *Ruth*, inspired by Huysmans. However, notwithstanding the critically acclaimed merit of a number of texts by the Young Estonia authors, an average Estonian would probably associate the movement primarily with their call to "be Estonians but [...] also become Europeans" (in Suits's "Noorte püüded") and would know Aavik as the influential language renewer who propagated his linguistic innovations via translations of Edgar Allan Poe's horror stories, rather than as the author of *Ruth*.

The Young Estonian language renewal was one of the most radical and extensive among such projects in the world. Over a short period of time it introduced numerous lexical items that are in common use today (about 30 artificially created stems and over 800 loan-words and derivatives of various origin) and even grammatical changes (reflexive verb forms, short plural and short superlative options, de-germanization of syntax). The Young Estonians see national language much in the same way as they see national literature: part of collective heritage, yes, but exactly for that reason open to individual talents to reimagine and improve. The reception of their endeavor and its ongoing role in the debates over the Estonian models of modernity and nationhood will be considered in the next subchapter.

Young Estonia as a modernist project: debates

The discussion of the Young Estonia movement remained topical in Estonia long since the movement's 100th anniversary in 2005. There are continuing debates, often much more highly charged, emotional and, indeed, personal than customary in academic conversation, on what this movement—the early phase of Estonian modernism—meant in the context of Estonian culture and what it did to that culture. All sides would probably agree that in more ways than one Young Estonia was engaged in a translation project, where the translation of numerous foreign texts was both an ongoing process for enhancing the Estonian language as well as a vehicle for popularizing the results of that work (Monticelli, "Keeleuuendus ja tõlkimine" I and II). However, what drove it—revolutionary creativity or slavish mimicry? What should we call it today: tour de force modernization or abasing "self-colonization" (Hennoste, "Noor-Eesti kui lõpetamata"; "Noor-Eesti enesekoloniseerimisprojekt")? What is the significance of the Young Estonians' translating the decadence and pessimism of French fin-de-siècle poets and the psychological nuances of D'Annunzio—topoi apparently alien for the Estonian peasant and petty bourgeois cultural tradition and their still overwhelmingly rural and agricultural society of the time? How to regard Young Estonia's aestheticist, radical—indeed, utopian—project of language-renewal, which drew to a great extent upon Estonian dialects and on Finnish, but also on a number of Western languages like French, Italian and English, as well as the "colonizer-languages", German and Russian?

At the start of his ground-breaking discussion of the formation, interpretations, and evaluations of the concept of modernism, Astradur Eysteinsson draws attention to the same phenomenon outlined above: how persistent, and also how highly charged the debates over the meaning and significance of "modernism" tend to be. There is a broad agreement what "modernism" refers to: "a paradigmatic shift, a major revolt [...] against the prevalent literary and aesthetic traditions of the Western world" that begins towards the end of the 19th century and gains ground during the first half of the 20th century (Eysteinsson 2).[4] However, there are a number of strikingly different, "often seemingly irreconcilable theories concerning the nature of the revolt" (Eysteinsson 2), its causes, origins, political affiliations, socio-cultural role and effects.

The term "modernism" in the above-referred sense of an innovative movement in the arts emerged only in the 1960s (Childs 12), when the core period of

---

4 Eysteinsson focuses on literary modernism and does not deal with other arts directly.

the movement itself was over. However, the term has not become a simple unambiguous marker, denoting a past and finished literary period with its particular aesthetic characteristics. Rather, there is a struggle over the meaning of the aesthetic and related broader socio-cultural and historical change "modernism" stands for. Significantly, the most recent wave of intensified theoretical interest in modernism started with the 20th-century *fin de siècle*, accelerated change and transformation of the models of modernity in different parts of the world.

Of course, any aesthetic concept may be, or in a certain context turn into, a field of major controversy. Yet I agree with Eysteinsson's appraisal that the special preoccupation with the case of modernism "springs from our awareness that through the concept we are 'constructing' our immediate past, we are creating a paradigm that we are not even certain we have surpassed, not to mention properly gauged and understood" (51-52). The concept of modernism is used in reference to and in the context of literature (or other arts), but it signals broader human concerns to do with tradition, change, formation of new traditions, and specifically with these concerns in relation to modernization and its discontents. The struggle over the meaning and significance of modernism, or particular modernist movements in a national cultural history is an aspect of the struggle over what counts as a proper story of the nation's modernization. Arguments concerning modernism's weight and role in a national literary canon, the role of the aesthetic transformation in the sociopolitical modernization process and its human cognitive purport, as well as the relationship between national and varying international impulses in a modernist movement—these are all facets of the debate about what is significant and/or meritorious about a particular past and present modern nationhood, and what is not.

The reception of Young Estonia has passed different phases reflecting the circumstances of the respective eras. In its own time, the beginning of the 20th century, it was strongly criticized by both the counter-Russification conservative nationalists and by the Estonian socialists for extra-literary reasons: being respectively either too alien and inappropriate for Estonians or too bourgeois and insufficiently class-conscious (Raun, "Eesti" 45). However, the standards of literary and critical professionalism set by Young Estonians, as well as much of their language renewal work, were gradually accepted and integrated even by their fierce opponents. By the interwar period, these aspects had largely entered the mainstream, although even the retrospective attitudes towards the movement itself remained ambivalent (Olesk and Laak 14-15).

After the Soviet occupation, during the Stalinist period, Young Estonia was unequivocally condemned (and the works banned) for its "decadence" and cosmopolitanism. Later in the Soviet period it was possible to reincorporate some figures with "progressive" leanings (Gustav Suits, Friedebert Tuglas) in the canon. The wave of innovative scholarly study and stage dramatizations of their work reflects Young Estonia's significance for that time. By the 1980s, the whole movement could be referred to as progressive (Olesk and Laak 16), though literary histories mostly focused more on individual authors than the in-depth interpretation of the Young Estonia phenomenon. Tammsaare who, though not part of the core group, still identified himself with the movement, was completely disassociated from it during the Soviet period. He was championed as the greatest realist novelist in the Estonian literature; his early stories with particularly characteristic modernist features were marginalized and left out of his collected works.

With the post-Soviet turn towards Western Europe, Young Estonia was publicly re-invented as a valuable new ally-ancestor. Its slogan "Let us be Estonians but let us also become Europeans" turned into a prominent part of the alternative history and identity juxtaposed to the one that had been hegemonic during the Soviet time. To provide a symptomatic example, the Estonian president Lennart Meri (1929–2006) evoked the movement in a future-oriented vision during his New Year speech on the 31st of December 1997. Talking about the recently commenced negotiations to join the European Union, Meri said that Estonians now had the obligation to imagine what Estonia would be like in the year 2005, the year of the 100th anniversary of Young Estonia: to project an Estonia that is part of 21st-century Europe and not just a visitor there. It is also significant, however, that, immediately after referring to Young Estonia, Meri mentioned in the same approving tone a critic of the movement, the conservative Jaan Tõnisson (1868–1941?). Meri, at that point, also explicitly emphasized the need for balance in politics, among other things the proverbial balance between being a European and an Estonian.

Further, once 2005 has arrived, in 21st-century arguments over Young Estonia, the debaters often make explicit references to their contemporary situation, and even if not, this co-text is strongly implied. The discussion dramatizes the extensive controversies over the situation and options of Estonia as a new member of EU, NATO and a part of the globalized world in a particular, sophisticated intellectual, dimension. For these reasons, I will outline the discussion at some length before contributing my own analysis in the next subchapter.

Daniele Monticelli argues that there are analogous features between the attacks against Young Estonia by their contemporary conservative critics and the statements by some Estonian nationalists in relation to the Bronze Soldier controversy in 2007. Both idealize Estonians' "traditional" culture as unique and idiosyncratic, at the same time demanding homogenization, isolation and conservation of the society to guard it. (Monticelli, "Noor-Eesti projektist" 276-277, 285.) Hennoste does not comment upon the Bronze Soldier parallel, but retorts to Monticelli that far from being promoters of cultural pluralism and multicenteredness, the Young Estonia movement, and the language-renewal leader Aavik in particular, were driving to impose their master system on Estonian society in the manner of arrogant colonizers ("Noor-Eesti enesekoloniseerimisprojekt").[5]

Hennoste, the most prolific present-day critic of Young Estonia, actually agrees with Monticelli that the vision the movement's nationally-minded opponents had of Estonian culture was rather stale and essentialist. Yet, for him the fault of Young Estonians lies in the fact that despite their early let-us-be-Estonians-let-us-become-Europeans slogan, they later entirely ignored the local dimension, and did not truly embrace the challenge of reinterpreting and repurposing 19th-century Estonianness for modern circumstances ("Noor-Eesti enesekoloniseerimisprojekt" 271).

According to Hennoste, for the Young Estonians Europe was the ideal to be copied without any need to note local cultural peculiarities, and they had little but disdain for their native culture. Moreover, they lacked true creativity and remained but imitators—thus also present-day Estonian culture is an inferior copy of the European original, and the renewed Estonian language "a pidgin" (Hennoste, "Noor-Eesti kui lõpetamata" 31). The literary scholar and cultural journalist Rein Veidemann appears to support Hennoste's views as he proposes that the Young Estonia jubilee debates and Hennoste's rephrasal of the Young Estonia slogan into "Let us be Estonians and Europeans but let us finally transform ourselves from a copy to an original!" ("Noor-Eesti kui lõpetamata") may have brought the Estonians to the end of one "cultural narrative" and—potentially—at the start of a new one ("Ühe suure" 295).

The literary scholar and author Aare Pilv, on the other hand, questions whether it is possible to become an original outside the copy/original dialectics. If we decide it is not, the appeal to turn ourselves into an original reads as very close to "let us become colonizers" (Pilv 9). This also automatically means becoming self-colonizers, Pilv continues, as self-colonization is the necessary first stage of becoming a colonizing culture. This is so because to become an "original" the culture first needs self-aware hierarchical *internal* splitting, a sense of

---

5   For partial expositions of Monticelli's and Hennoste's arguments in English, see Monticelli "(Trans)forming" and Hennoste "Europeanization" respectively.

more "central", "universalized" layers of the culture that the more "marginal" or "lower" ones of the *same* culture ought to aspire to copy (5). A more fruitful way to interpret Hennoste's appeal, Pilv adds, would be to read "let us become an original" as "let us leave the original/copy dialectics", i.e. let us note and accept that there are no originals in the traditional sense, but that our culture is not all of one piece, that there are internal alterities which need not necessary be seen as "other" or "secondary" in a negative sense (9).

Both Monticelli and Pilv emphasize the utopian drive of the Young Estonia movement. Drawing upon the translation theorist Lawrence Venuti, Monticelli analyzes the way the Young Estonians' defamiliarizing translations, oriented toward language renewal, participated in the more general cultural revolution. The texts had to be read with the help of attached dictionaries by Estonians at the time, as they were aimed less for them and more for an as yet non-existent "new cultural world" (Monticelli, "Keeleuuendus ja tõlkimine" I, 383). They projected "a utopian community" that was "yet not realized" (Venuti qtd. in "Keeleuuendus ja tõlkimine" I, 386). Pilv relates the movement's long-term interest in symbolist works with the Young-Estonians' inclination to the symbolists' metaphysical attitude which sees the existent and the concrete as simply symbols of, or references to, the ideal world.

Here it is interesting to note that Hennoste, who sees the Young-Estonians as imitators rather than innovators or utopians, denies for this very reason their being modernists at all. He contrasts them to true modernists in Europe and elsewhere who truly made "a leap to the future" ("Noor-Eesti enesekoloniseerimisprojekt" 268, 269-270). According to Hennoste the real modernists criticized the idea of European superiority and if they did borrow (which they, according to Hennoste, on the whole did not) they took from "primitive" cultures rather than the ones already canonized (269).

If the Young Estonians had chosen 20th-century European modernism as their example, instead of the outdated *fin de siècle,* Hennoste claims, they could have created a genuinely future-oriented and liberating culture (271). However, in their elitism and snobbish attitudes towards existing Estonian culture the Young Estonians failed to make modern Estonian culture a creative synthesized hybrid. Instead—and this I consider a truly thought-provoking claim from Hennoste that was not really taken up in the Young Estonia discussions—Estonian culture and society have turned out and remain an ill-functioning compound of, on the one hand, introverted essentialism and, on the other, idolized "colonial European values". Parts of society follow one course; other parts follow the other. This conflict is largely hidden as both sides have been ignoring or downplaying the existence of the other. Yet the outwardly dominant Young Estonia view, asserts Hennoste, has the upper hand in defining the course of society. There is no dialogue and no synthesis.[6]

The synthesis and the redefinition of what it means to be an Estonian in the modern world and in an independent state *was* attempted, according to Hennoste, but not by the Young Estonians. It was ventured by some young intellectuals of the next generation, born around 1900, who shared the experience of the War of Independence and gathered around the student society *Veljesto*.[7] Best exemplified in the writings of their leading theorist, the literary scholar and publicist August Annist, their values and ideals were non-elitist, social-liberal and ethnocultural. At the same time, they shared the Young Estonian (and National Awakening) belief in the power of highly developed culture to make a small nation great (Hennoste, "Noor-Eesti enesekoloniseerimisprojekt" 266-267). However, the turn in the 1930s to a different type of nationalism marginalized their approach, and their ideas have not really entered the present-day public discussion directly.

Young Estonia, modernity and modernism(s): a reading in contribution to the debates

Relating to the previous debates, in the following I will discuss exactly the *modernism* of Young Estonia, because there, I believe, lies the crux of the matter. It is important here to see the Estonian movement comparatively, placed in the context of modernism as an international phenomenon. Modernist art is often seen as a crisis, an interruption, in traditional aesthetics, or else as the carrier of an aesthetic that somehow *reflects* the broader historical crisis during a particular phase of rapid modernization. As suggested above, I support Eysteinsson's view that modernist movements ought to be considered more broadly, not only as purely aesthetic phenomena, but also as socio-cultural and political interruptions in their particular immediate modern circumstance which they see as flawed and barren. As Eysteinsson puts it: "In refusing to communicate according to established socio-semiotic contracts, they seem to imply that there

---

6   I opened the discussion of this polarization of values in Estonian society in Chapter One, with reference to the political theorist Tõnis Saarts's work.
7   Tiit Hennoste is an alumnus of the "Veljesto" society today, as is, for instance the Singing Revolution leader and a long-term leading Social Democrat politician Marju Lauristin. On the other hand, so was Johannes Aavik.

are other modes of communication to be looked for, or even some other modernity to be created" (7). This is the reason why modernist literature and manifestos stimulate so much general cultural and political debate in their context and even in their wake. This also explains why the controversy that modernism initiates is to a high degree fought in terms of what counts as pertinent or appropriate (use of) language.

In my analysis, Young Estonian texts are saturated by the same discourses and debate issues (technological change, urbanization, sense of acceleration, transforming generational and gender relationships, etc.) that surround late 19th-century and early 20th-century texts in Western societies (cf. Childs 20-23). Yet I am not suggesting that it is an imitative movement, rooted in the reading of foreign texts and not in the local experience. *All* literature and culture is to a degree transnational, but simultaneously it is also part of the sociopolitical and cultural environment from which it springs. Like other modernist movements, the Young Estonians write from and of their particular experience of modernization, to which they relate with a variety of—and often ambivalent—thoughts and feelings.[8] This experience involves a sense of political stagnation, frustration with the limitations on public debate and high-cultural life, but also the increased experience of city life, awareness of educational options and social mobility, rapid changes in human interaction, communication, travel, consumption, entertainment, etc. The writings of the Young Estonians relate to the perceived changes: accelerated time, excitement, disorientation and anxiety.

This combination is similar (though not identical) to the experience of modernization in many other societies, particularly to that of other "belated modernizers". However, the metaphor of family resemblance is a more illuminating explanatory tool here than the terms of originals and copies. There were no big cities in the beginning of 20th-century Estonia, but for the small group of first-generation urban intellectuals the shock of displacement seems to have compared to the shock experience of the city elsewhere (Hinrikus, *Dekadentlik* 42). Discussing the background of the Young Estonians, Aino Kallas describes the—sometimes superficially hardly visible—change in the Estonian life-world dramatically as a mental "salto mortale", and conjures a picture of a fluid, hopeful, overwrought, feverishly energetic society (11-12, 16-17).

---

8   Mirjam Hinrikus's *Dekadentlik modernsuskogemus A.H. Tammsaare ja nooreestlaste loomingus*, a study of what she terms "decadent discourses" in a body of texts by Tammsaare and other Young Estonians, supports this argument. Hinrikus strongly criticizes the view that the Young Estonian project was purely imitative and disassociated with their environment.

This vision is confirmed by mainstream history books which tell of a sharp acceleration in modernizing change at the end of the 19th and the beginning of the 20th century as the Russification-related administrative reforms were taking effect. However much Estonians may have resented Russification, it won them an important economic and administrative advantage compared to the Baltic Germans and opened new doors for self-advancement in those areas (Jansen, *Eestlane*; Kasekamp, *A History*). Kallas also links the Young Estonians' preference for the decadent and fantastic authors to their own state of nervous excitement and heightened sensitivity (17), which, however, equally strives towards crystallization in formal perfection (47).

The 100th anniversary of Young Estonia was based on the 1905 publication of the first of the movement's five literary albums. The beginnings of the movement date a few years earlier and in 1905 the press-ready manuscript had been stuck in the censor's office for about a year. However, the coincidence that ties the symbolic birthday of Young Estonia and the publication of its album demanding *"More culture! [...] More European culture!"* (Suits, "Noorte püüded" 17, emphasis in original) with the 1905 revolutionary demands for *political* modernization is not a simple historical accident, but points to deeper connections. Both the revolution and the appearance of artistic modernism shared the background of social dissatisfaction and fermentation, a sense of frustration in people increasingly modernized economically and technologically, who craved more satisfying avenues for *both* political and cultural participation and self-realization. Moreover, the Young Estonians were also actively involved in the 1905 revolution. They became strongly marked by the opening horizons the revolution initially evoked, on the one hand, and, on the other, by the following experience of political backlash, punitive expeditions, imprisonment or exile.[9]

Part of the Young Estonia nucleus group had already met in the underground societies of Tartu secondary school students who gathered to debate literature, philosophy and politics. Led by the future Young Estonian poet and critic Gustav Suits, the literary journal *Rays* (*Kiired*) was issued in 1901–1902 "to promote better Estonian literature". Other later Young Estonians, Johannes Aavik and Villem Grünthal-Ridala, who became (in)famous as promoters of radical modernization of the Estonian language, affiliated with similar student circles in

---

9   The historian Jüri Kivimäe finds that the most active promoters of the revolution were born on or around 1886, which coincides with Young Estonia's prevalent age group (29). Bernhard Linde and Friedebert Tuglas were born in exactly 1886, Villem Grünthal-Ridala and Jaan Oks in 1885, Gustav Suits in 1883, Johannes Aavik in 1880. The somewhat detached associates Aino Kallas and Anton Hansen Tammsaare were born in 1878.

the small town of Kuressaare. Suits later reminiscences about them as "very distinctive and original persons" in the "idyllic Kuressaare" who issued a hand-written newspaper titled *Young Estonian (Noor-Eestlane)*. They discussed Estonian concerns and language renewal, studied French and Italian as well as Finnish and Hungarian, and were interested in marvellous and imaginative writing such as works by French symbolists, Edgar Allan Poe, and Gabriele D'Annunzio. (Suits, "Lõpusõna" 638)

As the name Young Estonia suggests, the movement emphasizes its generational nature—and also indicates a contrast, a rupture, with their contemporary "Old" Estonia. The historian Toivo Raun argues that the generational gap between the 1880s generation with their elders goes beyond an ordinary generational clash ("Eesti lülitumine" 41-42).[10] The Young Estonians grew up in a markedly more urbanized, and technologically and economically rapidly modernized society. Estonians educated in earlier periods had lived in a predominantly German and agrarian world, but the new generation received their education entirely under Russification and was thus not inhibited by the accompanying language requirements like their parents had been. All core-group Young Estonians had an urban (small town) background either by birth or from early school years. Further, there were also many more Estonians acquiring secondary and higher education in their generation than there had been ever before. Most of the Young Estonians themselves received university education, while Suits, Tuglas and Grünthal-Ridala went as far as professorships in later life.

The most widely famous text in the first Young Estonia album (and probably in the movement's heritage altogether) is undoubtedly Gustav Suits's manifesto-like lead article "Aspirations of the Young" ("Noorte püüded"). Today, Estonians chiefly remember it by its epoch-making slogan: "Let us be Estonians but let us also become Europeans" (17). However, as Epp Annus has pointed out, the matter of Europe or discussion of appropriate outward influences for Estonia is not at all central in the article and does not take up much of its space (Annus, "Noorte" 527). Instead, most of the article deals with emphasizing the unacceptability of Estonians' current situation, laying out two main *internal* grounds for it, and then proposing a solution, making a spirited appeal to the reader to overcome the difficulties and to make the impossible possible.

The 19th-century National Awakening was like an idyllic springtime of beautiful and bold dreams, Suits suggests. "After the handsome spring there will come

---

10 Tammsaare's *Truth and Justice*, discussed in the previous chapter, is one of the central attempts to address and process that gap by literary means.

an even more beautiful summer!" it was hoped. "But the history of Estonian self-assertion is a story about a summer that never came." (Suits, "Noorte" 11)

The reasons for that were twofold. What the article stresses most is the lack of alliance and team spirit among Estonians. Suits is emphatic that it is not at all an *agreement* in views that is wanted. Quite the other way round, debate of ideas, non-subservience to dogmas, rigorous independent thought and critical spirit ought to be much more enthusiastically embraced by the young. What the article laments is the lack of tolerance, fairness and generosity towards opponents, and the absence of a shared joyful spirit of higher aspiration. The second reason (by implication also partially underlying the first one) is that, so Suits claims, 19th-century Estonian patriots had a wrong, disabling, detrimental sense of history.

> Much was written and spoken of the golden past of Estonia, of working for the public good and of other beautiful things. But the understanding of how to live soberly in the narrow frames of the present, how to really get work done for the public good, was quite dim. Estonia, fatherland, this was a word for evoking Sunday feelings, true everyday labor was not encompassed by that yet. (Suits, "Noorte" 11-12)

As the first chapters of this book show, the above judgement is not strictly true. The construction of a national historical consciousness, which incorporated a vision of a dignified pre-Christian past as a period of freedom and light, was certainly an important part of the ideological repertoire of 19th-century national activism, but in its heyday the movement was much more future- than past-oriented. Furthermore, considering the large-scale change accomplished—or even just attempted—by the constantly broadening circles of patriotic mobilizers and sympathizers, it is hardly fair to characterize them as idle dreamers. Thus I would guess that Suits's criticism of professions of patriotism remaining purely theoretical, his claim that "fatherland has become nothing but a worn-out clichéd sound" ("Noorte" 8), concern not so much the 1870s, but rather his own contemporaries who remain stuck in the faded glory of 19th-century history. Moreover, the rhetorical break with the past underlying the whole manifesto (note the "summer that never came", rather than "summer that has not yet come" (Annus, "Noorte" 529)), the emphasis on the current "time of transformation, rebirth", serve the appeal to concentrate all the powers to the present. The main point is not to lament previous mistakes, but rather to urge for a joyful drop of the burden of history, together with the dead weight of fear, inertia and pessimism.

Epp Annus thought-provokingly points out the analogies and shared spirit in Suits's "Aspirations of the Young" and Friedrich Nietzsche's essay "On the Use and Abuse of History for Life". There is no documentation that Suits had read the essay although he certainly read and referred to other texts by Nietzsche in 1903 and 1904 (Linde, "Noor-Eesti kümme aastat" 10). In contrast to Jüri Kivimäe (35), I agree with Annus that it hardly matters whether he had read this particular text. In a way, if he was *not* acquainted with that work, the strong similarities in both ideas and imagery even more persuasively indicate Suits's own modernist worldview. Both Suits and Nietzsche agree that history and tradition can have great value but both argue (Nietzsche, of course, much more extensively) that the "abuse" of history is detrimental "for life and action" (Nietzsche 1). The historical sense is something that makes one "active and progressive" modern people—people who live with a dynamic sense of change and hope for a better future (Nietzsche 6). Yet it could be considered a paradox of modernity that, to attain the hopeful enthusiasm and courage needed for taking action and rupturing with a past, one must draw upon the sense of the *unhistorical*, happy dedication to the moment. This is true of individuals, but also for cultures and nations.[11]

Suits and Nietzsche both make their strongest appeal to the young, though Suits in his finale qualifies it by counting in the young at heart. "People may speak against their crudeness and immoderation, but they are not yet old and wise enough to be content; above all they do not need to feign any ready-made culture" (Nietzsche 45).

It is important to note that neither in Suits's or Nietzsche's case is the revolt against the past, tradition, abstract, it is not an unspecific ahistorical patricide. Both emphasize the lack of spirited cultural interaction and synergy in the case of German and Estonian people respectively, and the resulting conventionality and cultural clumsiness. Nietzsche criticizes the ideology of science and positivistic historical consciousness. Suits criticizes the meaningless repetition of the 19th-century clichés that dominated his mental environment of theoretical patriotism, the fearful intolerance and the isolation from international cultural life.

---

11 It could also be noted here that both Suits and Nietzsche, though they became non-believers, were in their family upbringing deeply influenced by Lutheran Pietism (in Suits's case the Moravians), with its emphasis on religious enthusiasm and joyful rebirth, leaving the past behind. Thus the kinship in their modernist rhetorical strategies can perhaps also partly be taken back to this shared cultural heritage. Nietzsche is, of course, well known for his anti-Christian statements, but it can be convincingly argued that his philosophical drive has a "fundamentally religious nature", and one influenced by the Pietistic imagination (Fraser 43-44).

The proposed solution to find a way out of the dead end is in both cases literature and art. In the spirit of Nietzsche, Suits points out that education, the main reference point of the 19th century, alone will not help. Modern education is too particularistic, utilitarian and separates people in their specialities rather than unite them in joyful action. "Literature and art are the most important forces that can incite and bring together the aspirations and emotions of our contemporaries most widely, lend them stimulating, uplifting potentiality" (Suits, "Noorte" 18). Art and literature can undermine social and national prejudice, bring "light and freedom" into people's hearts ("Noorte" 18).[12] Later the Young Estonians were accused of aestheticism inappropriate for the political struggle, but as the above shows, art clearly was not understood as an aim in itself at the beginning of the movement. Its members merely envisioned their artistic, political and moral project differently from their predecessors.

In his well-known essay "Tradition and the Individual Talent" T. S. Eliot asserts: "if the only form of tradition, handing down, consisted in following the ways of the immediate generation before us in a blind or timid adherence to its successes, 'tradition' should positively be discouraged" (4). This I would describe as a very characteristic modernist view. Consequently, once it is accepted that the 19th-century tradition that an early modernist movement is revolting against is indeed not the only choice, this insight invites individual and collective explorations of other traditions that one could claim as one's heritage. Thus Gustav Suits writes towards the end of "Noorte püüded": "We want to search for such aims and forms to which we are, on the one hand, guided by the mentality of our own people, its natural qualities and needs, and on the other, by European culture" (19). It should be noted that Suits aims the double—or indeed plural, as Europe is not monolithic for the Young Estonians—heritage to *guide* Young Estonians, rather than command "blind or timid adherence" (Eliot 4). There are various ways to be tied to a tradition so understood: one can follow as well as "sift out, revaluate and rework" (Eysteinsson 137) and also parody, criticize, even denounce.

Furthermore, as has become clear from the above discussion of modernism, the choice of heritage is not an "innocent" artistic question but a highly charged issue of socio-cultural debate over what the most appropriate kinds of heritage are. Debating the choice of heritage is one of the significant ways to debate models

---

12 Jaanus Sooväli argues that Nietzschean "ideas such as creative tension, the storm and tempest (*Sturm und Drang*) of the youth, the intensity of life, and the accompanying longing for the heights of culture" also reached Suits and other Young Estonians through the mediation of the work of Georg Brandes (147).

of modernity. In this light it is noteworthy that Suits does altogether four separate things in his essay: makes a symbolic break with his immediate national environment that remains stuck in the 19th century; claims the heritage of European traditions instead; also claims the guide of the mentality and requirements (if not the culture) of his own people; makes an appeal that this people ought to create themselves a new and better national culture for the future.

This conjunction of foreign and domestic, future and past, is later echoed in many ways by different Young Estonians, very centrally in the work of the language renewal ringleader Johannes Aavik. In his *Uttermost Possibilities of Language Renewal* (*Keeleuuenduse äärmised võimalused*), he proposes radical changes to the existing Estonian language (the carrier of Estonian history and spirit of the nation, as Aavik's critics would remind him) for the very reason that "national culture is impossible without a cultivated language" (7). A people without such a language can have

> education, civilization—beautiful large cities, many factories, numerous railways, enough schools (in a foreign language), a plenty of doctors, lawyers, engineers, technicians, luxuriously designed interiors, widely travelled persons, gentlemen of fine manners, ladies of tasteful dress, elegant flirt and refined vices, but that kind of a people does not have a *national culture*. (Aavik, *Keeleuuenduse* 7, Aavik's emphasis).

For Aavik, language renewal is emphatically both a cultural and a political project. Because of the great historical disadvantages in the development of the Estonian people, its language too is stunted, crippled—a language bred in the low chimneyless huts of the peasants and showing the signs. However, all is not lost, one does not have to accept the natural development of a language, just like one (by implication) need not accept that the future is determined by the past. (Aavik, *Mis on keeleuuendus?* 8, Aavik, *Keeleuuenduse* 7-8) Provided one believes there can be a culturally and economically brighter future for the Estonians, one must create a more accomplished language that is better suited for this future and can help to bring it along. One ought not to see a national language primarily as a treasured legacy left by the ancestors, a natural carrier of ethnic individuality that must not be tampered with too much. No,

> first of all language ought to be seen as **a tool for human activity, an instrument, a MACHINE** for expressing thoughts and this often also in order to achieve aesthetic effects! (Aavik, *Keeleuuenduse* 8, Aavik's emphases).

If language is more akin to technology than to an organism, then technological innovation in the linguistic domain is only sensible.

Even if Aavik here seems to profess an instrumentalist view of language quite far from Herder's, his writings overall testify that language is much more for him than just one piece of technology among others. Having started from bitter dissatisfaction with the existing Estonian language, towards the end of his *Uttermost Possibilities of Language Renewal* he envisions a new Estonian language that is developed, nuanced, deep and sensitive, equipped to express "the highest thoughts and most visionary ideals", "some great and new truths, pinnacles of human achievement and goals" (Aavik, *Keeleuuenduse* 151). Thus, he sees language as a force that enables and builds culture, and not only nationally but internationally. If Estonians were to make their present under-development an advantage, Aavik urges, they could renew their language more boldly and creatively than any other nation has yet done and forge a language that is not only an equal among cultivated languages but that will become the example to all the rest of the world (*Keeleuuenduse* 137). The language question ought to be the primary one among the concerns of Estonian national culture, Aavik argues:

> if the renewal takes effect, we will acquire a language that has high value. This is a precious fortune, a treasure, the attainment of which is worth fighting for, toiling for and dedicating oneself to. This is a treasure that will give real value to the Estonian nation and will make life as an Estonian more fulfilled and beautiful. [...] Thus let us renew the language! Let us renew the written language! Let us renew madly! Let us not be afraid to go too far on that road! (*Keeleuuenduse* 150)

Thus, even as Aavik sees language as an instrument and often also describes the language renewal as something akin to a grand artistic project, he also sees it as the primary force that makes national and cultural existence possible, and indeed as a national treasure that can be passed on to future generations. In his writings Aavik uses a variety of metaphors to describe his understanding of what language is and what it does, but two especially repetitive ones (in addition to "the machine" mentioned above) are that of a musical instrument that needs tuning and that of a national house in need of development. These correspond to the two aspects in Aavik's thinking about language: one more poetic and individualist, the other more materialistic and collectivist. However, the two metaphors are not contradictory, and they are united by a stubborn, single-minded urgency in his demand for "a fever, a revolution in the life of the language" that has both political and artistic undertones. Thus, Aavik finishes his tractatus *What is Language Renewal? Its Justification and Programme* with the exhortation that, in order to succeed, the language renewal project commands two qualities from the Estonians: patriotism and aesthetic sense—and then he adds to them three more, as if to make practical success really sure: reason, courage and willpower (*Mis on keeleuuendus?* 37-39).

As mentioned in the beginning of the chapter, most discussions of Young Estonia emphasize the central, even emblematic, role translating played both for the Young Estonian language renewal and for the Young Estonia movement in general. This not only in the sense that translations of particular texts constitute a significant part of the Young Estonians' collective *oeuvre,* but also in the wider metaphorical sense of the reception of the foreign being of central importance for the movement (see e.g. Veidemann, "Maailmakirjanduse"; Monticelli, "Keeleuuendus ja tõlkimine" I and II).

From the viewpoint of the present argument, it is important to consider how translating foreign cultures and renewing the Estonian language functioned as an "interruption" in the immediate Young Estonian context of modernity, and why the controversy over the resulting competing models of modernity still lasts. Here the interaction between national and foreign, and the related interconnection between "national now" and "national in the future" must be analyzed. Furthermore, it is relevant to note more exactly not only on which foreign cultural texts and traditions the Young Estonians concentrated, but also what and how they "translated" from them.

Here I also want to draw attention to an issue that neither the critics nor the sympathizers of the Young Estonian translation-mindedness have truly considered: translation is one of the most characteristic traits of the modernist drive to "make it new", not only in small and/or "belated", but also in established and prestigious literary cultures. The translation theorist and historian Lawrence Venuti relates that, at the start of the 20th century, attitudes towards translation are thoroughly changed as the modernist movements turn them into a "focus of theoretical speculation and formal innovation" (71). Earlier, from the medieval period, hegemonic European aesthetics and literary history had perceived translation as being inferior to the original—a copy secondary both in terms of chronology and authenticity (Devy 182). A prevalent trope in the English tradition posits the translator as a servant who has the duty to obey the original unconditionally but who is potentially treacherous (Bassnett, "The Meek" 16).

For the modernists, however, translation is not a derivative and servile activity, but an important way to experiment with language and form in order to revitalize a literary culture (Venuti 71). Unlike the 19th century, when the English and French discourses of translation dominated internationally, the modernists find inspiration in the very different German tradition stemming from German Romanticism, hermeneutics and existential phenomenology: Herder, Goethe, Schiller, Schleiermacher, Humboldt etc. "They assume that language is not so much communicative as constitutive in its representation of thought and reality, and so translation is seen as an interpretation that necessarily transforms and reconstitutes the foreign text" (Venuti 71, see also Forster). This perspective inspires modernist texts in "foreignizing" translation that push the boundaries of the target language and culture, as well as the (superficial) opposite: the translator taking considerable liberty rewriting the original in the interests of his/her creative project.

One of the many examples of the combination of the two could be the American poet Ezra Pound's translation of Confucius in his *The Cantos*, where he develops a method of "ideogrammic" writing and uses Chinese characters in the English text. At the same time, the translation is not a "faithful" one, and, indeed, typically for modernist translators, Pound's understanding of the source language was quite limited (Yao 153-188). It is important to note that the translation of Confucius was also a political project: Pound believed that language expresses political blueprints precisely and that his translations improve the advancement of political thought. In his *Translation and the Languages of Modernism*, Yao studies the aesthetics and politics of the Irish modernist poet W.B. Yeats's translations of Sophocles in the framework of his development of Irish national drama. One of Yeats's goals was to dilute the predominance of English culture over the Irish one, not by shutting out all influence entirely but by multiplying its sources, promoting what he saw as a more balanced and creative way of development. In particular, Yeats argued that the Irish Literary Theatre should make "a point of performing Spanish, and Scandinavian, and French, and perhaps Greek masterpieces rather more than Shakespeare". It should open "its doors to the four winds of the world, instead of leaving the door that is towards the east wind open alone." (Yeats 75-76)

The quote above, with some change in the toponyms, could well have come from almost any of the Young Estonians. As far as foreign sources of heritage are concerned, the movement is correctly famous for its aim of freeing the Estonians from the "mental slavery" of German and Russian influence, promoting Finnish, Scandinavian, Italian, French, Belgian and Anglo-American stimuli instead. It ought to be added that although the Young Estonians did want to open their "doors to the four winds of the world", their anti-German-and-

Russian attitude in practice primarily concerned Russian "official culture" and the German *Trivialliteratur* dominating the Estonian scene. On the other hand, Russian symbolists got a lot of praise and attention from the Young Estonians, and so did, among others, Rilke, Nietzsche, Freud, Marx, and the infamous Otto Weininger. Occasionally the Young Estonian albums even published their contemporary Baltic German poets. Although the Young Estonians often talk about "Europe" in the singular, when one considers their practice, that is, the scope of translated authors represented in the Young Estonia publications, what actually emerges is a concept of multiplicity. Different sources are selected in order to balance one another out, so none will entirely dominate. This principle is continuously followed in translations, language renewal and in cultural orientation more generally.

Yet, not counting the very close Finnish ties often based on personal relationships,[13] the most famous (or infamous) cultural pre-occupations of the Young Estonians was probably their long-term attraction to French decadence.[14] Next to Suits's "The aspirations of the Young", Aavik's essay "Charles Baudelaire and Decadence" ("Charles Baudelaire ja dekadentismus") attracted the second-most attention at the time. This text, accompanied by translations of Baudelaire's work by Aavik gave the initial cause for associating the Young Estonians with France, as well as with perversion, pathology and general decadence (Sisask 24).

Why such a choice? Why would texts from Baudelaire's *Les Fleurs du Mal* and *Le Spleen de Paris* appear in the very first Young Estonian album, a step from Suits's manifesto denouncing pessimism and inertia, and proclaiming a time of transformation and rebirth? A good part of the answer to this question can be guessed from Aavik's accompanying essay. Despite his long-standing interest in Baudelaire as well as Poe (whom Aavik later translated with Baudelaire's version at the side), his introduction is quite cautious, even critical of what he describes as Baudelaire's tiredness of life and attraction to pathologies. However,

---

13 Several Young Estonians studied or spent long periods of time in Finland (Suits, Aavik, Ridala, Tuglas). The Finnish author Aino Kallas stood close to Young Estonia in her literary tastes and published a number of Finnish translations of Estonian texts, whereas the Young Estonians translated and published her essays and fiction. The connections extended to marital ties—Kallas was married to an Estonian, whereas Ridala, Suits and the later prominent Finnish dramatist Hella Wuolijoki (née Murrik, published under that name in the first Young Estonian albums) married Finns.

14 I am using "decadence" in accordance with the nowadays prevalent international usage, as proposed in the Estonian context by Mirjam Hinrikus: as a general term for early modernist writing, covering and/or overlapping with naturalism, symbolism, aestheticism, etc. In the French tradition *fin de siècle* covers much of the same meaning. The Young Estonians also talked about "decadence" ("dekadentismus"), but not consistently in the same meaning as the present-day one.

the tone of his essay changes towards the end when Aavik starts to talk about Baudelaire's and other decadents' revolution in language in a very approving way:

> In the field of language too the decadents have given birth to a revolution, demanding more freedom for language and breaking quite a few laws held sacred hitherto. The language of petrified grammars and the word resources of the pedantic dictionary of the Academy were insufficient to express the fine nuances of symbolism and mysticism. The Academy and the conservative critics mockingly called it the language of decadence [...] Théophile Gautier, however, in his preface to *Fleurs du Mal* [The reference is to Gautier's preface to the third edition of the collection—P.P.] cries with ardent admiration: "The poet of *Fleurs du Mal* loved the style which is inadequately called decadence, but is nothing but art arrived at the point of extreme maturity yielded by the slanting suns of aged civilizations: an ingenious, complicated style, full of shades and scholarship, constantly pushing back the boundaries of language, borrowing from all technical vocabularies, taking color from all palettes and notes from all keyboards, struggling to render what is most inexpressible in thought, what is vague and most elusive in the outlines of form, listening to translate the subtle confidences of neurosis, the dying confessions of passions grown depraved, and the strange hallucinations of the *idée fixe* which is turning to madness. The style of decadence is the ultimate word of logos, able to express everything, driven to the last finesse. ("Charles Baudelaire" 196)

As Kaia Sisask has perceptively noted, this is inherently an early expression of Aavik's main ideals of language which he later develops and familiarizes during the language renewal movement (25). It corresponds to Aavik's belief that language ought to be a fine machine or an instrument that allows the utmost technical precision and poetic nuance and through which—or even because of which—great and novel things can be thought, read, done and achieved. Throughout his many writings campaigning for language renewal Aavik insists that adopting a new, even "superior", word to express a concept does not mean that the older word(s) ought to disappear. The more the better, that much richer the language is. It is important to Aavik that even synonyms are not "the same", they always carry even ever so slight nuances of feeling or association which are nevertheless important and valuable. Aavik greatly appreciates the clarity, laconicity and "aristocratic gracefulness" of the French language ("Prantsuse"), but, on the other hand, he finds his contemporary French too conservative, poor in derivatives and thus stagnating (Chalvin 109)—from that aspect not a good example for Estonian.

Aavik's preoccupation with nuance and finesse is shared by other Young Estonians. Comparing the vocabulary for representing emotions and states of mind in Villem Grünthal-Ridala's experimental language-renewal-oriented translation of D'Annunzio's *The Victim* (*L'Innocente*, 1892) to the Italian original, Monticelli found that the Estonian text contained more, not fewer, different lexical items than the Italian one. The Italian novel is famous for its detailed dissection of psychology and on average introduces two new items of emotional vocabulary per page, yet the Estonian text still contains over 30% more of different shades, achieving it by using derivatives, dialect words, loans and artificial constructions. (Monticelli, "Keeleuuendus ja tõlkimine" II, see especially 481) Oscar Wilde's aphorism that "truth is entirely and absolutely a matter of style" makes perfect sense from the young Estonian perspective and Friedebert Tuglas enlarges it with: "no thought can be expressed in two ways with the thought remaining the same" ("Kirjanduslik stiil" 23).

Why such a preoccupation with translation, nuance and multiplicity of style? As we have already seen, the Young Estonians support the Herderian (and also modernist) understanding that culture is entirely or largely conditioned by language. If one wants to change the world, it is necessary to search for different modes of thinking and speaking and to persuade other people to do so as well (or at least follow the avant-garde's suit). The "old" language used in the 19th-century "chimneyless huts" is literally restricting. The modern world with all its choices, options, new knowledge, contacts, and experience needs a language that is infinitely varied and flexible and sophisticated enough to impress the civilized world (cf. Aavik *Mis on keeleuuendus?* 8-9). However, there seems to be yet another emotional component to the love of nuance. Aavik and other Young Estonians often depict positive linguistic or stylistic features with the words "refined" and "rich", also "graceful", "noble" and "aristocratic". "Poor" and "vulgar" are favorite insults, next to "ugly" and "stagnant". Socialists as some of them are, yet they have the need to find an array of aristocratic ancestors for themselves. The French and Italian decadent authors are a suitable option, whereas the local Baltic German nobility certainly is not.

In my analysis, the Young Estonians considered themselves strongly defined by their Estonian identity and were also politically national patriots. My research does not support Hennoste's conclusion that they became considerably less political in the later stages of the movement. Rather, the national-political and artistic-individualistic work intertwined throughout the considered period.

Chapter Four. Self-Colonizing Translations

In 1912, for example, Tuglas presented a bitter but quite characteristic and illuminating vindication of Young Estonia against its critics, discussing the role of foreign examples for the movement, as well as the Young Estonian stance to the Estonian nationhood. Once again he explains that to "find a cure" against a situation where Estonian culture experiences strong but narrow foreign influence, they want to get acquainted with many foreign cultures, the more different and contrastive to one another the better (264). The French "decadents" are useful: like all those guided by best instincts, the Young Estonians have looked for influences that would be "older", "more mature", "more perfect". "The French genius" can well help to "cultivate", "discipline" and "refine" a Northerner, as theexamples of Juhani Aho or Ivan Turgenev testify. (Tuglas, "Natuke Capitoliumist" 264-265)

One might nevertheless ask with Hennoste why the Young Estonians take so much trouble to cultivate and discipline their local culture even when met by protest and criticism. It is definitely no honor or pleasure for Tuglas to be born an Estonian, as he takes pain to make quite clear. "The Estonian nation is one of the feeblest among the civilized nations," he says ("Natuke Capitolimist" 263).

> But as it has so occurred that we [the Young Estonians—P.P.] have been born in this land and members of this nation, we have to work among those people and in this environment, and to express our thoughts in this language. To do anything else would be a violation of our souls. Because only in this frame can our ethnic psychology find logical realization for itself. (Tuglas, "Natuke Capitolimist" 264)

Tuglas's attitude here probably reflects Young Estonia's interest in the French literary critic and historian Hippolyte Taine (1828–1893). Aino Kallas often mentions the Young Estonians' style and mentality growing out of various aspects of their local geography and as she was one of the very few reviewers of the movement whom the members considered perceptive and fair, they presumably did not disagree with this approach. Tuglas also states on the topic of nationhood—note the echo of Suits's manifesto from 1905—that they do not consider any "demonstrations of Estonianness" or "professions of love" for fatherland necessary or useful, what is important for them is "being and working as an Estonian" (Tuglas, "Natuke Capitolimist" 263).

As I read him, Tuglas is saying that he is an Estonian, conditioned by this heritage whether he wants it or not, even if his Estonianness is different, not the kind his critics consider appropriate. This I see as a central reason why he is determined to push his ideas through—he is looking to realize himself in what he perceives as the only possible country he has. Taine's deterministic account of the relationship between the individual and his/her environment and its fatalistic interpretation by Tuglas may be highly debatable, but this is not the issue here. Rather, it is important to note that though Tuglas comes across as arrogant, he is not someone who peddles imported goods for prestige.

In summary of the above, Young Estonians constitute an important voice that reflected and contributed to the multiple-level modernization processes in Estonia at the time, partly generic, partly idiosyncratic as these were. However, I do not want to dismiss Hennoste's argument that this voice did not manage to address everyone in Estonia the same way and to the same extent, whether the reason was the self-righteousness and arrogance of the Young Estonians or something else. In the situation of rapid change that did not diminish but speeded up during the inter-war period, modernist antimimetic writing was but one literary response. Among others was the appearance of long family novels, written mostly in the realist style, depicting different fates in turbulent times across several generations. Such novels written by August Jakobson, Karl Ristikivi, A.H. Tammsaare and other were praised by the professional critics and enjoyed enormous popularity with broad readership, presumably offering an appropriate symbolic form for processing the sense of interaction between change and continuity that most people were experiencing.

The literary and cultural figure of Tammsaare is useful to keep in mind when making concluding remarks about Young Estonia's role for modern Estonian culture. Now that the strong connections of Tammsaare's creative biography to the Young Estonian project have been appropriately re-illuminated (Hinrikus, *Dekadentlik*), the potential of Young Estonia itself also becomes visible in more multiple facets. Tammsaare developed the Young Estonian heritage more broadly than anyone else amongst his cultural renewal peers, experimenting with varied combinations of modernist and realist modes and perceptively dramatizing the forces of modernization not only in urban but also in more counter-intuitive village settings. He narrativized the tradition and change of Estonian farming life in philosophical novels that were artistically sophisticated and internationally aware, but also locally engaged and idiosyncratically Estonian. Thus, it is not correct to say that Young Estonia did not and could not reach any synthesis between Estonian and European cultures.

However, as elaborated at the end of Chapter One, Tiit Hennoste is not alone to think that at the beginning of the 21st century there exists in Estonia an enmity along the same lines as the previous *fin de siècle*: the narrow and parochial national essentialists versus the arrogant and self-righteous cosmopolitans. Neither side has empathy or courtesy towards the other's view, and both consider the other a threat to good life in Estonia. The political theorist Tõnis Saarts's analysis ("Kahest demokraatiamudelist"; "The Bronze Nights") supports Hennoste's from a different disciplinary angle although it does not refer to Hennoste's work. Saarts describes the contestation in terms of two rival models of democracy in Estonia: the "nationalist defence democracy" and multiculturalist "citizen-centered democracy". He concludes that as both of these outlooks are democratic, the multiplicity of viewpoints is actually a positive phenomenon, whereas Hennoste holds the controversy barren and the lack of synthesis debilitating for the Estonian culture.

The above, of course, calls to mind many belated modernizers' conflicts between the "-philes" and the "westernizers", yet constitutes a specific case. I will try to approach these questions in the following subchapter by returning to the work of Andrus Kivirähk, the author who in today's Estonia holds a position not unlike Tammsaare did in his time. Though very different, Kivirähk's work often directly takes up Tammsaare's figures, storylines and concerns, and also shares with its predecessor the drive to process conflicts and dilemmas by dramatizing them into endless paradoxes and ambiguities. *The Man Who Spoke Snakish* clearly re-addresses the relationship between foreign and national, future and past that was essential for the Young Estonians at the beginning of the 20th century.

I will discuss the general poetic features and intertextual connections of Kivirähk's *The Man Who Spoke Snakish* and then, against that background, concentrate on its central trope, language: its function and main connotations in the novel. Furthermore, it will interest me how the understanding of language in the novel compares with the Young Estonian ideas of language in its communicative, constitutive and instrumental aspects. What is the purpose of language, what work does it do in the world of *The Man Who Spoke Snakish*, and what is the relationship between language and creativity? By reminding the reader that languages can be given up and forgotten, is Kivirähk, like modernists, radically criticizing "established socio-semiotic contracts" (Eysteinsson 7), is he implying "that there are other modes of communication to be looked for, or even some other modernity to be created" (Eysteinsson 7)? Finally, what are the ways in which different readers have interpreted the trope of Snakish and the novel generally?

Language, Abject and Imagination in *The Man Who Spoke Snakish*

Like *The Old Barny* carnevalizes the 18th-19th-century period, *The Man Who Spoke Snakish* is set in a timespace that could be described as a kind of a phantasmagoric 12th or 13th century, the period of Christian crusades against the pagan peoples along the southern and eastern coasts of the Baltic Sea. As we have seen, this is the period that since G. H. Merkel and the National Awakening has been known as the time the Germans colonized the Estonians, baptizing them to Christianity "with fire and sword", the beginning of the Jakobsonian "era of darkness", the "700-year night of slavery". Thus Kivirähk is, yet again, taking up a topos which already has strongly established significance in Estonian national cultural memory, historiography and fiction.

The novel is narrated by the protagonist Leemet, and the whole plot and story-world are perceived through him. Leemet in many ways conforms to the protagonist of the classical Walter Scott-type historical novel (Lukács, especially 36-37). He is an average, mediocre figure, yet with enough practical intelligence and human decency to make him sympathetic for the reader when he finds himself whirlwinded through history, entangled into others' affairs and acted upon from the outside. As Lukács observes in relation to Scott, such a protagonist functions as a focus through which to portray the moments of radical historical transition in a society; he serves as the neutral ground on which the opposing forces contest one another. However, if in Scott's novels the middling hero has empathy for the losing side but always ends up on the "progressive" side of history, serving as a symbolic figure of sociopolitical compromise and synthesis, in *The Man Who Spoke Snakish* nothing like that happens. As the historical forces push him here and there, Leemet becomes the last of his kind, someone who, in his own words, "got inside a past [era—P.P.] the last moment before its door closed" (197).

Leemet grows up among the Estonians who attempt to follow their historical lifestyle in the forest at the time that most of their peers are moving into European-inspired villages. However, he was born in the village (thus eyed with severe suspicion by some forest people) where his family had moved at his father's initiative and only later is brought back by his mother who never took to village life. As told by him, the story becomes one of a people who voluntarily give up their accustomed lifestyle to adopt a new culture considered "progressive", "developed", and "civilized", despite it being harder in terms of labor load and material quality of life. Together with other forest ways, people forget the snake tongue that enables them to control their forest environment at leisure, the language transmitted to them as the (younger) brethren of the snakes, the most revered species in the forest. In the village it makes more sense to switch to the "cultivated" languages like German and Latin—not only are the snakes considered the Devil's spawn by the Christians, it is simply not "progressive" to talk to savage creepy-crawlies if one can talk to civilized Europeans (195-196).[15]

In a word, the former forest folk starts to see and enact life in a—supposedly superior—Other's terms. Thus they voluntarily place themselves under the overlordship of the Other, the crusaders and the monks—the Europeans. In that way the founding national narrative of the destruction of a Golden Age by the foreign powers of fire and sword is subverted by Kivirähk's re-narrativization. The Estonians are not enslaved because of the superior military powers or better political condensation of the Germans/Europeans, but because of their own self-persuasion and credence that the Other's ways are superior. Indeed, the later prevalent discourse of the tragic inevitability of German victory now appears as part of the very same brainwashing process that once assured the foreigners' victory, one that might also be called self-colonization. Thus, even if the story is melancholy, it is not one lamenting Estonian victimhood in being crushed by an invincible enemy—the Estonians have considerable agency and they almost entirely seal their own fate (cf. Kaljundi).

Interestingly, another, in many ways very similar reinterpretation of the commencement of the "night of slavery" era is offered by the contemporaneous cinematic historical farce *Men at Arms* (*Malev* 2005, dir. Kaaren Kaer), in which the Estonians also voluntarily embrace the hard-working peasant lifestyle with Germans as the lords of the manor (Kaljundi). Yet the noteworthy difference between *The Man* and *Men at Arms* is that in the latter the Estonians do not consider the Germans or other Europeans superior to themselves. They beat the Germans on the battlefield, but they just enjoy their farming toil so much that they cannot conceive of a harsher punishment for the conquered enemy than to condemn them to the life of the idle gentry, deprived of the pleasures of physical farm labor.

To use the categories introduced in the Young Estonia discussion above, in *Men at Arms* they "colonize themselves" because of their 19th-century peasant mentality, not because of the *fin-de-siècle* "let-us-become-European" sentiment. The fun *Men at Arms* makes of the Estonian addiction to hard country work rather resembles Kivirähk's play *The Estonian Funeral*, not his *The Man*. It could be said

---

15 The Estonian word for wild, 'mets-' or 'metsik' is derived from 'mets' (forest, wood) like Latin *savage* is derived from 'silva'.

that the self-deprecating ethnic humor of *Men at Arms* and *Funeral* directed at the 19th-century peasant aspect of the Estonian self is light-hearted and self-affirming, whereas the one mocking the "parvenu" Young Estonian self in *The Man* is rather bitter and dark.

Moreover, the self-image of Estonians as naturally and at heart a farming people is also destroyed: the novel dramatizes the voluntary villagization of the forest-dwelling Estonians as the first round of self-loathing and self-colonization. Even the romantic view of Estonians as worshippers of spirits in sacred groves is undermined. In *The Man*, these traditions are fostered by the silly anti-village fundamentalists in the forest. These are characters a big step removed from the former commonsensical Snakish-speaking folk who enjoyed an occasional ceremony, but generally related to their habitat in more easy-going ways. The protagonist is deeply sad that the theatrical proceedings in the grove seem to become the feature of the era remembered by history instead of "all the good and beautiful things that had once been" (*The Man* 354).[16]

Similar to Scott's novels, *The Man* could also be described as a *Bildungsroman*, one of the postcolonial kind where the personal formation of the protagonist is shaped by the trials, decisions and opportunities relating to his troubled identity as a member of an identity collective. Indeed, despite its chimeric setting, the plot and motif pattern of the Kivirähk's novel perfectly correspond to those of the postcolonial *Bildungsromane* discussed in Chapter Three. The text has a number of Scott-like plot twists that the reader may expect to produce a serendipitous conclusion and offer some symbolic hope—a synthesis of the historical confrontations in the novel, a promise of a new start. However, all these moments turn around and lead to nothing but more hopelessness.

In one such plot line, Leemet saves the life of his childhood mate Hiie, the last young woman still in the forest, and falls in love with her. There is a pre-nuptial mood signalling a potential for renewal in traditional life. However, the bride suddenly gets killed at the wedding. Later, Leemet has a relationship with the village beauty Magdaleena, to whose half-German baby he plans to teach Snakish like his uncle once taught him. The situation yet again seems overripe with the symbolism of a potential "social contract" and renewal, as Magdaleena tells

---

16 The critic Linda Kaljundi, a medieval historian in her primary specialization, admires Kivirähk's witty insightfulness in this respect. The present-day Estonian understanding of the pagan religious world, she points out, is indeed almost entirely formed through the sources and thus the perspective of the medieval Christianizers. Thus the generations of Estonian patriots who have tried to rekindle the grove fairy world to return to their original culture can actually also be blamed for self-colonization, if one wishes.

Chapter Four. Self-Colonizing Translations

Leemet: "You and I have to bring up my son together, so he can learn about the old and the new world equally. Then there will be at least one man like that, not only just people who don't know either one properly" (*The Man* 352). However, violent death yet again interferes out of the blue. Magdaleena and the baby are killed in a bloodshed, and the couple's utopia never gets a chance. When Leemet decides to return to the forest, this is only to witness the death of his mother and all his snake friends who also get killed (*The Man* 382-385).

Is there a particular force behind the annihilation of everything that constitutes Leemet's world and that might offer a positive conclusion to his coming-of-age story? As said above, the Germans only play a small role. The snakes and Leemet's mother are killed by the villagers who have forsaken the snakes as allies. The deaths of Leemet's girlfriends, however, are caused by the fundamentalists among the forest folk themselves, depicted as at least equally as misguided and cruel as the villagers. Even with only a few people left in the forest, there continues a deadly enmity over what the true laws and customs of Estonianness are and who constitutes a traitor in breach of them. There is a hint of similarity in the mood of the dark plot's enrolment with that of Chinua Achebe's *Things Fall Apart*, the famous realist novel dealing with the Christianization and colonization of Nigeria in the 19th century. In *The Man* things fall apart as well, they are not blown apart from the outside.

The Estonian critics have mostly read the underlying message of the novel to be that the (Estonian) nation will be irredeemably dead if one does not stop aping the foreign ways and forgetting its own: dead with finality and without a hope of resurrection in a meaningful sense. "But an age will not dawn one day," as Kaljundi summarizes the morale of the novel in the title of her review.[17] It is one of Leemet's greatest regrets that the forest people will only be remembered as a caricature through the distorted lens of the holy grove extremists and of the superstitious villagers, not in their own terms. The biological existence of "the Estonians" will go on, but, as Leemet sees it, this will be an existence in a changed world and for quintessentially different people, with no continuity or understanding in anything that matters.

If Estonian national discourses predominantly build on the tropes of resurrection and rebirth, *The Man* seems to present, for once, the other side of the coin, that of dying and decomposition. The motifs of death, decay, the rotting

---

17 The paraphrasing reference is to the last stanza of *Kalevipoeg*: "But one day an age will dawn / when all spills, at both their ends, / will burst forth into flame; / and this stark fire will sever / the vise of stone from Kalevipoeg's hand. / Then the son of Kalev will come home / to bring his children happiness / and build Estonia's life anew" (Kreutzwald 266).

and smell of putrefying bodies accompany the whole account. The narrator may contemplate the twists and turns of history in a rather Tammsaare-like way and note that "one day this new world with its gods and iron men will be forgotten, and something new will be invented", just like the lifeworld of the Snakish speakers was replaced (*The Man* 440). However, the idea of history as a series of transformations and new beginnings does not gladden or hearten him, nor even relieve his anger at the devalidation of his accepted order of the world.

Leemet starts his narration with a vivid picture of the animals in the forest baffled by his words in Snakish. As Snakish is now heard so seldom, the wildlife is no longer properly trained in the rituals of submission the language ought to trigger in them, and instead seem to consider attacking or fleeing the "strange freak" they see in Leemet (*The Man* 1-2). He reacts with rage and and fiercely continues hissing in Snakish, driving the animals' confusion to extreme distraction until they physically explode (2). "Inside me there is a strange hatred," he says, "toward the newcomers who don't know the old ways and just gambol through the forest, as if it had been created at the dawn of time just for them to loll about in" (2).

As critics and other readers usually take Snakish to stand for the threatened Estonian language, the voice of the protagonist-narrator is also conflated with that of the historical author of the work. Kivirähk's own paratexts give ambivalent messages in this respect. In some interviews he supports the parallel between Snakish and Estonian, as well as the interpretation of the work as a "novel of warning" for the latter's disappearance (see e.g. Grünfeldt), in others he emphasizes that Leemet's voice was a "role", not the author's credo, and hopes the novel will not be read as if it was written "against Europe or progress" (Rooste). "It could even be interpreted from the European perspective," Kivirähk says, that is, reading the forest people not as Estonians, but as Europeans who are entering an era of marginalization (Rooste).

Thus, it is important to consider how "reliable" Leemet is as a narrator: does the poetics of the novel encourage the reader to trust him? His character, drawn as boyish, unpretentious, jocular, yet also elegiac (and in those qualities not unlike Kivirähk's own public persona) and finally tragic, is clearly destined to win the reader's empathy. However, it can also be noticed that the overall value structure of the novel (the "implied author") does not support the narrator's account and judgement fully but leaves space for paradoxes and ironies. His account does not go uncontested, even if most of the challengers are presented—by his own narrative, of course—as negative figures. Several readers do pay attention to this feature of the novel. For example, Meelis Fiedenthal, a theologist and science fiction author, underlines that Leemet is not a neutral chronicler but represents "the party of snakes": the village elder Johannes or the holy grove sage Ülgas would each have told the whole story very differently.[18]

Whereas Ülgas and Johannes are presented as bigoted, ridiculous and ultimately vicious, there is also a fourth camp in the story that is seen sympathetically: the human ape couple Pirre and Rääk, the last surviving representatives of *their* kind. The apes relativize Leemet's apparently sensible credo of not abandoning one's original nature and healthy common sense by gently disapproving of the "regressive" trendy habits of the forest folk such as cooking their meat too thoroughly or using iron implements robbed from Germans instead of "our own stones" (*The Man* 64). How far back does one have to go to find authenticity? the reader is provoked to ask. And if the raw-meat-eating apes are not necessarily more sensible than Leemet, why should one consider Leemet more sensible than the bread-eating villagers?

The human ape couple themselves have a rather liberal attitude towards the world, allowing them to unashamedly enjoy their preferred lifestyle without any desire to force it upon anyone else. Thus, they also represent a contrast that humorously highlights the complex-laden violent culture wars going on between the rest of the characters. Leemet learns from the apes that, whereas the forest humans are not able to communicate to any insects in Snakish, the primeval human apes who pronounced the language in a more nuanced way, could (*The Man* 66). Pirre and Rääk retain the ability to command the lice, which they train as pets, but other insects are out of their reach too. Like all creatures who cannot be addressed in Snakish, the insects are considered worthless and beyond the pale by the forest people. Leemet does not stop to consider the implications of the information that it is the humans themselves who lack the special language skills for communicating to the insects.

This leads us to the central question of how language and languages have been conceptualized in the novel and the role they carry in the disappearing world of the forest Estonians. The Snake language has three main functions for them: it allows to converse with the snakes; to control and make use of most other animal life; and to raise from sleep a powerful creature called the Northern Frog who, once awake, destroys all enemies who attack Estonians, allowing the latter to collect the war booty. The latter function is often at the center of

---

18 True, of course, that the Ülgases and Johanneses have had a lot of chance to present their cases, as Ülgas represents the fetishization of the pre-Christian Golden Age and Johannes not only the catching-up-with-Europe discourse, but also that of the resurrection from the ashes central to Estonian modernity (which is reversed in *The Man*).

the readers' attention, so although Snakish is taken to stand for the threatened Estonian language (and culture more generally), it is associated with a kind of unifying national code of action, rather than an organically enfolding carrier of culture, an instrument of poetic self-expression or simply a specific means for intersubjective communication. Raising the Northern Frog to fight the enemy requires ten thousand men to address him together in Snakish. By the time the novel begins this is not possible anymore, as the tradition of learning Snakish has been forsaken.

The linguist Martin Ehala writes:

The old Estonians had their secret weapon—the Northern Frog who slept in its primeval cave but woke up and came to the aid of his people when ten thousand men called him in the words of Snakish. This nicely highlights the two unavoidable conditions for a collective's vitality: a shared cultural and linguistic code (the mastery of Snakish) and internal coordination (10,000 men together) are what enable collective purposeful action. Thus, the Northern Frog is nothing but the latent collective will that a well-functioning ethnos is able to express at decisive moments. The particular Snakish used to call the Frog varies with different peoples, but in principle there is no people without its Frog. The Estonians have it too, and most recently it responded to our call at the time of the Singing Revolution. (Ehala, "Õhuke riik")

Ehala's analysis is insightful, but a more thorough consideration of the pragmatics and functions of the particular Snakish can help to understand why its collective's vitality withered. The forest people's Snakish is for them more like an instrumentalized code, an effectual tool, than a national language. People *speak* Estonian, Snakish is used firstly for achieving instrumental ends and only secondarily for (by the time the novel begins generally very superficial) socializing with the snakes. It lacks both the aesthetic and the affective dimensions that Estonians associate with collective singing.

At the same time, for the narrator and other forest people the Snake language, rather than the Estonian language, constitutes a strict symbolic order. The hierarchy of all the creatures of the forest is based upon and expressed through Snakish. The snakes, who as benevolent elder brothers originally gave their language to the forest people, are the top of the hierarchy, followed by the Snakish-speaking humans. The bears have only rudimentary skills in Snakish and are also otherwise a simple, instinct-driven race the forest folk looks down upon, though they can communicate and like to seduce forest females who consider these affairs pleasurable but socially embarrassing. For most animals, like elks, wild boar, or wolves, the words of Snakish are simply a kind of a magic spell, and the orders given in this language they must—quietly—obey. This enables the forest folk to use them for food, clothes and transport effortlessly and to live in a kind of a (consumer) paradise without having to do hard work.

The creatures who do not understand the Snake language and do not respond to their power are considered despicable and their life worthless. This includes hedgehogs and the above-mentioned insects, but also Germans and villagers. A human who does not respond to a greeting hissed in Snakish, the snake king explains to Leemet early in the novel, can be killed: "he's no longer one of us. He is like a hedgehog or an insect and we don't pity him" (*The Man* 39). The reception of *The Man* has often remarked how the forest folk live in perfect harmony with their natural environment. The literary scholar Cornelius Hasselblatt has even called it the first Estonian ecological novel ("Eesti"). However, the harmony is hierarchical and exploitative.

Ironically, against these despicable creatures who do not understand Snakish only physical means of coercion can be used and these are mostly far less effective than the symbolic spell of Snakish. In cases where the power of the Snakish is counteracted or diminished, the animals rebel and the illusion of harmony quickly disappears. Not only do the wild animals resist taking orders (*The Man* 1-2), but the domesticated wolves also immediately turn against their masters when their ears are deafened, making them unable to hear Snakish. The reader may wonder how various forest *people* felt being part of the order based on the language of the snakes. Meelis Friedenthal, for example, suggests that the reason why the humans started to leave the forest for villages was to escape this violent and restrictive system. This would also explain, he writes, why the villagers so quickly forgot their Snakish and felt nothing but extreme abhorrence against the snakes afterwards.

The whole novel is full of instances of visceral repugnance and horror in reaction to an "other" culture that could be best understood through Julia Kristeva's concept of abjection. According to Kristeva, abjection is a human reaction of abhorrence to a threatened collapse of an established symbolic order through the disappearance of the distinction between subject and object or between self and other. The clearest example of what causes abjection is a corpse, an object which once was a subject and traumatically reminds one of human materiality. Bodily wastes, food, filth, etc. are also typical causes of abjection and different cultures regulate all these through varied taboos (Douglas, *Purity and Danger*). Ultimately, abjection is directed at the part of ourselves that we exclude in order to submit to the symbolic order. The abject "disturbs identity, system, order" (4), but it is not fully foreign: it is also the "recognition of the *want* on which any being, meaning, language, or desire is founded" (5).

The village food makes the forest children vomiting sick (*The Man* 121). The symbolically aberrant animals who do not understand Snakish provoke outrage and sadistic violence in Leemet (1-2). The villagers in their turn see the foresters as filthy and bestial (22), benighted (24), associating with horrendous devil's spawn, that is, snakes (*The Man* 113-14, 194, 382-385), etc. Leemet repeatedly describes the cultural aspirations of the villagers in terms of their desire of being homosexually dominated or castrated by the Europeans (the latter in order to become a fashionable castrato singer) which Leemet, unsurprisingly, finds abhorrent (215-216, 266-267, 339-340). It is interesting that while the novel is (hetero)sexually libidinous and decidedly unpuritanical, its only pervasive fear and taboo is that of being unmanned by the decadent Europeans.

This line of tropology is related to the early 20th-century concern that the Young Estonians poison healthy Estonian (peasant) minds with foreign perversion and decadence, but also with the 21st-century "defensive nationalist" (to use Saarts's term introduced above) criticism of the onslaught of "European" values (multiculturalism, civic nationhood, "political correctness") that "ravage" the Estonian "national body" (Loog) and "castrate" its history (Suurkask). "Citizen-centered" Estonians answer by expressing their distaste for this rhetoric, charging the opponents with chauvinism and xenophobia, in more radical occasions with forms of Nazism.

In *The Man Who Spoke Snakish*, however, the Snake language itself, first associated with the naturalized social order, also comes to be connected to death and to abjection as this social order falls apart. From about a quarter into the novel, Snakish is associated with the smell of death, as its power starts to disappear, crumble and fade. This happens with yet another false hopeful turn in the plot (157-159). Leemet and his uncle Vootele, the man who taught him Snakish and one of the most likable carriers of the forest culture in the whole novel, sit pleasantly together, eating elk meat in the uncle's cellar. There is a fresh spring beginning and hope is in the air. Suddenly the uncle chokes on a bone and dies on the spot.

Trying to carry the dead uncle out of the cellar, Leemet breaks his own arm and thus remains stuck with the putrefying body for weeks. Having loved his uncle, he is now horrified of him as an abject "monster" of bulging features and repulsive smell. With a feverish brain, Leemet imagines to be talking to the Northern Frog in Snakish and that vision saves him because his hissing is heard

Chapter Four. Self-Colonizing Translations

far away where his human whimper could not have been. On the other hand, the smell of death never leaves his nose and always remains associated with the snake language. "Sometimes it seems to have gone. For many days I can't smell it," Leemet relates, "but in a moment it again strikes my nose, ranker than ever, and turns my stomach. It was the last gift I got from my beloved uncle who taught me my Snakish and who mouldered away beside me." (164)

Similarly to *The Man*, in Kivirähk's earlier novels *The Old Barny* and *Butterfly* (*Liblikas*, 1999) death is also a strongly thematized force that the characters must day-to-day reckon with. However, only in *The Man* does death win hands down and without any hope of an afterlife. Looking for possible explanations in the features that differentiate *The Man* from the author's previous novels, we are back to the above-mentioned instrumentality of the Snake language, and to the related values of pragmatic common sense and positivism that—in contradiction to *The Old Barny* and *Butterfly*—characterize all the likeable characters in *The Man*.

Both the protagonist of *Butterfly*, an endlessly role-playing actor of the Young Estonia period and self-confessed unreliable narrator, and *The Old Barny*'s aesthetically imaginative proto-artist Liina enact creative ideals that, like for Kivirähk generally, are incorporated in play, spectacle, the truth of masks (cf. the essay "The Truth of Masks" by Oscar Wilde, a favorite of the Young Estonians). In *The Man* snakes impress on Leemet early on that "nature always remains the same" (49). In *The Butterfly* it is the Grey Dog, death and life's tedium personified in one, who makes comparable arguments and hates the actors for "living many lives", making a joke of death and thus breaking all the laws of the natural world order (Kivirähk, *Liblikas* 140-141).

Differently from the villagers who sing and the human apes who make cave paintings of their history, the forest folk in *The Man* seem to practice no arts and reduce the aesthetic to the decorative. Furthermore, their disregard for the transcendental and for the beautiful makes spirituality meaningless (for Leemet's family) or turns it into sterile monologous ideology (for the nativist sacred grove worshippers among the forest Estonians). Leemet's uncle tells him:

> One person believes in spirits and visits the sacred grove, and another believes in Jesus and goes to the church. It's just a matter of fashion. There is nothing useful to be done with a god, they are more like brooches or necklaces, just for decoration. For hanging around your neck, or for playing with. (*The Man* 27-28)[19]

---

[19] Here I have modified the translation to render the original more closely.

The above quotation contrasts with the key monologue of the protagonist of *Butterfly*: "I have to say I like useless things and purposeless activities [...] With great respect I also look at all sorts of circus junk and bits and pieces, little many-colored pins and balls, which lack any sensible application," he says (*Liblikas* 110). And before that: "I have always admired the circus—to think of it, a man walks on a thin rope instead of striding on sturdy pavement! There is nothing sillier, it doesn't lead him anywhere and he would certainly get on much quicker taking a horse cab, not to mention an automobile, but I like it." (*Liblikas* 110)

The circus and the theatre *seem* to have no practical purpose, but in truth they are ways to create alternative worlds next to the one pre-given (*Liblikas* 110-111). Thus, artists are comparable with revolutionaries, but importantly their new worlds remain not only non-coercive, but also variable and non-totalizing (111, 129-130). Contrary to *The Man*, in which the characters quarrel over the right way of being an Estonian, the protagonist of *Butterfly* talks with pleasure of his multiple personae, transcending time, space and ethnicity: born an Estonian at the end of the 19th century, he has spoken words written by people dead long before his birth, and has been English, Spanish, even Ancient Roman (111).

In keeping with their worldview, the forest people in *The Man* use the Snake language in an instrumentalized manner that can well be described by Heidegger's critical concept of *Gestell*, the "enframing" accomplished by modern Western technology (Heidegger, *The Question of Technology*, see especially 21, 23-24). Through this enframing, Heidegger says, nature and the world in general, including ultimately humans, are made to be regarded as "orderable" "standing-reserve" (*Bestand*), "stock", resource (17-18). Nature is viewed as a "coherence of forces calculable in advance" (21), temporarily an object of scientific research, "until even the object disappears into the objectlessness of standing-reserve" (19), that is, viewed as without autonomy, mere means to an end, exploitable and consumable.[20]

The danger that Heidegger identifies is not the instrumentalizing worldview as such, but its totalizing quality, the disproportionate imbalance between instrumental efficiency and other values. According to Heidegger, in Ancient Greece the idea of technology involved an experience of the coming together of usefulness (*techné*), as well as beauty (*poesis*), truth/knowledge (*aletheia, episteme*) and holiness (*promos*). A successful, rewarding adoption of a technique or a tool occurred only on the condition that all four aspects of the "single manifold" (Heidegger, *Basic Writings* 316) were present.

---

20 This is in line with the instrumentalized lifeless aspect of *techné* discussed by Pheng Cheah in connection to Indonesian and Kenyan *Bildungsromane* (Chapter One).

The Snake language does not function as a vehicle of nuanced self-expression, poetic or otherwise. It resembles a coded socioeconomic ideology, coated as common sense, rather than a multidimensional national language. It is noteworthy that its users are interested in the exactness of pronunciation (which may increase the effect of the words), but not in expressing shades of meaning or broadening the boundaries of what can be thought and felt via a language, as was the case with the Young Estonians' project. As mentioned above, Aavik too likes to think of language as an instrument or a machine, but if in his case the characteristic instrument is a violin, for *The Man* it could be a mechanical tool of armament.

Finally, while *The Man* has often been interpreted as a novel of warning against the threat of losing the Estonian language, symbolized by Snakish, it ought to be noted that the *literal* Estonian language is actually also constantly used in the novel. Its Estonian characters have not forgotten this language; in fact, it seems almost too resilient to believe. In contrast to the Snake language, it appears to be adapting well in different contexts, being employed by the human apes, the forest people, and the villagers alike, for trivial as well as philosophical conversations. It shows the ability to change, characteristic to a living language. Leemet is a character likely to win the reader's empathy, but what he tells us is full of paradoxes. It is no wonder that Kivirähk's oeuvre has resisted a neat classification either as a voice of "nationalist defence democracy" or the cosmopolitan "citizenship-centered democracy" in Estonia. The reception of *The Man* has been varied as there are no unambiguous answers. Rather, the novel presents a stage set that can enable the reader—and not only the Estonian reader—to think across and beyond this type of dichotomy.

* * *

Both parts of the chapter are set at the time of a crucial phase of modernization. Young Estonia acted within the dynamics of the great rupture of *fin-de-siècle* Europe and its own position in the world of Czarist Russia. Kivirähk's *The Man* is written in a globalized 21st-century world, with Estonia being a full member of the European Union, which it voluntarily joined. Yet in both cases there is a central tension between the aspiration to preserve what is perceived as a natural and authentic culture, and the aspiration to learn from foreigners for what is perceived as improvement/modernization of one's culture. These aspirations interact and develop in an environment where the native population feels itself to be acting in the forcefield of more dominant players, politically or economically. As we have seen, the 21st-century situation of globalization and that of old-school colonialism can create partly similar reactions and concerns (how much are we in control of our history and our future? what can we do about it?), even if there is also a great deal of difference between the two.

Afterword

In this book, I have continually emphasized the importance of studying the history of the multiple strands of discourses and practices that feed into the construction of a modern nation—native and borrowed, old and new, deliberately created or spontaneously arisen. It is even more important, moreover, to note that, in order to contribute to the nation-building process, any of these elements has to resonate with at least part of the population. The historian also must ask if, how, why it happens or discontinues to be the case, and what are the effects. My case study was Estonia, a postcolonial country, whose self-understanding is strongly built on repeating stories of rupture and forever continuing struggles for agency. The book, however, is not meant only for Estonians; that is why I chose to write it in English. A major part of my ambition for creating a historically informed case study of discourses of modernization, was to identify new (or forgotten) sociopolitical imaginaries, new cultural capital for others facing the challenges of the present-day globalized world and looking for resources to come up with novel solutions. By way of conclusion, I will be highlighting this potential of Estonian history one more time—I will be arguing, in other words, why Estonian history matters today beyond its own borders.

In his *Modernity: Understanding the Present*, Peter Wagner expresses the hope that societies with a vibrant operative experience of thoroughgoing social transformation can offer inspiring examples of collective creativity and collective action for the current global situation. What is more, they can do it *in contrast* to Western societies where institutional stability and low-participation representative democracy have been the norm since WWII. The practice of democracy as "management" (rather than leadership) of the polis, almost as if predetermined by the laws of economics, has outrun its course, now unable to provide even what it promised—political stability and consumer-citizen satisfaction. Societies with a richer, or more recent, historical experience of steering drastic institutional change in a situation of unfortunate socio-political heritage and strong outward pressures may be more tuned to the current polycentric global environment.

A significant turning point in contemporary Estonian historical memory that continues to play a role in the collective political imaginary to this day is the Singing Revolution of the end of the 1980s and beginning of the 1990s where profound transformations in the model of modernity were conceptualized and carried out in a short period of time. Such a turnaround can provide a good occasion to examine how exactly such major socio-cultural and political change is possible and how it comes about. How, individually and collectively, is the leap between the space of experience and the horizon of expectations taken? How do new discourses emerge and spread themselves despite the clear dominance of the existing ones? How, through co-ordinated, but still multi-level, multi-faceted action, are institutions and practices transformed (with unintended consequences and new social problems also replacing the former ones)?

My own perspective on the Singing Revolution is unavoidably multifaceted: that of an active participant, of a young student whose interest in the phenomenon of major social change was triggered by this experience, and that of a scholar trying to think herself—and her compatriots—through these many-layered historical events. Having both an insider position and a scholarly viewpoint, from which I can discuss the Singing Revolution as a dynamic field of individual and collective action, I cannot but see it as something more innovative and creative than a "return to the West", or a return to a pre-existing normality. Therefore, it seems paradoxical that exactly when Estonians were carrying through this major transformation with a wide variety of expectations for the future, in the West leading theorists spoke about the end of history with no substantial change possible. Even more ironically, by the mid-1990s Estonians, too, were advised that they should consider becoming "just another boring Nordic state" as their next ambitious goal (cf. "Toomas Ilves").

We knew that history did not end in the 1990s, and if some of us were convinced to forget it, we have surely been reminded of that lately. As I am finishing this book, in December 2022, a chain of global crises is afoot and we are participating in major changes. What is important to remember, then, is that the mechanisms of change, and the ways in which people define and address the agenda relevant for their social situation always depend on the particular historical circumstance—societies' collective self-understanding, the available political imaginary, dynamics of leadership, the nature of outward pressures. They necessarily need to be studied in their concreteness, and they can never be resurrected in the form of an exact past model. Yet, this does not mean that other people, at other times and/or places cannot be inspired by them and draw upon them as common human cultural capital to develop new dimensions in their own social, cultural and political imagination.

Works Cited

Aavik, Johannes. "Charles Baudelaire ja dekadentismus." ["Charles Baudelaire and Decadence"] *Noor Eesti I album*. [Ed. Gustav Suits. Tartu]: "Kirjanduse Sõprade" Kirjastus, 1905. 194-196.
—. *Keeleuuenduse äärmised võimalused*. [*The Uttermost Possibilities of the Language Renewal*] Tartu: Istandik, 1924.
—. *Mis on keeleuuendus? Ta põhjendus ja ta programm*. [*What is Language Renewal? Its Justification and Programme*] Tartu: Reform, 1916.
—."Prantsuse stiili iseärasustest." ["About the Peculiarities of the French Style"] *Noor-Eesti* 5-6 (1910–1911): 617-622.
Achebe, Chinua. "The African Writer and the Biafran Cause." *The Conch* 1 (1969): 8-14.
—. "The Novelist as Teacher." *New Statesman* January 1965: 161-162.
Adams, Jüri. "Tundmatu Kontantin Päts." ["The Unknown Konstantin Päts"] *Eesti riik*. Vol. 2. By Konstantin Päts. Eds. Toomas Karjahärm, Hando Runnel. Tartu: Ilmamaa, 2001. 9-28.
Ahl, Nils C. "Le dernier sifflement." ["The Last Hiss"] *Le Monde* 14.02.2013. <http://www.lemonde.fr/livres/article/2013/02/14/le-dernier-sifflement_1832309_3260.html> 16 July 2017.
Alenius, Kari. "The Birth of Cultural Autonomy in Estonia: How, Why, and for Whom?" *Journal of Baltic Studies* 38.4 (2007): 445-462.
—. "Under the Conflicting Pressures of the Ideals of the Era and the Burdens of History: Ethnic Relations in Estonia, 1918–1925." *Journal of Baltic Studies* 35.1 (2004): 32-49.
Allik, Jaak. "Mees, kelle elu ja loomingut juhtis vastutustunne." ["A Man Whose Life and Creative Work were Guided by his Sense of Responsibility"] *Postimees* 04.09.2007. <http://kultuur.postimees.ee/1698885/mees-kelle-elu-ja-loomingut-juhtis-vastutustunne> 17 October 2016.
Almberg, Antti and Lydia Koidula. *Koidula ja Almbergi kirjavahetus*. [*Correspondence between Koidula and Almberg*] Ed. August Anni. Tartu: Eesti Kirjanduse Selts, 1925.
Alvarez, Roman and Carmen-Africa Vidal (eds.). *Translation, Power, Subversion*. Clevedon, Philadelphia, Adelaide: Multilingual Matters LTD, 1996.
Anderson, Benedict. *Imagined Communities*. Rev. ed. London and New York: Verso, 1983.

Anepaio, Terje. "Eesti mäletab?! Repressiooniteema retseptsioon Eesti ühiskonnas." ["Estonia Remembers?! The reception of the Topic of repressions in the Estonian Society"] *Mälu kui kultuuritegur. Etnoloogilisi perspektiive. Studia ethnologica Tartuensia* 6. Eds. Ene Kõresaar and Terje Anepaio. Tartu: Tartu Ülikool, 2003. 206-230.

Annist, Aet. "Kuhu kadus ettevõtlikkus? Vaatlusi sotsialismijärgsest külast." ["Where did the Entrepreneurial Spirit Go? Observations from a Post-Socialist Village"] *Vikerkaar* 4-5 (2013): 108-123.

Annus, Epp. "Anton Hansen Tammsaare." *Eesti Kirjanduslugu*. Eds. Epp Annus, Luule Epner, Ants Järv, Sirje Olesk, Ele Süvalep, Mart Velsker. Tallinn: Koolibri, 2001. 275-291.

—. "Kirjanduskaanon ja rahvuslik identiteet." ["Literary Canon and National Identity"] *Keel ja Kirjandus* 1 (2000): 10-17.

—. *Kuidas kirjutada aega*. [*How to Write Time*] Tallinn: Underi ja Tuglase Kirjanduskeskus, 2002.

—. "Noorte püüded ja rõõmus ajalugu: Gustav Suits ja Friedrich Nietzsche." ["The Strivings of the Young people and the Gay History: Gustav Suits and Friedrich Nietzsche"] *Keel ja Kirjandus* 7 (2005): 526-534.

—. "The Problem of Soviet Colonialism in the Baltics." *Journal of Baltic Studies* 43.1 (2012): 32-49.

—. "Tõe ja õiguse lõppköide: tagasivaated ja kokkuvõtted." ["The Last Volume of *Truth and Justice*: Recollections and Summaries"] *Tõde ja õigus*. Vol. 5. By Anton Hansen Tammsaare. Tallinn: Avita, 2004. 359-376.

Appadurai, Arjun. *Modernity at Large: Cultural Dimensions of Globalization*. Minneapolis, Minn.: University of Minnesota Press, 1996.

Aristotle. *The Complete Works of Aristotle*. Vol. 2. The rev. Oxford translation. Ed. Johnathan Barnes. Princeton: Princeton University Press, 1984.

Ashcroft, Bill, Gareth Griffiths, Helen Tiffin. *The Empire Writes Back: Theory and Practice in Post-colonial Literatures*. 2nd rev. ed. London, New York: Routledge, 2002.

—. *Postcolonial Studies: The Key Concepts*. London, New York: Routledge, 2005.

Attridge, Derek and Marjorie Howes (eds.). *Semicolonial Joyce*. Cambridge: Cambridge University Press, 2000.

Aun, Karl. *Der Völkerrechtliche Schutz nationaler Minderheiten in Estland von 1917 bis 1940*. [*The Protection of National Minorities under International Law in Estonia from 1917 to 1940*] Hamburg: Hansischer Gildenverlag J. Heitmann, 1951.

Baak, J.J. van. *The Place of Space in Narration: A Semiotic Approach to the Problem of Literary Space. With an Analysis of the Role of Space in I.E. Babel's* Konarmija. Amsterdam: Rodopi, 1983.

Bakhtin, M.M. *The Dialogic Imagination: Four Essays by M.M. Bakhtin*. Transl. Caryl Emerson and Michael Holquist. Ed. Michael Holquist. Austin: University of Texas Press, 1981.

—. *Problems of Dostoevsky's Poetics*. Ed. and transl. Caryl Emerson. Minneapolis: University of Minnesota Press, 1984.

—. *Speech Genres and Other Late Essays*. Transl. Vern W. McGee. Ed. Caryl Emerson, Michael Holquist. University of Texas Press, 2004 [1986].

Bal, Mieke. *Travelling Concepts in the Humanities: A Rough Guide*. Toronto, Buffalo, London: University of Toronto Press, 2002.

Balina, Marina and Evgeny Dobrenko. Introduction. *Petrified Utopia: Happiness Soviet Style*. Eds. Marina Balina and Evgeny Dobrenko. London and New York: Anthem Press, 2009. xv-xxvi.

Barthes, Roland. *Image-Music-Text*. New York: Hill and Wang, 1977.

—. *Writing Degree Zero & Elements of Semiology*. London: Jonathan Cape, 1984.

Bassnett, Susan. "The Meek or the Mighty: Reappraising the Role of the Translator." *Translation, Power, Subversion*. Eds. Roman Alvarez and Carmen-Africa Vidal. Clevedon, Philadelphia, Adelaide: Multilingual Matters LTD, 1996. 10-24.

— and André Lefevere. General Editor's Preface. *Translation, Rewriting, and the Manipulation of Literary Fame*. Ed. André Lefevere. London and New York: Routledge, 1992. vii-viii.

— and Harish Trivedi (eds.). *Post-Colonial Translation: Theory and Practice*. London and New York: Routledge, 1999.

Baudelaire, Charles. "The Painter of Modern Life." [1863]. Penn Libraries. <http://www.writing.upenn.edu/library/Baudelaire_Painter-of-Modern-Life_1863.pdf> 15 October 2014.

Bauman, Zygmunt. *Intimations of Postmodernity*. London: Routledge, 1994.

Bayly, C. A. *The Birth of the Modern World 1780-1914: Global Connections and Comparisons*. Oxford: Blackwell, 2004.

Belgum, Kirsten. *Popularizing the Nation. Audience, Representation, and the Production of Identity in* Die Gartenlaube *1853-1900*. Lincoln and London: University of Nebraska Press, 1998.

Bendix, Reinhard. *Nation-Building and Citizenship: Studies of Our Changing Social Order*. New York: Wiley and Sons, 1964.

Benveniste, Emil. *Problems in General Linguistics*. Transl. Mary Elizabeth Meek. Coral Gables: University of Miami Press, 1973.

Berger, Stefan. "Germany: Ethnic Nationalism Par Excellance?" *What is a Nation? Europe 1789-1914*. Eds. Timothy Baycroft and Mark Hewitson. Oxford: Oxford University Press, 2006. 42-62.

Berlin International Film Festival. "37th Berlin International Film Festival February 20—March 3, 1997 [sic]." *Berlinale Archive: Annual Archives: 1987 Yearbook*. <http://www.berlinale.de/en/archiv/jahresarchive/1987/01_jahresblatt_1987/01_Jahresblatt_1987.html> 30 June 2014.

Bhabha, Homi K. "DissemiNation: Time, Narrative and the Margins of the Modern Nation." *Nation and Narration*. Ed. Homi K. Bhabha. London and New York: Routledge, 1991. 291-322.

—. *The Location of Culture*. London and New York: Routledge, 1994.

—. "On Writing Rights." *Globalizing Rights: The Oxford Amnesty Lectures 1999*. Ed. M.J. Gibney. Oxford: Oxford University Press, 2003. 162-183.

—. "Representation and the Colonial Text: A Critical Exploration of Some Forms of Mimeticism." *The Theory of Reading*. Ed. Frank Gloversmith. Brighton: Harvester, 1984. 93-120.

Boden, Ragna. "Soviet World Policy in the 1970s—A Three-Level Game." Eds. Marie-Janine Calic, Dietmar Neutatz, Julia Obertreis. *The Crisis of Socialist Modernity: The Soviet Union and Yugoslavia in the 1970s*. Göttingen: Vanderhoeck and Ruprecht, 2011. 184-203.

Boes, Tobias. *Formative Fictions: Nationalism, Cosmopolitanism and the Bildungsroman*. Ithaca: Cornell U. Press and Cornell U. Library, 2012.

—. "Modernist Studies and the Bildungsroman: A Historical Survey of Critical Trends." *Literature Compass* 3.2 (2006): 230-243.

Bourdieu, Pierre. *Distinction: A Social Critique of the Judgement of Taste*. Transl. Richard Nice. Cambridge, Mass.: Harvard University Press, 1984.

—. *The Field of Cultural Production: Essays on Art and Literature*. Ed. Randal Johnson. Cambridge: Polity, 1993.

Brandenberger, David. *National Bolshevism: Stalinist Mass Culture and the Formation of Modern Russian National Identity, 1931-1956*. Cambridge, Mass., and London, England: Harvard University Press, 2002.

Brockmann, Stephen. "Literature and Convergence: The Early 1980s." *Beyond 1989: Re-reading German Literature since 1945*. Ed. Keith Bullivant. Oxford: Berghahn Books, 1997. 49-67.

Brown, David. *Contemporary Nationalism: Civic, Ethnocultural and Multicultural Politics*. London and New York: Routledge, 2000.

Buckler, Julie A. "What Comes after 'Post-Soviet' in Russian Studies?" *PMLA* 124.1 (2009): 251-263.

Buckley, Jerome Hamilton. *Season of Youth: The Bildungsroman from Dickens to Golding*. Cambridge, MA: Harvard University Press, 1974.

Butler, Marilyn. *Romantics, Rebels and Reactionaries: English Literature and Its Background, 1760-1830*. New York and Oxford: Oxford University Press, 1982.

Byrne, Eleanor. "Healing and Reconciliation: Post-Colonial Fictions of Adoption. Presentation at the conference of the Association for Commonwealth Literature and Language Studies, Vancouver 17-22 August 2007. Abstract." <http://ocs.sfu.ca/aclals/viewabstract.php?id=129 > 2 May 2014.

Calhoun, Craig. *Nations Matter: Culture, History and the Cosmopolitan Dream*. London and New York: Routledge, 2007.

Campbell, Colin. *The Romantic Ethic and the Spirit of Modern Consumerism*. Oxford: Blackwell, 1987.

Campbell, Mavis C. *Nova Scotia and the Fighting Maroons: A Documentary History*. Williamsburg, Virginia: Dpt. of Anthropology, College of William and Mary, 1990.

Carey, Henry. F. and Rafal Raciborski. "Postcolonialism: A Valid Paradigm for the Former Sovietized States and Yugoslavia?" *East European Politics and Societies* 18.2 (2004): 191-235.

Carrère d'Encausse, Hélène. "Determinants and Parameters of Soviet Nationality Policy." *Soviet Nationality Policies and Practices*. Ed. Jeremy R. Azrael. New York, London, Sidney, Toronto: Praeger Publishers, 1978. 39-59.

Casanova, Pascale. *The World Republic of Letters*. Transl. M. B. DeBevoise. Cambridge, US, London, UK: Harvard University Press, 2004.

Casement, Ann. "The Shadow." *The Handbook of Jungian Psychology: Theory, Practice and Applications*. Ed. Renos K. Papadopoulus. London and New York: Routledge, 2006. 94-112.

Cassirer, Ernst. *An Essay on Man: An Introduction to a Philosophy of Human Culture*. New Haven, CT: Yale University Press, 1962.

Castells, Manuel. *Communication Power*. New York: Oxford University Press, 2009.

Castle, Gregory. *Reading the Modernist Bildungsroman*. Gainesville, FL: University Press of Florida, 2006.

Chakrabarty, Dipesh. *Provincializing Europe: Postcolonial Thought and Historical Difference.* Princeton and Oxford: Princeton University Press, 2000.

Chalvin, Antoine. "Johannes Aavik ja prantsuse keel." ["Johannes Aavik and the French Language"] *Methis* 1-2 (2008): 104-115.

Chang, Nam Fung. "Polysystem Theory and Translation." *Handbook of Translation Studies.* Vol. 1. Eds. Yves Gambier and Luc Van Doorslaer. Amsterdam: John Benjamins, 2010. 257-263.

Chatterjee, Partha. *The Nation and Its Fragments: Colonial and Postcolonial Histories.* Princeton: Princeton University Press, 1993.

Cheah, Pheng. "Of Other Worlds to Come." *Delimiting Modernities: Conceptual Challenges and Regional Responses.* Eds. Sven Trakulhun and Ralph Weber. Lanham: Lexington Books, 2015. 3-23.

—. *Spectral Nationality: Passages of Freedom From Kant to Postcolonial Literatures of Liberation.* New York: Columbia University Press, 2003.

Childs, Peter. *Modernism.* London and New York: Routledge, 2000.

Chrisman, Laura. "Nationalism and Postcolonial Studies." *The Cambridge Companion to Postcolonial Literary Studies.* Ed. Neil Lazarus. Cambridge: Cambridge University Press, 2004. 183-198.

Clavin, Matt. "Race, Rebellion, and the Gothic: Inventing the Haitian Revolution." *Early American Studies* 5.1 (2007): 1-29.

Collier, Stephen. *Post-Soviet Social: Neoliberalism, Social Modernity, Biopolitics.* Princeton: Princeton University Press, 2011.

Comenius, John Amos. *The Great Didactic.* London: A and C. Black, 1896. *Internet Archive.* <http://www.archive.org/details/greatdidacticjo00keatgoog> 1 December 2009.

Connor, Walker. "When Is a Nation?" *Ethnic and Racial Studies* 13.1 (1990): 92-103.

Cooper, Frederick. *Colonialism in Question. Theory, Knowledge, History.* Berkeley, Los Angeles, London: University of California Press, 2005.

Crowner, David and Gerald Christianson. General Introduction. *The Spirituality of German Awakening.* Eds., transl. David Corowney and Gerald Christianson. Mahwah, NJ: The Paulist Press, 2003. 5-44.

Culler, Jonathan. "Anderson and the Novel." *Diacritics* 29.4 (1999): 20-39.

Darden, Keith A. *Liberalism and Its Rivals: The Formation of International Institutions among the Post-Soviet States.* Cambridge and New York: Cambridge University Press, 2009.

Davies, Christie. "Exploring the Thesis of the Self-Deprecating Jewish Sense of Humor." *Humor—International Journal of Humor Research,* 4.2 (2009): 189-210.

"Declaration of Independence." 24 February 1918. State portal Eesti.ee. <http://www.president.ee/en/republic-of-estonia/declaration-of-independence/index.html> 26 November 2016.

Deutsch, K. W. *Nationalism and Social Communication: An Inquiry into the Foundations of Nationality.* Cambridge, Mass.: Technology Press of the Massachusetts Institute of Technology, and New York: Wiley, 1953.

Devy, Ganesh. "Translation and Literary History: An Indian View." *Post-Colonial Translation: Theory and Practice.* Eds. Susan Bassnett and Harish Trivedi. London and New York: Routledge, 1999. 182-188.

Dickens, Eric. "Old Barny—or, Is Humour Translatable?" *Estonian Literary Magazine* 14 (2002). <http://elm.estinst.ee/issue/14/old-barny-or-humour-translatable/ > 4 January 2018.

Dijk, van Rijk. "Pentecostalism, Cultural Memory and the State: Contested Representations of Time in Postcolonial Malawi." *Memory and the Postcolony: African Anthropology and the Critique of Power.* Ed. Richard Webner. Ch. 6. London and New York: Zed Books, 1998. 155-181.

Dittmar, Heinrich. *Die Weltgeschichte in einem leicht überschaulichen, in sich zusammenhängenden Umrisse für den Schul- und Selbstunterricht. Zweite Hälfte. Geschichte der Welt nach Christus.* [*World History in a Short Coherent Outline for Schools and for Independent Study. Second Half. History of the World after Christ*] Heidelberg: Karl Winter, 1859.

Dostoevsky, Fyodor. *The Brothers Karamazov.* Transl. Richard Pevear and Larissa Volokhonsky. New York: Vintage, 1990.

Douglas, Mary. *Purity and Danger: An Analysis of Concepts of Pollution and Taboo.* London and New York: Routledge, 2002.

"The Easter Morning Sunrise Service." April 2007. This Month in Moravian History. Moravian Archives. <http://www.moravianchurcharchives.org/documents/07aprilEaster.pdf> 30 October 2009.

Eellend, Johan. "Agrarianism and Modernization in Inter-War Eastern Europe." *Societal Change and Ideological Formation Among the Rural Population of the Baltic Area 1880–1939.* Ed. Piotr Wawrzeniuk. Huddinge: Södertörns högskola, 2008. 35-56.

Ehala, Martin. "The Bronze Soldier: Identity Threat and Maintenance in Estonia." *Journal of Baltic Studies* 40.1 (2009): 139-158.

—. "Õhuke riik ja Põhja Konn." ["The Thin State and the Northern Frog"] *Postimees.* 17.03.2007. <http://rooma.postimees.ee/170307/ esileht/arvamus/250426.php> 30 April 2013.

Eisenstadt, Shmuel N. *Comparative Civilizations and Multiple Modernities.* Leiden: Brill, 2003.

—. *Modernization, Protest and Change.* Englewood Cliffs: Prentice Hall, 1966.

—. ed. *Multiple Modernities.* New Brunswick, N.J.: Transaction Publishers, 2002.

Eliot, T.S. "Tradition and Individual Talent". *Perspecta.* Vol. 19. (1982) [1919]: 36-42.

"Empire, Union, Center, Satellite. The Place of Post-Colonial Theory in Slavic/Central and Eastern European/(Post-)Soviet Studies. A Quetionnaire." *Ulbandus* 7 (2003): 5-25.

Epner, Luule. "Proosa ja draama kodumaal: stalinismi kammitsas." ["Prose and Drama in Estonia: In the Fetters of Stalinism"] *Eesti Kirjanduslugu.* Eds. Epp Annus, Luule Epner, Ants Järv, Sirje Olesk, Ele Süvalep, Mart Velsker. Tallinn: Koolibri, 2001. 378-386.

Erll, Astrid and Ansgar Nünning (eds.). *A Companion to Cultural Memory Studies.* In collab. with Sara Young. Berlin and New York: De Gruyter, 2010.

Estes, Clarissa Pinkola. *Women Who Run With the Wolves: Myths and Stories of Wild Woman Archetype.* New York: Ballantine Books, 1992.

Estonica. The Encyclopedia on Estonia. "History." <http://www.estonica.org> 7 December 2009.

Esty, Jed. *Unseasonable Youth: Modernism, Colonialism, and the Fiction of Development.* Oxford and New York: Oxford U. Press, 2012.

Even-Zohar, Itamar. *Papers in Historical Poetics.* Tel Aviv: Porter Institute for Poetics and Semiotics, 1979.

Eysteinsson, Astradur. *The Concept of Modernism.* Ithaca: Cornell U. Press, 1990.

Fahlbusch, Erwin et al., eds. *Encyclopedia of Christianity*. Leiden: W.B. Eerdmans, 1999-2008.
Forster, Michael N. *After Herder: Philosophy of Language in the German Tradition*. Oxford: Oxford U. Press, 2010.
Foucault, Michel. *The Archeology of Knowledge*. Transl. Sheridan Smith. London: Tavistock, 1972 [1969].
—. *The Foucault Reader*. Ed. Paul Rabinow. Transl. Donald F. Bouchard and Sherry Simon. New York: Pantheorn, 1984.
Fraser, Giles. *Redeeming Nietzsche: On the Piety of Unbelief*. London and New York: Routledge, 2002.
Freeman, Arthur J. "Zinzendorf's Theology: A Gift to Enable Life." *Zinzendorf: The Ecumenical Pioneer*. <http://www.zinzendorf.com/freeman.htm> 30 October 2009.
Friedenthal, Meelis. "Mees, kes teadis ussisõnu." ["The Man Who Knew Snakish"] *Kirikiri* 14 November 2007. <http://www.kirikiri.ee/article.php3?id_article=396> 30 April 2013.
Fukuyama, Francis. *The End of History and the Last Man*. New York: Free Press, 1992.
Furedi, Frank. *On Tolerance: A Defence of Moral Independence*. London: Continuum, 2011.
Gaonkar, Dilip Parameshwar (ed). *Alternative Modernities*. Durham, NC.: Duke University Press, 2001.
Garve, Horst. *Konfession und Nationalität. Ein Beitrag zum Verhältnis von Kirche und Gesellschaft in Livland im 19. Jahrhundert*. [*Denomination and Nationality. On the Relationship Between Church and Society in Livonia in the 19th Century*] Marburg/Lahn: J.G. Herder-Institut, 1978.
Gellner, Ernest. *Nationalism*. London: Phoenix, 1997.
—. *Nations and Nationalism*. Ithaca: Cornell University Press, 1983.
Genette, Gérard. *Narrative Discourse: An Essay in Method*. Ithaca, New York: Cornell University Press, 1995.
—. *Narrative Discourse Revisited*. Ithaca, New York: Cornell University Press, 1994.
—. *Paratexts: Thresholds of Interpretation*. Cambridge: Cambridge University Press, 1997.
George, Olankunle. *Relocating Agency: Modernity and African Letters*. Albany: State University of New York Press, 2003.
Giddens, Anthony. *The Consequences of Modernity*. Cambridge: Polity Press, 1991.
Gikandi, Simon. "Postcolonial Theory and the Spectre of Nationalism." *Clio* 22. 09.2006. <http://www.highbeam.com/doc/1G1-157946468.html> 20 January 2014.
Ginzburg, Carlo. "Making Things Strange: The Pre-History of a Literary Device." *Representations* (1996): 8-28.
Goethe, Johann Wolfgang von. *Faust I & II*. Collected Works in 12 Volumes. Volume 2. Ed. and transl. Stuart Atkins. Princeton and Oxford: Princeton University Press, 2014.
Gollin, Gillian Lindt. *Moravians in Two Worlds: A Study of Changing Communities*. New York: Columbia University Press, 1967.
Greenblatt, Stephen. *Shakespearean Negotiations: The Circulation of Social Energy in Renaissance England*. Berkeley: University of California Press, 1989.
Greenfeld, Liah. *Nationalism: Five Roads to Modernity*. Cambridge, Mass.: Harvard University Press, 1992.
Grigorjan, Rafik and Igor Rosenfeld. *Iseseisvuse anatoomia*. [*The Anatomy of Independence*] Tartu: Kripta, and St. Petersburg: Bazunov, 2004.

Grimes, Alan Pendleton. *American Political Thought*. Rev. ed. New York: Holt, Rinehart and Winston, 1960 [1955].

Grišakova, Marina. "Mõtteid Tammsaarest, Nietzschest ja Dostojevskist." ["Thoughts about Tammsaare, Nietzsche and Dostoevsky"] *Vikerkaar* 1-2 (2005): 80-86.

Gronow, Jukka. *The Sociology of Taste*. London, Routledge, 1997.

Grünfeldt, Inna. "Ussisõnad pälvisid Vildelt võidupärja." ["Snakish was Awarded Vilde's Victory Wreath"] *Virumaa Teataja* 05.03.2008. <http://www.virumaateataja.ee/2314213/ussisonad-palvisid-vildelt-voiduparja> 30 April 2013.

Habermas, Jürgen. *Strukturwandel der Öffentlichkeit: Untersuchungen zu einer Kategorie der Bürgerlichen Gesellschaft*. Mit einer Vorwort zur Neuauflage [The Structural Transformation of the Public Sphere: An Inquiry into a Category of the Bourgeois Society. With a Preface for the New Edition] 1990. Frankfurt am Main: Suhrkamp, 1990 [1962].

Hanke, Lewis. *Aristotle and the American Indians: A Study in Race Prejudice in the Modern World*. London: Hollis and Carter, 1959.

Hardin, James N. "Reflection and Action: Essays on the Bildungsroman: Introduction." *Reflection and Action. Essays on the Bildungsroman*. Ed. James N. Hardin. Columbia, S.C.: University of South Carolina Press, 1991. ix-xvii

Hasselblatt, Cornelius. "Eesti esimene ökoromaan." ["The First Estonian Ecological Novel"] *Looming* 8 (2007): 1262-1267.

—. "Sajand hiljem. Mida Noor-Eesti tegi ja mida ta ei teinud." ["A Century Later: What Young Estonia Did and What It Did Not Do"] *Methis* 1-2 (2008): 44-57.

Haug, Toomas. *Klassikute lahkumine: 25 kirjatööd*. [*The Departure of the Classics: 25 Writings*] Tallinn: Eesti Keele Sihtasutus, 2010.

Heidegger, Martin. *Basic Writings*. Ed. David Farrell Krell. New York: Harper & Row, 1977.

—. *The Question Concerning Technology and Other Essays*. Transl. William Lovitt. New York and London: Garland Publishing, Inc., 1977.

Heller, Agnes. *A Theory of Modernity*. Oxford: Blackwell, 1999.

Hennoste, Tiit. "Europeanization as Self-Colonization in Estonian Literature at the Beginning of the 20th Century: the Case of the Young Estonia Movement." *Letonica* 28 (2014): 11-24.

—. "Heroism ja eksistentsialism. Mõttevahetus: Eesti eksistentsiaalsusest." ["Heroism and Existentialism. An Exchange of Ideas: Estonian Existentiality"] *Looming* 8 (2011): 1139–1148.

—. "Noor-Eesti enesekoloniseerimisprojekt. Teine osa. Olulised kirjandusmõtteviisid ja nende suhted kolonialismiga 20. sajandi algupoole Eesti kirjanduses." ["The Self-Colonization Project of Young Estonia. Part II. Modes of Literary Thinking and Relations with Colonialism in Estonian Literature of the Beginning of the 20th Century"] *Methis* 1-2 (2008): 262-275.

—. "Noor-Eesti kui lõpetamata enesekoloniseerimisprojekt." ["Young Estonia – An Unfinished Project of Self-Colonization"] *Noor-Eesti 100. Kriitilisi ja võrdlevaid tagasivaateid*. Tallinn: TLÜ Kirjastus, 2005. 9-38.

—. "Postkolonialism ja Eesti. Väga väike leksikon." ["Postcolonialism and Estonia. A Very Small Lexicon"]. *Vikerkaar* 4-5 (2003): 85-100.

Hermans, Theo (ed.). *The Manipulation of Literature: Studies in Literary Translation*. London and Sydney: Croom Helm, 1985.

—. *Translation in Systems: Descriptive and System-Oriented Approaches Explained*. Manchester: St. Jerome, 1999.
Hiden, John W. and David J. Smith. "Looking beyond the Nation State: A Baltic Vision for National Minorities between the Wars." *Journal of Contemporary History* 41.3 (2006): 387-399.
Hillerbrand, Hans (ed.). *Encyclopedia of Protestantism*. New York: Routledge, 2003.
Hinrikus, Mirjam. *Dekadentlik modernsuskogemus A.H. Tammsaare ja nooreestlaste loomingus*. [*The Experience of Decadent Modernity in the Texts of A. H. Tammsaare and Young-Estonia*] Dissertationis literarum et contemplationis comparativae Universitatis Tartuensis. Tartu: Tartu Ülikooli Kirjastus, 2011.
—. "Spleen the Estonian Way: Estonian Literary Decadence in J. Randvere's *Ruth* (1909), Friedebert Tuglas' *Felix Ormusson* (1915), and Anton Hansen Tammsaare's Novellas *Noored hinged* (1909) and *Kärbes* (1917)." *Interlitteraria* 11.2 (2006): 305-321.
Hoagland, Ericka A. "The Postcolonial Bildungsroman." *A History of the Bildungsroman*. Ed. Sarah Graham. Cambridge: Cambridge University Press, 2019. 217-38.
Hobsbawm, E. J. *Nations and Nationalism since 1780: Programme, Myth, Reality*. Rev. ed. Cambridge: Cambridge University Press, 1997.
Honour, Hugh. *The New Golden Land: European Images of America from the Discoveries to the Present Time*. London: Allen Lane, 1976.
Hope, Nicholas. "Interwar Statehood: Symbol and Reality." *The Baltic States: The National Self-Determination of Estonia, Latvia and Lithuania*. Ed. Graham Smith. New York: St. Martin's Press, 1994. 41-68.
Horn, W.O. "Huaskar. Eine Erzählung aus der ersten Hälfte des sechzehnten Jahrhundert." ["Huaskar. A Story from the First Half of the Sixteenth Century"] *Gesammelte Erzählungen*. Neue Volks-Ausgabe. VII. Band. Frankfurt a. M.: J. D. Sauerländers Verlag, 1861. 293-401.
—. *Die Spinnstube, ein Volksbuch für das Jahr [...]*. [*Spinning Room, a Volksbuch for the year [...]*] Frankfurt a. M.: J.D. Sauerländers Verlag, 1846-67.
Housden, Martyn. "Cultural Autonomy in Estonia: One of History's "Curiosities"? *The Baltic States and their Region: New Europe or Old?* Ed. David J. Smith. Amsterdam, New York: Rodopi, 2005. 227-249.
Hroch, Miroslav. "From National Movement to the Fully-formed Nation: The Nation-building Process in Europe." *Mapping the Nation*. Ed. Gopal Balakrishnan. New York and London: Verso, 1996. 78-97.
—. *Social Preconditions of National Revival in Europe. A Comparative Analysis of the Social Composition of Patriotic Groups among the Smaller European Nations*. Transl. Ben Fowkes. Cambridge, etc.: Cambridge University Press, 1985. [1968].
Hünefeldt, Christine. *A Brief History of Peru*. New York: Facts on File, 2010.
Huntington, Samuel P. *Political Order in Changing Societies*. New Haven: Yale U. Press, 1968.
Illingworth, Dustin. "Andrus Kivirähk's *The Man Who Spoke Snakish*." Book Reviews. *The Words Without Borders. Writing From the Edge: Estonian Literature*. October 2015. <http://www.wordswithoutborders.org/book-review/andrus-kiviraehks-the-man-who-spoke-snakish-dustin-illingworth> 25 October 2016.
Ilmjärv, Magnus. *Hääletu alistumine: Eesti, Läti ja Leedu välispoliitilise orientatsiooni kujunemine ja iseseisvuse kaotus 1920. aastate keskpaigast anneksioonini*. [*Silent Submission. Forma-*

tion of Foreign Policy of Estonia, Latvia and Lithuania : period from mid 1920's to annexation in 1940] Tallinn: Argo, 2010.
Isaac, Jeffrey C. "The Meanings of 1989." *The Revolutions of 1989*. Ed. Vladimir Tismăneanu. London and New York: Routledge, 1999. 121-59.
Ivanov, Andrei. *Peotäis põrmu*. [*A Handful of Dust*] Tallinn: Varrak, 2011.
Jaaksoo, Andres. "Kadri Jalakas jätkab lendu." ["Kadri Jalakas Continues Her Flight"] *Postimees* 28.06.2004. <http://www.postimees.ee/ 1416135/kadri-jalakas-jatkab-lendu> 1 July 2014.
—. Personal interview. 28 April 2014.
Jaanus, Maire. "Estonia and Pain: Jaan Kross's *The Czar's Madman*." *Baltic Postcolonialism*. Ed. Violeta Kelertas. Amsterdam and New York: Rodopi, 2006. 309-329.
Jansen, Ea. *Carl Robert Jakobson muutuvas ajas. Märkmeid, piirjooni, mõtteid*. [*Carl Robert Jakobson in the Changing Time. Notes, Outlines, Thoughts*] Tallinn: Eesti Raamat, 1987.
—. *Eestlane muutuvas ajas. Seisusühiskonnast kodanikuühiskonda*. [*The Estonian in the Changing Time. From Estate Society to Civil Society*] Summary in English. Tartu: Eesti Ajalooarhiiv, 2007.
Jantz, Harold. "Amerika im deutschen Dichten und Denken." ["America in German Literature and Thought"] *Deutsche Philologie im Aufriss* 7.3 (1962): 309-372.
Jeffries, Ian. *The Countries of the Former Soviet Union at the Turn of the Twenty-First Century: The Baltic and European States in Transition*. London: Routledge, 2004.
Jusdanis, Gregory. *Belated Modernity and Aesthetic Culture. Inventing National Literature*. Minneapolis and Oxford: University of Minnesota Press, 1991.
—. *The Necessary Nation*. Princeton and Oxford: Princeton University Press, 2001.
Kahu, Meelik. *Võti C.R. Jakobsoni maailmavaate mõistmiseks. Tema kirjanduslik lemmikkangelane ja võrdkuju*. [*A Key to Understand C.R. Jakobson's Worldview. His Favorite Literary Character With Whom He Identified*] Kurgja: Eesti NSV Kultuuriministeerium, 1964.
Kalda, Maie. "Mitte ainult vanemale koolieale." ["Not Only for High School Students"] *Keel ja Kirjandus* 10 (1963): 634-636.
Kalev, Leif, Ott Lumi, and Tõnis Saarts. "Eesti poliitiline kultuur: poliitikastiilid ja poliitikaprotsess." ["Political Culture in Estonia: Political Styles and Political Process"] *Riigikogu Toimetised* 19 (2009). <http://rito.riigikogu.ee/wordpress/wp-content/uploads/2016/03/Eesti-poliitiline-kultuur-poliitikastiilid-ja-poliitikaprotsess-Leif-Kalev-Ott-Lumi-T%C3%B5nis-Saarts.pdf> 2 November 2016.
Kaljundi, Linda. "Aga ükskord ei alga aega." ["But an Age will not Dawn One Day"] *Vikerkaar* 9 (2007). http://www.vikerkaar.ee/ ?page=Arhiiv&a_act=article&a_number=4612 2 May 2013.
Kallas, Aino. *Noor-Eesti. Näopildid ja sihtjooned*. [*Young Estonia. Portraits and Principles*] Transl. Friedebert Tuglas. Tartu: Noor-Eesti Kirjastus, 1921.
Karulis, Konstantins. *Latviešu etmologijas vardnica*. [*Latvian Etymological Dictionary*] Riga: Avots, 1992.
Kasekamp, Andres. *A History of the Baltic States*. London and New York: Palgrave Macmillan, 2010.
—. *The Radical Right In Interwar Estonia*. Basingstoke, London: Macmillan Press; New York: St. Martin's Press, 1999.
Kaskla, Edgar. "The National Woman: Constructing Gender Roles in Estonia." *Journal of Baltic Studies* 34.3 (2003): 298-312.

Kaus, Jan. "Kuidas õigus võidab tõe: näiteid Dostojevski ja Tammsaare toel." ["How Justice Trumps Truth: Examples Based on Tammsaare and Dostoevsky"] *Tõde ja õigus: kirjandus, mis kunagi valmis ei saa.* Eds. Toomas Haug and Maarja Vaino. Tallinn: A.H. Tammsaare Muuseum, 2007. 17-27.

Keller, Margit. *Representations of Consumer Culture in Post-Soviet Estonia: Transformations and Tensions.* Dissertationes de mediis et communicationibus universitatis tartuensis (3). Tartu: Tartu University Press, 2004.

Kelley, Donald R. "The Soviet Debate on the Convergence of the American and Soviet Systems." *Polity* 6.2 (1973): 174-196.

Kelly, Catriona. "A Joyful Soviet Childhood: Licensed Happiness for Little Ones." *Petrified Utopia: Happiness Soviet Style.* Eds. Marina Balina and Evgeny Dobrenko. London: Anthem Press, 2009. 3-18.

Kemiläinen, Aira. *Auffassungen über die Sendung des Deutschen Volkes um die Wende des 18. und 19. Jahrhunderts.* [*Views on the Mission of the German People at the Turn of the 18th and 19th centuries*] Annales Academiae Scientarum Fennicae. Vol. 101. Helsinki: Suomalainen Tiedeakatemia, 1956.

Kerr, C[larke] et al. *Industrialism and Industrial Man.* Cambridge, MA: Cambridge University Press.

Kharkhordin, Oleg. *The Collective and the Individual in Russia: A Study of Practices.* Berkeley; Los Angeles; London: University of California Press, 1999.

Kiiks. "E. Tode *Piiririik*". ["E. Tode's *Border State*"] Web blog post. *Kiiksu lugemisarhiiv.* 14.02.2011. <http://lugemisarhiiv.blogspot.com.ee/2011/02/e-tode-piiririik.html> 08. October 2016.

Kiin, Sirje; Ruutsoo, Rein; Tarand, Andres. *40 kirja lugu.* [*The Story of the Letter of 40*] Tallinn: Olion, 1990.

Kirkus Reviews. "*The Man Who Spoke Snakish* by Andrus Kivirähk, translated by Christopher Moseley." *Kirkus.* 17.08.2015. <https://www.kirkusreviews.com/book-reviews/andrus-kivirahk/the-man-who-spoke-snakish/> 26 October 2016.

Kirss, Tiina. "Interstitial Histories: Ene Mihkelson's *Labour of Naming.*" *Baltic Postcolonialism.* Ed. Violeta Kelertas. Amsterdam; New York: Rodopi, 2006. 387-407.

—. "Rändavad piirid: postkolonialismi võimalused." ["Travelling Boundaries: the Possibilities of Postcolonialism"] *Keel ja Kirjandus* 10 (2001): 673-682.

Kisseljova, Ljubov. "Vene ajalugu ja kultuur Jaan Krossi romaanis *Keisri hull.*" ["Russian History and Culture in Jaan Kross's Novel *The Czar's Madman*"] *Keel ja Kirjandus* 5 (2010): 321-330.

Kivimäe, Jüri. "Noor-Eesti tähendust otsides: vanu ja uusi mõtteid." ["In Quest of the *Meaning of Young Estonia*: Old and New Reflections"] *Methis* 1-2 (2008): 21-43.

Kivirähk, Andrus. "Eesti küsimus on ikka sündimuse küsimus." ["The Estonian Question is still related to the Birth Rate"] Interview by Jürgen Rooste. *Sirp* 23.02.2007. <http://www.sirp.ee/index.php?option=com_content&view=article&id=1428:eesti-k-simus-on-ikka-s-ndimuse-k-simus&catid=7:kirjandus&Itemid=9&issue=3148> 2 May 2013.

—. "Helesinine vagun." ["The Blue Carriage"] *Papagoide päevad. Näidendid.* By Andrus Kivirähk. Tallinn: Eesti Keele Sihtasutus, 2002. 209-267.

—. *Ivan Orava mälestused ehk Minevik kui helesinised mäed.* [*Memoirs of Ivan Orav, or the Past as Azure Mountains*] Tallinn: Andrus Kivirähk, 1995.

—. *Liblikas*. [*Butterfly*] Tallinn: Tuum, 1999.
—. *The Man Who Spoke Snakish*. [2007] Transl. Christopher Moseley. New York: Grove Atlantic, Black Cat, 2015.
—. *Rehepapp ehk November*. [*The Old Barny, or November*] Tallinn: Varrak, 2000.
Knauft, Bruce M. (ed). *Critically Modern: Alternatives, Alterities, Anthropologies*. Bloomington and Indianapolis: Indiana University Press, 2002.
—. Critically Modern: Introduction. *Critically Modern. Alternatives, Alterities, Anthropologies*. Ed. Bruce M. Knauft. Bloomington and Indianapolis: Indiana University Press, 2002. 1-54.
Knellwolf, Christa. "The Exotic Frontier of Imperial Imagination." *Eighteenth Century Life* 26. 3 (2002): 10-30.
Kohn, Hans. *The Idea of Nationalism: A Study in Its Origins and Background*. New York: Macmillan, 1944.
Koidula, Lydia. [on the title page: Johan Jansen] *Juudit ehk Jamaika saare wiimsed Maroonlased*. [*Juudit, or the Last Maroons of the Island of Jamaica*] Tartu: Laakmann, 1870.
—. [on the title page: Johan Jansen] *Martiniiko ja Korsika*. [*Martinique and Corsica*] Tartu: Laakmann, 1869
—. [on the title page: Johan Jansen] *Perúama wiimne Inka*. [*The Last Inca of Peru*] Tartu: Laakmann, 1866.
Kõresaar, Ene. *Elu ideoloogiad. Kollektiivne mälu ja autobiograafiline minevikutõlgendus eestlaste elulugudes*. [*Ideologies of Life. Collective Memory and Autobiographical Meaning-Making of the Past in Estonian Post-Soviet Life Stories*] Tartu: Eesti Rahva Muuseum, 2005.
—. "Nostalgia ja selle puudumine eestlaste mälukultuuris. Eluloouurija vaatepunkt." ["Nostalgia and its Absence in Estonian Remembrance Culture: the View of a Biography Researcher"] *Keel ja Kirjandus* 10 (2008): 760-771.
Koselleck, Reinhart. *Futures Past. On the Semantics of Historical Time*. Transl. Keith Tribe. New York: Columbia University Press, 2004 [1979].
Kõvamees, Anneli. "Minevik ja tulevik. Mälestus ja unistus." ["Past and Future. Memory and Daydream"] *Tõde ja õigus: kirjandus, mis kunagi valmis ei saa*. Eds. Toomas Haug and Maarja Vaino. Tallinn: A.H. Tammsaare Muuseum, 2007. 29-37.
Kreutzwald, F. R. *Kalevipoeg. An Ancient Estonian Tale*. Transl. Jüri Kurman. Moorestown, N.J.: Symposia Press, 1982.
—. Preface. *Kalevipoeg. An Ancient Estonian Tale*. By F.R. Kreutzwald. Transl. Jüri Kurman. Moorestown, N.J.: Symposia Press, 1982. ix-xii.
Kristeva, Julia. *Powers of Horror: An Essay on Abjection*. Transl. Leon S. Roudiez. New York: Columbia University Press, 1982.
Kroeker, Travis P. and Bruce K. Ward. *Remembering the End: Dostoevsky as Prophet* to Modernity. Boulder and Oxford: Westview Press, 2001.
Kross, Jaan. *The Czar's Madman*. Transl. Anselm Hollo. London: Harvill Press, 1992.
—. "Kirjanikuna päikeseriigis." ["In the State of the Sun as a Writer"] Interview by Toomas Haug. *Looming* 2 (1995): 231-241.
Krull, Hasso. *Katkestuse kultuur*. [*Culture of Rupture*] Tallinn: Vagabund, 1996.
Krusten, Reet. "Silvia Rannamaa ja Kadri Jalakas täna." ["Silvia Rannamaa and Kadri Jalakas Today"] *Looming* 3 (1978): 508-512.
Kruus, Hans. *Eesti küsimus*. [*The Estonian Question*] Eds. Toomas Karjahärm and Hando Runnel. Tartu: Ilmamaa, 2005.

Kulli, Jaanus. "Koolipäev Nüganeniga vana Mauruse koolis." ["A Schoolday with Nüganen in the Old Maurus's School"] Õhtuleht 12.02.2005. <http://www.ohtuleht.ee/index.aspx?id=169915> 19 January 2009.

Laak, Marin. "Ajalik ja ajatu *Piiririik*." ["Border State—the Historical and the Eternal"] *Piiririik*. By Emil Tode. Ed. Mart Orav. Eesti Lugu. Vol. 46. Tartu and Tallinn: Eesti Päevaleht and Akadeemia, 2009. 131-143.

Laanes, Eneken. "Confession: Performative Production of Gender and Memory in Tõnu Õnnepalu's *Border State*." *Querelles. Jahrbuch für Frauen- und Geschlechterforschung* 13 (2008): 133-154.

—. "Jakob Mättik Jaan Krossi "Keisri Hullus": jutustajast tegelaseks." ["Jakob Mättik in Jaan Kross' "The Czar's Madman": from Narrator to Character"] Summary in English. *Kultuuri maailmad. Cultural Worlds*. Ed. Mihhail Lotman. Tallinn: Acta Collegii Humaniorum Estoniensis 4 (2004): 201-219.

—. *Lepitamatud dialoogid*. [*Unresolved Dialogues: Subjectivity and Memory in Post-Soviet Estonian Novel*] Tallinn: Underi ja Tuglase Kirjanduskeskus, 2009.

—. "Tunnistaja lahkumine. In memoriam Jaan Kross." ["The Departure of the Witness. In Memoriam Jaan Kross"] *Postimees* 28.12.2007. <http://www.postimees.ee/1742247/tunnistaja-lahkumine> 16 October 2018.

Laar, Mart. Äratajad. *Rahvuslik ärkamisaeg Eestis 19. sajandil ja selle kandjad*. Tallinn: [*Awakeners. The National Awakening in Estonia in the 19th century and Its Bearers*] Grenader Kirjastus, 2006.

Laasik, Andres. "Lastekodu müürid hoidsid inimest vangis." [The Walls of the Orphanage Kept Humans in Prison] *Eesti Päevaleht* 19.10.2012. <http://epl.delfi.ee/news/kultuur/lastekodu-muurid-hoidsid-inimest-vangis?id=65133438> 12 October 2016.

Lagerspetz, Mikko. "Postsocialism as a Return: Notes on a Discursive Strategy." *East European Politics and Societies* 13.2 (1999): 16-28.

— and Henri Vogt. "Estonia." Ch. 3. *The Handbook of Political Change in Eastern Europe*. Eds. Sten Berglund, Tomas Hellén, Frank H. Aarebrot. Cheltenham, UK: Edward Elgar, 1998. 55-88.

— and Henri Vogt. "Estonia." Ch. 3. *The Handbook of Political Change in Eastern Europe*. Eds. Sten Berglund, Joakim Ekman, Frank H. Aarebrot. 2nd ed. Cheltenham, UK: Edward Elgar, 2004. 57-94.

— and Henri Vogt. "Estonia." Ch. 4. *The Handbook of Political Change in Eastern Europe*. Eds. Sten Berglund, Joakim Ekman, Kevin Deegan-Krause, Terje Knutsen. 3rd ed. Cheltenham, UK: Edward Elgar, 2013. 51-83.

Laulud.ee. Eestikeelsed laulusõnad. [Song Lyrics in Estonian] <http://www.laulud.ee/laul/koit_tonis_magi-574.aspx> 20 January 2014.

Lauristin, Marju. *Punane ja sinine: peatükke kirjutamata elulooraamatust: valik artikleid ja intervjuusid 1970-2009*. [*Red and Blue: Some Chapters from the Unwritten Memoir. A Selection of Unwritten Articles and Interviews 1970–2009*] Tallinn: AS Eesti Ajalehed, 2010.

— and Peeter Vihalemm. "The Political Agenda During Different Periods of Estonian Transformation." *Journal of Baltic Studies* 40.1 (2009): 1-28.

Lehiste, Ilse. "Book Review. Border State by Tõnu Õnnepalu. Translated by Madli Puhvel. Evanston, Illinois: Northwestern University Press, 2000. 100 pp. ISBN 0-8101-1779-7 (Cloth), 0-8101-1780-0 (Paper). From the original Estonian text: Piiririik, by Emil Tode. Tallinn: Tuum. 1993." *Translation Review* 61.1 (2012): 68-69.

Lejeune, Philippe. "The Autobiographical Contract." *French Literary Theory Today: A Reader.* Ed. Tzvetan Todorov. Transl. R. Carter. Cambridge: Cambridge University Press, 1982. 192-222.
Levy, Marion J. *Modernization and the Structure of Societies.* Princeton: Princeton University Press, 1966.
Lieber, Francis. *On Civil Liberty and Self-Government.* 3rd rev. ed. Ed. Theodore D. Woolsey. Philadelphia: J.B. Lippincott & Co., 1891.
Liiv, Juhan. *Meel paremat ei kannata. Valik luulet eesti ja inglise keeles./The Mind Would Bear No Better. A Selection of Poetry in Estonian and English.* Ed. Jüri Talvet. Transl. Jüri Talvet and H.L. Hix. Tartu: Tartu Ülikooli Kirjastus, 2007.
—. *Vari.* [*The Shadow*] [1894] Tallinn: Eesti Raamat, 1966.
Lima, Maria Helena. "Decolonizing Genre: Caribbean Women Writers and the Bildungsroman." Diss. University of Maryland College Park, 1993.
Linde, Bernhard. *"Noor-Eesti" kümme aastat.* [*The Ten Years of "Young Estonia"*] Tartu, 1918.
Lodge, David. *Small World: An Academic Romance.* London: Secker and Warburg, 1984.
Loog, Alvar. "Poliitiline korrektsus ja rahvuslik enesetapp". ["Political Correctness and National Suicide"] *Sirp* 22.09.2006. <http://www.sirp.ee/index.php?option=com_content&view=article&id=3845:poliitiline-korrektsus-ja-rahvuslik-enesetapp&catid=9:sotsiaalia&Itemid=13&issue=3127> 30 April 2013.
Lopez, Alfred J. *Posts and Pasts. A Theory of Postcolonialism.* New York: State University of New York, 2001.
Lotman, J.M. "O metayazike tipologitsheskih opisanii kultury." *Stati po semiotike i tipologii kultury.* ["On the Metalanguage of the Typological Descriptions of Culture"] Vol. 1. Tallinn: Aleksandra, 1992. 386-406.
—. *Universe of the Mind.* Transl. Ann Shukman. London and New York: I.B. Tauris, 2001 [1990].
Luik, Viivi. "Kõne koolimaja haual." ["A Sermon at the Grave of the Schoolhouse"] *Kõne koolimaja haual. Artiklid ja esseed 1998-2006.* By Viivi Luik. Tallinn: Tuum, 2006. 105-109.
Lukács, Georg. *The Historical Novel.* Transl. Hannah Mitchell and Stanley Mitchell. Lincoln, London: University of Nebraska Press, 1983.
Macura, Vladimir. "Epopöa lõpp." ["The End of the Epic"] *Tammsaare maailmakirjanikuna. Kolm välismaa Tammsaare-uurijat.* Ed. Elem Treier. Transl. Leo Metsar. Tallinn: Olion, 2001. 181-188.
—. "Tragöödia, mis polnud saatuslik." ["A Tragedy that Was not Fatal"] *Tammsaare maailmakirjanikuna. Kolm välismaa Tammsaare-uurijat.* Ed. Elem Treier. Transl. Leo Metsar. Tallinn: Olion, 2001. 175-180.
Mälksoo, Lauri. *Illegal Annexation and State Continuity: The Case of the Incorporation of the Baltic States by the USSR: A Study of the Tension between Normativity and Power in International Law.* Leiden: Martinus Nijhoff Publishers, 2003.
Mayer, Theresa Hammond. *American Paradise: German Travel Literature from Duden to Kisch.* Heidelberg: Carl Winter Universitätsverlag, 1980.
McClain, William and Lieselotte E. Kurth-Vogt. "Clara Mundts Briefe an Hermann Costenoble. Zu L. Mühlbachs historischen Romanen." ["Clara Mundt's Letters to Hermann Costenoble. On Mühlbach's Historical Novels"] *Archiv für Geschichte des Buchwesens* 22 (1981): 917-1248.

McClintock, Anne. "The Angel of Progress: Pitfalls of the Term 'Post-Colonialism'." *Colonial Discourse and Post-Colonial Theory*. Eds. Patrick Williams and Laura Chrisman. New York: Columbia University Press, 1994. 291-304.

Meri, Lennart. "Vabariigi presidendi uusaastatervitus 1997/1998." ["The New Year's Greeting by the President of the Estonian Republic 1997/1998"] *Vabariigi presidendi kõned 1992–2001*. < https://vp1992-2001.president.ee/est/k6ned/K6ne.asp?ID=4060> 16 July 2017.

Merkel, Garlieb Helwig. *Die Letten vorzüglich in Liefland am Ende des philosophischen Jahrhunderts. Ein Beytrag zur Völker- und Menschenkunde*. [*Latvians, especially in Livonia at the End of the Philosophical Century. A Contribution to the Study of Nations and People*] Wedemark: Verlag Harro v. Hirschheydt, 1998 [1796].

—. *Liiwimaa esiaeg. Mälestusesammas papi- ja rüütliwaimule*. [*The Prehistory of Livonia. A Monument to the Spirit of Priests and Knights*] Vol. 1. Partial transl. A. F. Tombach. Peterburi: Ühiselu, 1909 [*Die Vorzeit Lieflands: Ein Denkmahl des Pfaffen- und Rittergeistes*. 2 vols. Berlin: Vossische Buchhandlung, 1798].

Meyer, Birgit. "'Make a Complete Break with the Past': Memory and Postcolonial Modernity in Ghanaian Pentecostal Discourse." Ch. 7. *Memory and the Postcolony: African Anthropology and the Critique of Power*. Ed. Richard Webner. London and New York: Zed Books, 1998. 182-208.

Miller, Alexandria. "On the Advantage and Disadvantage of History for Life." The Modernism Lab at Yale University 2010. <https://modernism.research.yale.edu/wiki/index.php/ On_the_Advantage_and_Disadvantage_of_History_for_Life > 16 October 2016.

Miller, Michael B. *The Bon Marché: Bourgeois Culture and the Department Store, 1869–1920*. Princeton, NJ: Princeton University Press, 1981.

Mills, Sara. *Discourse*. London and New York: Routledge, 2003.

Miłosz, Czesław. *Witness of Poetry*. The Charles Eliot Norton Lectures. Cambridge, MA: Harvard University Press, 1984.

Mits, Krista. "Pilk ingliskeelse kirjanduse tõlgetele 18. sajandi lõpust 20. sajandi algusveerandini." ["A Look at Estonian Translations of English Literature from the Late 18th Century to the First Quarter of the 20th Century"] *Methis* 9-10 (2012): 70-87.

Monticelli, Daniele. "Keeleuuendus ja tõlkimine Noor-Eesti kultuurilise utoopia raames. Villem Ridala tõlgitud "Süütu" näitel." ["Language Renewal and Translation in the Context of the Estonian Cultural Movement "Young-Estonia": An Analysis of Villem Grünthal-Ridala's Translation of Gabriele D'Annunzio's "The Victim""] Part I. *Keel ja Kirjandus* 5 (2006): 379-386.

—. "Keeleuuendus ja tõlkimine Noor-Eesti kultuurilise utoopia raames. Villem Ridala tõlgitud "Süütu" näitel." ["Language Renewal and Translation in the Context of the Estonian Cultural Movement "Young-Estonia": An Analysis of Villem Grünthal-Ridala's Translation of Gabriele D'Annunzio's "The Victim""] Part II. *Keel ja Kirjandus* 6 (2006): 477-490.

—. "Noor-Eesti projektist tänapäeva Eesti kultuurilis-poliitilise reaalsuse taustal. Kriitilised ülestähendused." ["The Young-Estonia's Project of Renewal on the Background of the Cultural-Political Discourse of Present Estonia. Some Critical Observations"] *Methis* 1-2 (2008): 276-287.

—. "(Trans)forming National Images in Translation. The Case of the "Young Estonia" Movement." *Interconnecting Translation Studies and Imagology*. Eds. Peter Flynn, Joep Leerssen, Luc van Doorslaer. Amsterdam and Philadelphia: John Benjamins, 2016. 277-297.

—, Piret Peiker, Krista Mits. "Jamaicast Pariisi ning sealt Tartusse tagasi. Lydia Koidula maailmavaatest ja mugandamisstrateegiatest tema saksa eeskujude valguses." ["From Jamaica to Paris and Back to Tartu Again. On Lydia Koidula's Worldview and Adaptation Strategies in the Light of her German Examples"] *Keel ja Kirjandus* 12 (2018): 915-941.

Moore, D.C. "Is the Post- in Postcolonial the Post- in the Post-Soviet? Toward a Global Postcolonial Critique." *PMLA* 116.1 (2001): 111-128.

Moretti, Franco. *Distant Reading*. London: Verso, 2013.

—. *The Way of the World: The Bildungsroman in European Culture*. New ed. London and New York: Verso, 2000 [1987].

Mügge, Theodor. *Eduard Montague. Neue Novellen*. Vol. 5. Hannover: Verlag von C.F. Rius, 1846. 1-178.

Mühlbach, Luise. *Kaiserin Josephine. Ein Napoleonisches Lebensbild*. [*The Empress Josephine. A Historical Sketch of the Days of Napoleon.*] Vol. 1. Berlin: O. Janke, 1861.

Müller-Salget, Klaus. *Erzählungen für das Volk. Evangelische Pfarrer als Volksschriftsteller im Deutschland des 19. Jahrhunderts*. [*Stories for the People. Pastors as Volksschriftsteller in the 19th Century Germany*] Berlin: Erich Schmidt Verlag, 1984.

Muuli, Kalle. *Isamaa tagatuba: Mart Laari valitsus 1992-1994*. [*The Back Room of the Pro Patria Party: Mart Laar's Government 1992-1994*] Tallinn: Tulimuld, 2012.

Nagai, Kaori. "Glossary of Terms Used." *The Cambridge Introduction to Postcolonial Literatures in English*. By C. L. Innes. Cambridge: Cambridge University Press, 2007. 233-241.

Nichols, Mary P. *Citizens and Statesmen: A Study of Aristotle's Politics*. Lanham, MD: Rowman and Littlefield, 1998.

Nietzsche, Friedrich. "On the Use and Abuse of History for Life." *Untimely Meditations*. Transl. Ian C. Johnston (amended in part by The Nietzsche Channel), [1874]. College of Liberal Arts, The University of Texas at Austin. <http://la.utexas.edu/users/hcleaver/330T/350kPEENietzscheAbuseTableAll.pdf> 12 November 2016.

Nimni, Ephraim (ed.). *National Cultural Autonomy and its Contemporary Critics*. London and New York: Routledge, 2006.

Niranjana, Tejaswini. *Siting Translation: History, Post-Structuralism and the Colonial Context*. Berkeley: University of California Press, 1992.

Nonini, Donald M. and Aihwa Ong. "Chinese Transnationalism as an Alternative Modernity." *Ungrounded Empires: The Cultural Politics of Modern Chinese Transnationalism*. Eds. Donald M. Nonini and Aihwa Ong. New York: Routledge, 1997. 3-33.

Noor-Eesti 100. [*Young Estonia 100*] Eesti Kirjandusmuuseum. < http://www2.kirmus.ee/nooreesti/> 21 August 2007

Nyatetu-Waigwa, Wangari wa. *The Liminal Novel: Studies in the Francophone-African Novel as Bildungsroman*. New York: Peter Lang, 1996.

Olesk, Sirje. "Kirjanduse võimalused kodumaal." ["The Options for Literature in Estonia"] *Eesti Kirjanduslugu*. Eds. Epp Annus, Luule Epner, Ants, Järv, Sirje Olesk, Ele Süvalep, Mart Velsker. Tallinn: Koolibri, 2001. 345-352.

— and Marin Laak. "Noor-Eesti rollist eesti kirjandus- ja kultuuriloos." ["The Role of Young Estonia in Estonian Literary and Cultural History"] *Methis* 1-2 (2008): 7-20.

Õnnepalu, Tõnu. *Border State*. Transl. Madli Puhvel. Evanston, Illinois: Northwestern University Press, 2000.

—. "Kohaloleku kunst—intervjuu Tõnu Õnnepaluga." ["The Art of Being There – Interview with Tõnu Õnnepalu"] Interview by Anari Koppel. *Müürileht* 11.08.2014. <https://www.muurileht.ee/kohaloleku-kunst-intervjuu-tonu-onnepaluga/> 25 August 2016.

—. "Piiririigis, ükskõik kus. Seletus." ["One is in a Border State Anywhere. Explanation"] *Eesti Ekspress* 27 March 1997: B3.

Parming, Tönu. *The Collapse of Liberal Democracy and the Rise of Authoritarianism in Estonia*. London, Beverly Hills: Sage Publications, 1975.

Parsons, Talcott. *Societies: Evolutionary and Comparative Perspectives*. Englewood Cliffs: Prentice Hall, 1966.

—. *The System of Modern Societies*. Englewood Cliffs: Apprentice Hall, 1971.

Päts, Konstantin. "Parlamentaarse vabariigi riigipea küsimus: riigivanem või president." ["The Question of the Head of State in a Parliamentary Republic: State Elder or President"] *Eesti riik*. Vol. 2. By Konstantin Päts. Eds. Toomas Karjahärm and Hando Runnel. Tartu: Ilmamaa, 2001 [1927]. 273-279.

—. "Põhiseaduse sünnivalud." ["The Birth Pangs of the Constitution"] *Eesti riik*. Vol. 2. By Konstantin Päts. Eds. Toomas Karjahärm and Hando Runnel. Tartu: Ilmamaa, 2001 [1920]. 135-146.

—. "Riigieelarve ja riigikorralduse põhimõisted." ["State Budget and the Main Concepts of Polity"] *Eesti riik*. Vol. 2. By Konstantin Päts. Eds. Toomas Karjahärm and Hando Runnel. Tartu: Ilmamaa, 2001 [1922]. 173-214.

—. "Vähemusrahvuste omavalitsuste ajutise korraldamise seaduse esimesel lugemisel." ["At the First Reading of the Law of Temporary Organization of National Minorities' Self-Governments"] *Eesti riik*. Vol. 2. By Konstantin Päts. Eds. Toomas Karjahärm and Hando Runnel. Tartu: Ilmamaa, 2001 [1923]. 215-220.

Peegel, Juhan. "Eesti varasema ajalehestiili arengujooni. J.V. Jannseni 150. sünniaastapäevaks." ["The Development of the Style Characteristics of Early Estonian Journalism"] *Keel ja Kirjandus* 5 (1969): 288-292.

Peiker, Piret. "A.H. Tammsaare's *Truth and Justice* as a Postcolonial Bildungsroman." *Journal of Baltic Studies* 46 (2) 2015: 199-216.

—. "An Account of One's Own: Narrating I-s in Postcolonial Literatures." *New Britain: The Heritage of the Past and the Challenge of the Future: Proceedings of the Second Tartu Conference of British Studies 24-26 August 1998*. Ed. Pilvi Rajamäe. Tartu: Tartu University Press, 1999. 94-108.

—. "Estonian Nationalism through the Postcolonial Lens." *Journal of Baltic Studies* 47 (1) 2016: 113-132.

—. "History, Politics and Myth: Lydia Koidula's Novella *Juudit, or the Last Maroons of Jamaica*." *Novels, Histories, Novel Nations: Historical Fiction and Cultural Memory in Finland and Estonia*. Eds. Linda Kaljundi, Eneken Laanes, Ilona Pikkanen. Helsinki: Suomalaisen Kirjallisuuden Seura, 2015. 98-120.

—. "Postcolonial Change: Power, Peru and Estonian Literature." *Baltic Postcolonialism*. Ed. Violeta Kelertas. Amsterdam: Rodopi, 2006.

—. "Postcommunist literatures: A Postcolonial Perspective." *Eurozine* 2006. <http://www.eurozine.com/articles/2006-03-28-peiker-en.html> 10 August 2014.
—. "Rahvusvaheline kultuurimälu ja ümberkirjutus Koidula *Juuditis*." ["International Cultural Memory and Rewriting in Koidula's *Juudit*"] *Keel ja Kirjandus* 8-9 (2013): 591-606.
Petersoo, Pille and Marek Tamm (eds.). *Monumentaalne konflikt: mälu, poliitika ja identiteet tänapäeva Eestis*. [*Monumental Conflict: Memory, Politics and Identity in Contemporary Estonia*] Tallinn: Varrak, 2008.
Petőfi, Sándor. "A kutyák dala". "A farkasok dala". ["The Song of the Dogs". "The Song of the Wolves"] *Kolozsvári Szalonna*. <https://kolozsvaros.com/2016/06/03/a-kutyak-dala-a-farkasok-dala/> 15 December 2015.
Pilv, Aare. "'Sa oled mul teine': Teisesusest eesti kultuuri eneseanalüüsis." ["'You are My Second One': The Role of Otherness in the Self-Analysis of the Estonian Culture"] *Rahvuskultuur ja tema teised*. Ed. Rein Undusk. Tallinn: Underi ja Tuglase Kirjanduskeskus, 2008. 67-92.
Plakans, Andrejs. *A Concise History of the Baltic States*. Cambridge: Cambridge University Press, 2011.
Plath, Ulrike. *Esten und Deutsche in den baltischen Provinzen Russlands. Fremdheitskonstruktionen, Lebenswelten, Kolonialphantasien 1750–1850*. [*Estonians and Germans in the Baltic Provinces of Russia. Constructions of Difference, Life-Worlds, Colonial Phantasies 1750–1850*] Wiesbaden: Harrassowitz Verlag, 2011.
Platt, Kevin M.F. and Benjamin Nathans. "Socialist in Form, Indeterminate in Content: The Ins and Outs of Late Soviet Culture." *Ab Imperio* 2 (2011): 301-324.
Põldmäe, Rudolf. *Vennastekoguduse Kirjandus*. [*Literature of the Moravian Brethren Community*] Tartu: Ilmamaa, 2011.
Poselyagin, Nikolai and Elena Strukova. "Lotman v perestroetshnoi presse (1986–1992)." ["Lotman in the Perestroika Period Media (1986–1992)"] *Slutshainost' i nepredskazuemost' v istorii kul'tury. Materialy vtoryh Lotmanskih dnei v Tallinskom universitete (4-6 iyunya 2010)*. Ed. Igor Pilshchikov. Tallinn: Tallinn University Press, 2013. 533-551.
Puhvel, Madli. *Symbol of Dawn: The Life and Times of the 19th-Century Estonian Poet Lydia Koidula*. Tartu: Tartu University Press, 1995.
Pye, Michael. "Rationality, Ritual and Life-Shaping Decisions in Modern Japan." *Japan and Asian Modernities*. Ed. Rein Raud. London, New York, Bahrain: Kegan Paul, 2007. 1-27.
Rannamaa, Silvia. Autori järelsõna. [Author's Afterword]. *Kadri. Kasuema*. By Silvia Rannamaa. Tallinn: Eesti Raamat, 1978. 374-375.
—. *Kadri. Kasuema*. [*Kadri. Stepmother*] Tallinn: Eesti Raamat, 1978 [*Kadri* 1959; *Kasuema* 1963].
—. *Kasuema*. [*Stepmother*] Tallinn: Eesti Raamat, 1965 [1963].
—. *Kohtumine lastekirjanikuga 14.06.2002* [DVD]. [*Meeting with a Children's Author*] Interview by Andres Jaaksoo. Tallinn: Tallinna Keskraamatukogu, 2002.
—. *Maast madalast*. [*Since Tender Age*] Tallinn: Eesti Raamat, 1990.
Raud, Rein. "A Comparative Analysis of Challenge Discourses: 'Overcoming Modernity' and the 'Asian Values' Debate." *Japan and Asian Modernities*. Ed. Rein Raud. London, New York, Bahrain: Kegan Paul, 2007. 167-182.
—. Introduction. *Japan and Asian Modernities*. Ed. Rein Raud. London, New York, Bahrain: Kegan Paul, 2007. iii-x.
—. (ed.). *Japan and Asian Modernities*. London, New York, Bahrain: Kegan Paul, 2007.

Raun, Toivo U. "1905 as a Turning Point in Estonian History." *East European Quarterly* 13.3 (1980): 327-333.
—. "Eesti lülitumine modernsusesse. "Noor-Eesti" roll poliitilise ja sotsiaalse mõtte mitmekesistamisel." ["The Role of Young Estonia in the Diversification of Political and Social Thought"] *Tuna* 2 (2009): 39-50.
—. *Estonia and the Estonians.* Updated second edition. Stanford: Hoover Institution Press, 2001.
—. "Nineteenth- and Early Twentieth-Century Estonian Nationalism Revisited." *Nations and Nationalism.* 9 (1) 2003: 129-147.
— and Andrejs Plakans. "The Estonian and Latvian National Movements: An Assessment of Miroslav Hroch's Model." *Journal of Baltic Studies* 21 (2) 1990: 131-144.
— and Andrejs Plakans. "The Latvian and Estonian National Movements 1860-1914." *The Slavonic and East European Review.* 64.1 (1986): 66-80.
Redfield, Marc. *Phantom Formations. Aesthetic Ideology and the Bildungsroman.* Ithaca, NY and London: Cornell University Press, 1996.
Remael, Aline and Ilse Logie (eds.). *Translation as Creation: The Postcolonial Influence.* Special issue of *Linguistica Antverpiensia (New Series)* 2. Antwerpen: Hogeschool Antwerpen, Hoger Instituut voor Vertalers en Tolken, 2003.
Rigney, Ann. Postface: Multidirectional Fictions. *Novels, Histories, Novel Nations: Historical Fiction and Cultural Memory in Finland and Estonia.* Eds. Linda Kaljundi, Eneken Laanes, Ilona Pikkanen. Helsinki: Suomalaisen Kirjallisuuden Seura, 2015. 322-328.
Robe, Stanley L. "Wild Men and Spain's Brave New World." *The Wild Man Within: An Image in Western Thought from Renaissance to Romanticism.* Eds. Edward Dudley, Maximilian E. Novak. Pittsburgh: University of Pittsburgh Press, 1972. 39-54.
Rohtmets, Helen. "Birth of a State: Formation of Estonian Citizenship (1918–1922)." *Citizenship in Historical Perspective.* Eds. Steven G. Ellis, Guðmundur Hálfdanarson, Ann Katherin Isaacs. Pisa: Plus Pisa University Press, 2006. 289-303.
—. *Eesti kodakondsuse kujunemine: põhimõtted ja praktika.* [*The Evolution of Estonian Citizenship: Priciples and Practice*] Master's thesis. University of Tartu, 2005.
Roosalu, Triin. "Income Inequality and Equality." Chap. 3.2. *Estonian Human Development Report 2012/2013. Estonia In The World.* Eds. Mati Heidmets, Marju Lauristin, Jüri Sepp, Erik Terk, Anu Toots. Tallinn: Eesti Koostöökogu, 2013. 114-121.
Rooste, Jürgen. "Eesti küsimus on ikka sündimuse küsimus." ["The Estonian Question is still related to the Birth Rate"] *Sirp* 23.02.2007. <http://www.sirp.ee/s1-artiklid/c7-kirjandus/eesti-k-simus-on-ikka-s-ndimuse-k-simus/> 12 November 2016.
Rosa, Hartmut. *Social Acceleration: A New Theory of Modernity.* New York: Columbia U. Press, 2013.
—. "Social Acceleration: Ethical and Political Consequences of a Desynchronized High-Speed Society." *High-Speed Society: Social Acceleration, Power, and Modernity.* Eds. Hartmut Rosa and William E. Scheuerman. University Park: Pennsylvania U. Press, 2009. 77-114.
—. "The Universal Underneath the Multiple: Social Acceleration as a Key to Understanding Modernity." *Modernity at the Beginning of the 21st Century.* Ed. Volker H. Schmidt. Newcastle: Cambridge Scholars Publishing, 2007. 37-61.

— and William E. Scheuerman. Introduction. *High-Speed Society: Social Acceleration, Power and Modernity*. Eds. Hartmut Rosa and William E. Scheuerman. University Park: Pennsylvania U. Press, 2009. 1-29.

Rösselt, Friedrich. *Lehrbuch der Weltgeschichte für Töchterschulen und zum Privatunterricht heranwachsenden Mädchen.* [*Textbook of World History for Girls' Schools and for Adolescent Girls' Indepent Study*] Vol. 3. Breslau, Max und Comp, 1858.

Rostow, Walt W. *The Stages of Economic Growth: A Non-Communist Manifesto.* London: Cambridge University Press, 1960.

Saariluoma, Liisa. *Erzählstruktur und* Bildungsroman. Wielands Geschichte des Agathon, Goethes Wilhelm Meisters Lehrjahre. [*Narrative Structure and* Bildungsroman. *Wieland's* The History of Agathon *and Goethe's* Wilhelm Meister's Apprenticeship] Würzburg: Königshausen & Neumann, 2004.

Saarsen, Kaarin. "Väljasaatmine Eestist jätkub." ["Exiling from Estonia Continues"] *Stokholmi Eesti Päevaleht. Estniska Dagbladet.* 04. 03. 1988.

Saarts, Tõnis. "The Bronze Nights: The Failure of Forced Europeanization and the Birth of Nationalist Defensive Democracy." *Eurozine* 10.10.2008. http://www.eurozine.com/articles/ 2008-10-10-saarts-en.html 20 May 2013.

—. "Kahest demokraatiamudelist ja Eesti demokraatia tuumpingest." ["Two Models of Democracy and the Core Tension of Estonian Democracy"] *Vikerkaar* 6 (2012): 78-88.

—. "Kas teine Eesti on olemas?" ["Does the Second Estonia Exist?"] *Postimees* 10.06.2002. <http://arvamus.postimees.ee/1938665/kas-teine-eesti-on-olemas > 27 November 2016.

Salupere, Malle. *Koidula. Ajastu taustal, kaasteeliste keskel.* [*Koidula. Against the Background of Her Era, in the Midst of Her Fellow-Travellers*] Tallinn: Tänapäev, 2017.

Savisaar, Edgar. *Kõned.* [*Speeches*] Tallinn: Olion, 1990.

Scaglione, Aldo. "A Note on Montaigne's Des Cannibales and the Humanist Tradition." *First Images of America: The Impact of the New World on the Old.* Ed. Fredi Chiappelli. Berkeley and Los Angeles: University of California Press, 1976. 63-70.

Schöpflin, George. "The Functions of Myth and a Taxonomy of Myths." *Myths and Nationhood.* Eds. Geoffrey Hosking and George Schöpflin. New York: Heinemann, 1997. 19-35.

—. "Nationalism Theory and Estonia." Unpublished manuscript.

—. "Nationhood, Modernity, Democracy. Manifestations of National Identity in Modern Europe." *Eurozine* 17.11.2005. <http://www.eurozine.com/ articles/2005-11-17-schopflin-en.html> 2 December 2008.

—. "The Small States of Europe and Large Whirlpools. The Implications of a Multi-Polar World." *Estonian Foreign Policy Yearbook 2009.* Ed. Andres Kasekamp. Tallinn: Estonian Foreign Policy Institute, 2009. 7-21.

Schorske, Carl E. *Fin-de-Siécle Vienna: Politics and Culture.* New York: Knopf, 1980.

Selg, Peeter. "A Political-Semiotic Introduction to the Estonian "Bronze-Night" Discourse." *Journal of Language and Politics* 12.1 (2012): 80-100.

Shannon, Ashley Elizabeth. *Romantic Peripheries: The National Subject and the Colonial Bildungsroman in Edgeworth, Scott, Child and Hogg.* PhD. diss. Texas University at Austin, 2003.

Shelley, Louise I. *Policing Soviet Society: The Evolution of State Control.* New York: Routledge, 1996.

Siimisker, Helene. *A. H. Tammsaare: lühimonograafia.* [*A.H. Tammsaare: A Short Monography*] Tallinn: Eesti Riiklik Kirjastus, 1962.
Simpson, Anthony. "Memory and Becoming Chosen Other: Fundamentalist Elite-Making in a Zambian Mission School." Ch. 8. *Memory and the Postcolony: African Anthropology and the Critique of Power.* Ed. Richard Webner. London and New York: Zed Books, 1998. 209-228.
Sisask, Kaia. *Noor-Eesti ja* esprit fin de siècle. *Puhta kunsti kreedo maailma- ja inimesetunnetust restruktureeriv roll 20. saj. alguse Eestis.* [*The Young Estonia Movement and* esprit fin de siècle. *The Role of Literary Aestheticism in Estonia at the Beginning of the 20th Century*] PhD. diss. Tallinn University, 2009. <www.e-ait.tlulib.ee> 10 August 2014.
Slater, Don. *Consumer Culture and Modernity.* Cambridge: Polity, 1997.
Slonimsky, Aleksandr. ""Vdrug" u Dostoevskogo." [""Suddenly" in Dostoevsky's Work"] *Kniga i revolyutsiya* 8.20 (1922): 9-16.
Smelser, Neil J. *Social Change in the Industrial Revolution.* London: Routledge and Kegan Paul, 1959.
Smith, David J. "Non-Territorial Cultural Autonomy as a Baltic Contribution to Europe Between the Wars." *The Baltic States and their Region: New Europe or Old?* Ed. David J. Smith. Amsterdam, New York: Rodopi, 2005. 211-226.
Sooväli, Jaanus. "Friedrich Nietzsche's Influence on the Estonian Intellectual Landscape." *Studia Philosophica Estonica.* 8.2 (2015): 141-155.
Spivak, Gayatri Chakravorty. "Nationalism and the Imagination." *Lectora* 15 (2009): 75-98.
Steinberg, Mark D. *Proletarian Imagination: Self, Modernity and the Sacred in Russia, 1910–1925.* Ithaca, NY; London: Cornell University Press, 2002.
Steinbrink, Bernd. *Abenteuerliteratur des 19. Jahrhunderts in Deutschland. Studien zu einer vernachlässigten Gattung.* [*Adventure Literature in the 19th Century Germany. A Study of a Neglected Genre*] Tübingen: Max Niemeyer Verlag, 1983.
Steinby, Liisa and Michael Schmidt (eds.). *Augenblick, Lebenszeit, Geschichte, Ewigkeit. Die Zeit in Goethes Werken.* [*Moment, Lifetime, History, Eternity. Time in Goethe's Texts*] Heidelberg: Winter, 2017.
Streeck, Wolfgang. "The Study of Organized Interests: Before 'the Century' and After." *The Diversity of Democracy: Corporatism, Social Order and Political Conflict.* Eds. Colin Crouch and Wolfgang Streeck. Cheltenham: Edward Elgar, 2006. 3-45.
Suits, Gustav. Lõpusõna. [Afterword]. *Noor-Eesti. Kirjanduse, kunsti ja teaduse ajakiri* 5-6 (1910/1911): 637-641.
—. "Noorte püüded." ["The Aspirations of Young People"] *Noor-Eesti I album.* [Tartu]: "Kirjanduse Sõprade" Kirjastus, 1905. 3-19.
Suny, Ronald Grigor. "Nationalism, Nation Making and the Postcolonial States of Asia, Africa and Eurasia." *After Independence: Making and Protecting the Nation in Postcolonial and Postcommunist States.* Ed. Lowell W. Barrington. Ann Arbor: University of Michigan Press, 2006. 279-295.
—. *The Revenge of the Past. Nationalism, Revolution and the Collapse of the Soviet Union.* Stanford, CA: Stanford University Press, 1993.
Suurkask, Heiki. "Kastreeritud ajalugu." ["Castrated History"] *Eesti Päevaleht.* 08.03.2007. <http://www.epl.ee/news/ arvamus/heiki-suurkask-kastreeritud-ajalugu.d?id=51078538> 30 April 2013.

Suzuki, Takaaki. "Modernity and the Transformation of the Japanese State." *Japan and Asian Modernities*. Ed. Rein Raud. London, New York, Bahrain: Kegan Paul, 2007. 43-66.

Sztompka, Piotr. *The Sociology of Social Change*. Oxford: Blackwell, 1993.

Taagepera, Rein. *Estonia: Return to Independence*. Boulder, CO: Westview Press.

Tali, Piret. "Eesti riigi vanune Kadri kasuema Silvia Rannamaa." ["Kadri's Stepmother Silvia Rannamaa – the Same Age as the Estonian State"] *Eesti Päevaleht* 04.06.2005. <http://epl.delfi.ee/news/kultuur/eesti-riigi-vanune-kadri-kasuema-silvia-rannamaa.d?id=51012215> 1 June 2014.

Talvet, Jüri. "Juhan Liiv and His Existential Poetry." *Meel paremat ei kannata. Valik luulet eesti ja inglise keeles./The Mind Would Bear No Better. A Selection of Poetry in Estonian and English*. By Juhan Liiv. Ed. Jüri Talvet. Transl. Jüri Talvet and H.L. Hix. Tartu: Tartu Ülikooli Kirjastus, 2007. 29-52.

Tamm, Triinu. "Prantslased ussisõnade lummuses." ["The French Bewitched by Snakish"] *Looming* 3 (2013). <http://www.looming.ee/2013/06/prantslased-ussisonade-lummuses/> 23 August 2014.

Tammsaare, Anton Hansen. "Lunastusest." ["On Salvation"] Anton Hansen Tammsaare *Kogutud teosed*. Vol. 16. Tallinn: Eesti Raamat, 1988. 603-606.

—. "Spengleri Õhtumaa allakäigust." ["On Spengler's *The Decline of the West*"] Anton Hansen Tammsaare *Kogutud teosed*. [Collected Works] Vol. 16. Tallinn: Eesti Raamat, 1988. 526-548.

—. *Tõde ja õigus*. [*Truth and Justice*] Vol. 1. Tallinn: Eesti Raamat, 1964 [1926].

—. *Tõde ja õigus*. [*Truth and Justice*] Vol. 2. Tallinn: Eesti Raamat, 1965 [1929].

—. *Tõde ja õigus*. [*Truth and Justice*] Vol. 3. Tallinn: Eesti Raamat, 1968 [1931].

—. *Tõde ja õigus*. [*Truth and Justice*] Vol. 5. Tallinn: Eesti Raamat, 1969 [1933].

—. "Tõest ja õigusest. Kiri Andres Prantspillile." ["On *Truth and Justice*. Letter to Andres Prantspill] *Tulimuld* 3 (1954): 131-133.

—. "Vaim ja võim." ["Intellect and Power"] Anton Hansen Tammsaare *Kogutud teosed*. Vol. 17. Tallinn: Eesti Raamat, 1990. 212-215.

Taylor, Charles. *Sources of the Self: The Making of the Modern Identity*. Cambridge, Mass.: Harvard University Press, 1989.

—. "Two Theories of Modernity". *The International Scope* 3.5 (2001): 1-9. <http://www.mercaba.org/SANLUIS/Filosofia/autores/Contempor%C3%A1nea/Taylor,%20Charles/Two%20theories%20of%20modernity.pdf> 19 June 2015.

Tchassovskaia, Bella. *Eesti temaatika vene ajalehtedes 1930ndatel aastatel*. [Estonia in the Russian Newspapers of the 1930s] B.A. diss. Tartu University, 2001.

Teder, Eerik. "A.H. Tammsaare ja F. Dostojevski." ["A.H. Tammsaare and F. Dostoevsky"] *Keel ja Kirjandus* 7 (1997): 459-469.

Theodorsen, Cathrine. "Political Realism and the Fantastic Romantic: German Liberal Discourse and the Sámi in Theodor Mügge's Novel *Afraja* (1854)." *Nordlit* 23 *Arctic Discourses* (2008): 355-370.

Thorhalsson, Baldur and Rainer Kattel. "Neo-Liberal Small States and Economic Crisis: Lessons for Democratic Corporatism." *Journal of Baltic Studies* 44.1 (2013): 83-103.

Thorsen, Dag Einar. "The Neoliberal Challenge: What is Neoliberalism?" Working paper 10.10.2009. Department of Political Science, University of Oslo. <http://folk.uio.no/daget/neoliberalism2.pdf> 20 January 2014.

Tocqueville, Alexis de. *Democracy in America*. Vol. 2. Ed. Phillips Bradley. Transl. Henry Reeve. London: David Campbell, 1994.
"Toomas Ilves, Estonia's American European." *The Economist* 29.10.1998. <http://www.economist.com/node/174163 > 29 December 2016.
Toury, Gideon. *Descriptive Translation Studies and Beyond*. Amsterdam and Philadelphia: John Benjamins, 1995.
—. *In Search of a Theory of Translation*. Tel Aviv: The Porter Institute for Poetics and Semiotics, Tel Aviv University, 1980.
Treier, Elem. *Tammsaare elust härra Hansenina*. [*On Tammsaare's Life as Mr. Hansen*] Tallinn: Olion, 2002.
—. *Tammsaare ja tema "Tõde ja õigus"*. [*Tammsaare and his Truth and Justice*] Tallinn: Olion, 2000.
Trejo-Mathys, Jonathan. "Translator's Introduction: Modernity and Time." *Social Acceleration: A New Theory of Modernity*. New York: Columbia U. Press, 2013. xi-xxxi.
Trivedi, Harish. "Translating Culture vs. Cultural Translation." *91st Meridian* 1 (2005). <http://iwp.uiowa.edu/91st/vol4-num1/translating-culture-vs-cultural-translation> 12 October 2014.
Tuglas, Friedebert. "A.H. Tammsaare. Kriitiline essee." ["A.H. Tammsaare. An Analytical Essay"] Tartu: Odamees, 1918.
—. "Kirjanduslik stiil." ["Literary Style"] *Noor-Eesti IV album*. [Ed. Gustav Suits. Tartu]: Noor-Eesti, 1912. 23-100.
—. [Felix]. "Natuke Capitoliumist ja hanidest." "Shortly on the Capitol and the Geese" *Noor-Eesti IV album*. [Ed. Gustav Suits. Tartu]: Noor-Eesti, 1912. 257-268.
Turtola, Martti. *Kindral Laidoner ja Eesti Vabariigi hukk 1939-1940*. [*General Laidoner and the Demise of the Estonian Republic 1939-1940*] Transl. Maimu Berg. Tallinn: Tänapäev, 2008.
—. *President Konstantin Päts: Eesti ja Soome teed*. [*President Konstantin Päts: The Roads Taken by Estonia and by Finland*] Transl. Maimu Berg. Tallin: Tänapäev, 2003.
Tuumalu, Tiit. "Emil Tode "Piiririiki" saadab Euroopas tõlkeedu." ["Emil Tode's *Border State* Enjoys Translation Success in Europe"] *Postimees* 06.12.1995. <http://www.postimees.ee/2465319/emil-tode-piiririiki-saadab-euroopas-tolkeedu> 8 October 2016.
Tymoczko, Maria. "Translation and Political Engagement: Activism, Social Change and the Role of Translation in Geopolitical Shifts." *The Translator* 1 (2000): 23-47.
—. *Translation in a Postcolonial Context: Early Irish Literature in English Translation*. Manchester: St. Jerome Publishing, 1999.
Undla-Põldmäe, Aino. *Koidulauliku valgel. Uurimusi ja artikleid*. [*In the Light of the Singer of the Dawn. Studies and Articles*] Tallinn: Eesti Raamat, 1981.
—. "Lydia Koidula ja Julius Jannsen Ameerika avastamisest." ["Lydia Koidula and Julius Jannsen on the Discovery of America"] *Keel ja Kirjandus* 8 (1981): 465-470.
Undusk, Jaan. "Abielu kui utoopia. Sissejuhatus ühte kirjanduslikku motiivi." ["Marriage as a Utopia. Introduction to a Literary Motif"] *Uurimusi keelest, kirjandusest ja kultuurist*. Eds. Mihhail Lotman and Tõnu Viik. Tallinn: *Acta Collegii Humaniorum Estoniensis* 2 (1995): 126-138.
—. "Die Ehe als Utopie. Einführung in ein literarisches Motiv." ["Marriage as a Utopia. Introduction to a Literary Motif"] *Literaturbeziehungen zwischen Deutschbalten, Esten und Letten. Zwölf Beiträge zum 7. Baltischen Seminar 1995*. Ed. Michael Garleff. Lüneburg: Carl Schirren Gesellschaft, 2007. 185-201.

—. "Eesti lugu: Emil Tode "Piiririik"." ["Estonia's Story: Emil Tode's *Border State*"] *Eesti Päevaleht* 31.07.2009. <http://epl.delfi.ee/news/ kultuur/eesti-lugu-emil-tode-piiririik?id=51174562> 15 October 2016.

—. "Eesti lugu: Jaan Kross "Keisri hull". ["Estonia's Story: Jaan Kross's *The Czar's Madman*"] *Eesti Päevaleht* 27.12.2008. <http://epl.delfi.ee/news/kultuur/eesti-lugu-jaan-kross-keisri-hull?id=51153618> 16 October 2016.

—. "Eksistentsiaalne Kreutzwald." *Vikerkaar* 10-11 (2004): 133-152.

—. "Isiksusest, häbist ja süüst." ["On Personality, Shame, and Guilt"] Tuglas-seura. <http://www.tuglas.fi/isiksusest-habist-ja-suust> 15 October 2016.

—. "Kolm võimalust kirjutada eestlaste ajalugu. Merkel—Jakobson—Hurt." ["Three Ways to Write the History of Estonians. Merkel—Jakobson—Hurt"] *Keel ja Kirjandus* 11 (1997): 721-734.

Vaan, Laura. *Propagandatalitus Eesti Vabariigis autoritaarsel ajajärgul*. [*Propaganda Service During the Authoritarian Period of the Estonian Republic*] MA diss. Tartu University, 2005.

Välipõllu, Hilja. "Kadri õnn ja kolm k-d. Rmt: S. Rannamaa. Kadri." ["Kadri's Happiness and three k-s. Review of S. Rannamaa's *Kadri*"] *Keel ja Kirjandus* 7 (1961): 570-572.

Väljataga, Märt. "Orja teadvus varjus ja valguses." ["Slave Mind in Shadow and in Light"] *Looming* 12 (2006): 1884-1892.

Veidemann, Rein. "Jaan Kross ja eesti müüt." ["Jaan Kross and the Estonian Myth"] *Eesti Päevaleht* 19.02.2000. <http://epl.delfi.ee/news/kultuur/jaan-kross-ja-eesti-muut?id=50783569> 16 October 2016.

—. "Maailmakirjanduse retseptsiooniplahvatus Eestis." ["The Explosion of World Literature Reception in Estonia"] *Keel ja Kirjandus* 11 (2005): 865-872.

—. "Ühe (suure) kultuurinarratiivi saatus: Noor-Eesti" ["The Fate of a (Grand) Cultural Narrative: Young Estonia"] *Methis* 1-2 (2008): 288-297.

Velsker, Mart. "Nüüdiskirjandus. Uue luule aastad." ["Contemporary Literature. The Years of New Poetry"] *Eesti Kirjanduslugu*. Eds. Epp Annus, Luule Epner, Ants Järv, Sirje Olesk, Ele Süvalep, Mart Velsker. Tallinn: Koolibri, 2001. 624-645.

—. "Stalinismi taandumine ja 1960. aastad. Kirjandus ja ühiskond: sulaaja kirjandus." ["The Relaxation of Stalinism and the 1960s. Literature and Society: The Literature of the Khrushchev Thaw Period"] *Eesti Kirjanduslugu*. Eds. Epp Annus, Luule Epner, Ants Järv, Sirje Olesk, Ele Süvalep, Mart Velsker. Tallinn: Koolibri, 2001. 412-419.

Venuti, Lawrence. "1900s-1930s." Ed. Lawrence Venuti. *Translation Studies Reader*. 2nd ed. London, New York: Routledge 2004. 69-74.

Vinkel, Aarne. *Eesti rahvaraamat. Ülevaade XVIII- ja XIX sajandi lugemisvarast*. [*Estonian Volksliteratur. Overview of the Reading Materials in the 18th and 19th Century*] Tallinn: Eesti Raamat, 1966.

—. "Juhan Liiv." *Eesti kirjanduse ajalugu*. Vol. 3. Ed. Heino Puhvel. Tallinn: Eesti Raamat, 1969. 100-136.

—. "Mats Kirsel ja rõhumisevastane temaatika eesti rahvaraamatus." ["Mats Kirsel and Anti-Oppression Thematic in Estonian *Volksliteratur*"] *Keel ja Kirjandus* 10 (1960): 605-611.

Vladiv, Slobodanka. "Dostoevsky's Major Novels as Semiotic Models." *Dostoevsky Studies* 9 (1988): 158-63.

Võõbus, Arthur. *Studies in the History of the Estonian People*. Vol. 5. Stockholm: Estonian Theological Society in Exile, 1979.

Vries, Ad de. *Elsevier's Dictionary of Symbols and Imagery.* Rev. by Arthur de Vries. 2nd enlarged edition. Amsterdam [etc.]: Elsevier, 2004.
Vucetic, Srdjan. "Identity is a Joking Matter: Intergroup Humor in Bosnia." *Spacesofidentity.net* 01.04.2004. <http://soi.journals.yorku.ca/index.php/soi/article/view/801118> 18 October 2017.
Vucheva, Elitsa. "Estonians Least Religious in the World." *EU Observer* 11.02.2009. <https://euobserver.com/social/27587> 1 January 2017.
Wagner, Peter. *Modernity as Experience and Interpretation: A New Sociology of Modernity.* Cambridge: Polity Press, 2008.
—. *Modernity: Understanding the Present.* Cambridge: Polity Press, 2012.
—. *Progress: A Reconstruction.* Cambridge: Polity Press, 2015.
"The Warwick Debates". The Ernest Gellner Resource Site. <http://www.lse.ac.uk/researchAndExpertise/units/gellner/Warwick.html > 29 November 2016.
Wassermann, Renata R. Mautner. *Exotic Nations. Literature and Cultural Identity in the United States and Brazil, 1830-1930.* Ithaca and London: Cornell University Press, 1994.
Weber, Max. *Economy and Society.* Totwa, NJ: Bedminster Press, 1968 [1921].
—. "Politics as a Vocation." *Max Weber: Essays in Sociology.* Eds. and transl. H.H. Gerth and C. Wright Mills. New York: Oxford University Press, 1946 [1919]. 77-128.
—. *The Protestant Ethic and the Spirit of Capitalism.* London and New York: Routledge, 2001 [1904-1905].
—. "Science as a Vocation." *Max Weber: Essays in Sociology.* Eds. and transl. H.H. Gerth and C. Wright Mills. New York: Oxford University Press, 1946 [1919]. 129-156.
Weinrich, Harald. *Tempus: Besprochene und erzählte Welt.* [*Tempus: The World of Discussion and the World of Narration*] 6th rev. ed. München: C.H. Beck, 2001 [1964].
Werbner, Richard (ed.). *Memory and the Postcolony: African Anthropology and the Critique of Power.* London and New York: Zed Books, 1998.
White, Hayden. "The Noble Savage Theme as Fetish." Hayden White. *Tropics of Discourse: Essays in Cultural Criticism.* Baltimore and London: The John Hopkins University Press, 1985. 183-196.
Widdowson, Peter. *Literature.* London; New York: Routledge, 1999.
Wilde, Oscar. "The Truth of Masks—A Note on Illusion." Read book online. <http://www.readbookonline.net/readOnLine/481/ > 2 May 2013.
Williams, Raymond. *Culture and Society.* London: Chatto and Windus, 1958.
—. *Keywords: A Vocabulary of Culture and Society.* Rev. ed. New York: Oxford University Press, 1985.
—. *The Long Revolution.* London: Chatto and Windus, 1961.
Wilson, Kathleen. "The Performance of Freedom: Maroons and the Colonial Order in Eighteenth-Century Jamaica and the Atlantic Sound." *William & Mary Quarterly* 66.1 (2009): 45-86.
Winks, Robin W. and Joan Neuberger. *Europe and the Making of Modernity 1815-1914.* New York and Oxford: Oxford University Press, 2005.
Woolsey, Theodore D. Introductory. *On Civil Liberty and Self-Government.* By Francis Lieber. 3rd rev. ed. Ed. Theodore D. Woolsey. Philadelphia: J.B. Lippincott & Co., 1891. 5-10.
Yack, Bernhard. *The Fetishism of Modernities: Epochal Self-Consciousness in Contemporary Social and Political Thought.* Notre Dame, IN: University of Notre Dame Press, 1997.

—. *Nationalism and the Moral Psychology of Community.* Chicago: The University of Chicago Press, 2012.

Yao, Steven G. *Translation and the Languages of Modernism: Gender, Politics, Language.* New York: Palgrave Macmillan, 2002.

Yeats, W.B. *Explorations.* London: Macmillan, 1962.

Young, Robert. *Colonial Desire; Hybridity in Theory, Culture and Race.* London: Routledge, 1995.

Yurchak, Alexei. *Everything Was Forever Until It Was No More: The Last Soviet Generation.* Princeton: Princeton University Press, 2007.

Zaslavsky, Victor. "The Soviet Union." *After Empire: Multi-Ethnic Societies and Nation-Building: The Soviet Union and the Russian, Ottoman and Habsburg Empires.* Eds. Karen Barkey and Mark von Hagen. Boulder, CO: Westview Press, 1997. 73-96.

Zubkova, Jelena. *Baltimaad ja Kreml 1940–1953.* [*The Baltic States and the Kremlin 1940–1953*] Transl. Margus Leemets. Tallinn, Varrak, 2009.

Index

A
Aavik, Johannes, 232, 236, 238n, 240, 245–47, 249–51, 266
Achebe, Chinua, 27, 258
Adams, Jüri, 65
Ahl, Nils C., 228n
Aho, Juhani, 252
Alcott, Louisa May, 181
Alencar, José de, 103
Alenius, Kari, 59
Alexander I of Russia, 192, 196
Alexander II of Russia, 44
Alliksaar, Artur, 70
Almberg, Antti, 105n, 151, 153
Amaru, Túpac, 103
Anderson, Benedict, 24–25, 88, 227
Annist, August, 238
Annus, Epp, viii, 30n, 75, 219n, 241, 243
Aristotle, 109

B
Bakhtin, Mikhail, 24, 106–7, 165, 167, 211, 212–13, 215, 216
Bal, Mieke, 28n, 29
Barth, Fredrik, 18n
Barthes, Roland, 122
Bassnett, Susan, 103
Baudelaire, Charles, 3, 232, 249–50
Bauer, Otto, 60, 63, 64
Bauman, Zygmunt, 204n
Bayly, Christopher, 8, 14, 17
Beecher-Stowe, Harriet, 25
Benveniste, Émile, 122
Bhabha, Homi K., 86, 88, 104, 107–8, 209
Bock, Katharina von, 192n
Bock, Timotheus Eberhard von, 192–97
Boes, Tobias, 162–63, 166–67
Bourdieu, Pierre, 28n, 206n
Brandes, Georg, 244n
Brezhnev, Leonid, 179, 191
Brontë, Charlotte, 107
Brown, David, 55–56, 64, 90
Burnett, Francis, 181
Butler, Marilyn, 28n
Byrne, Eleanor, 172

C
Cabral, Amílcar, 87n
Calhoun, Craig, 84, 88
Campbell, Colin, 207n
Campe, J. H., 122n
Casanova, Pascale, 25–27, 38, 228
Cassirer, Ernst, 163
Castells, Manuel, 17

Castle, Gregory, 167–68
Césaire, Aimé, 87n
Chakrabarty, Dipesh, 16n, 21, 218n
Charles V, 102, 126, 136, 137, 141
Chautebriand, François René de, 112, 139, 141
Cheah, Pheng, 15n, 88–89, 93, 162, 163, 265n
Christianson, Gerald, 43
Coetzee, J. M., 107
Comenius, John Amos, 40, 41
Confucius, 248
Connor, Walker, 45
Conrad, Joseph, 108
Cooper, Frederick, 5
Cooper, James Fenimore, 103, 141
Corneille, Pierre, 156
Cortés, Hernán, 112
Crowner, David, 43
Culler, Jonathan, 25

D

D'Alembert, Jean-Baptiste le Rond, 156
D'Annunzio, Gabriele, 232, 233, 241, 251
Davies, Christian, 229–30
Defoe, Daniel, 107, 112
Dickens, Charles, 25
Dickens, Eric, 228
Diderot, Denis, 156
Dilthey, Wilhelm, 162, 166, 167
Dittmar, Heinrich, 122n, 154–55
Dostoevsky, Fyodor, 212, 215–17, 219–20, 221–22, 224
Durkheim, Émile, 4, 9

E

Eellend, Johan, 68n
Eggert, Hartmut, 152
Ehala, Martin, 261
Eisenstadt, Shmuel N., 7n
Eliot, T. S., 173, 244
Esty, Jed, 167, 168n

Even-Zohar, Itamar, 100, 106n
Eysteinsson, Astradur, 233–34, 238

F

Faehlmann, Friedrich Robert, 39, 43
Fallersleben, August Heinrich Hoffmann von, 105
Fanon, Frantz, 87n
Fichte, Johann Gottlieb, 89n, 162
Foucault, Michel, 2n, 5
Francke, August Hermann, 41
Freiligrath, Friedrich, 105
Freud, Sigmund, 249
Friedenthal, Meelis, 262
Friedman, Milton, 85
Fukuyama, Francis, 208
Furedi, Frank, 92

G

Gagarin, Yuri, 182, 188–89
Gautier, Théophile, 250
Gellner, Ernest, 34–36
Genette, Gérard, 119
George, Olakunle, 16n
Gikandi, Simon, 86, 88
Glaubrecht, Otto von, 117
Goethe, Johann Wolfgang von, 161, 162, 166, 167, 212–13, 215, 216, 224, 248
Gorbachev, Mikhail, 69, 73, 79, 80
Greenblatt, Stephen, 28n
Greenfeld, Liah, 33, 55, 56
Grimes, Alan, 62
Gronow, Jukka, 204n
Grünthal-Ridala, Villem, 232, 240, 241, 251
Guys, Constantin, 3

H

Habermas, Jürgen, 6, 52–53
Harvey, David, 15n
Hasselblatt, Cornelius, 262
Hasselblatt, Werner, 60

Index

Hegel, Georg Wilhelm Friedrich, 89n, 103
Heidegger, Martin, 265
Hennoste, Tiit, 231, 236-38, 251, 252, 253-54
Herder, Johann Gotfried, 10n, 26-27, 33, 38, 49, 57, 59, 64, 88, 103, 114, 161-62, 221, 246, 248, 251
Hinrikus, Mirjam, 212n, 239n, 249n
Horn, W.O., 101-2, 106, 108, 111, 113, 118, 120, 121, 122, 124-43
Housden, Martyn, 60
Hroch, Miroslav, 16n, 19, 37-38, 39, 44, 45, 47-48, 49, 53
Humboldt, Alexander von, 112
Humboldt, Wilhelm von, 161, 162, 167, 248
Hunfalvy, Pál, 105n
Huntington, Samuel P., 11
Hurt, Jakob, 43n, 48, 49, 50, 105n
Hus, Jan, 40
Huysmans, Joris-Karl, 232

J

Jaaksoo, Andres, 181, 184n, 189
Jaanus, Maire, 196
Jakobson, August, 253
Jakobson, Carl Robert, 43n, 45, 49, 105n, 116, 144, 255
Jannsen, Emilie, 104
Jannsen, Johann Voldemar, 43n, 44, 48n, 49, 104, 105, 117, 119
Jannsen, Lydia. *See* Lydia Koidula
Jansen, Ea, 16n, 22, 48, 52-53
Josephine, Empress of the French, 153-54
Joyce, James, 168n
Jusdanis, Gregory, 27, 28, 29

K

Kalev, Leif, 90n
Kaljundi, Linda, 184n, 231, 257n, 258
Kallas, Aino, 67, 239-40, 249n, 252

Kant, Immanuel, 89n
Kaya, Ibrahim, 7
Keller, Margit, 204, 206
Kelly, Catriona, 183
Kerr, Clark, 11n
Khrushchev, Nikita, 69-70, 72, 179, 190
Kiin, Sirje, 80
Kirsel, Mats, 117, 118
Kirss, Tiina, 173
Kivimäe, Jüri, 240n, 243
Kivirähk, Andrus, 32, 96-97, 227-31, 254-59, 264-66
Knauft, Bruce, 7-8, 14
Kohn, Hans, 55, 56, 57
Koidula, Lydia, 25, 31, 43n, 45, 48n, 49, 72, 99, 101-5, 108, 111, 113, 114, 116-22, 124-25, 126-38, 140-41, 143-59, 172, 176n
Koselleck, Reinhart, 8-9
Kotzebue, August von, 118n
Kõvamees, Anneli, 214
Kreutzwald, Friedrich Reinhold, 39, 43, 105n
Kristeva, Julia, 262
Kross, Jaan, 70, 72, 164, 173, 179, 190-92, 228
Krull, Hasso, 94
Krusten, Reet, 180-81, 182n, 188
Kulli, Jaanus, 20
Kundera, Milan, 206n

L

Laanes, Eneken, 192n, 209
Laar, Mart, 48-49
Lagerspetz, Mikko, 94
Las Casas, Bartolomé de, 10, 102, 103, 118, 10n, 124-27, 129, 130, 131, 132, 133-34, 135, 137, 142, 143
Lauristin, Marju, 238n
Lefevere, André, 103
Lejeune, Philippe, 123
Lenin, Vladimir, 76
Lévi-Strauss, Claude, 139

Lieber, Francis, 60, 62
Liiv, Juhan, 147, 164, 173-79, 183, 191, 200, 201, 202, 204, 209
Lima, Maria Helena, 163
Lincoln, Abraham, 60, 102
Linde, Bernhard, 240n
Lopez, Alfred, 171
Lorca, Federico García, 173
Lotman, Juri (Yuri), 119n, 217
Lübbe, Hermann, 9
Luik, Viivi, 95-96, 208
Lukács, Georg, 255
Lumi, Ott, 90n
Luther, Martin, 9, 114

M

Maeterlinck, Maurice, 232
Mägi, Tõnis, 81
Manco Inca Yupanqui, 103n
Mann, Thomas, 192
Marie Antoinette, 154
Martini, Fritz, 166n
Marx, Karl, 9, 89n, 207n, 249
Masing, Otto Wilhelm, 193
McClintock, Anne, 2n
Medem, Vladimir, 60
Meri, Lennart, 235
Merkel, Garlieb Helwig, 38, 44, 49, 57, 105, 114-15, 126, 157, 221, 255
Meyer, Birgit, 96n
Miller, Hillis J., 106
Miller, Michael B., 205n
Miłosz, Czesław, 168-69, 170-71
Minaudier, Jean-Paul, 228
Mits, Krista, 101n
Molotov, Vyacheslav, 82
Montaigne, Michel de, 156
Montesquieu, 156
Monticelli, Daniele, 229, 235-37, 251
Moore, David, 75
Moretti, Franco, 28n, 163, 165-66, 167, 171, 216
Morgenstern, Karl, 166-67

Mügge, Theodor, 101, 143-51, 152
Mühlbach, Luise (Clara Mundt), 101, 152-54, 156
Müller, Adam, 113
Müller-Salget, Klaus, 131,
Mundt, Theodor, 152
Mylius, Christlob, 112

N

Naipaul, V.S., 107, 108, 171
Napoleon I, 153, 156
Nietzche, Friedrich, 4
Nüganen, Elmo, 220
Nyatetu-Waigwa, Wangari wa, 171

O

Obama, Barack, 15
Oks, Jaan, 240n
Olearius, Adam, 115n
Olesk, Sirje, 181n
Õnnepalu, Tõnu, 164, 173, 198-99, 204, 205, 207

P

Pareto, Vilfredo, 10n
Parsons, Talcott, 12
Päts, Konstantin, 60, 61-62, 64-65, 66, 68
Paullu Inca, 102n
Peegel, Juhan, 120
Peter I of Russia, 21, 196
Peterson, Kristjan Jaak, 39
Petőfi, Sándor, 178-79
Philippe I, Duke of Orléans, 155
Pilv, Aare, 236-37
Pizarro, Francisco, 102, 125-26, 127, 132n
Plath, Ulrike, 115n
Poe, Edgar Allan, 232, 241, 249
Poma, Guamán, 103
Pound, Ezra, 248
Pranspill, Andres, 220-21
Pushkin, Alexander, 183

R

Racine, Jean-Baptiste, 156
Raleigh, Walter sir, 112
Rannamaa, Silvia, 164, 173, 179, 180–90, 191, 201, 207
Raud, Rein, 16n, 20
Raun, Toivo, 43, 45–46, 241
Raynal, Abbé, 156
Renner, Karl, 60, 63–64
Rhys, Jean, 107
Ribbentrop, Joachim von, 82
Rigney, Ann, 30
Rilke, Rainer Maria, 249
Rimbaud, Arthur, 232
Ristikivi, Karl, 253
Rizal, José, 25
Robespierre, Maximilian, 9
Rosa, Hartmut, 9–11, 15, 32, 208, 231
Rosenplänter, Johann Heinrich, 39
Rösselt, Friedrich, 154–55
Rostow, Walt W., 11n
Rousseau, Jean-Jacques, 103, 108, 110, 111–12, 114, 115, 139, 156, 203
Ruutsoo, Rein, 80

S

Saarts, Tõnis, 90, 238n, 254, 263
Said, Edward, 74
Saint-Pierre, Jacques-Henri Bernardin de, 112, 139
Saussure, Ferdinand de, 107
Savisaar, Edgar, 80
Schiller, Friedrich, 161, 162, 167, 248
Schlau, Wilfried, 22
Schlegel, Friedrich, 113
Schlegel, Joachim-Hans, 181n
Schleiermacher, Friedrich, 248
Schöpflin, George (György), 16, 17–18, 34, 178n
Schorske, Carl E., 16n
Scott, Walter, 152, 255, 257
Shannon, Ashley Elizabeth, 171
Simmel, Georg, 9
Simpson, Anthony, 96n
Sisask, Kaia, 250
Slater, Don, 203–4, 206
Smith, Anthony, 34–36
Sooväli, Jaanus, 244n
Sophocles, 248
Spengler, Oswald, 10n, 212, 220–21
Spivak, Gayatri, 75
Stalin, Yosif, 70, 76, 182, 184n
Steinberg, Mark D., 16n
Suigusaar, Mihhail, 153
Suits, Gustav, 232, 235, 240–45, 249, 252
Sztompka, Piotr, 12–13

T

Taagepera, Rein, 71, 124n
Taine, Hippolyte, 252, 253
Tallima Paap, 42
Tamm, Marek, 90n
Tamm, Triinu, 228
Tammsaare, Anton Hansen, 32, 66, 67, 164, 174, 190, 210–15, 217–25, 228, 235, 239n, 240n, 241n, 253, 254, 259
Tarand, Andres, 80
Taylor, Charles, 4–5, 7
Thatcher, Margaret, 85
Theodorsen, Cathrine, 143
Thiong'o, Ngũgĩ wa, 27, 88
Tocqueville, Alexis de, 62
Tode, Emil, 198, 202
Toer, Praemodya Ananta, 88
Toynbee, Arnold J., 10
Tuglas, Friedebert, 67, 232, 235, 240n, 241, 249n, 251, 252–53
Turgenev, Ivan, 252

U

Undla-Põldmäe, Aino, 122n
Undusk, Jaan, 191–92, 200

V

Vahtre, Lauri, 124

Välipõllu, Hilja, 185
Väljataga, Märt, 177n
Valk, Ülo, 124
Van Baak, J.J., 119n
Van Dijk, Rijk, 96
Venuti, Lawrence, 237, 247
Verhaeren, Émile, 232
Verlaine, Paul, 232
Vinkel, Aarne, 101n
Vladiv, Slobodanka, 217
Voltaire, 110, 114, 156
Vucetic, Srdjan, 230

W

Wagner, Peter, 5–7, 14–15, 62, 269
Walcott, Derek, 171
Wassermann, Renata R. Mautner, 138, 139
Weber, Max, 4, 9, 11n
Webster, Jean, 181
Weininger, Otto, 249
Weinrich, Harald, 123n
White, Hayden, 110, 115, 117, 118
Widdowson, Peter, 24
Wilde, Oscar, 125n, 251, 264
Williams, Raymond, 28n
Willmann, Friedrich Wilhelm, 117
Wilson, Kathleen, 144n
Wilson, Woodrow, 59
Woolsey, Theodore, 62
Wuolijoki, Hella, 249n
Würdig, Ludwig, 101n

Y

Yack, Bernard, 5, 84, 89n
Yeats, William Butler, 248
Yrjö-Koskinen, Yrjö Sakari, 105n, 116
Yurchak, Alexei, 71n, 72n, 78–80

Z

Zaslavsky, Victor, 77
Zinzendorf, Nicholas Ludwig von, 40, 41n, 42
Zola, Émile, 205n

Index

Index

Index

Index

www.ingramcontent.com/pod-product-compliance
Lightning Source LLC
Chambersburg PA
CBHW052128070526
44586CB00016B/2134